FORECASTING

STUDIES IN THE
MANAGEMENT SCIENCES

Editor in Chief

ROBERT E. MACHOL

Volume 12

NORTH-HOLLAND PUBLISHING COMPANY — AMSTERDAM · NEW YORK · OXFORD

FORECASTING

Edited by

S. MAKRIDAKIS
S. C. WHEELWRIGHT

1979

NORTH-HOLLAND PUBLISHING COMPANY – AMSTERDAM · NEW YORK · OXFORD

This North-Holland/TIMS series is a continuation of the Professional Series in the Management Sciences, edited by Martin K. Starr

North-Holland ISBN for this volume: 0 444 85294 8

Reprinted from TIMS Studies in the Management Sciences, Volume 12

Published by:

NORTH-HOLLAND PUBLISHING COMPANY
AMSTERDAM · NEW YORK · OXFORD

Sole distributors for the U.S.A. and Canada:

ELSEVIER NORTH-HOLLAND, INC.
52 VANDERBILT AVENUE
NEW YORK, NY 10017

Printed in The Netherlands

TABLE OF CONTENTS

TIMS Studies in the Management Sciences 12 (1979) vii
© North-Holland Publishing Company

PREFACE

The Institute of Management Sciences had two objectives when it initiated publication of its special issues of *Management Science* in December of 1971. The first was perhaps best captured by the subtitle of those special issues — "The Professional Series in the Management Sciences". This objective was intended to describe recent research and thought concerning selected fields of interest to management scientists. The second objective was to gather that research and related application experience into a single publication that could serve as a critical mass for those whose professional activities dealt mainly with that subject matter.

Since the publication of the first two special issues, *Marketing Management Models* and *Game Theory and Gaming* the concept has proven so successful that not only have a number of other topics been included in the series but it has become necessary to create a new series — The North-Holland/TIMS Studies in the Management Sciences — under the direction of its own Editor-in-Chief, Robert E. Machol. To ensure that the same standards of quality would be met for this new series as for *Management Science*, outside reviewers have continued to be used for all manuscripts submitted to the editors for each title in this series.

Given our long-term interest and involvement in the field of forecasting and our desire to make available to both practitioners and researchers the most recent concepts and knowledge about forecasting, it was natural that we would approach TIMS and propose a special issue on forecasting. After several iterations and contributions from Martin Starr, Robert Machol, and others, the original concept reached its final form as represented by this publication. We are most appreciative to the authors who submitted manuscripts for this publication, the reviewers who provided candid and insightful evaluations of those manuscripts, and the many individuals involved in the final production of this publication.

Spyros Makridakis
INSEAD, Fontainebleau, France
Steven C. Wheelwright
Harvard Business School, Boston, Mass., May 1978

TIMS Studies in the Management Sciences 12 (1979) 1–15
© North-Holland Publishing Company

FORECASTING: FRAMEWORK AND OVERVIEW

Spyros MAKRIDAKIS
INSEAD, Fontainebleau, France

and

Steven C. WHEELWRIGHT
Graduate School of Business Administration, Harvard University

1. Introduction

Forecasting the future has long been a challenge for mankind. Fortune tellers, astrologers, priests, and prophets have sought to fulfill man's need to predict the future and reduce its uncertainties. These predictions have not been just an intellectual curiosity. Knowledge of the future has always promised advantage and opportunity of many kinds.

In today's society few believe that the most appropriate forecasting methodology is looking at the stars or studying palms. Superstition has given way to rationality and scientific reasoning, and the quest for knowledge of the future has moved from the supernatural towards the scientific.

Since the early nineteenth century mathematicians — Herschel and Schuster, for example — and later statisticians such as Yule, and economists have attempted to forecast by analyzing past data patterns and extrapolating them into the future. These pioneers developed the basic approaches that became popular between 1940 and 1960. However, application of these approaches was constrained by a shortage of reliable data and limited computing capabilities. The Second World War and the commercial development of computers provided the impetus for widespread development of more formal, if not more scientific, ways of analyzing and forecasting.

Forecasting developments during recent decades have come from several major groups, frequently working independently, but each making contributions that moved the field of forecasting toward its present advanced stage. Statisticians developed regression methods and autoregressive/moving average (ARMA) schemes, while engineers developed filtering methods. Economists first developed decomposition approaches and later econometric models. Operations researchers developed the widely used smoothing models, while long-range planners concentrated on techniques known as technological or qualitative methods. Last but not least, practitioners in business and government developed what have been referred to as judgmental methods such as the jury of executive opinion, sales force composite, and customer expectations.

The work in these various disciplines led to advances of both a theoretical and technical nature. Concurrent with these advances, computers became widespread, providing the data processing power needed to overcome what had been tedious and time-consuming calculations.

Although interest and knowledge in the forecasting field has grown exponentially in the past 20 years, much still remains to be done. Knowledge of applications has lagged behind the major theoretical and technical advances. Such difficulties must be overcome before forecasting can become more of a science. It is hoped that this publication will contribute to standardizing the *art* of forecasting and moving it toward a science.

The goals of this publication are sixfold. The first goal is to provide some framework and historical perspective that can be used to better understand the range of methodologies available, their distinct differences, and the way in which they might be evaluated and matched to specific forecasting situations. The second is to provide an overview of those major categories of forecasting methodologies for which considerable research has been done and in which science has been applied to standardize methodologies.

The third objective is to present extensions of existing forecasting techniques, the types of problems being dealt with in those extensions, and the most current research and thought as to what is likely to be successful in pursuing those developments. The fourth is to provide practitioners with results addressing the practical and organizational aspects of forecasting. These aspects have often been overlooked with a tendency to expect that they would disappear if the technical aspects of the methodologies were sufficiently robust. Unfortunately, that has not been the case, and the need to address directly such organizational problems in forecasting is now becoming more widely recognized.

The fifth objective is to summarize the state of the field at the present time and suggest where it is likely to go in the future. While such long-term forecasts about forecasting are risky, it is hoped that they will help to identify those efforts that might be most beneficial.

The sixth and final purpose is to make clear that forecasting is an interdisciplinary field and appropriately so. A serious mistake often made by forecasters is to view forecasting as the proprietary domain of a single discipline. Much can be gained by combining the efforts of all those disciplines that have contributed to forecasting and by communicating developments in all fields of related endeavor.

The papers included in this publication are organized into five categories, corresponding closely to the first five goals described above. The sixth objective is covered implicitly in the range of subjects and disciplines represented in this publication. The remainder of this introduction will present an overview of each of these five categories and the articles they include, together with a framework for classifying the various forecasting methodologies available.

2. Framework for forecasting

The future has always held both promises and threats, opportunities and dangers. Today's managers understand the future much better than those of past eras, but there is still considerable uncertainty about what the future holds. Scientific progress has gradually reduced the magnitude of this uncertainty. However, the amount of reduction has varied considerably from one area to another.

Perhaps the greatest advances in forecasting have been made in the physical sciences. There, research has led to the identification of a number of phenomena that can be predicted, often with almost perfect accuracy. In fact, the patterns of many of the laws of nature — for example, the exact time of sunrise or the precise moment of high tide — have become so well-known that they are no longer thought of as being in the realm of forecasting.

Unfortunately, progress in the social sciences, particularly those aspects related to economic and business situations, has not been nearly as great. That is due, in part, to the nature of the phenomena, their complexity, and the impact of individual choices of consumers and organizations on outcomes. Historically, judgmental approaches have been used in forecasting these situations. Only in recent decades have more systematic approaches and scientific tools been developed and applied to any great extent. The desire for such techniques has been spurred not only by recognition of the benefits to managers and administrators from improved forecasting, but also by the need for such forecasts so that the recent emphasis on planning can lead to more meaningful results.

It is unfortunate, yet true, that not only is forecasting in the social sciences less exact than in the natural sciences, but even the tools for evaluating applications in the social sciences are inexact. Thus, while managers would like to receive an answer to the question, "How accurate or appropriate are different methodologies?" the answer is, "It depends," or "We don't know."

Sometimes quantitative techniques of forecasting can be very accurate, while other times they do not perform as well as simple naive methods. However, a key point is that often informal or judgmental approaches can be even less accurate than quantitative ones. That is particularly true where the forecasting of repetitive events is concerned — a fact that has been documented extensively in the psychological literature. In addition, as experienced forecasters have learned, accuracy is not the only important criterion. Many other criteria are relevant to evaluating alternative methodologies, which further complicates the selection of an appropriate forecasting methodology.

Forecasting is only useful when its results are applied in planning or decision making. Practical applications may derive from theory, but they require considerable modifications before they can be used. Strong bridges are required to connect theory and practice, and many problems must be solved before forecasting methods *can be used* efficiently and effectively in management situations. Thus, the practice of forecasting in business and economics becomes of utmost importance.

The article by Robert L. McLaughlin, "Organizational Forecasting: Its Achievements and Limitations," presents a historical perspective on this theory-practice gap. McLaughlin summarizes the efforts that have come from several disciplines and suggests one framework for integrating those into an eclectic approach. While not as scientific as some might desire, the framework and approach outlined by McLaughlin do capture much of what business and government practitioners have developed, based on their experience in the forecasting field. A key strength of this perspective is that it deals with many of the major problems that these practitioners have found to be most pressing. McLaughlin also suggests some useful insights on how these problems can be overcome.

3. Existing forecasting methodologies

The range of existing forecasting methodologies can be described by considering several frameworks suggested for their classification. One of the simplest of these is summarized in table 1. This framework employs two dimensions for describing forecasting situations – the type of pattern experienced and the type of information available [2]. The upper left-hand quadrant of the table represents situations for which time-series methods are appropriate – where quantitative historical data are available and where it is anticipated that the historical pattern will continue into the future. The lower left-hand quadrant represents situations for which

Table 1
Classification of forecasting techniques.

Type of pattern	Type of information available	
	Quantitative	Qualitative of technological
History repeats itself	Time series methods Exponential smoothing Decomposition/census II Filters Autoregressive/moving average Leading indicators Various forms of trend extrapolations	Exploratory methods Anticipatory surveys Catastrophe theory Delphi Historical analogies Life-cycle analysis Morphological research Jury of executive opinion Sales force composite
External factors determine events	Explanatory methods Regression Econometric models Multivariate ARMA Input/output	Normative methods Cross-impact matrices Relevance trees Delphi System dynamics Market research

explanatory or causal approaches – based on quantitative historical data – are appropriate, where the pattern depends on external factors as well as historical data on the item being forecast. The methodologies in both the upper and lower left-hand quadrants assume a continuation into the future of a historical pattern, although the number of variables used in indentifying and predicting that pattern is different for the two quadrants.

The upper right-hand quadrant of table 1 presents those methods commonly referred to as exploratory. These methods are appropriate for situations involving subjective or qualitative data in which historical patterns are expected more or less to repeat themselves. This category includes many of the traditional approaches used in business, such as jury of executive opinion and sales force composite. Finally, the lower right-hand quadrant shows those normative methodologies which, while based on qualitative or subjective data, consider the impact of factors chosen by management on the future outcome for a specific event.

In the classification scheme of table 1, moving from top to bottom represents increasing complexity in terms of the number of variables and thus a need for substantially more data. Moving from left to right represents a move from systematic, mathematically based approaches, to subjective or judgmentally based approaches.

A second classification scheme that is somewhat similar to that shown in table 1 has been described by Chambers, Mullnick, and Smith [1]. This approach is based on matching methodologies with the forecasting needs as determined by the product life cycle. As a product enters a market in its early stages of growth and development, there is likely to be little quantitative data available, and thus qualitative forecasting approaches must be used. These would generally be exploratory methods, as opposed to normative, simply because most products must compete with existing items in the marketplace, and the impact of management action is very difficult to predict. As the product enters the rapid growth stage, additional quantitative data become available, and either time-series or explanatory methods can be employed. Finally, for mature products with slower growth, even more data are available and explanatory or causal methods can be used to relate product demand to general economic factors. In addition economic cycles often become a major determinant of the level of demand for products during periods of change in the pace of economic activity. For mature products with strong brand images, normative approaches may be most appropriate, since management may be able to exert major influences on the entire market.

Still a third approach to categorizing existing forecasting methods is that outlined in table 2. This framework identifies several different criteria for evaluating forecasting methodologies and uses those criteria to match the situation with the most appropriate forecasting approach [4,5]. The most important criterion in table 2 is the time horizon of forecasting. That is because the time horizon often determines the relative importance of different pattern elements (stationary, nonstationary, seasonal, and cyclical) and indicates the types of pattern that must

Table 2
Formal forecasting methodologies

Factors	Quantitative methods							
	Time-series methods							
	Naive			Smoothing				De-
		For example						
	Mean	$\hat{X}_t = X_{t-1}$	$\hat{X}_t = 1.05X_{t-L}$	Simple	Linear and higher order	Adaptive	Generalized	Classical
Time horizon of forecasting								
Immediate (less than 1 mo.)	X	X		X		X	X	
Short (1–3 mos.)	X	X		X	X	X	X	X
Medium (3 mos.– 2 yrs.)			X					
Long (2 yrs and more)								
Type of data pattern								
Horizontal	X	X		X		X	X	X
Trend			X		X		X	X
Seasonal					X		X	X
Cyclical								X
Costs (0 smallest to 1 highest)								
Development	0.1	0	0	0.05	0.1	0.1	0.5	0.4
Storage requirements:								
program	0.09	0	0	0.08	0.15	0.13	0.4	0.2
data	0.1	0.001	0.001	0.006	0.05	0.005	0.1	0.20
Running	0.03	0	0	0.005	0.05	0.01	0.1	0.2
Complexity (0 smallest to 1 highest)								
Learning time	0.1	0	0	0.05	0.1	0.1	0.6	0.1
Ease of understanding and interpreting results	1	1	1	1	0.9	0.8	0.5	0.8
Data requirements †	30	1	1	2	3–7	3	4–8	5*L
Accuracy	No conclusive statement of forecasting accuracy can be made. It varies wit:							

† L is the length of seasonality.

7

composition		ARMA		Filters		Leading indicators			Leading extrapolation	
Census II, BE, Berlin, Others	Foran	Univariate	Multivariate *	Kalman	Adaptive	Composite	Pyramid of indicators	Paired indiced	Linear	Exponential
X	X	X	X	X	X	X	X	X		
			X						X	X
									X	X
X	X	X	X	X	X					
X	X	X	X	X	X				X	X
X	X	X	X	X	X					
X	X					X	X	X		
0.6	0.5	0.7	0.8	0.9	0.5	0	0.2	0.5	0.2	0.25
0.6	0.5	0.6	0.8	0.7	0.4			0.5	0.15	0.16
0.25	0.06	0.25	0.4	0.3	0.25		0.15	0.30	0.15	0.15
0.6	0.2	0.7	0.9	0.6	0.4			0.3	0.1	0.1
0.6	0.3	0.7	1.0	1.0	0.4	0	0.1	0.3	0.05	0.1
0.7	0.7	0.4	0.1	0.2	0.6	1	0.9	0.7	1	0.9
72	24	30–6*L	60–8*L	60–8*L	20–4*L			3*L	10–30	10–30

the situation.

* Multivariate ARMA methods are not strictly time series.

Table 2 (continued)

Factors	Qualitative methods							
	Explanatory					Others		
	S-curve	Simple regression	Multiple regression	Econometric models	Input/output	Inventory control	Quality control	Combining various methods
Time horizon of forecasting								
Immediate (less than 1 mo.)		X				X	X	X
Short (1–3 mos.)		X	X	X				X
Medium (3 mos.–2 yrs.)			X	X	X			X
Long (2 yrs and more)	X					X		X
Type of data pattern								
Horizontal					X	X	X	X
Trend	X	X	X	X				X
Seasonal		X	X	X				X
Cyclical		X	X	X	X			X
Costs (0 smallest to 1 highest)								
Development	0.30	0.2	0.5	0.9	1.0	0.4	0.3	0.6
Storage requirements:								
program	0.18	0.15	0.33	1.0	0.6	0.5	0.3	0.4
data	0.15	0.2	0.45	1.0	1.0	0.5	0	0.6
Running	0.1	0.1	0.21	0.9	0.6	0.01		0.2
Complexity (0 smallest to 1 highest)								
Learning time	0.15	0.2	0.5	0.9	0.6	0.4	0.2	0.5
Ease of understanding and interpreting results	0.8	0.7	0.3	0.1	0.6	0.7	0.9	0.6
Data requirements [†]	10–30	30	30– $6*L$	Few 100	Few 1,000			
Accuracy	No conclusive statement of forecasting accuracy can be made. It varies with							

	Subjective assessment					Technological Exploratory					Normative			
	Decision analysis	Sales force estimates	Juries of executive opinion	Surveys	Market research	Delphi	Catastrophe theory	Historical analogies	Life-Cycle analysis	Morphological research	Cross-Impact matrices	Relevance trees	Delphi	Systems dynamics
		X		X										
	X	X	X	X	X		X							X
	X				X	X	X	X	X	X	X	X	X	X
	0.5	0.1	0.1	0.1	0.5	0.5	0.7	0.5	0.5	0.9	0.8	0.8	0.5	0.8
	0.8	0.1	0.1	0.3	0.9	0.5	1.0	0.6	0.6	0.9	0.8	0.6	0.5	0.8
	0.7	1	1	1	0.7	1	0.4	0.8	0.7	0.5	0.8	0.7	1	0.4

the situation.

be handled in specific forecasting situations. Another important factor is accuracy. However, little knowledge is available to make conclusive statements about the relative accuracy of one method versus another. The other criteria in table 2 — type of data pattern, cost, complexity, and data requirements — can be used as an additional screen of those methodologies that fit a given situation. This framework has been used as the basis for selecting appropriate methodologies through a comprehensive set of interactive computer programs, SIBYL/RUNNER [3].

Using key elements of each of these three frameworks, the articles included in the second segment of this publication describe and illustrate the major types of methodologies. In the first paper in this segment, "Forecasting with Exponential Smoothing and Related Methods", Johnson and Montgomery cover what many practitioners commonly think of as the simplest and broadest group of time-series methods. These include such approaches as those developed by Holt, Brown, and Winters. Such methods have found their widest application in inventory and production control systems where the time horizon is relatively short and the number of items for which forecasts must be prepared is large, making cost an important consideration.

In the Burman article, "Seasonal Adjustments — A Survey", the methods of decomposition and seasonal adjustment of time series are described. Some of these methodologies have the longest history of application by government and business forecasters. They are based on identifying the seasonal components of a time series, as well as the trend-cycle pattern. Such methods, even though not problem free, provide a unique and highly useful approach for forecasting and monitoring of macro data or sales figures.

The category of time-series approaches known as autoregressive/moving average (ARMA) methods has been advanced in the last four decades and has become extremely popular as a result of the work by Box and Jenkins. Much of this work is summarized in the paper, "Time-Series Model Building and Forecasting: A Survey", by Paul Newbold. While statistically much more general than the exponential smoothing approaches developed in the 1950s, the ARMA methodology is complex and often difficult to apply. However, as pointed out by Newbold, ARMA methods tend to be somewhat more accurate and more informative than many of the exponential smoothing approaches, when used by the experienced forecaster.

Related to the time-series approaches described in the first three articles of this segment is the approach known as filtering. Based on work done in the engineering field, methodologies in this category have only recently been applied in business and government forecasting situations. In the article, "Kalman Filters and Their Application to Forecasting", Mehra summarizes the key aspects of this filtering approach to forecasting, with particular emphasis on the original work done by Kalman and Bucy. Mehra suggests that this approach is likely to find increased application and adoption in the future, since filters are the most general of all time-series methods.

Moving from time-series methodologies to explanatory approaches, the article,

"An Econometric Approach to Forecasting Demand and Firm Behavior", by Corbo and Pindyck provides an overview of an economic approach to forecasting and its application in a major utility. In the stable period of the sixties, such econometric models gained widespread acceptance. As Corbo and Pindyck point out, it was not until the more unstable economic period of the seventies that many forecasters began to recognize that both time-series and econometric approaches had their advantages and appropriate applications on an outgoing basis.

Some of the recent work that has sought to extend the use of explanatory approaches in forecasting is summarized in the article, "Input-Output Methods in Forecasting", by Blin, Stohr, and Bagamery. While more cumbersome than either time-series or standard econometric approaches, this methodology considers additional factors external to the organization that might be extremely important in providing more accurate forecasts for the future. These factors relate to the interrelationships between various sectors of the economy and the demands placed on one sector to achieve a certain output level in another.

In the final article of this segment, Helmer, one of the original developers of the Delphi method, summarizes some of the issues and concerns relevant to selecting a qualitative or technological approach to forecasting. In addition, "The Utility of Long-Term Forecasting", considers the record of such approaches during the past decade and discusses some of the challenges facing the field.

While these seven articles on existing forecasting methodologies do not cover all of the major categories of methods, they refer to the techniques that are used most frequently and suggest the major considerations in applying each approach. Furthermore, they provide additional in-depth references and an up-to-date, state-of-the-art account of the various techniques.

4. Applications and extensions of existing forecasting methodologies

While the previous section indicated the existence of a wide range of forecasting methodologies, there is ample opportunity to extend the range of situations to which those can be applied and to make modifications in the methodologies that will further enhance their usefulness and applicability. The aim of the third segment of the book is to address some of the major problems and issues that can be overcome by such extensions. Some of the difficulties that have led to these extensions include the following:

1. Some of the more complicated quantitative methodologies require subjective assessment and experienced judgment to apply the method appropriately.
2. The mathematics of some methods are sufficiently complex that interpreting the resulting forecasts is extremely difficult for the practitioner.
3. For many forecasting situations, no methodology is currently available.
4. Criteria for selecting the most appropriate methodology may be largely subjective and ill defined.

5. Most methodologies require either judgmental inputs exclusively, or quantitative data inputs exclusively, making it difficult to combine the two types of data.
6. Recognition and development of new application areas with increased importance require that existing methodologies be adapted to fit those application areas.

The articles in this third section represent work that has been motivated by one or more of the above considerations.

In the first article, "Forecasting and Whitening Filter Estimation", Parzen extends and modifies existing autoregressive/moving average approaches so that model identification can be handled systematically (less subjectively) and to a certain extent, automatically. The outcome of using such a methodology can result in formulations that are more intuitive and that can be interpreted directly in a manner more useful to the practitioner. While still in its theoretical development, this approach to time-series forecasting holds substantial potential for overcoming some of the complexities and difficulties of the Box-Jenkins ARMA methods.

In the article by Steece and Wood, "A Cost Minimization Forecasting Methodology for a Classified Inventory Environment", the emphasis is on expressing individual inventory item demand as a fraction of aggregate classification demand for which a sophisticated ARMA model is developed. The individual item demand is found by multiplying the aggregate demand by fractional estimates developed through exponential smoothing models. The approach suggested is illustrated in a hospital environment where it is shown to minimize forecasting errors and costs.

Accuracy has long been considered one of the major criteria for evaluating forecasting methodologies. However, very little attention has been paid to measures other than mean squared error for optimizing the parameters of a model. In the article, "Time-Series Analysis and Forecasting with an Absolute Error Criterion", Cogger evaluates the use of a linear loss function as a criterion for measuring the forecasting accuracy of ARMA models. Cogger's efforts are of particular interest as computing costs become a less important factor in model optimization.

The possibility of combining different methodologies to fit the needs of a given situation better is considered by Reinmuth and Geurts in "A Multideterministic Approach to Forecasting". The authors give an example of how combining forecasts through a straightforward regression approach provides more accurate predictions than individual methods. The results of using alternative criteria for combining forecasting methodologies are also presented and compared. This article identifies several issues that must be dealt with before such combinations can be made and the benefits to be gained from using the information available in both types of approaches can be realized.

In the final article for this segment, "Inflation's Turn", Moore describes a forecasting methodology currently used at the National Bureau of Ecomonic Research. Using leading indicators, Moore applies this method to forecasting the rate of inflation, a particularly timely area of application, given today's economic environment.

5. Practical and organizational aspects of forecasting

Much of the literature on forecasting tends to describe the problems of forecasting as technical in nature, related to inappropriate methodologies or inaccurate application of the various techniques available. However, recent experience indicates that even the existence of methodologies that fit well in a given situation does not ensure successful forecasting. Both practical problems — those related to a changing environment that may affect the future performance of what has historically been an excellent approach for a given situation — and organizational considerations may affect successful forecasting.

The impact of changes in the environment have received some attention in the recent literature and are addressed by several articles in this segment. In addition, the organizational problems, which are frequently underestimated or ignored completely, are considered. Many of the contributing authors whose works are included in this part have found that these two aspects of forecasting can best be examined through specific examples of forecasting applications and resulting performance.

In the first article, "Lessons from the Track Record of Macroeconomic Forecasts in the 1970s", McNees evaluates the performance of economic forecasts in the early seventies. In doing so, he highlights many of the problems that have led to a much poorer performance in the turbulent seventies than was anticipated in view of the record of the relatively stable sixties. The underlying causes of these problems, possible models of solution, and the checks and balances that might be used to more quickly reflect changing levels of accuracy in such economic forecasts are also discussed.

Building on the fact that economic forecasting has not performed adequately in recent years, in the second article, "Forecasting Considerations in a Rapidly Changing Environment", Beckenstein identifies several factors that must be understood and addressed if forecasting is to perform as well in a changing environment as in a stable one. Because of the aggregate nature of the economic forecasts considered in this article, the methodologies examined are mainly of an explanatory nature.

Practitioners must regularly make immediate and short-term forecasts to support scheduling and operational planning. Many, however, have neither the time nor the training for selecting and properly using the most appropriate forecasting methodology available. In the article, "Automatic Forecasting", Coopersmith describes and evaluates one system, FLEXICAST, that can automatically select a forecasting model and provide suitable forecasts without human intervention.

One of the attractions of econometric and regression methods of forecasting is that they explicitly account for the impact of external factors on the forecast. However, as the environment changes, the relationship between those external factors also changes. In the article "An Application of Regression Smoothing for Forecasting Customer Utility Bills", Freeland and Bonini consider the impact of a changing environment by examining the evolution over time of the coefficients of a regression model. They then illustrate how a smoothing approach can be used to update those coefficients as new data become available, thus realizing the benefits of both time-series and regression methods in a single application.

In the final paper of this segment, "On Specifying a Quantitative Forecasting Model", Fildes and Howell direct their attention to several important issues that must be addressed in selecting a quantitative forecasting approach for a given situation. They emphasize that the practical organizational aspects of the situation must be adequately considered and that forecasting accuracy must not be based solely on fitting a forecasting model to past data but must also consider how well the model does in forecasting post sample periods. Several examples of the problems that can rise and limit the effectiveness of forecasting are included.

6. Conclusions

The final segment of the book provides a summary of the current challenges in forecasting and tries to identify some likely directions of future forecasting developments by considering two questions:
Where are we now in terms of forecasting?
Where do we want to be and are we likely to get there?

In the past few years the somewhat deteriorating performance of quantitative methods in forecasting the economy, has raised the major issue of the appropriate role of such methodologies, as compared to subjective or judgmental methods. In the article "Intuitive Predictions: Biases and Corrective Procedures", Kahneman and Tversky review some of the weaknesses of judgmental forecasting procedures and suggest some ways for overcoming them. The major theme of this article is that human judgment suffers from systematic bias, "mental astigmatism as well as from myopia". The authors have some suggestions as to what should be done to improve judgmental forecasts, but this area definitely requires further research efforts.

In the final article, the editors have sought to tie together several of the issues that have been raised in each of the segments of this publication and to suggest needs for further developments. Based on these needs, some modest predictions of directions to be taken are presented. Although only time will tell the accuracy of these forecasts of forecasting, it is hoped that this description of current problems facing the field and the suggestion of some alternative scenarios and directions of future research, will more broadly define the opportunities for future work and will enhance the possibilities for progress.

References

[1] J.C. Chambers, S.K. Mullick and D.D. Smith, An Executive's Guide to Forecasting (Wiley, New York, 1974).

[2] S. Makridakis and S.C. Wheelwright, Forecasting: issues and challenges for marketing management, Journal of Marketing (October 1977), 24–38.

[3] S. Makridakis and S.C. Wheelwright, Interactive Forecasting, 2nd. ed. (Holden-Day, San Fransico, 1978).

[4] S. Makridakis, and S.C. Wheelwright, Forecasting: Methods and Applications (Wiley, New York, 1978).

[5] S.C. Wheelwright and S. Makridakis, Forecasting Methods for Management, 2nd. ed. (Wiley, New York, 1977).

TIMS Studies in the Management Sciences 12 (1979) 17–30
© North-Holland Publishing Company

ORGANIZATIONAL FORECASTING:
ITS ACHIEVEMENTS AND LIMITATIONS

Robert L. McLAUGHLIN

President, Micrometrics, Inc.

Historical developments in organizational forecasting are presented and changes in scope and emphasis over time are noted. Forecasting is looked at as a vehicle for planning and decision making which must be integrated into the overall structure of a business firm to be effective. The author suggests that this is only possible through an eclectic approach that combines existing forecasting methodologies with judgement inputs from those directly responsible for planning and decision making.

1. Introduction

Forecasting is an aid to decision making. It has little other practical value. Consequently, forecasting will be used and judged according to the contribution it makes in guaranteeing the success of decision makers. In the uncertain worlds of managers sales executives, traffic controllers, military strategists, production schedulers, weather forecasters, highway designers, product planners, economic policy makers, and others in supervisory positions, the decision is the *raison d'etre* and, since decisions are invariably made for the future, they will be based on forecasts — good or bad, implied or explicit.

Forecasts become ingredients of power and are important inputs into almost all decisions affecting the future of the organization. Inescapably, then, they get caught in the crossfire of management factionalism. In the period since World War II, great progress has been made in the technical aspects of forecasting, but bringing managerial consensus to forecasts and implementing them as optimal decision tools is still a problem. In fact, in this sphere, it almost seems that "the more things change the more they remain in the same".

Much of the technology in our society is developed at our universities, research foundations, and government agencies, but it generally takes several years before the work of theorists trickles down to industry and other sectors for use in decision making. As a practicing forecaster since 1950, primarily in manufacturing companies, my career parallels the period of the technological revolution in forecasting that stems primarily from the computer. For the practitioner, who is usually charged with many responsibilities in addition to forecasting, the period posed three special problems: 1) the constant struggle to keep up with the technical state of the art, 2) the difficulty of implementing technical advances in one's own specific applications, and 3) the challenge of both teaching and winning the cooperation of a continuously changing team of managers, who are indispensable to forecasting in an organization.

In the early postwar period, organizational forecasting was highly judgmental because the amount of arithmetic and statistical analysis that the practitioner could use was severely restricted. What was it like before the computer? Fortunately, The Conference Board conducted a remarkable survey in the late 1940s that shows how corporations forecasted their sales at the time. The results of the survey, in which 107 major corporations participated, describe the state of the art. Looking back

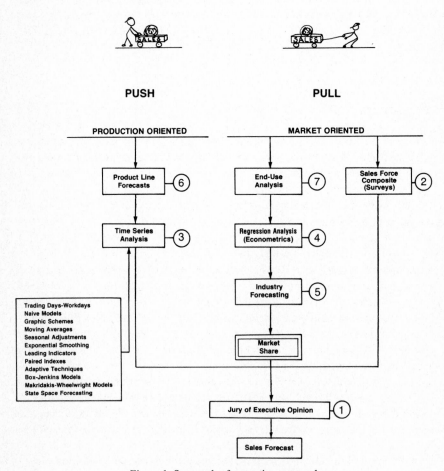

Figure 1. Seven sales forecasting approaches.

now one is impressed by the seven approaches used: 1) jury of executive opinion, 2) sales force composite, 3) time series analysis, 4) regression analysis, 5) industry forecasting, 6) product-line forecasting, and 7) end-use analysis. It is remarkable how difficult it is to add an eighth category — even now. These seven approaches, arranged as a total forecasting system, are shown in fig. 1.

Production-oriented approaches, highlighted by an array of time-series analysis techniques, can be seen at the left of the figure. Essentially, these are pushing techniques in which history is extrapolated into the future. At the right are the market-oriented approaches, pulling techniques in which the forecasts are generated by analysis of the environment. The survey method or sales force composite is commonly used. The more formal method of end-use analysis — going through regression to an industry forecast — requires the forecaster to consider market share. [1] As the figure shows, all forecasts, being instruments of power, must flow through a jury of executive opinion from whence approval comes.

These approaches have been effective in the countless companies that have used them. Although it is difficult to add an eighth category, the computer has made a great change in the frequency of use of these approaches. Approaches 3 and 4 have become widely used primarily because virtually all organizations now have access to a computer. Both approaches require great quantities of arithmetic, and the computer has made them practical forecasting tools. Before the advent of the computer, they were understood for the most part, but could not be effectively used. Whether the computer represented a change in kind or degree for the organizational forecaster is perhaps arguable, but what is not arguable is that the computer changed forecasting irrevocably.

2. The computer revolution in forecasting

The arrival of the computer in the 1950s and its proliferation in the 1960s created a dramatic revolution in forecasting. Although the techniques employed today were known before the advent of the computer, the computer made the required arithmetic possible. Forecasters in the 1950s were extremely limited in their ability to implement techniques they thoroughly understood. They simply could not justify the clerical expense needed to use them. In most organizations, it was probably cheaper to make the mistake. Since World War II, there have been roughly four periods from the point of view of the forecasting practitioner. These periods, except for the first, depend increasingly on the computer.

1. The judgmental period (1945-1955). In spite of the fact that the computer did not appear until the late 1950s, practitioners did surprisingly well in much of their forecasting. In looking back it seems that they were always short of statistical

---

[1] Market share is shown as a double-line in fig. 1 and is not one of the seven approaches to forecasting.

support, but they were nonetheless able to exert their logic and lead their companies much of the time with well-worked judgmental forecasts. A new product forecast developed in 1953 in General Electric Company's Electronics Division is a good example. It was a twelve-year forecast with 1964 as the horizon. A few data points of history, an analysis of industry acceptance, interviews with prospective users, a laboratory test to estimate the life cycle for predicting the replacement market, and probability paper to make a straight line of the S-curve were used to produce a remarkably accurate forecast than enabled the management to make reasonable decisions.

2. The univariate period (1955-1965). The decade from 1955 to 1965 can be recalled as the univariate period in which practitioners learned how to use the computer for analyzing and forecasting single time series. It was first used for short-term monthly forecasts with a time horizon a few months into the future. In making the great machine serve, a long list of contributors comes to mind, but three giants dominated the path toward implementation of computer technology: Julius Shiskin [28] in economics, and Robert G. Brown [2,3] and Peter R. Winters [33] in operations research. At the same time, a fourth giant − Geoffrey H. Moore − was enabling a whole generation of economic forecasters to use leading indicators [22].

3. The multivariate period (1965-1975). The decade from 1965 to 1975 can be cited as the multivariate period, in which practitioners learned how to use the computer in analyzing more than one variable by the use of regression analysis. Although statisticians developed the transfer function for forecasting one variable from another and economists made progress in the indicator approach by storing, analyzing and graphing large numbers of variables, the greatest breakthrough of the era was the development of econometric models. Again, the list of contributors is long, but one giant stands above all others: Lawrence R. Klein [12,13]. Around the middle of the 1960s, quarterly econometric models of the U.S. economy became available to industry practitioners, first at the Wharton School and later at several other places. Econometrics enabled organization forecasters to develop medium-term quarterly forecasts, extending the horizon to the end of the following year for budgets. The econometricians toward the end of the 1960s lengthened the horizon with long-range forecasts, enabling practitioners to develop long-term annual models going out five to ten years. These were useful for capacity planning.

4. The total forecast period (1975-   ). In the 1974-75 recession, the practice of forecasting in organizations entered a new period. The initial breakthrough of the computer and the 20 years of learning how to use it are past, but the problem of implementing this know-how remains. It is no longer cheaper to make the mistake than to obtain statistical information, but forecasters must still teach other managers how to use these techniques and must win their support. How many technical people are still frustrated after all these years by the task of explaining semilog paper? And how many have convinced managers that they should work with seasonally adjusted data? In the next few years, the computer will be taken for granted. The new phase will be the development of a total

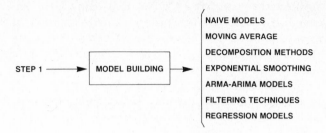

Figure 2. Objective models.

forecasting system that incorporates objective models, eclectic systems, and systematic judgmental inputs.

These three parts of a total forecasting system are worth discussing separately. The objective models, of course, were made possible by the computer. They represent step 1 of a total forecasting system and are summarized in fig. 2.

Though the computer progress from 1955 to 1975 was extraordinary, the future remains unknown, and it is difficult to predict exactly what will happen. The computer gave us excellence in the objective side of forecasting, but the subjective side is another story. In areas that the computer cannot handle, very little progress has been made. Perhaps that was best suggested by Brown [3] in (1962; p. iv): when he said, "80 to 95 percent of the problems encountered are quite routine, they can be handled by the computer. Thus, the analyst has from five to twenty times as much effort available to spend on the exceptions that really do require his skill, judgment and experience."

What progress has been made in developing the "skill, judgement and experience" that Brown talked of in 1962? The answer, to put it generously, is very little. Brown himself set the tone by ignoring the problem and devoting his writing to the objective aspect. Of the subjective aspect, which at one point he called "management's occult conjectures," he frankly declared, "I shall have very little to say . . . except to get more skill, better judgment, and longer experience" [3].

3. The development of a total forecasting system

Objective computer models were first developed for use at the item level, where they mechanically forecasted the many specific items that were too numerous to control personally. Projects were generally under the direction of the operations research department or production control. While operations researchers were building exponential smoothing models for item-level forecasts, marketing researchers were building more general models encompassing broad product lines as well as the business as a whole. The marketing research models were most often built around Shiskin's Census Method II, leading indicators, and business cycle analysis. It gradually became evident that the models of the two disciplines could be brought together. The time-series techniques of the operations researcher could also be useful at the higher levels of aggregation that were of interest to the marketing researcher — categories, colors, sizes, and product lines.

Going up the rungs of aggregation showed up a difficulty in the use of computer forecasting models. Managers generally welcome help but often balk at taking responsibility for results they do not personally control. An objective forecast is not easy to adjust — particularly by one who does not understand its derivation in the first place. The objective computer models were widely acceptable down at specific item levels, but with each step up the pyramid of aggregation, these forecasts met more and more opposition.

Fig. 3 shows a pyramid of different levels of aggregation for the entire operation in a typical manufacturing company. At the top, the corporation as a total entity has its own problems of forecasting and generally has the staff to perform the function. Nevertheless, top-level forecasts cannot be developed in a vacuum. They must rely on successful forecasts at lower levels, all the way down to the irreducible item level. The second level of aggregation is generally called the group in larger firms and represents families of businesses. At the third level are the divisions, each of which is that critical institution of industry, the autonomous profit center. Within divisions are product lines that may have dozens of distinct product categories, which in turn may be broken into models. Finally, there are the actual items themselves, which can number in the hundreds or the hundreds of thousands. For example, the item is the yellow-handled screwdriver with the 6-inch blade, standard tip, made of boron steel. Someone personally — or mechanically by computer —

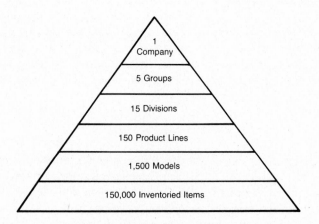

Figure 3. The pyramid of aggregation.

must forecast each of the thousands of items. But every entity, at all levels of the pyramid of aggregation, must also be forecasted in some way.

The objective computer models are not enough. Lack of managerial cooperation is not the only problem. The fact is that a forecaster must build methods for getting at what Brown called the exceptions. The most neglected area of forecasting is that part that is exceptional. Forecasters, who must anticipate change, face this dilemma: objective models tend to be averaging processes, but every real-world forecast brings one head-on against a unique event, — rampant with exceptions and special considerations. The truth is that what is about to happen in the next discrete period is not adequately explained by averages, even though averages do represent the proper place to begin. What Brown passed over is often the most important forecasting problem. It is now clear that forecasters must bring together the objective and the subjective if they are to create a total forecasting system.

In developing eclectic systems, the forecaster must understand the intricacies of the business being forecasted. Every business has its own peculiar characteristics, and in some cases two competing companies can have considerably different forecasting needs. For example, one company may sell its output directly to other manufacturers, while a competitor may sell its output through distributors. Even though these two companies are in the same industry, the inventory requirements can be very different and quite different forecasting methods may be needed. These characteristics dictate the kinds of eclectic systems that may be required. If forecasts begin with objective models, they can be altered by different methods of dealing with the exceptional. Some of these methods are shown in fig. 4. Objective models themselves, of course, are one of the many methods included in an eclectic system, but the other methods tend more toward the qualitative than the quantitative. At the simplest level, a table of raw data as issued by the accounting department ought to be the first item in a list of system components. Equally simple, graphic systems may be the most overlooked of all methods. A picture is still worth a thousand words and much can be decided just by studying a series of graphs of orders, sales, shipments, backlogs, inventories, production rates, and so on. Surveys are another way of developing information for making better decisions. These not only include the sales force composite, but may deal with market shares developed

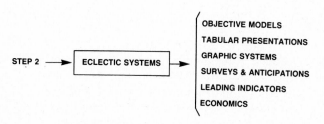

Figure 4. Components of an eclectic system.

by surveying companies or surveys of potential buyers. Indicators continue to be a source for making better forecasts. The search for leading indicators is a useful pursuit, if for no other reason than that the economy itself exhibits a timing spectrum that ranges over several years. This fact was demonstrated by the use of indicator pyramids, which showed that dozens of indicators arrayed according to their timing at peaks and troughs produce the picture of a business cycle constantly in the process of peaking and troughing [18]. In addition, the whole field of economics is filled with material for aiding the forecaster. Indicator pyramids were summarized into a five-phase economic forecasting system that ran from first cause policy indicators, through the conventional leading, coinciding, and lagging indicators, to the final effect price indexes [18].

One computer program that was specifically designed to optimize the use of objective models and eclectic systems was FORAN II, a program with a two-page printout for each product line. It includes naive models, moving averages, leading indicators, paired indexes, and ratio variables; correlation, econometrics and graphic schemes; and raw forecasts, optimal forecasts, and final forecasts [16]. It also extends the ability of the forecaster to use judgmental inputs.

4. The use of skill, judgment and experience

Having successfully built objective models and supported them with the added knowledge gained from various eclectic systems, the forecaster in a large organization still faces what may be his most difficult challenge — getting at the vital information stored in the minds of other managers. Each decision-making manager has a set of informed opinions that represent information of value to the forecaster. In many organizations, this information may be the true mother-lode, the missing link in building a total forecasting system. The computer models can represent an objective first premise to be adjusted by subjective information — first from the eclectic systems and finally from the managers themselves.

The forecasting program within an organization should not be wholly identified with a single personality. No one has a secret formula, a sixth sense or a crystal ball. Although it is wise for one person to coordinate the forecasting program (in the larger manufacturing companies, the coordinator is most likely to be the marketing research manager), important decision makers within the organization should participate actively. The informed opinions of people such as product managers, sales managers, and production managers are imperative to forecasting accuracy — especially in the short term, where these people have an acute sense of the imminent. Consensus in putting the forecast together is vital for another reason as well. If the key people who manage the organization do not participate, they may feel threatened, and they will often lack confidence in the forecast. Such attitudes can cause forecasts to play a minor role in the planning function. The purpose of the search for consensus is to arrive at a single forecast acceptable to all critical decision

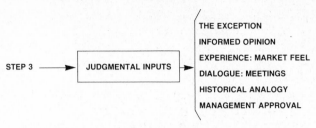

Figure 5. Components of judgmental inputs.

makers. The alternative is to have more than one forecast, which in a large organization can quickly lead to competing forecasts.

Fig. 5 lists some of the inputs of skill, judgment, and experience that can be obtained from managers. The exception is always the thing that must be pinpointed, if exceptions are impending – and they usually are. The exception cannot be averaged; it is unique. For example, how badly may the impending strike affect sales? Only experience and informed opinion can help adjust the objective forecast for such an event. The value of dialogue should not to be overlooked. Expose the forecast to those who are knowledgeable about the operation and debate will ensue. The process of dialogue itself is a superb learning device, and large organizations constantly make the process available through meetings. Historical analogy, particularly in the absence of statistics such as new product forecasts, can be used to advantage in developing forecasts.

No matter what technique is employed or how much work is entailed, ultimately a forecast must be approved by those in management. In bringing managers into the forecasting operation, two basic problems must be resolved: 1) only those managers should be enlisted who really have useful information obtainable by interview and dialogue, and 2) a system should be developed to get the information with the least amount of their time and aggravation. In effect, a system should be designed that begins with an objective set of recommended forecasts that can be subjectively altered by a jury of executive opinion through the process of dialogue.

Fig. 6 illustrates how a consensus forecast can be developed within an organization – in this case a manufacturer. The plan shown in the flow diagram in fig. 6 assumes that the marketing research manager is the coordinator of the sales forecast. In this specific case, the forecast is developed deductively using the general-to-particular or top-down approach, probably beginning at the divisional level of the pyramid of aggregation and going down from there. However, at the same time, the operations research department is developing bottom-up forecasts starting at the item level and aggregating upwards. The two forecasts are later compared. A basic difference between the two is that the operations research work is going on continuously, whereas the more general marketing research forecast is developing at monthly or even quarterly intervals.

On the first Wednesday of the month, the accounting department releases data

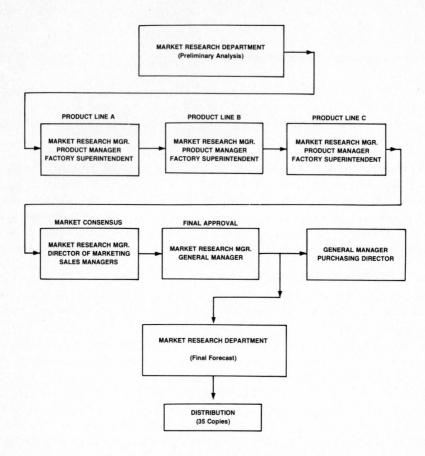

Figure 6. Chronology of a consensus sales forecast.

for the preceding month. These include such vital statistics as orders received, sales billed, warehouse shipments, production rates, prices, inventories, order backlogs, and the like. The marketing research department processes much of these raw data with various computer programs such as Census II and FORAN II so that they can be analyzed. In the first couple of hours on Thursday – forecast day – the market- ing research manager analyzes the printouts and develops recommended forecasts. About mid-morning the research manager goes to the various product line offices and holds meetings with key personnel. There may be any number of broad product lines from a few to a dozen. At these meetings the marketing research manager presents the recommended forecasts for discussion. The meetings are short and attended by a minimum of informed managers. Those present besides the marketing research manager include a representative from sales (in the larger companies, usually the product manager) and a representative from production.

Consensus at the product line level is sought at these first meetings. The research manager contributes the recommended forecasts, based first on objective models, which may then be altered by the results of various eclectic approaches. In the dialogue that ensues, such questions as "Did you know we are negotiating a large military order?" will come from the product manager. The production representative may say, "Did you know we're planning to shut down machine number 3 for repairs the second week of February? If we can't build it, you can't sell it." Thus by a simple process of dialogue, it is possible to develop a method for systematically adjusting objective forecasts with subjective information. Still, it is not easy to discipline managers to attend a fifteen-minute monthly meeting. These are the busiest people in an organization and there is considerable call on their time. Nevertheless, it has been found that recommended objective forecasts only rarely survive these dialogues unchanged. Such is the prevalence of the exceptional. The degree of change in forecasts made necessary by the exceptional is much greater than generally supposed. What is important in the system described is that, as each product line meeting ends, there is general agreement. The system is designed to enhance consensus, integrate the objective and subjective, and bring speed to a difficult operation.

The product line meetings generally end around noon. The forecasts generated at these morning meetings are the crux of the system. They are brought together into a total sales forecast for consideration by the top marketing executives at a meeting early in the afternoon. At this meeting the director of marketing, sales managers, distribution managers, advertising managers, and the like should be brought into the dialogue. Once again the marketing research manager presents the forecasts – this time, as amended at the product line meetings. Often at the general marketing consensus meeting, the very important subject of pricing will enter the discussions. Though organizations differ considerably, the product manager frequently will have price authority only within a range, but the top marketing executives will have considerable price authority.

Following the marketing consensus, the forecast is taken to the general manager for final approval. After this final step, the general manager may meet with the purchasing manager to plan the purchase of materials and parts. At times of capacity operation, the purchasing department will be represented at the product line meetings. It may be at such times that bottlenecks will develop that can prevent production from meeting the plan.

The marketing research manager returns to his office late in the day to prepare the final forecast for distribution to all decision makers. This entire once-a-month operation will take the better part of a day for the marketing research manager. In addition, provision must be made for revisions. The easiest approach to revisions is to have the product manager phone the marketing research manager weekly. At these phone meetings the status of the monthly forecast can be reviewed and weekly revisions made where necessary.

The three-step process just described of starting with objective models (quantitative), testing them with eclectic systems (both quantitative and qualitative) and, finally, subjecting them to the dialogue of judgmental consensus (qualitative) may be the nearest we can come to developing a total forecasting system for all levels of the pyramid of aggregation: the organization. Its use extends far beyond the manufacturing concern described here.

In economic forecasting, the three-step system has been developed into a fine art in universities and the federal government. The University of Michigan, the University of Georgia, and the University of California at Los Angeles (UCLA) have all had top econometric projects for some time, but the father of these quarterly models and perhaps the best in terms of the three-step system, is clearly that of the Wharton School. Since before 1965, its econometric project has issued quarterly forecasts of the U.S. economy. Its procedure is to run an objective model of the economy, adjusted by a highly important middle exercise in which the Wharton School's own experts discuss and, through its own eclectic methods, produce step two: the pre-meeting solution.

Wharton then holds its quarterly meeting with the 50 or so principal subscribers to the model. At these quarterly consensus meetings, experts from various sectors of the economy have the chance to question the output of the model. This step-three exercise is particularly useful where the experts involved have qualitative information that can make a contribution toward a better ultimate solution. After the meeting, Wharton issues its post-meeting solution, which incorporates the knowledge gained at the quarterly meeting from the practitioners, especially those who have expertise in special sectors of the economy. Dialogue again becomes the essence, changing the purely objective into a finely honed post-meeting solution.

The federal government too has an excellently developed third step in which experts from the various economic agencies conduct dialogues through what are called the *troika* and the *quadriad*. The former includes representation from the Office of Management and Budget, the Treasury, and the President's Council of Economic Advisers. When the independent Federal Reserve Board joins the group, it is called the quadriad. Not only is the administration's economic plan subjected to these committees. Once through them, the plan goes before the committees of Congress and then the Congress itself.

In the economic sphere, the step-three exercise of judgmental dialogue does not give much heed to short-term operating forecasts, its principal use in manufacturing companies. Rather, the economists are interested primarily in the medium-term budget forecasts that center essentially on the business cycle. To a lesser extent, they concern themselves with the long-term capacity forecast.

In building the total forecasting system for the organization, many levels of development must be considered. Certainly the short-, medium-, and long-term horizons are among them. The integration of the work of many disciplines into the system – statistics, mathematics, economics, engineering, operations research, and marketing research to mention the most obvious – must also be considered. The various forecasting problems related to the different levels of aggregation are also important. But, above all, the three-step system of objective models, eclectic systems, and judgmental dialogue must be developed. In my opinion, this system is essential to the successful utilization of forecasting.

References

[1] G.E.P. Box and G.M. Jenkins, Time Series Analysis: Forecasting and Control (Holden Day, San Francisco).
[2] R.G. Brown, Statistical Forecasting for Inventory Control (McGraw-Hill, New York, 1959).
[3] R.G. Brown, Smoothing Forecasting and Prediction of Discrete Time Series (Prentice-Hall, Englewood Cliff N.J. 1963).
[4] J.C. Chambers et al, How to choose the right forecasting technique, Harvard Business Review, July-August (1971) 45–74.
[5] C.F. Christ, Econometric Models and Methods (Wiley, New York, 1966).
[6] J.S. Duesenberry, G. Fromm, L.R. Klein and E. Kuh, The Brookings Quarterly Econometric Model of the United States (Rand McNally, Chicago, 1965).
[7] S. Eilon and J. Elmaleh, Adaptive limits in inventory control, Management Science, April, 1970.
[8] M.K. Evans, Macroeconomic Activity (Harper and Row, New York, 1969).
[9] M.K. Evans and L.R. Klein, The Wharton Econometric Forecasting Model (University of Pennsylvania, Philadelphia, 1968).
[10] A.C. Harberger, The Demand for Durable Goods (University of Chicago Press, Chicago, 1960).
[11] H.S. Houthakker and L.D. Taylor, Consumer Demand in the United States (Harvard University Press, Cambridge, Mass., 1970).
[12] L.R. Klein, Essays in industrial econometrics, Vols. 1–3 (University of Pennsylvania, Philadelphia, 1971).
[13] Lawrence, R. Klein, An introduction to econometrics (Prentice-Hall, Englewood Cliffs, N.J., 1962).
[14] F.R. Macauley, The Smoothing of Time Series (University Microfilms, Inc., Ann Arbor, Mich., 1931).
[15] M.D. McCarthy, The Wharton Quarterly Econometric Forecasting Model (Mark III) (University of Pennsylvania, Philadelphia, 1972).
[16] R.L. McLaughlin and J. Boyle, Short-term forecasting (American Marketing Assn., Chicago, 1968).
[17] R.L. McLaughlin, The paired index as a leading indicator, Proceedings of the Business and Economics Section (American Statistical Association; New York, 1971).
[18] R.L. McLaughlin, A new five phase economic forecasting system, The Journal of Business Economics, Sept., 1975.
[19] S. Makridakis, A. Survey of Time Series (European Institute of Business Administration (INSEAD) Fontainebleau, France, 1974).
[20] S. Makridakis, A. Hodgsdon and S. Wheelwright, An interactive forecasting system, The American Statistician (American Statistical Assn., November, 1974).
[21] S. Makridakis and S. Wheelwright, Interactive Forecasting (Holden Day, San Francisco, 1977).

[22] G.H. Moore, Business cycle indicators Vols. 1-2 (Princeton University Press for National Bureau of Economic Research, Princeton, N.J., 1961).

[23] G.H. Moore, Tested knowledge of business cycles, 42nd Annual Report of the National Bureau of Economic Research (National Bureau of Economic Research, New York, 1962).

[24] T.H. Naylor and T.G. Seaks, Box—Jenkins methods: an alternative to econometric models, International Statistical Review, Vol. 40, No. 2, (1972) 123—137.

[25] C.R. Nelson, Applied Time Series Analysis (Holden Day, San Francisco, 1973).

[26] R.S. Preston, The Wharton Annual and Industry Forecasting Model (University of Pennsylvania, Philadelphia, 1973).

[27] S.D. Roberts and R. Reed, The development of a self-adaptive forecasting technique, AIIE Transactions, December, 1969.

[28] J. Shiskin, Electronic computers and business indicators (National Bureau of Economic Research, Occasional Paper 57, NYC).

[29] J. Shiskin, Signals of Recession and Recovery (National Bureau of Economic Research, New York, 1961).

[30] D.B. Suits, Forecasting and analysis with an econometric model, American Economic Review, March, 1962.

[31] D.W. Trigg, and A.G. Leach, Exponential smoothing with an adaptive response rate. Operations Research Quarterly, March, 1967.

[32] D.C. Whybark, A Comparison of Adaptive Forecasting Techniques, Paper number 302, March, 1971, Krannert Graduate School, Purdue University, Lafayette, Ind.

[33] P.R. Winters, Forecasting sales by exponentially weighted moving averages, Management Science, April, 1960.

TIMS Studies in the Management Sciences 12 (1979) 31–44
© North-Holland Publishing Company

FORECASTING WITH EXPONENTIAL SMOOTHING
AND RELATED METHODS

Lynwood A. JOHNSON and Douglas C. MONTGOMERY

Georgia Institute of Technology

An overview of exponential smoothing methods and their use in forecasting time series is given. Both the multiple smoothing and direct smoothing formulations of the general procedure are presented. The equivalence of exponential smoothing to other time series analysis methods is noted. There is also a discussion of the properties and characteristics that make exponential smoothing useful in practical forecasting situations, particularly those involving a large number of time series.

1. Introduction

Exponential smoothing methods are widely used for modeling and forecasting time series. Their popularity is due at least in part to their simplicity and the relatively high forecast accuracy that may often be obtained without extensive modeling effort. The purpose of this paper is to give a brief overview of exponential smoothing, pointing out the various forms of the parameter estimation and forecasting equations that are in common use, and noting several important extensions or variations of the basic technique. We shall also discuss some of the characteristics of exponential smoothing that make it a desirable approach to forecasting, particularly in situations where there are a large number of time series to be forecast.

2. Description of exponential smoothing methods

The basic methodology of exponential smoothing is well known. In the general form of the procedure, estimates of the parameters of the underlying time series model are updated recursively each period, as soon as the new observation for that period becomes available. Forecasts for future periods are then made using the revised parameter values. The exact nature of the smoothing (updating) and forecasting equations depends upon the assumed characteristics of the time series process. In section 2.1, we give an intuitive development of the simplest forms of exponential smoothing to illustrate the procedure.

Much of the original work in this area is by Brown [3], [4]. Holt [18] and Winters [32] also have made significant contributions to exponential smoothing methodology, devising somewhat different procedures for dealing with trends and seasonals from those advocated by Brown and Meyer [6] generalized exponential smoothing to the case of a polynomial trend. The resulting procedure, which we shall summarize briefly in section 2.2, usually is called *multiple exponential smoothing.* Meyer [21] extended the exponential smoothing process to a more general time series in which the independent variables could be polynomial, exponential, or trigonometric functions of time, thus allowing the analyst to incorporate both trend and seasonal variation into his model. Brown [4], [5] has done much to popularize this method, referring to it as *adaptive smoothing.* Because it leads to a procedure in which estimates of the model parameters are updated *directly* instead of implicitly through use of exponentially smoothed statistics, other authors have called this approach *direct smoothing* (for example, see Montgomery and Johnson [23]). Direct smoothing methods are described in section 2.3.

2.1. A heurtistic development of exponential smoothing

A heuristic development of exponential smoothing that has considerable intuitive appeal is often given. Suppose that the average level of the time series is nearly constant over time, or if it is changing, it is doing so very slowly. Consequently, we might model the series as

$$x_t = b + \epsilon_t, \tag{1}$$

where b is the expected value of demand in any local segment of time, and ϵ_t is a random error component with mean zero and variance σ_ϵ^2. To forecast a future observation, we must estimate the unknown parameter b. Suppose that at the end of period T, we have available the estimate of b made at the end of the previous period $T - 1$, denoted by S_{T-1}, and the current period's observation x_T. S_{T-1} was used as the forecast for period T, made at the end of period $T - 1$. A reasonable way to obtain a new estimate of b is to adjust the old estimate by some fraction α ($0 < \alpha < 1$) of the forecast error realized in the current period. This forecast error is $X_T - S_{T-1}$ and the new estimate of b is

$$S_T = S_{T-1} + \alpha(x_T - S_{T-1}). \tag{2}$$

Rearranging (2) yields

$$S_T = \alpha x_T + (1 - \alpha)S_{T-1}. \tag{3}$$

The operation defined by (3) is called simple or first-order exponential smoothing, and α is called the smoothing constant. Since S_T estimates b, and in light of the assumption of a constant time series model (1), the forecast of an observation in any future period $T + \tau$ made at the end of period T is

$$\hat{x}_{T+\tau}(T) = S_T. \tag{4}$$

Now suppose that the time series model contains a linear trend, say

$$x_t = b_1 + b_2 t + \epsilon_t. \tag{5}$$

If first-order exponential smoothing were applied to the observations generated from this process, S_T would lag behind the true signal by an amount equal to $(\beta/\alpha)b_2$, where $\beta = 1 - \alpha$. That is, $E(S_T) = E(x_T) - (\beta/\alpha)b_2$. One approach used to compensate for this lag is to apply the exponential smoothing operator to the output of (3), resulting in

$$S_T^{[2]} = \alpha S_T + (1 - \alpha) S_{T-1}^{[2]}. \tag{6}$$

The operation in (6) is called double exponential smoothing. Now $E(S_T^{[2]}) = E(S_T) - (\beta/\alpha)b_2$, so that a logical way to estimate b_2 at the end of period T is by

$$\hat{b}_2(T) = (\alpha/\beta)(S_T - S_T^{[2]}).$$

Consequently, a reasonable correction for the lag in S_T is

$$\hat{x}_T = 2S_T - S_T^{[2]}.$$

To forecast the observation for period $T + \tau$ at the end of period T using double exponential smoothing, we use the forecast function

$$\hat{x}_{T+\tau}(T) = \hat{x}_T + \tau \hat{b}_2(T) = 2S_T - S_T^{[2]} + \tau(\alpha/\beta)(S_T - S_T^{[2]})$$

$$= (2 + \alpha\tau/\beta)S_T - (1 + \alpha\tau/\beta)S_T^{[2]}. \tag{7}$$

Note that this forecast function is just a linear combination of the two smoothed statistics S_T and $S_T^{[2]}$.

These two forms of exponential smoothing are widely used in practice. They are special cases of multiple exponential smoothing, which is summarized in the next section.

2.2. Multiple exponential smoothing

In this section we shall briefly summarize the multiple exponential smoothing procedure of Brown and Meyer [6]. We shall think of a time series as a realization of a discrete stochastic process $\{x_t, t = 0, 1, ...\}$. Suppose that the time series can be modeled by an nth degree polynomial

$$x_t = \mu_t + \epsilon_t = b_1 + b_2 t + \frac{b_3 t^2}{2!} + \dots + \frac{b_{n+1} t^n}{n!} + \epsilon_t, \tag{8}$$

where μ_t is the mean of the process and ϵ_t is a random variable having expectation $E(\epsilon_t) = 0$ and variance $V(\epsilon_t) = \sigma_\epsilon^2$. Exponential smoothing of order p is defined as

$$S_T^{[p]} = \alpha S_T^{[p-1]} + (1 - \alpha) S_{T-1}^{[p]}, \tag{9}$$

where we let $S_T^{[1]} = S_T = \alpha x_T + (1 - \alpha) S_{T-1}$, α is the exponential smoothing constant, usually (but not necessarily) defined so that $0 < \alpha < 1$, and T denotes the current time period.

The parameters $\{b_i\}$ in (8) are based on the original time origin. In most forecasting systems it is convenient to use a *current* origin model; that is, the origin of time for the model should be the end of the current period T. On a current origin basis, the observation for period $T + \tau$ becomes

$$x_{T+\tau} = a_1(T) + a_2(T)\tau + a_3(T)\frac{\tau^2}{2!} + \dots + a_{n+1}(T)\frac{\tau^n}{n!} + \epsilon_{T+\tau}, \tag{10}$$

where the $\{a_i(T)\}$ are the current-origin analogs of the $\{b_i\}$ in (8). Brown and Meyer [6] have shown that the following relationship holds between the first $n + 1$ exponentially smoothed statistics and the coefficients in the current-origin model:

$$E(S_T^{[p]}) = \sum_{k=0}^{n} (-1)^k \frac{a_{k+1}(T)}{k!} \frac{\alpha^p}{(p-1)!} \sum_{j=0}^{\infty} j^k (1-\alpha)^j \frac{(p-1+j)!}{j!},$$

$$p = 1, 2, \dots, n+1. \tag{11}$$

In matrix notation, (11) becomes

$$E(\mathbf{S}_T) = \mathbf{M}\mathbf{a}(T), \tag{12}$$

where $\mathbf{S}_T' = [S_T^{[1]}, S_T^{[2]}, \dots, S_T^{[n+1]}]$, $\mathbf{a}'(T) = [a_1(T), a_2(T), \dots, a_{n+1}(T)]$, and $\mathbf{M}$ is an $(n + 1) \times (n + 1)$ matrix with elements

$$M_{pk} = \frac{(-1)^k}{k!} \frac{\alpha^p}{(p-1)!} \sum_{j=0}^{\infty} j^k (1-\alpha)^j \frac{(p-1+j)!}{j!}, \tag{13}$$

which can be written in closed form. If the inverse of $\mathbf{M}$ exists, then we have

$$\mathbf{a}(T) = \mathbf{M}^{-1} E(\mathbf{S}_T), \tag{14}$$

which expresses the model coefficients in terms of the expected values of the first $n + 1$ exponentially smoothed statistics. When the elements of $E(\boldsymbol{S}_T)$ are replaced by the observed values $\boldsymbol{S}_T$, it seems reasonable to estimate $\boldsymbol{a}(T)$ by

$$\hat{a}(T) = M^{-1}S_T. \tag{15}$$

These estimates, computed at the end of period T, could be used to forecast the observation at period $T + \tau$ as

$$\hat{x}_{T+\tau}(T) = \hat{a}_1(T) + \hat{a}_2(T)\tau + \hat{a}_3(T)\frac{\tau^2}{2!} + ... + \hat{a}_{n+1}(T)\frac{\tau^n}{n!}, \quad \tau \geqslant 1. \tag{16}$$

This result is usually called the *fundamental theorem of exponential smoothing*. In practice, once the order of the polynomial model approximating the time series is known, we need only update the elements of the vector $\boldsymbol{S}_T$ through (9), revise the estimates of the model parameters through (15), and generate the required forecasts from (16). If we define $\tau' = [1, \tau, \tau^2/2!, ..., \tau^n/n!]$, we may combine (15) and (16) to obtain the forecast function

$$\hat{x}_{T+\tau}(T) = \tau' M^{-1}S_T. \tag{17}$$

Thus we may calculate the forecast directly as a linear combination of the $n + 1$ exponentially smoothed statistics, as in (4) and (7), the forecast functions for first-order and double exponential smoothing. D'Esopo [14] has shown that the estimates of the model parameters obtained by this process are optimal with respect to a discounted least squares criterion. Furthermore, (12) could be used to obtain starting values of the exponentially smoothed statistics from initial estimates of the model parameters.

2.3. Direct smoothing procedures

The multiple exponential smoothing procedures described in section 2.2 can be applied to time series models containing only polynomial terms. Meyer [21] and Brown [3] show that the exponential smoothing concept can be extended to the general model

$$x_t = \sum_{i=1}^{k} b_i z_i(t) + \epsilon_t, \tag{18}$$

where the $\{z_i(t)\}$ are either polynomial, exponential, or trignometric functions of time (often called "fitting functions"). As in section 2.2, it is customary to express the model on a current-origin of time basis, so that the observation at time $T + \tau$ is represented by

$$x_{t+\tau} = \sum_{i=1}^{k} a_i(T)z_i(\tau) + \epsilon_{T+\tau}. \qquad (19)$$

We estimate the model parameters $\{a_i(t)\}$ by the method of discounted least squares. This involves choosing the $\{a_i(T)\}$ to minimize

$$SS_E = \sum_{j=0}^{T-1} \beta^j [x_{T-j} - \sum_{i=1}^{k} a_i(T)z_i(-j)]^2, \quad 0 < \beta < 1,$$

resulting in

$$\hat{a}(T) = G^{-1}(T)g(T),$$

where

$$G(T) = \sum_{j=0}^{T-1} \beta^j z(-j) z'(-j),$$

$$z(t) = [z_1(t), z_2(t), ..., z_k(t)]',$$

and

$$g(T) = \sum_{j=0}^{T-1} \beta^j x_{T-j} z(-j).$$

It can be shown [23, pp. 79–83] that for large T the following recursive relationship can be used to compute $\hat{a}(T)$ from $\hat{a}(T-1)$:

$$\hat{a}(T) = L'\hat{a}(T-1) + h e_1(T), \qquad (20)$$

where L is a $k \times k$ matrix of elements $\{L_{ij}\}$ such that

$$z(t) = Lz(t-1),$$

$e_1(T) = x_T - \hat{x}_T(T-1)$ is the single-period forecast error, $G^{-1} = \lim_{T\to\infty} G^{-1}(T)$, and $h = G^{-1}z(0)$ is called the *smoothing vector*.

In computing h, the steady-state or limiting value of G is required. If the model consists of polynomial, exponential, or trignometric terms, then the required G and L matrixes will exist. The parameter updating (20) is usually called *general exponential smoothing, adaptive smoothing,* or *direct smoothing.* Note that estimates of the model parameters are modified each period for two reasons. The first is to shift the origin of time to the end of the current period, and the second is to revise the estimates according to the current forecast error. These two purposes are accomplished by the first and second terms, respectively, of (20).

Once the smoothed parameter estimates have been obtained, the forecast made at time T of the expected value of the time series variable in period $T + \tau$ is obtained from

$$\hat{x}_{T+\tau}(T) = \sum_{i=1}^{k} \hat{a}_i(T) z_i(\tau).$$

If the model contains only polynomial terms, then the direct smoothing approach is equivalent to multiple exponential smoothing with $\alpha = 1 - \beta$, as discussed in section 2.2. The only difference is that the calculations are organized somewhat differently; that is, the estimates of the model parameters are revised directly from (20) instead of indirectly through the exponentially smoothed statistics [see (15)]. Thus direct smoothing often leads to a more intuitively appealing forecasting system, in that the parameter updating equations can be explained more easily to nontechnical management.

When the time series contains growth or seasonal variation, then transcendental terms can be incorporated into the direct smoothing model. For example, if the series contains a simple, symmetric seasonal pattern observed monthly, superimposed on a linear trend, then an appropriate model would be

$$x_{T+\tau} = a_1(T) + a_2(T)\tau + a_3(T) \sin \frac{2\pi\tau}{12} + a_4(T) \cos \frac{2\pi\tau}{12} + \epsilon_{T+\tau}. \qquad (21)$$

More complex seasonal patterns are usually modeled by adding sine—cosine pairs with appropriately chosen harmonic frequencies (see Brown [4] and Montgomery and Johnson [23]). Spectral analysis methods are often helpful in selecting both the fundamental and harmonic frequencies for these models.

A major difficulty in the application of these models is developing the smoothing vector h. For some model structures it is possible to find G in closed form, thus yielding h as a relatively simple function of the discount factor β. For other models, however, finding a closed form expression for G may be extremely difficult, and numerical generation of h may be necessary. This difficulty in generating smoothing vectors for a suitable range of values of the discount factor β has limited the application of direct smoothing models. Brown [4] and Montgomery and Johnson [23] list the elements of h for various values of β for several important model structures. Brown [5] gives a good discussion of the computational problem.

2.4. Other exponential smoothing methods

Both the multiple exponential smoothing and direct smoothing techniques summarized in sections 2.2 and 2.3 can be developed formally from the discounted least-squares criterion. There are also several heuristic exponential smoothing procedures in wide use that are not based on least squares. Perhaps the best known of these is an approach to forecasting a seasonal time series due to Winters [32]. Winters' method assumes that the time series is represented by the model

$$x_t = (b_1 + b_2 t) c_t + \epsilon_t, \tag{22}$$

where b_1 is the permanent component, b_2 is a linear trend component, and c_t is a multiplicative seasonal factor defined so that over a season of length L we have $\Sigma_{t=1}^{L} c_t = L$. Winters [32] describes a simple procedure for revising the estimates of the parameters in (22). This updating procedure is intuitively appealing, but it does not result from any formal mathematical criterion.

From (22) we note that Winters' method would be suitable for a time series in which the amplitude of the seasonal pattern increases as the average level of the series $(b_1 + b_2 t)$ increases. This is a result of the multiplicative structure of the seasonal factors. A direct smoothing model with this property might be

$$x_t = b_1 + b_2 t + (b_3 + b_4 t) \sin \frac{2\pi \tau}{12} + (b_5 + b_6 t) \cos \frac{2\pi \tau}{12} + \epsilon_t,$$

which is often called a *growing sine wave model*. In practice, one might prefer Winters' method for such series because of the relatively simpler parameter updating procedure and the widespread availability of computer programs.

It is possible to devise alternate model structures to (22) and their associated parameter updating procedures. For example, suppose that the amplitude of the seasonal pattern is independent of the average level of the series. This implies an additive seasonal model, say

$$x_t = b_1 + b_2 t + c_t + \epsilon_t. \tag{23}$$

Note that the direct smoothing analog of this model is given by (21). Montgomery and Johnson [23, pp. 108–111] give the heuristic parameter updating equations for this model, and show that initial parameter estimates can be obtained by least squares. Pegels [26] gives a good summary of various model structures that admit simple heuristic parameter updating equations. Many other variations and applications of exponential smoothing have appeared in the literature. For example, see Chen and Winters [8], Crane and Crotty [13], Bamber [2], Cohen [11], and McClain and Thomas [19].

2.5. Relationship of exponential smoothing to ARIMA models

In certain special cases, exponential smoothing is mathematically equivalent to the autoregressive integrated moving average (ARIMA) model popularized by Box and Jenkins [7]. For example, Muth [24] and Harrison [16] observed that forecasting with first-order exponential smoothing is equivalent to forecasting with an ARIMA (0, 1, 1) model (i.e. an ARIMA model with 0 autoregressive parameters, 1 difference to obtain stationarity, and 1 moving average parameter). More recently, Goodman [15] and Cogger [10] have shown that the forecasts produced by multiple exponential smoothing of order k are optimal in a minimum mean square error sense for a restricted class of ARIMA (0, k, k) processes. McKenzie [20] has extended these results to direct smoothing models in which the model may contain transcendental terms. Thus, exponential smoothing methods are really just special cases of the more general ARIMA model structure.

Although their equivalence to certain ARIMA model forms suggests that exponential smoothing would be useful only for a small variety of time series, practical experience indicates that the opposite is true. Cox [12] noted that first-order exponential smoothing performed well for a number of series that were not of moving average form, and in fact, derived an optimal value of the smoothing constant α for forecasting a first-order stationary autoregressive process. Pandit and Wu [25] suggest exponential smoothing as the optimal forecasting procedure for a uniformly sampled autoregressive moving average process, and show that various special cases of this model imply values for the smoothing constant. The general implication is that there are a wide variety of actual time series for which exponential smoothing methods will perform satisfactorily.

3. Characteristics of smoothing methods

There are a number of aspects to the application of exponential smoothing and related methods that explain their popularity. Essentially these methods are relatively easy to develop and install, have good operating characteristics, yield reasonable accuracy, and generally can be explained to nontechnical management involved in the forecasting system.

Exponential smoothing methods are ideally suited for situations in which a relatively large number of time series must be forecast on a periodic basis, as in forecasting for inventory control purposes. A common model form, perhaps containing trend and seasonal terms, can be used for large groupings of items, with the parameters of the model varying from item to item. Model initialization is relatively simple, using either available historical data or subjective considerations to establish the initial parameter values. These methods require limited data storage. Only evaluation of simple algebraic expressions is necessary to revise periodically a model's parameters. The rate of smoothing can be modified, either by external intervention or adaptively through internal logic, to adjust the responsiveness of the model to forecast error.

Periodic forecasts of the expected value of the time series variable in any future period are calculated by evaluating the model for the lead time of interest, as indicated by (17). For those smoothing models derived using a discounted least squares criterion, it also is possible to develop relatively simple algebraic functions that permit the forecasts to be stated in terms of a prediction interval. The prediction interval is based on a specified probability of the interval containing the true realization of the time series variable. It is usually possible to develop closed form expressions for the cumulative forecast over a number of future periods, as a function of the forecast lead time. This is useful in inventory control, for example, where procurement lead times vary among items.

Exponential smoothing methods are very compatible with efforts to control forecasting performance. Error analysis of often based on tracking signal tests. Two forms of the tracking signal are in common use. One version, based on the cumulative forecast error, is due to Brown [4]. Let $Y(T)$ be the cumulative forecast error at the end of period T. This is a measure of forecast bias. For computation, we use

$$Y(T) = Y(T-1) + e_1(T).$$

If an estimate of the standard deviation of Y, say $\hat{\sigma}_Y$, is available, then we would conclude that the forecasts are biased if $|Y(T)|$ exceeds some multiple, say K_1, of $\hat{\sigma}_Y$. It is customary to base this test on the smoothed mean absolute deviation

$$\hat{\Delta}(T) = \alpha|e_1(T)| + (1-\alpha)\hat{\Delta}(T-1),$$

rather than $\hat{\sigma}_Y$. The smoothed mean absolute deviation is related to the standard deviation of the one-step ahead forecast error by $\hat{\sigma}_e = 1.25\,\hat{\Delta}(T)$, assuming that the forecast errors are approximately normally distributed. The ratio $Y(T)/\hat{\Delta}(T)$ is called the *cumulative error tracking signal,* computed at time T. If the ratio

$$|Y(T)/\hat{\Delta}(T)| > K_2, \tag{24}$$

we conclude that the forecasts are biased, and that some intervention in the forecasting system is necessary. If a relationship between σ_Y^2 and σ_e^2 can be found, then this can be used to determine the critical value of K_2 in (24) (see [4, pp. 288–289] and [23, pp.163–165]). When dealing with complex smoothing models, one usually chooses K_2 directly. Typical values are $4 \leqslant K_2 \leqslant 6$.

The second type of tracking signal, due to Trigg [28], is based on the smoothed error. We define the smoothed error as

$$Q(T) = \alpha e_1(T) + (1-\alpha)Q(T-1).$$

The ratio $Q(T)/\hat{\Delta}(T)$ is called the *smoothed error tracking signal.* The hypothesis of an unbiased forecast would be rejected if

$$|Q(T)/\hat{\Delta}(T)| > K_3.$$

Appropriate values of K_3 are $0.2 \leqslant K_3 \leqslant 0.5$. For a discussion of the relative advantages of the two types of tracking signals see [23, pp. 166–167].

A principal advantage of exponential smoothing is the ease with which the model can be adjusted when the tracking signal indicates an out-of-control condition. The rate of smoothing can be increased by utilizing a larger smoothing constant, or by employing a new smoothing vector h in (20) based on a smaller discount factor. If a direct smoothing formulation is employed, one may also directly modify the parameter estimates $\hat{a}(T)$. This is possible in situations where the parameters have a logical interpretation to the forecast manager (as, for example, the parameter representing trend).

In addition to external intervention by an analyst, it is possible to design internal adaptive control procedures for adjusting the smoothing constants, so that the effects of dynamic changes in the time series can be automatically incorporated into the forecasting procedure. A number of authors have devised procedures for automatic control of a single exponential smoothing constant; for example, see Chow [9], Trigg and Leach [29], and Whybark [31]. Their procedures can be used directly with multiple smoothing models, and with minor variations, on direct smoothing models. Roberts and Reed [27] and Montgomery [22] have proposed techniques for the automatic control of several smoothing constants, as would be required for Holt–Winters type models. Harrison and Davies [17] have suggested forecast control procedures based on the cumulative sum of forecast errors. The ability to automatically adapt smoothing constants to changing conditions is an important extension of exponential smoothing. This capability does not yet exist for other types of forecasting systems, although Bagshaw and Johnson [1] have recently proposed procedures that may be useful in designing a self-adaptive ARIMA forecasting model.

The problem of selecting the form of the model is relatively straightforward. Historical data can be analyzed to determine the presence of trend and seasonality, and if seasonality is a consideration, what are the important frequencies. A model can then be constructed to include the relevant terms, and the direct smoothing procedure can be used. Generally, fewer historical data are required to obtain good initial parameter estimates in exponential smoothing than is usually suggested in time series analysis procedures. This is due, at least in part, to the dependency of time series procedures on autocorrelation analysis to determine model structure, and relatively long series must be used to obtain stable estimates of autocorrelation coefficients. However, even if no useful historical data are available, a time series model can be formed through subjective consideration of the expected future nature of the time series. The ability to rationally select model forms that have a high likelihood of being representative of a future time series, when there is limited valid historical information, is an important characteristic of direct smoothing methods.

When compared to more complex methods of time series analysis and to methods involving development of multiple regression models to exploit causal or correlative relationships between other time series and the time series of interest, both of which require more development and operating effort, exponential smoothing methods often are preferred because of the attributes and advantages mentioned previously. From an economic point of view, the value of any increased forecasting accuracy resulting from use of more sophisticated methods is more than offset by the lower cost and greater operating flexibility afforded by exponential and direct smoothing procedures. The objective of forecasting is to reduce the uncertainty in decision making, thereby averting a portion of the opportunity losses associated with the uncertainties. Because many time series contain a strong random component that cannot be forecast in any case, increased expenditures on forecasting systems reach a point of diminishing returns far short of perfect accuracy. Usually the optimal level of effort is in the range of expenditure required for exponential smoothing and associated methods. To see this, note that the variance of forecast error is a function of the variance of the time series process plus the variance resulting from improper model identification and errors in parameter estimation, or more formally

$$V(\text{Forecast Error}) = V(\text{Process})[1 + c], \qquad c \geqslant 0.$$

Perfect forecasting would yield $c = 0$. If c is much less than 1, the variance of forecast error is basically a function of the noise in the process, and less influenced by the relative accuracy of the forecasting method used.

For a more complete discussion of the characteristics and advantages of exponential smoothing methods, see [4], [23] and [30].

4. Summary

Smoothing methods provide a means of periodically revising the parameters in a time series model by means of algebraic equations that combine prior parameter estimates with current forecast error experience to obtain new parameter estimates. The following are some of the more important reasons for the widespread use of these methods:

(1) The selection of the form of the time series model can be done in a rational manner based either on objective historical data or subjective consideration of the future. A modest amount of historical data is usually sufficient for determining initial parameter values.

(2) Determination of initial values for model parameters is usually easily done.

(3) Model parameters often have intuitive meaning to the forecaster.

(4) Only limited data storage is required.

(5) The same model form may be used for a large number of time series.

(6) Periodic revision of model parameters is easily accomplished by means of simple algebraic expressions.

(7) Forecast generation based on the model is straightforward extrapolation over the lead time of interest.

(8) Forecasts can often be stated in terms of prediction intervals with little additional effort.

(9) Cumulative forecasts can usually be expressed as closed form expressions involving the model's parameters and the lead time length.

(10) The relation between stability and responsiveness of the forecasting procedure can be adjusted easily by changing the rate of smoothing.

(11) Tracking signal tests for forecast control are easy to apply, with corrective action on out-of-control situations being possible either automatically through programmed logic or through external intervention.

(12) The cost of developing the model and operating it is less than that of more sophisticated time series methods and causal models, while the accuracy obtained in the forecasting stage (as opposed to the parameter estimation or fitting stage) is often comparable.

References

[1] M. Bagshaw and R.A. Johnson, Sequential procedures for detecting parameter changes in a time-series model, Journal of the American Statistical Association 72, No. 359 (1977) 593–597.

[2] D.J. Bamber, A versatile family of forecasting systems, Operational Research Quarterly 20 (1969) 111–121.

[3] R.G. Brown, Statistical Forecasting for Inventory Control (McGraw-Hill, Inc., New York, 1959).

[4] R.G. Brown, Smoothing, Forecasting and Prediction of Discrete Time Series (Prentice-Hall, Inc., Englewood Cliffs, N.J., 1962).

[5] R.G. Brown, Decision Rules for Inventory Management (Holt, Rinehart and Winston, Inc., New York, 1967).

[6] R.G. Brown and R.F. Meyer, The fundamental theorem of exponential smoothing, Operations Research 9, No. 6 (1960) 673–685.

[7] G.E.P. Box and G.M. Jenkins, Time Series Analysis, Forecasting, and Control, 2nd ed. (Holden-Day, Inc., San Francisco, 1976).

[8] G.K.C. Chen and P.R. Winters, Forecasting peak demand for an electric utility with a hybrid exponential model, Management Science 12, No. 12 (1966) 531–537.

[9] W.M. Chow, Adaptive control of the exponential smoothing constant, Journal of Industrial Engineering 16, No. 5 (1965) 314–317.

[10] G.D. Cohen, Bayesian adjustment of sales forecasts in multi-item inventory control systems, Journal of Industrial Engineering 17, No. 9 (1966) 474–479.

[11] K.O. Cogger, The optimality of general-order exponential smoothing, Operations Research 22, No. 4 (1974) 858–867.

[12] D.R. Cox, Prediction by exponentially weighted moving averages and related methods, Journal of the Royal Statistical Society B23, No. 2 (1961) 414–422.

[13] D.B. Crane and J.R. Crotty, A two-stage forecasting model: exponential smoothing multiple regression, Management Science 13, No. 8 (1967) 501–507.

[14] D.A. D'Esopo, A note on forecasting by the exponential smoothing operator, Operations Research 9, No. 5 (1961) 686–687.

[15] M.L. Goodman, A new look at higher-order exponential smoothing for forecasting, Operations Research 22, No. 4 (1974) 880–888.

[16] P.J. Harrison, Exponential smoothing and short-term sales forecasting, Management Science 13, No. 11 (1967) 821–842.

[17] P.J. Harrison and O.L. Davies, The use of cumulative sum (CUSUM) techniques for the control of routine forecasts of product demand, Operations Research 12, No. 2 (1964) 325–333.

[18] C.C. Holt, Forecasting trends and seasonals by exponentially weighted moving averages, O.N.R. Memorandum No. 52 (Carnege Institute of Technology, 1957).

[19] J.O. McClain and L.J. Thomas, Response-variance tradeoffs in adapative forecasting, Operations Research 21, No. 2 (1973) 554–568.

[20] E. McKenzie, An analysis of general exponential smoothing, Operations Research 24, 11 (1976) 131–140.

[21] R.F. Meyer, An adaptive method for routine short-term forecasting, Proceedings of the 3rd International Conference on Operational Research (English Universities Press, London, 1964, 882–895).

[22] D.C. Montgomery, Adaptive control of exponential smoothing parameters by evolutionary operation, AIIE Transactions 2, No. 3 (197) 268–269.

[23] D.C. Montgomery and L.A. Johnson, Forecasting and Time Series Analysis (McGraw-Hill, Inc., New York, 1976).

[24] J.F. Muth, Optimal properties of exponentially weighted forecasts of time series with permanent and transitory components, Journal of the American Statistical Association 55, No. 290 (1960) 299–306.

[25] S.M. Pandit and S.M. Wu, Exponential smoothing as a special case of a linear stochastic system, Operations Research 22, No. 4 (1974) 868–879.

[26] C.C. Pegels, A note on exponential forecasting, Management Science 15, No. 5 (1969) 311–315.

[27] S.R. Roberts and R. Reed, The development of a self-adaptive forecasting technique, AIIE Transactions 1, No. 4 (1969) 314–322.

[28] D.W. Trigg, Monitoring a forecasting system, Operational Research Quarterly 15 (1964) 271–274.

[29] D.W. Trigg and A.G. Leach, Exponential smoothing with an adaptive response rate, Operational Research Quarterly 18 (1967) 53–59.

[30] S.C. Wheelwright and S. Makridakis, Forecasting Methods for Management, 2nd Edition (Wiley, New York, 1977).

[31] D.C. Whybark, A comparison of adaptive forecasting techniques, The Logistics and Transportation Review 8 (1970).

[32] P.R. Winters, Forecasting sales by exponentially weighted moving averages, Management Science 6, No. 3 (1960) 324–342.

TIMS Studies in the Management Sciences 12 (1979) 45–57
© North-Holland Publishing Company

SEASONAL ADJUSTMENT – A SURVEY

J. Peter BURMAN

Bank of England, London

This paper gives a brief history of moving average methods of seasonal adjustment since 1960 and a comparative description of the main steps in four additive and multiplicative methods used officially. These steps are trend removal, choice of smoothing, smoothing of the seasonal pattern, and subtraction from, or division into, the original series. Two mixed additive-multiplicative methods are also mentioned. The properties of an ideal adjustment procedure are listed and reference is made to analyses of the performance of the various methods. Unfortunately, these properties are either satisfied by all methods or they conflict with one another. In addition, the paper summarizes the contributions to the Washington Conference of 1976, at which leading time series theorists and applied statisticians discussed ways of improving seasonal adjustment methods. An optimal method of adjustment, signal extraction, was proposed but its properties still need to be tested practically. The concluding section looks at the possibilities of new methods coming into use in the next few years.

1. Description of moving average methods

Because of the comparatively recent growth of demand for economic information and the high cost of collection, economic time series are usually monthly or quarterly and are comparatively short. They have short-term irregularities and often a periodicity associated with the calendar year. Moving average (m.a.) methods assume that the series consists of three components – trend-cycle (T), seasonal (S) and irregular (I), that is, $Y = T + S + I$ (additive), or $Y = TSI$ (multiplicative), or sometimes $Y = TS_1 + S_2 + I$ (mixed).

S may be a strictly periodic series (with a period of one year), but usually it is thought of as varying slowly over time. T is taken to be a smooth series, that may have cycles, provided their periods are substantially greater than one year. Already it is apparent that a subjective element is present: How smooth must T be? Can oscillations of, say, 18 months be distinguished from the seasonal pattern? And, most importantly, how rapidly may S vary over the years? The authors of the methods described below have taken different views about these questions (see, for example, the discussion on smoothing).

The earliest practical method of analysis for series with moving seasonality was published by the U.S. Bureau of the Census in 1957, but its large-scale use depended on the development of the computer. At a conference on this subject held by the OECD in Paris [22], the Bureau presented the latest version of its

Table 1
Comparison of Main Steps in Four Seasonal Adjustment Methods

	X.11	EEC Seabird	Bank of England (BE)	Berlin
Type of model	Additive or multiplicative (ratios)	Additive only; multiplicative assumed covered by rapid adjustment of scaling factor (see below)	Additive or multiplicative (log transform)	Additive
Trend removal	9, 13, or 23-term weighted average (at 2d iteration); symmetric, end terms lost	19-term weighted average; symmetric in central part, skew for end terms	13-term weighted average (except 1st harmonic which uses 25-term weighted and 13-term unweighted averages); symmetric, end terms lost	Regression of cubic (plus harmonic variables) fitted to 23 observations, 12 before and 10 after the term being estimated
Components of pattern	12 months constrained to sum to zero	11 harmonics (excluding insignificant ones) [a]	11 harmonics	11 harmonics (excluding insignificant ones) [a]
Choice of smoothing	–	–	Pooled von Neumann ratio as criterion of moving pattern	–
Smoothing seasonals	{3}{3} 1st round {3}{5} 2d round	{5}	Fixed or exponential (λ = 0.9, 0.8, or 0.7) or {3}{5} or {5}	Regression of 11 harmonic variables (plus 5th degree polynomial) fitted to 45 observations, 23 before and 21 after the term being estimated

Special feature	—	Seasonal split into pattern (moving 5-year average) and scaling factor (moving 12-month average) [a]	—	—
Manner of replacing extremes	Graduated weights between 1.5 and 2.5 sigma [a]	Effect of extremes muted by various steps with truncation; [a] also extremes identified and given zero weight [a]	Graduated weights between 2.0 and 2.5 sigma [a]	Identified by comparison with previous 24 terms; replaced by upper/lower bound of selected confidence intervals [a]
Quarterly version	Yes	No	Yes	Yes
Trading-day adjustment	Yes	No	Not included but has been used in separate program	No

[a] These steps create non linearity in the filters

method, the X.10. Following criticisms of this method by a U.S. official committee [25] and by Nerlove [20], it was replaced in 1965 by the X.11, which has come into worldwide use. At the same time the author developed an optimal filter method [4], modified in 1967, which is currently used at the Bank of England (called BE below). A little later Nullau published an article on the BERLIN method [21] used at the German Institute for Economic Research, and Mesnage the SEABIRD method [18] developed by himself and Bongard [1], which is used by the Statistical Office of the European Economic Community. Mesnage and Bongard have recently announced their intention of replacing SEABIRD by a new method, called DAINTIES [2]. In 1974 den Haan described [15] the Dutch Central Planning Bureau mixed additive-multiplicative method (CPB), which was followed by the Durbin-Murphy mixed method [10], which has been used experimentally by the United Kingdom (CSO).

Why such a proliferation of methods? One reason was a dislike of the iterative features of X.11, and another the search for a clearer theoretical model. Some thought that X.11 was too flexible for very irregular series; that is it would give excessive movement in the seasonal pattern. Others, on the contrary, thought it not flexible enough. Very few comparisons of performance have been published [11,7] because of the extreme difficulty in agreeing on criteria and the absence of clear-cut results.

To explain this situation, one must look at the differences between four of the methods applied to monthly series, using the additive model for simplicity. Table 1 shows the essential features of these methods. Each one starts by 1) removing trend (leaving $(S + I)$, 2) choosing the smoothing average (this step applies only to be BE method), 3) smoothing $(S + I)$ by using the selected average to give S, and 4) subtracting S from Y to give the seasonally adjusted series.

A property of most seasonal adjustment methods is their symmetry; each filter is symmetric when applied to the central portion of the series. For terms near the ends, asymmetric filters have to be used, but they have what may be called weak symmetry: seasonally adjusting the reverse of the original series gives the same result as seasonally adjusting the original series and reversing it.

All the methods described here have weak symmetry, except BERLIN. Its asymmetric filter for trend removal may displace the estimated peak and trough of the business cycle and have undesirable effects on the seasonal adjustment. X.11 uses the $\{12\}\{2\}$ monthly filter [1] for the preliminary estimate of S, then, because it is thought that this filter does not remove all the trend, a 13-term weighted average of the preliminary adjusted series is used to obtain the trend for the final S. It is not possible to use the second filter on the first round, because it distorts the seasonal pattern. BE uses a similar 13-term weighted average, but recovers the original seasonal pattern by harmonic analysis [4, section 6], avoiding iteration. SEABIRD and BERLIN also avoid iteration. However, apart from asymmetry, differences in trend

---

[1] This filter is a 2-month average of a 12-month average.

removal are not likely to cause major differences in the results, because any trend not removed by these filters is very much attenuated by the smoothing filter.

The critical features are:

1. The choice of model (additive, multiplicative, or mixed).
2. The smoothing average used for $(S + I)$.
3. The manner of treating extreme or maverick observations.

With regard to model choice, SEABIRD and BERLIN offer only an additive model, but the former analyzes S into a normalized pattern and a scale factor – this factor being estimated over a very short period and so, it is hoped, adapting to a rapildy growing series. The user chooses the model in the other two methods. Unless the series shows little growth, he will try both models and select the one that gives the more stable S. Usually that will also be the one with the smaller number of mavericks.

The manner of smoothing determines the flexibility of a method. X.11 has {3} {5} year smoothing on its final round, after modification of extreme values. SEABIRD smooths the normalized pattern of S over five years, but the scaling factor over one year. Thus it is considerably more flexible than X.11, its values of S are more erratic for a given month, and they do not sum to approximately zero over a year. For BERLIN the smoothing average covers 45 months (again asymmetric), which makes it, too, more flexible than X.11. In BE, S is analyzed into 11 harmonic components, each of which is smoothed independently, the appropriate average being chosen automatically. In practice, BE is less flexible than X.11 because most of the components are smoothed by longer averages than {3} {5}. Criteria for judging the appropriateness of the smoothing are discussed in the next section.

Unlike the case in linear regression, extreme observations in m.a. seasonal adjustment are very important, and the treatment varies a good deal. In X.11 a root mean square (sigma) of I is estimated over spans of five years, and (in the standard option) extremes beyond 2.5 sigma are totally rejected. A new sigma is calculated for the remaining observations and again extremes beyond 2.5 sigma are rejected, while those between 1.5 and 2.5 sigma are given reduced weight. In BE the weights are tapered to zero between 2.0 and 2.5 sigma, there is no iteration, and the interaction of two adjacent extremes is allowed for. The purpose of tapering is that when the seasonal adjustment is updated the treatment of an extreme should not change abruptly. SEABIRD deals with isolated extremes (they occur only rarely) but also has an elaborate system of truncating outliers from a group of observations, which is applied at various stages.

The two mixed additive-multiplicative methods (CPB and CSO) are not shown in table 1. They have only been used with the unemployment series in various countries, since there are economic reasons why mixed models should be valid in this case and it is particularly difficult to discriminate between pure additive and pure multiplicative models. But large numbers of parameters are needed to define the seasonal pattern and there tends to be collinearity between corresponding components of S_1 and S_2. In CPB the number of parameters is reduced by assuming, first, a fixed ratio between the additive and multiplicative components, and, second, a linear or quadratic trend in the seasonal pattern. CSO also uses a special feature from SEABIRD − the division of the seasonal pattern between a normalized shape and a (varying) scale factor. It also has a very thorough method of allowing for interactions between adjacent extremes. The limited use of these methods reflects the amount of judgment of individual results that is needed.

2. Comparative behaviour of moving average methods

The following properties are required by the user of seasonally adjusted series [11,17]:
1. No residual seasonality − for example, the correlogram should show no peak at lag 12.
2. Idempotency (no further adjustment when applied a second time).
3. Rapid response to changes in the seasonal pattern.
4. Minimum revisions when updating (stability).
5. No overadjustment − evidenced by a negative correlation at lag 12.
6. Aggregation consistency − when a total series and its components are adjusted separately, the former should still equal the sum of the latter.

Arranging the methods in order of flexibility, one finds that the more flexible methods have a more rapid response, but less stability. The diagram below indicates the order of flexibility for the four methods.

Fixed seasonal	BE	X.11	BERLIN	SEABIRD

increasing flexibility $\longrightarrow$

Fase et al. [11] showed that none of the moving average methods left any significant *residual seasonality*. They found that BE scored best for *idempotency* (apart from the fixed pattern methods, which are completely idempotent). On *stability* only the fixed pattern methods were rated satisfactory, X.11 and BE were indecisive and SEABIRD poor. There was not much difference in average stability between BE and X.11 because, although BE is less flexible, it is liable sometimes to larger revisions when the choice of smoothing parameters changes on updating. (See, for example, the results for U.S. housing starts, which have an almost fixed pattern, in the author's discussion on Kuiper (Burman [6]).) The same reference shows that both BE and X.11 tend to give slight overadjustment, but it is usually smaller for the former. The *aggregation* problem disappears if the method is strictly linear; but unfortunately all four methods have nonlinear features, for example, omission of nonsignificant components of S and modification of extreme observations (see table 1).

The conflict between rapid response and minimum revisions can only be resolved by recourse to some wider criterion. The author has suggested testing which method of adjustment is a better aid to forecasting, since this is one the the prime reasons for adjusting. But objective forecasting of a single series involves a model and an obvious choice is the well-known Box—Jenkins class. Extensive testing was carried out [6,7] with both real and simulated series. Each series was seasonally adjusted and a Box—Jenkins nonseasonal model fitted; the forecasts were combined with forecast S to give a forecast of the original series. SEABIRD did not perform well in these tests, but the comparisons between BE and X.11 were totally inconclusive. In this context it is relevant that Whittle [27, p. 38] found that a model which is not very close to the true model of a series may nevertheless have almost as good predictive power as the latter.

Several writers have suggested using spectral analysis to provide a criterion of seasonal adjustment [20,14,5]. The spectrum of a series measures the average proportion of its variance that can be attributed to oscillations in different frequency bands. For a monthly economic series there is a lot of spectral power in the low frequencies (say, periods of two years or less), which we recognize as the trend-cycle component. For seasonal series there are also peaks at frequency 1/12 (one year) and multiples of this up to 6/12 (two months) (see figure 1).

The ideal method of seasonal adjustment would remove the seasonal peaks in the spectrum, leaving the troughs alone, so that the adjusted series would have a fairly smooth spectrum (still with the trend peak at low frequencies). But it is impossible to estimate the spectrum to reasonable accuracy with less than about 150 observa-

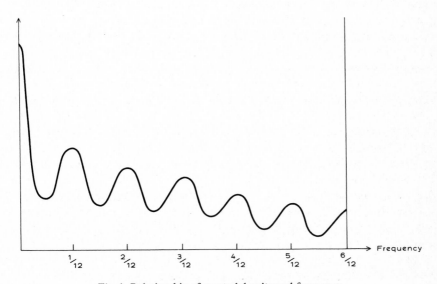

Fig. 1. Relationship of spectral density and frequency.

tions (12 years) and often statisticians are adjusting only 7 to 8 years' data. Also, even with longer series, there are few statistical tests of whether a spectrum is smooth or whether one method of adjustment removes significantly more power than another at interseasonal frequencies. So spectral methods have not yet been successfully used to discriminate between methods (see [17]).

3. NBER-Census conference on seasonal analysis

Because of the variety of empirical methods of seasonal adjustment used by official statisticians and the difficulties they present to the practitioners of forecasting (who do not necessarily understand the properties of each method), the National Bureau of Economic Research and the U.S. Bureau of the Census decided to hold a conference on this subject. It took place in Washington, D.C., on September 9 and 10, 1976, and was very successful in bringing together official statisticians and academics. They explored the philosophy of seasonal adjustment, the advantages of the existing empirical and new theoretical methods, and the problems of handling groups of related series. The papers and contributions by discussants are to be published shortly, but they are summarized here under six topical headings.

Objectives and framework of seasonal analysis

Kallek, an official statistician, and Granger from the academic viewpoint, presented thoughtful analyses of the problems encountered in establishing the objectives and framework of seasonal analysis [16,13]. Another academic, Tukey, in his discussion on Granger's paper, demonstrated clearly that no method of adjustment of a seasonal series can make it indistinguishable from a series that was never seasonal in the first place. An adjusted series will always have dips in its spectrum at seasonal frequencies.

Description and analysis of seasonal adjustment procedures in use

Kuiper surveyed existing empirical methods [17] (discussed earlier in this paper) and described a new version of X.11 – the X.11 ARIMA method developed by Dagum [9] at Statistics Canada. In this method the missing observations required to estimate symmetric averages at the ends of the series are supplied by a Box–Jenkins ARIMA model. The paper concluded that it was very difficult to rank the performance of methods, apart from BERLIN, which failed one of Kuiper's tests, and X.11 ARIMA, which seemed to have some advantage in terms of minimum revisions.

Specific problems in existing methods

Among the specific problems dealt with were the treatment of extreme observations and movable public holidays, and the difficulties of model selection in mixed additive-multiplicative models.

New methods for analyzing seasonal problems

In many ways the contributions on new methods were the most important aspect of the conference. There were papers by Pierce [23] and by Box, Hillmer and Tiao [3] on the signal extraction method of seasonal adjustment first proposed by Grether and Nerlove [14]. The method, as described by Box et al., consists of the following steps:

Step 1. Fit Box–Jenkins seasonal model

$$y_t = \frac{\theta(B)\Theta(B^s)}{\phi(B)\Phi(B^s)} e_t = f(B) e_t \quad \text{(say)}$$

where B is the lag operator, e_t is a series of independently, identically distributed random variables (white noise), the function is normalized by making the coefficient of B^0 unity, and s is the period of seasonality.

Step 2. The spectrum of this series is:

$$g(\omega) = f(z)f(z^{-1}) \sigma_e^2$$

where $z = e^{i\omega}$ and σ_e^2 is the variance of e_t [27, chapter 3]. Assume that y_t is the sum of two independent series generated by ARIMA models, representing the seasonally adjusted series and the seasonal component:

$$y_t = f_a(B)d_t + f_s(B)b_t = p_t + s_t$$

$$\text{Then } g(\omega) \equiv f_a(z)f_a(z^{-1}) \sigma_d^2 + f_s(z)f_s(z^{-1}) \sigma_b^2;$$

that is, the spectrum of y_t is the sum of the spectra of p_t and s_t. The models of the latter are chosen so that the spectrum of p_t is smooth, usually with a peak at zero frequency, while that of s_t has peaks at the (s) seasonal frequencies and not at zero. This requires that the denominator of the y_t model be factorized: the denominator of $f_a(B)$ containing $\phi(B)$ and factors corresponding to *real positive* roots of $\Phi(B^s) = 0$; and the denominator of $f_s(B)$ containing the remainder of $\Phi(B^s)$. As the author pointed out in the discussion on [3], a feasible partition can be obtained by expressing $g(\omega)$ as a rational function of $\cos \omega$, and then applying the technique of partial fractions, but that is not the only feasible solution.

Step 3. Box et al. make the partition unique by the principle of minimum signal extraction (MSE); that is, find the minimum of the spectrum of s_t and subtract from it the corresponding white noise. Denoting this minimum by $\epsilon^* \sigma_e^2$, and the revised spectra by asterisks:

$$g_a^*(\omega) = f_a(z)f_a(z^{-1}) \sigma_d^2 + \epsilon^* \sigma_e^2 = h_a(z, z^{-1}) \sigma_e^2,$$

$$g_s^*(\omega) = f_s(z)f_s(z^{-1}) \sigma_b^2 - \epsilon^* \sigma_e^2 = h_s(z, z^{-1}) \sigma_e^2,$$

where σ_d^2 and σ_b^2 have been expressed as known fractions of σ_e^2, and h_a and h_s are symmetric functions of z, z^{-1},

Step 4. The MSE filters for p_t and s_t are respectively:

$$\frac{h_a(B, F)}{f(B)f(F)} \quad \text{and} \quad \frac{h_s(B, F)}{f(B)f(F)} \quad \text{(where } F \text{ is the forward shift operator).}$$

The proof is in Whittle [27]. This is a doubly infinite filter, but Cleveland [8] showed that it could be applied to the forecast and backcast series derived from y_t to give the asymptotic estimates $E(p|y)$ and $E(s|y)$.

Step 5. Obtain a power series expansion of the filter for p_t (this is the simpler one), using the recurrence formulae of Box et al. [3] Appendix).

Step 6. Forecast and backcast y_t to the point where the coefficients of B^n and F^n in the filter are small.

Step 7. Apply the filter to the extended series y_t to obtain $\hat{p}_t; \hat{s}_t = y_t - \hat{p}_t$.

Pierce [23] uses a slightly different ARIMA model and applies trend removal and seasonal smoothing filters successively, instead of in a combined moving average. He considers carefully the difficult problem of model identification, and he extends this process to include the possibility of removing seasonal means from the series (deterministic seasonality) before applying the filters.

Econometric modeling and seasonality

The contribution on econometric models contained interesting papers by Wallis [26] and by Plosser [24]. These point out that a system of simultaneous equations in seasonally adjusted time series could give incorrect estimates of the relationships, if the adjustment procedure was inappropriate. In principle, a better method is to use an extended system with the structural equations linking the unadjusted series by rational lags, and further equations representing the exogenous variables in terms of ARIMA seasonal models. The error terms in the structural equations would also in general have rational lag structures. An alternative formulation of the system (the final equations) expresses the current value of each endogenous variable in terms of its own past values and the current and past values of the exogenous variables. In this form, certain restrictions on the form of the rational lag operators are required if the model is to be valid. In spite of these restrictions and the length of the series used (over 200 observations in both papers), there are serious problems in determining the correct model specification (Box–Jenkins 'identification'). It seems highly improbable that this approach could be used for any but the smallest econometric models, and then only when exceptionally long runs of data are available.

Aggregation and seasonal analysis

Comments on aggregation dealt mainly with the important practical question of how to seasonally adjust the components of a series — for example, a regional or commodity breakdown — so that they are consistent with the adjusted total. Geweke [12] points out that for maximum use of information the components and total should be adjusted simultaneously unless the components are completely independent. He sketches out an extension of the signal extraction method which would enable this to be done, but the procedure in his one empirical example is rather *ad hoc,* and needs to be generalized. Box et al. [3] also touch on the seasonal adjustment of multiple series, of which the aggregation problem is a special case. Suppose, for example, that a series is a sum of two components Y_{1t} and Y_{2t}: these may be expressible as rational lag functions of two independent while noises a_{1t}, a_{2t}. Geweke constructs the spectral matrix (auto-spectra and cross-spectra) of the two series: this is Hermitian. The spectral matrix $S(\omega)$ must then be partitioned into seasonal and nonseasonal parts $[S^s(\omega)$ and $S^n(\omega)]$. Geweke does not say how, but a feasible solution can probably be obtained by a generalization of the partial fraction technique suggested by the author for the univariate case. Geweke shows that $S^n(\omega)S(\omega)^{-1}$ is a valid signal extraction filter, but does not indicate how to choose the optimum filter (minimum signal extraction).

4. Conclusion

At least two of the traditional moving average methods in current use appear to give satisfactory results over a wide range of series, but there are some series — for example erratic series or those subject to abrupt changes in seasonality — for which they are not satisfactory; and there is a feeling among economic model builders that inappropriate seasonal adjustment may give rise to incorrect economic relationships. The main difficulty with the traditional methods is in finding the right trade-off between flexibility and stability, and it is clear that no method is optimal.

Recent advances in the theory of ARIMA models, as discussed at the September 1976 Washington Conference, have shown that the optimal method is a minimum signal extraction filter (MSEF). Given that a model has been fitted to a series, MSEF provides the best linear filter for estimating the terms of the adjusted series. These filters have the property of weak symmetry defined earlier.

The method is also applicable in principle to multivariate series, and would provide an optimal solution to the aggregation problem.

This method is a big step forward, but many practical questions must be resolved before MSEF is acceptable for large-scale use by official statisticians. Among these questions are the following:
1. What range of ARIMA models will be entertained?
2. Case studies have shown that models with different structures — for example, varying degrees of differencing — can be fitted equally well to a single economic series, partly because the series are relatively short. How can one choose between them? If the accumulation of more data indicates a change of model, will that cause larger revisions to earlier figures than traditional methods?
3. A simple model can be adequately fitted with, say, 100 observations (8 years of monthly data), but what should official statisticians do if, as is now the case, they

have to provide seasonal adjustments for 5 to 6 years' data?
4. If the series is long enough to fit an ARIMA model, can the Box–Jenkins identification procedure be reduced to a set of automatic rules suitable for an organization with hundreds or thousands of series to adjust?

It will still be necessary to identify extreme observations, estimate modified values
for them, and refit the model. Length-of-month or number-of-working-days effects
in monthly series will also need to be tested and, if found, removed before reestimation. The U.S. Bureau of the Census is going to experiment with the X.11-ARIMA
program. This method could be brought into use fairly quickly.

The next few years should be an interesting period for all concerned with seasonal adjustment because, for the first time, there has been a meeting of minds
between time-series theorists and applied statisticians who are responsible for publishing adjusted series. If signal extraction methods are adopted, they will allow, in
theory, for more rapid adaptation to sudden change than the traditional methods;
but that implies the risk of larger revisions if the change is really only part of the
irregular component. Meanwhile, private users of economic series are probably well
advised to use seasonally adjusted series in economic models (other than very small
ones). They should also be aware that there are other methods of adjustment than
X.11 and should be prepared to try these if the adjustments provided by the latter
seem unsatisfactory.

References

[1] J. Bongard, Some remarks on moving averages, Seasonal adjustment on Electronic Com-
    puters OECD (1960) 361–390.
[2] J. Bongard, Aspects de la theorie des moyennes mobiles, paper presented at the Confer-
    ence on Seasonal Adjustment, Free University Amsterdam, April 1–2, 1976 (unpub-
    lished).
[3] G.E.P. Box, S.C. Hilmer and G.C. Tiao, Analysis and modelling of seasonal time series,
    paper presented at the NBER-Census Conference on Seasonal Analysis of Economic Time
    Series, Washington, D.C., September 9–10, 1976 (to be published).
[4] J.P. Burman, Moving seasonal adjustment of economic time series, Journal of the Royal
    Statistical Society, Series A 128 (1965) 534–538.
[5] J.P. Burman, Assessment of a seasonal adjustment procedure by spectral analysis, Journal
    of the J. Institute of Statisticians 17 (1967) 247–256.
[6] J.P. Burman, Comments on John Kuiper's paper, NBer-Census Conference on Seasonal
    Analysis of Economic Time Series, Washington, D.C., September 9–10, 1976 (to be pub-
    lished).
[7] J.P. Burman, Seasonal adjustment of artificial series generated from a Box–Jenkins Model,
    paper presented at the Conference on Seasonal Adjustment, Free University Amsterdam,
    April 1–2, 1976 (unpublished).
[8] W.P. Cleveland, Analysis and forecasting of seasonal time series, PH.D. dissertation Univer-
    sity of Wisconsin (1972).
[9] E.B. Dagum, Seasonal factor forecasts from ARIMA models, contributed papers, 40th Ses-
    sion of International Statistical Institute (1975) 206–219.

[10] J. Durbin and M.J. Murphy, Seasonal adjustment based on a mixed additive-multiplicative model, Journal of the Royal Statistical Society, Series A 138 (1975) 385–410.

[11] M.M.G. Fase, J. Koning and A.F. Volgenant, An experimental look at seasonal adjustment, De Economist 121 (1973) 441–480.

[12] J. Geweke, Temporal and sectoral aggregation of seasonally adjusted time series, paper presented at the NBER-Census Conference on Seasonal Analysis of Economic Time Series, Washington, D.C., September 9–10, 1976 (to be published).

[13] C.W.J. Granger, Seasonality: causation, interpretation and implications, paper presented at the NBER-Census Conference on Seasonal Analysis of Economic Time Series, Washington, D.C., September 9–10, 1976 (to be published).

[14] D.M. Grether and M. Nerlove, Some properties of optimal seasonal adjustment, Econometrica 38 (1970) 682–703.

[15] R.J.A. Haan, A mechanized method of seasonal adjustment (Central Planning Bureau Holland, 1974).

[16] S. Kallek, Overview, paper presented at the NBER-Census Conference on Seasonal Analysis of Economic Time Series, Washington, D.C., September 9–10, 1976 (to be published).

[17] J. Kuiper, A survey and comparative analysis of various methods of seasonal adjustment, paper presented at the NBER-Census Conference on Seasonal Analysis of Economic Time Series, Washington, D.C., September 9–10, 1076 (to be published).

[18] M. Mesnage, Elimination des variations saisonnieres: la nouvelle methode de l'OSCE, Etudes et Enquetes Statistiques, 1968, No. 1, 7–78.

[19] M. Mesnage, Utilisation de Filtres Lineaires a Coefficients Constants pour la Desaisonnalisation des Series Chronologiques, paper presented at the Conference on Seasonal Adjustment, Free University, Amsterdam, April 1–2, 1976.

[20] M. Nerlove, Spectral analysis of seasonal adjustment procedures, Econometrica 32: 3 (1964) 241–285.

[21] B. Nullau, The Berlin method – A new approach to time series analysis (German Institute for Economic Research, Berlin, 1969).

[22] Seasonal Adjustment on Electronic Computers (Organization for Economic Cooperation and Development, Paris, 1960).

[23] D.A. Pierce, Seasonal adjustment when both deterministic and stochastic seasonality are present, paper presented at the NBER-Census Conference on Seasonal Analysis of Economic Time Series, Washington, D.C., September 9–10, 1976 (to be published).

[24] C. Plosser, Time series analysis, seasonality in econometric models, paper presented at the NBER-Census Conference on Seasonal Analysis of Economic Time Series, Washington, D.C., September 9–10, 1976 (to be published).

[25] President's Committee to Appraise Employment and Unemployment Statistics, Measuring employment and unemployment (Washington, D.C., 1962).

[26] K.F. Wallis, Seasonal adjustment and multiple time series, paper presented at the NBER-Census Conference on Seasonal Analysis of Economic Time Series, Washington, D.C., September 9–10, 1976 (to be published).

[27] P. Whittle, Prediction and regulation by linear least-square methods (EUP, London, 1963).

TIMS Studies in the Management Sciences 12 (1979) 59–73
© North-Holland Publishing Company

TIME-SERIES MODEL BUILDING AND FORECASTING:
A SURVEY

Paul NEWBOLD

University of Nottingham

Stimulated primarily by the work of Box and Jenkins [8], a good deal of attention has been given to the subject of time-series model building in the last few years, both in the theoretical and applied literature. The objective of this paper is to review briefly the Box–Jenkins methodology, to survey important developments since 1970, and to indicate the range of applications of the procedures in practical forecasting problems.

1. Introduction

The time-series approach to model building propounded by Box and Jenkins [8] can be viewed as consisting of the following stages:
1. The specification of a class of models that the investigator is prepared to consider as potential generators of a set of data.
2. The choice of a particular model, for subsequent analysis, from the general class. The properties of the available data will inevitably play a very important role in model selection, though theoretical considerations about the data-generating process should certainly not be ignored.
3. The statistical estimation of the parameters of the selected model.
4. The checking of the adequacy with which the selected model explains the given data. Any inadequacies revealed may lead to respecification of the model, followed by reestimation and rechecking, so that model building can be thought of as an iterative process that terminates when an apparently satisfactory model has been found.
5. The application of the fitted model, for example, in the production of forecasts.

The essence of the time-series approach of Box and Jenkins is contained in steps 2 and 4 above, where data is employed in the selection and verification of a model for subsequent analysis. The simplest problem in time-series analysis concerns the situation in which observations on only a single series are available. This problem will be discussed in the following two sections. The final section deals with the situation in which simultaneous observations on several related series are available.

2. The Box–Jenkins approach to univariate model building

Suppose that n equally spaced observations through time, $X_1, X_2, ..., X_n$, are available on a process X, and forecasts of future values X_{n+h}, $h \geqslant 1$, are required. In this section we summarize very briefly the methodology developed by Box and Jenkins [8] for attacking this problem.

Obviously the number of ways in which forecasts could be based on the given data is infinite, and it would seem essential, in practice, to impose restrictions on the forms of forecast functions contemplated. It is usual, at least as a starting point, to consider only forecasts that are linear functions of the data.

In trying to determine what kind of models might adequately represent actual data, one important point is the fact that many observed series, particularly in economics and business, follow quite smooth paths through time rather than exhibiting variation about a fixed mean level. This characteristic is noted in spectral terms by Granger [28]. This particular kind of behavior generally dominates all other characteristics of a series, making them difficult to detect and analyze. It can often be removed by differencing, that is by considering the series $x_t = X_t - X_{t-1} = (1 - B)X_t$, where B is a back-shift operator on the index of the time series, so that $B^j X_t \equiv X_{t-j}$. Occasionally higher order differencing is required, so that the transformation $x_t = (1 - B)^d X_t$, where d is some positive integer, is used. An important principle in time-series analysis involves the desirability of fitting a model with as few coefficients as possible, provided an adequate description of the data is achieved. Taken together these considerations led Box and Jenkins to employ, for nonseasonal series, the so-called ARIMA (autoregressive integrated moving average) class of models:

$$(1 - \phi_1 B - \phi_2 B^2 - ... - \phi_p B^p)(1 - B)^d X_t$$

$$= \theta_0 + (1 - \theta_1 B - \theta_2 B^2 - ... - \theta_q B^q)a_t, \tag{1}$$

where a_t is a process with mean zero, fixed variance through time and with a_t and a_s uncorrelated for $t \neq s$. Such processes are called white noise and are, of course, unpredictable in a linear sense from their own past. The time-series model, then, can be thought of as a linear transformation of the data to white noise. Alternatively it can be viewed as an attempt to decompose X_t additively to a component dependent on past history and an unpredictable, purely random, component (a_t).

For seasonal time series of period s (that is, $s = 4$ for quarterly data and $s = 12$ for monthly data) Box and Jenkins generalise the model (1) to

$$(1 - \phi_1 B - \phi_2 B^2 - ... - \phi_p B^p)(1 - \phi_{1,s} B^s - ... - \phi_{p_s,s} B^{p_s s})$$

$$\times (1 - B)^d (1 - B^s)^{d_s} X_t = (1 - \theta_1 B - \theta_2 B^2 - ... - \theta_q B^q)$$

$$\times (1 - \theta_{1,s} B^s - ... - \theta_{q_s,s} B^{q_s s})a_t. \tag{2}$$

The problem of selecting a specific model from the general class involves, for example, choosing appropriate values for the integers p, d, and q of (1). In order to achieve this, one calculates from the data statistics whose behavior characterizes particular individual models. Box and Jenkins suggest use of sample autocorrelations and partial autocorrelations. The coefficients of the selected model are estimated by a nonlinear regression algorithm, and the residuals from the fitted model provide useful information about its adequacy. In particular, the behavior of these residuals should closely resemble that of a white noise series, and hence their autocorrelations should not be too large. An overall portmanteau test of model adequacy can be based on the first 20 or so of these residual autocorrelations. Further details of the test are given by Box and Pierce [11]. Box and Jenkins show how a fitted model of the form (1) or (2) can be projected forward to obtain forecasts of future values, together with standard errors and confidence intervals.

The basic Box—Jenkins methodology will not be discussed in further detail here as many adequate expositions already exist, for example, in the books by Box and Jenkins [8], Nelson [49], Chatfield [18], and Granger and Newbold [31], and in articles by Box and Jenkins [7], Naylor, Seaks, and Wichern [47], Chatfield and Prothero [19], and Newbold [52]. These sources also contain a wide range of practical illustrations of the methodology.

Box—Jenkins techniques can readily be viewed as competitors of the many exponential smoothing procedures in widespread use for short-term forecasting in industry (see, for example, Brown [15], Harrison [37,38] and Winters [69]). Compared with the latter, the former have an important advantage and an important disadvantage, both springing from the same source. Within the time-series model-building framework, the facility to allow a wide range of possible forecasting models and to select the model eventually used on the basis of the properties of the data allows for extra versatility compared to exponential smoothing procedures in which an underlying generation process is effectively assumed a priori. On the other hand, the processes of model selection and verification, by their very nature, render a Box—Jenkins analysis relatively slow and expensive, in terms of computing and skilled manpower, compared to exponential smoothing.

One would expect, because of its extra versatility and as a compensation for its extra cost, a Box—Jenkins analysis to produce, on the average, more accurate forecasts than exponential smoothing procedures. Evidence for this is provided by Reid [61,62] and Newbold and Granger [54]. These authors analyzed large collections of actual time series and found, in the great majority of cases, that Box—Jenkins forecasts outperformed their simpler competitors. Such results are to be expected since – as noted for example by McKenzie [46], Cogger [22], and Godolphin and Harrison [27] – many exponential smoothing predictors can be derived as special cases of particular members of the ARIMA class of time-series models. Results which appear, on the surface, to favor exponential smoothing predictors over Box—Jenkins models in empirical comparisons are presented by Groff [34]. However, these results are explained by the fact that, over a number of series, Groff was evaluating the performance of various individual members of the ARIMA class (1). Thus the performance of the Box—Jenkins methodology was not really being evaluated since, for any specific series, the data was not used to select, and verify the adequacy of, a particular model from the general class.

The various books and articles mentioned above contain numerous illustrations of the Box—Jenkins approach applied to a wide range of time series, many of which concern economic or product demand data. Other published studies include Thompson and Tiao [64] on the forecasting of telephone installations and removals, and Brubacher and Wilson [16] who discuss a forecasting model for electricity demand. Univariate time-series models have also been used as benchmarks against which the performance of a more sophisticated forecasting model can be judged, for example Nelson [48] and Christ [20]. Finally, as will be seen in the final section of this article, the construction of univariate models is often a useful first step in multivariate time-series model building.

3. Recent innovations in univariate model building

The work of Box and Jenkins has stimulated considerable further research into time-series model building methods. The object of this section is to survey some of the most interesting and potentially useful developments in each of the stages described in the first section.

3.1. The class of models

A restriction to linear forecast functions is, of course, a mathematical convenience, but one which cannot always be easily defended in practical applications. The difficulty in relaxing this restriction is that enormous problems are created in trying to determine which particular nonlinear function might be appropriate in any given situation. One simple possibility, which can be incorporated into an analysis without too much extra difficulty, is to assume a model not necessarily linear in X_t, but in $T(X_t)$ where $T(\cdot)$ is some parametric function. Thus, in model (1) or (2), X_t is replaced by $T(X_t)$. A class of transformations that has proved useful in a number of contexts in statistics is the class of power transformations:

$$T(X_t) = \frac{X_t^\lambda - 1}{\lambda}; \qquad \lambda \neq 0$$

$$= \log X_t; \qquad \lambda = 0$$

(3)

introduced by Box and Cox [6]. The parameter λ is then regarded as an extra coefficient to be estimated, by maximum likelihood methods.

The fitting of a model of this kind to sales data is discussed by Wilson [67] and Box and Jenkins [9]. Some problems caused by the use of instantaneous transformations of this type are considered by Granger and Newbold [31]. These authors show how, given that a model has been built in terms of $T(X)$, forecasts of the original process X can be made. They also point out that, in general, the autocovariance function and ARIMA structure is not invariant under instantaneous transformations, and hence that difficulties arise in model selection. A more general treatment of nonlinearity extends the class of models (1) to include so-called bilinear models.

It is often the case that time-series met in practice do not exhibit sufficient stability for fixed coefficients models of the form (1) or (2) to be appropriate. A situation of this kind that is relatively easy to deal with arises when disturbing influences occur at known points in time. For example, a change in advertising strategy might be expected to influence the time series of a firm's monthly sales. Box and Tiao [12] attack this problem by the method of intervention analysis, which is the time-series analogue of dummy-variable methods in regression analysis. Suppose, in general, there are M dummies $D_{j,t}$, $j = 1, 2, ..., M$. The model (1) is then extended to

$$X_t = \sum_{j=1}^{M} \frac{\omega_{0,j} + \omega_{1,j}B + ... + \omega_{r_j,j}B^{r_j}}{1 - \delta_{1,j}B - ... - \delta_{s_j,j}B^{s_j}} D_{j,t}$$

$$+ \frac{1 - \theta_1 B - ... - \theta_q B^q}{(1 - B)^d (1 - \phi_1 B - ... - \phi_p B^p)} a_t. \tag{4}$$

For example, Box and Tiao consider a series on the monthly rate of change of consumer prices in the United States. The data set includes the months September through November 1971 when Phase I of a government-imposed price policy was in operation. Phase II followed immediately and extended to the end of the data set. The model achieved by Box and Tiao for these data was of the form

$$X_t = \omega_{0,1}D_{1t} + \omega_{0,2}D_{2t} + [(1 - \theta B)/(1 - B)] a_t, \tag{5}$$

where $D_{1,t} = 1$ for September–November 1971

               $= 0$ otherwise,

$D_{2t} = 1$ from December 1971 onwards

               $= 0$ otherwise.

A further example given by Box and Tiao concerns monthly averages of levels of oxidant in downtown Los Angeles. It was felt likely that this series would be affected by the introduction of a law on the chemical composition of locally sold gasoline and by later regulations on engine design. These factors can again be accounted for within the framework of the general model (4). Several further practical illustrations are given by Glass, Willson and Gottman [26].

A related but intrinsically more difficult problem arises when one suspects that a series may contain several changes in structure at unspecified points in time. This situation is considered by Harrison and Stevens [39,40], who develop a methodology for analyzing such series based on Kalman filtering rather than the Box—Jenkins model-building approach that is the subject of this survey.

3.2. Model selection

The choice, based on sample autocorrelations and partial autocorrelations, of a specific model from the general class (1) or (2) is often quite difficult. Frequently it appears that there is little to choose between two or three alternative structures, though as noted by Box and Jenkins [9] this may simply result from the fact that the models themselves are practically identical. For example, Granger and Newbold [32] consider a series of 204 monthly values of an index of help-wanted advertisements in the United States. Although one would hope with such an unusually large sample size to be able to make a clear-cut choice, it was found impossible to distinguish on the evidence of the data between two alternative structures, which when fitted to the data led to the estimated equations

$$(1 - 0.11B - 0.34B^2 - 0.16B^3)(1 - B)X_t = a_t, \tag{6}$$

and

$$(1 - 0.45B - 0.31B^2)(1 - B)X_t = (1 - 0.36B)a_t. \tag{7}$$

The reason for this can be seen by multiplying through equation (7) by $(1 - 0.36B)^{-1}$ to give

$$(1 - 0.09B - 0.34B^2 - 0.12B^3 - 0.04B^4 - 0.02B^5 - ...)X_t = a_t, \tag{8}$$

which differs very little from equation (6). Hence the models (7) and (6) are very similar, and it is not terribly important to distinguish between them, since both will give similar forecasts of future values.

In spite of these comments, however, it must be admitted that practitioners would greatly welcome further tools to aid in model selection. One possibility, which has not been explored in any great empirical detail, is the use of inverse autocorrelations proposed by Cleveland [21]. A more radical approach is to seek a procedure that automatically selects and estimates an appropriate model. Such a method will be discussed later in this section.

3.3. Coefficient estimation

For most general purposes the least squares procedure of Box and Jenkins for estimating the parameters of model (1) or (2) has proved satisfactory. However, for shorter series, particularly if the true parameters are thought to lie close to the boundary of the parameter surface, [1] a full maximum likelihood procedure, based on an assumption of normality, may be more efficient, though computationally more expensive. A closed form expression for the exact likelihood function for the model (1) is derived by Newbold [51]. This function must be maximized numerically, and some discussion of the computational difficulties involved and means for overcoming them is given by Osborn [55] and Dent [25].

Estimators that are close to maximum likelihood are derived and studied by Anderson [4], and a number of writers have proposed estimators based on the sample spectral density (see Hannan [35]). In fact, a large number of estimators of the parameters of the model (1) have been suggested over the years, though there exists remarkably little evidence about the small sample properties of these estimators. A rare exception is the study by Nelson [50].

3.4. Checking model adequacy

Box and Jenkins suggest a number of checks on the adequacy of representation of a fitted model to a given data set, including the commonly calculated portmanteau statistic of Box and Pierce [11]. Let n be the number of observations used to fit the model (1), that is, the total number of available observations less the required degree of differencing d. Denote by $\hat{a}_t$ the residuals from the estimated model and let the autocorrelations of these residuals be written as

$$\hat{r}_k = \frac{\sum_{t=k+1}^{n} \hat{a}_t \hat{a}_{t-k}}{\sum_{t=1}^{n} \hat{a}_t^2}; \qquad k = 1, 2, 3, ... \tag{9}$$

Consider the statistic

$$Q = n \sum_{k=1}^{m} \hat{r}_k^2 . \tag{10}$$

---

[1] This is restricted by the requirement that the coefficients of model (1) for example, are such that the roots of the two polynomial equations in B, $(1 - \phi_1 B - \cdots - \phi_p B^p) = 0$ and $(1 - \theta_1 B - \cdots - \theta_q B^q) = 0$, all have moduli greater than unity. The first condition ensures the stationarity of the differenced series, while the seond guarantees uniqueness of representation of the model.

P. Newbold, Time-series model building and forecasting

Box and Pierce show that, under the null hypothesis of model adequacy, if m is sufficiently large (usually taken to be 15 or 20) the quantity (10) is asymptotically
distributed as χ^2 with $(m-p-q)$ degrees of freedom. The null hypothesis is
rejected for unusually high values of the statistic. However, Nelson [50] noted in a
simulation study of first-order moving average processes that for sample sizes commonly found in practice the true significance levels can be much lower than the
asymptotic values. The reasons for this phenomenon are demonstrated more generally by Davies, Triggs and Newbold [24].

In an attempt to get around this difficulty, Ljung and Box [45] consider the
alternative statistic

$$Q' = n(n+2) \sum_{k=1}^{m} (n-k)^{-1} \hat{r}_k^2. \tag{11}$$

Davies [23] has shown that, although the true significance levels of this statistic can
be rather high, they are typically closer to the asymptotic values than those of
(10). Thus, if a portmanteau test is to be carried out, the available evidence suggests
that it should be based on Q' rather than Q.

An alternative test of model adequacy, or model stability, is proposed by Box
and Tiao [14], based on one-step-ahead post-sample prediction errors.

3.5. Forecasting

The usual procedure for calculating standard errors and confidence intervals for
forecasts based on model (1) or (2) does not take into account errors in estimating
the model parameters. A method for doing so has been developed by Yamamoto
[70,71].

3.6. An integrated model selection and estimation procedure

The necessity to use skilled manpower at the model selection stage of the Box–
Jenkins procedure renders it, on occasion, unattractive because of the costs
involved. If selection could in some way be made automatic, these costs would
be reduced. One possible approach is from Akaike [1,2,3] and is further discussed by Jones [44] and Shibata [63]. The procedure is to select a number of
models from the general class (1) and to estimate the coefficients of each by maximum likelihood. The model for which the maximized log likelihood less the total
number of estimated coefficients is largest is then selected.

The practical possibilities of this approach have not as yet been evaluated in any
great detail, but the results of Shibata suggest that it is likely to lead to the fitting
of overelaborate models disturbingly frequently. Moreover, the need to compute
maximum likelihood estimators for a range of models makes it rather expensive.

4. Multivariate time-series model building

It must be stated at the outset that practical procedures for multivariate time-series model building are, at the present time, much less well developed than those for the single series case. Considerable research effort has been spent on this problem in recent years and a number of alternatives have been suggested, though practical experience in this area is quite limited.

The simplest possible situation is where past values of a series X_2 are useful in predicting X_1, but past X_1 is irrelevant to the prediction of X_2. In the terminology of Granger [29], X_2 "causes" X_1 but there is no feedback from X_1 to X_2. For such processes Box and Jenkins [8] propose the model

$$x_{1,t} = \frac{\omega_0 + \omega_1 B + ... + \omega_r B^r}{1 - \delta_1 B - ... - \delta_s B^s} x_{2,t} + \frac{1 - \theta_1 B - ... - \theta_q B^q}{1 - \phi_1 B - ... - \phi_p B^p} a_t, \qquad (12)$$

where $x_{1,t}$ and $x_{2,t}$ are appropriately differenced versions of the original series, and a_t is a white noise process independent of $x_{2,t}$. Box and Jenkins describe a model-building procedure, that experience indicates generally works satisfactorily. This can be extended to the case where there are several x variables on the right-hand of (12). The use of these techniques in fitting equations to macroeconomic data is illustrated by Wall et al. [65].

The practical difficulties involved in model building increase enormously when there is feedback between series. For the bivariate case, in such circumstances, Granger and Newbold [32,33] consider, by analogy with (12), the model

$$x_{1,t} = \frac{\omega_{1,0} + \omega_{1,1} B + ... + \omega_{1,r_1} B^{r1}}{1 - \delta_{1,1} B - ... - \delta_{1,s_1} B^{s1}} x_{2,t}$$

$$+ \frac{1 - \theta_{1,1} B - ... - \theta_{1,q_1} B^{q1}}{1 - \phi_{1,1} B - ... - \phi_{1,p_1} B^{p1}} a_{1,t}$$

$$x_{2,t} = \frac{\omega_{2,1} B + ... + \omega_{2,r_2} B^{r2}}{1 - \delta_{2,1} B - ... - \delta_{2,s_2} B^{s2}} x_{1,t} + \frac{1 - \theta_{2,1} B - ... - \theta_{2,q_2} B^{q2}}{1 - \phi_{2,1} B - ... - \phi_{2,p_2} B^{p2}} a_{2,t},$$

$$\qquad (13)$$

where $a_{1,t}$ and $a_{2,t}$ are independent white noise series. Granger and Newbold develop and illustrate with economic data a methodology for building such models.

The more general multivariate time-series problem, where one has data on a vector of series $x_t' = (x_{1,t} x_{2,t} ... x_{M,t})$ which may be suitably differenced versions of M original series, is generally considered in terms of a model analogous to (1):

$$(I - \Phi_1 B - ... - \Phi_p B^p) x_t = (I - \theta_1 B - ... - \theta_q B^q) a_t, \qquad (14)$$

where I is the $M \times M$ identity matrix, the Φ_i and θ_j are $M \times M$ matrices of coefficients and a_t is a white noise vector series, so that

$$E(a_t a_s') = \Sigma; \qquad t = s$$

$$= 0 \qquad \text{otherwise}$$

(15)

where Σ is a positive definite matrix.

Models of the type (14) were first studied in any great detail by Quenouille [60]. More recently the problem of fitting such models to data has been examined by Jenkins [43] and Wallis [66]. These authors consider, without loss of generality, models of the form (14) with the coefficient matrices $\Phi_j, j = 1, 2, ..., p$ taken to be diagonal.

The problem of selecting a particular multivariate model from a general class of models is a very difficult one and remains an area of active research interest. It might be thought that, since sample autocorrelations are of great value in the univariate model selection problem, the cross-correlations

$$r_k^{(ij)} = \frac{\Sigma(X_{i,t} - \bar{X}_i)(X_{j,t-k} - \bar{X}_j)}{[\Sigma(X_{i,t} - \bar{X}_i)^2 \Sigma(X_{j,t} - \bar{X}_j)^2]^{1/2}}; \qquad k = ..., -1, 0, 1, ... \quad (16)$$

would be equally useful in the present context. In fact this is not so, since although the quantities (16) do contain information about the interrelationship between X_i and X_j, this information is inextricably intertwined with information about the individual autocorrelations of these series. Indeed, unless great care is taken, use of the statistics (16) can produce very misleading conclusions, as illustrated by Box and Newbold [10].

Since the individual autocorrelations make it difficult to analyze interrelationships, a first step followed in many investigations of multivariate series is to fit univariate models of the form (1) or (2) to some or all of the individual series. The cross-correlations

$$r_k^{*(ij)} = \frac{\Sigma \hat{a}_{i,t} \hat{a}_{j,t-k}}{[\Sigma \hat{a}_{i,t}^2 \Sigma \hat{a}_{j,t}^2]^{1/2}}; \qquad k = ..., -1, 0, 1, ... \quad (17)$$

between the residuals $\hat{a}_{i,t}$ and $\hat{a}_{j,t}$ from these fitted models are rather easier to interpret that the quantities (16). Jenkins [43] employs these statistics to suggest an appropriate model of the type (14), and Granger and Newbold [32,33] use them to select a model from the class (13). They are also used by Haugh and Box [42] to select models from the class (12) and by Pierce [58] to assess causal direction. Wallis [66] notes that the forms of the fitted univariate models can themselves be useful in suggesting an appropriate multivariate model. On the other hand, a methodology that does not involve initially building univariate models is proposed by

Caines and Chan [17]. It must be emphasized, however, that whatever procedure is employed multivariate model selection is a far more uncertain business than univariate selection.

Multivariate time-series models are generally estimated by methods that are close to maximum likelihood. The estimation of the parameters of (14) is considerd by Wilson [68], Hannan [35] and Osborn [56].

Checks on the adequacy of a fitted model can be based on the autocorrelations and cross-correlations of the residuals, which should behave approximately as multivariate white noise. However, since model selection is such a tenuous process, it is probably more important to experiment by trying a number of alternative structures and retaining that which best fits the data.

After one achieves a fitted model, the projection forward of this model to obtain forecasts is quite straightforward. Of course, the object of the whole exercise is to achieve better forecasts than can be obtained from univariate models alone. A discussion and illustration of the gains that can be obtained using the model (12) is given in Pierce [57].

In moving from univariate to multivariate problems, the difficulties faced in building time-series models grow rapidly, and it appears unlikely that models of the type (14) can be handled by time-series methods alone unless there are only a few series or the relationships involved are particularly simple. Neither does it seem desirable to rely on time-series models exclusively, since one will almost certainly have available theoretical results on the data-generating process. The most useful approach would seem to be to attempt to build behavioral models, but with particular attention paid to time-series problems, such as lag and error structures. As an alternative, Box and Tiao [13] fit multivariate time-series models by canonical analysis to data of Quenouille [60], but lay great stress on achieving models with clear econmic interpretation. Attempts to reconcile and compare behavioral models traditionally used in econometrics with time-series models such as (14) have been made by Zellner and Palm [72] and Prothero and Wallis [59]. The great advantage of employing behavioral models is that they impose restrictions on the class of models that need to be considered, thus simplifying the model selection problem. The simplest model of this type is a linear regression with an error term of the form (1) or (2). For example, in order to forecast demand for telephones in Australia, Bhattacharyya [5] relates demand to installation and rental charges, the achieved model having a seasonal time-series error structure. It should be stressed that a behavioral mode alone is generally inadequate, since misleading conclusions can be drawn if insufficient attention is paid to time-series error structure, as shown by Granger and Newbold [30] and Newbold and Davies [53].

Multivariate time-series analysis is an area with many unsolved problems, that are attracting the attention of an increasing number of researchers. It must be expected that the methods described in this section will be exploited and extended a great deal in the next few years. It is difficult to anticipate progress, but probably the marriage between time-series methods and the traditional behavioral model-building approach, which is already under way in econometrics, offers the most fruitful possibilities. It is difficult at this stage, since practical experience is so limited, to assess which of the purely time-series procedures is likely to prove most valuable. All possess useful features that could prove important in particular empirical investigations.

References

[1] H. Akaike, Autoregressive model fitting for control, Annals of Institute of Statistical Mathematics 23 (1971) 163–180.

[2] H. Akaike, Use of an information theoretical quantity for statistical model identification, Proceedings of 5th Hawaii Conference on System Sciences, 1972.

[3] H. Akaike, Information theory and an extension of the maximum likelihood principle, in: B.N. Petrov and F. Cyaki, eds., 2nd International Symposium on Information Theory (Akademiai Kiado, Budapest, 1973).

[4] T.W. Anderson, Maximum likelihood estimation of parameters of autoregressive processes with moving average residuals and other covariance matrices with linear structure, Annals of Statistics 3 (1975) 1283–1304.

[5] M.N. Bhattacharyya, Forecasting the demand for telephones in Australia, Applied Statistics 23 (1974) 1–10.

[6] G.E.P. Box and D.R. Cox, An analysis of transformations, Journal of the Royal Statistical Society B25 (1964) 211–243.

[7] G.E.P. Box and G.M. Jenkins, Some recent advances in forecasting and control, Applied Statistics 17 (1968) 91–109.

[8] G.E.P. Box and G.M. Jenkins, Time Series Analysis, Forecasting and Control (Holden-Day, San Francisco, 1970).

[9] G.E.P. Box and G.M. Jenkins, Some comments on a paper by Chatfield and Prothero and on a review by Kendall, Journal of the Royal Statistical Society A136 (1973) 337–345.

[10] G.E.P. Box and P. Newbold, Some comments on a paper of Coen, Gomme and Kendall, Journal of the Royal Statistical Society A134 (1971) 229–240.

[11] G.E.P. Box and D.A. Pierce, Distribution of residual autocorrelations in autoregressive integrated moving average time series models, Journal of the American Statistical Association 65 (1970) 1509–1526.

[12] G.E.P. Box and G.C. Tiao, Intervention analysis with applications to economic and environmental problems, Journal of American Statistical Association 70 (1975) 70–79.

[13] G.E.P. Box and G.C. Tiao, A. canonical analysis of multiple time series, Biometrika 64 (1977) 355–365.

[14] G.E.P. Box and G.C. Tiao, Comparison of forecast and actuality, Applied Statistics 25 (1976) 195–200.

[15] R.G. Brown, Smoothing, Forecasting and Prediction of Discrete Time Series (Prentice-Hall, Englewood Cliffs, N.J., 1962).

[16] S.R. Brubacher and G.T. Wilson, Interpolating time series with application to the estimation of holiday effects on electricity demand, Applied Statistics 25 (1976) 107–116.

[17] P.E. Caines and C.W. Chan, Feedback between stationary stochastic processes, IEEE Transactions on Automatic Control (1975) 498–508.

[18] C. Chatfield, The Analysis of Time Series: Theory and Practice (Chapman and Hall, London, 1975).

[19] C. Chatfield and D.L. Prothero, Box–Jenkins seasonal forecasting problems in a case study, Journal of the Royal Statistical Society A136 (1973) 295–315.

[20] C.F. Christ, Judging the performance of econometric models of the U.S. economy, International Economic Review 16 (1975) 54–74.

[21] W.S. Cleveland, The inverse autocorrelations of a time series and their applications, Technometrics 14 (1972) 277–293.

[22] K.C. Cogger, The optimality of general order exponential smoothing, Operations Research 22 (1974) 858–867.

[23] N. Davies, Mis-specified models in time series analysis, Ph.D. dissertation, Department of Mathematics, University of Nottingham, 1977.

[24] N. Davies, C.M. Triggs and P. Newbold, Significance levels of the Box–Pierce portmanteau statistic in finite samples, Biometrika 64 (1977) 517–522.

[25] W. Dent, Computation of the exact likelihood function of an ARMA process, Journal of Statistical Computation and Simulation (1977) 193–206.

[26] G.V. Glass, V.L. Willson and J.M. Gottman, Design and Analysis of Time Series Experiments (Colorado Associated University Press, Boulder, 1975).

[27] E.J. Godolphin and P.J. Harrison, Equivalence theorems for polynomial-projecting predictors, Journal of the Royal Statistical Society B37 (1975) 205–215.

[28] C.W.J. Granger, The typical spectral shape of an economic variable, Econometrica 34 (1966) 150–161.

[29] C.W.J. Granger, Investigating causal relations by econometric models and cross-spectral methods, Econometrica 37 (1969) 424–438.

[30] C.W.J. Granger and P. Newbold, Spurious regressions in econometrics, Journal of Econometrics 2 (1974) 111–120.

[31] C.W.J. Granger and P. Newbold, Forecasting transformed series, Journal of the Royal Statistical Society B38 (1976) 189–203.

[32] C.W.J. Granger and P. Newbold, Forecasting Economic Time Series (Academic Press, New York, 1977).

[33] C.W.J. Granger and P. Newbold, Identification of two-way causal systems, in: M.D. Intriligator, ed., Frontiers of Quantitative Economics III (North-Holland, Amsterdam, 1977).

[34] G.K. Groff, Empirical comparison of models for short range forecasting, Management Science 20 (1973) 22–31.

[35] E.J. Hannan, The estimation of mixed moving average autoregressive systems, Biometrika 56 (1969) 579–594.

[36] E.J. Hannan, The estimation of ARMA models, Annals of Statistics 3 (1975) 975–981.

[37] P.J. Harrison, Short term sales forecasting, Applied Statistics 14 (1965) 102–139.

[38] P.J. Harrison, Exponential smoothing and short term sales forecasting, Management Science 13 (1967) 821–842.

[39] P.J. Harrison and C.F. Stevens, A Bayesian approach to short term forecasting, Operational Research Quarterly 22 (1971) 341–362.

[40] P.J. Harrison and C.F. Stevens, Bayesian forecasting, Journal of the Royal Statistical Society B38 (1976) 205–228.

[41] L.D. Haugh, The identification of time series interrelationships with special reference to dynamic regression, Ph.D. dissertation, Dept. of Statistics, University of Wisconsin, Madison, 1972.

[42] L.D. Haugh and G.E.P. Box, Identification of dynamic regression (distributed lag) models connecting two time series, Journal of American Statistical Association 72 (1977) 121–130.

[43] G.M. Jenkins, The interaction between the muskrat and mink cycles in North Canada, in: L.C.A. Corsten and T. Postelnicu, eds., Proceedings of the 8th International Biometric Conference Constanta Romania, 1974.

[44] R.J. Jones, Fitting autoregressions, Journal of the American Statistical Association 70 (1975) 590–592.

[45] G.M. Ljung and G.E.P. Box, A modification of the overall χ^2 test for lack of fit in time

series models, Technical Report 477 (Department of Statistics, University of Wisconsin, Madison, 1976).

[46] E. McKenzie, A comparison of standard forecasting systems with the Box–Jenkins approach, The Statistician 23 (1974) 107–116.

[47] T.H. Naylor, T.G. Seaks and D.W. Wichern, Box–Jenkins methods: an alternative to econometric models, International Statistical Review 40 (1972) 123–137.

[48] C.R. Nelson, The prediction performance of the FRB-MIT-PENN model of the U.S. economy, American Economic Review 62 (1972) 902–917.

[49] C.R. Nelson, Applied Time Series Analysis for Managerial Forecasting (Holden-Day, San Francisco, 1973).

[50] C.R. Nelson, The first order moving average process: identification, estimation and prediction, Journal of Econometrics 2 (1974) 121–141.

[51] P. Newbold, The exact likelihood function for a mixed autoregressive-moving average process, Biometrika 61 (1974) 423–426.

[52] P. Newbold, The principles of the Box–Jenkins approach, Operational Research Quarterly 26 (1975) 397–412.

[53] P. Newbold and N. Davies, Error mis-specification and spurious regressions, International Economic Review 19 (1978) 513–519.

[54] P. Newbold and C.W.J. Granger, Experience with forecasting univariate time series and the combination of forecasts, Journal of the Royal Statistical Society A137 (1974) 131–146.

[55] D. Osborn, Maximum likelihood estimation of moving average processes, Annals of Economic and Social Measurement 5 (1976) 75–87.

[56] D. Osborn, Exact and approximate maximum likelihood estimators for vector moving average processes, Journal of the Royal Statistical Society B39 (1977) 114–118.

[57] D.A. Pierce, Forecasting in dynamic models with stochastic regressors, Journal of Econometrics 3 (1975) 349–374.

[58] D.A. Pierce, Relationships – and the lack thereof – between economic time series with special reference to money reserves and interest rates, Journal of American Statistical Association 72 (1977) 11–21.

[59] D.L. Prothero and K.F. Wallis, Modelling macroeconomic time series, Journal of the Royal Statistical Society A139 (1976) 468–486.

[60] M.H. Quenouille, The Analysis of Multiple Time Series (Griffin, London, 1957).

[61] D.J. Reid, A comparative study of time series prediction techniques on economic data, Ph.D. dissertation, Department of Mathematics, University of Nottingham.

[62] D.J. Reid, A review of short term projection techniques, in: H.A. Gordon, ed., Practical Aspects of Forecasting (Operational Research Society, London, 1975).

[63] R. Shibata, Selection of the order of an autoregressive model by Akaike's information criterion, Biometrika 63 (1976) 117–126.

[64] H.E. Thompson and G.C. Tiao, Analysis of telephone data, Bell Journal of Economics and Management Science 2 (1971) 514–541.

[65] K.D. Wall, A.J. Preston, J.W. Bray and M.H. Peston, Estimates of a simple control model of the U.K. economy in: G.A. Renton, ed., Modelling the Economy (Heinemann, London, 1975).

[66] K.F. Wallis, Multiple time series analysis and the final form of econometric models, Econometrica 45 (1977) 1481–1497.

[67] G.T. Wilson, Contribution to discussion of paper by Chatfield and Prothero, Journal of Royal Statistical Society A136 (1973) 315–319.

[68] G.T. Wilson, The estimation of parameters in multivariate time series models, Journal of the Royal Statistical Society B35 (1973) 76–85.

[69] P.R. Winters, Forecasting sales by exponentially weighted moving averages, Management Science 6 (1960) 324–342.

[70] T. Yamamoto, Asymptotic mean square error of multi-step prediction from mixed auto-regressive moving average models, Discussion paper 7521 (C.O.R.E., Université Catholique de Louvain, 1975).
[71] T. Yamamoto, Asymptotic mean square prediction error for an autoregressive model with estimated coefficients, Applied Statistics 25 (1976) 123–127.
[72] A. Zellner and F. Palm, Time series analysis and simultaneous equation econometric models, Journal of Econometrics 2 (1974) 17–54.

TIMS Studies in the Management Sciences 12 (1979) 75–94
© North-Holland Publishing Company

KALMAN FILTERS AND THEIR APPLICATIONS TO FORECASTING

Raman K. MEHRA

President, Scientific Systems, Inc., Cambridge, Massachusetts

This paper presents a survey of Kalman filtering techniques and their applications to fore-casting. First, a Bayesian approach is used to derive the general nonlinear filtering equations. It is then shown how the Kalman filtering equations follow directly from these equations for the Gauss-Markov model. The discussion also covers the advantages and limitations of Kalman fil-ters as well as various extensions that have been developed in the engineering literature over the last fifteen years. Adaptive Kalman filters and multiple Kalman filters that are expected to play an important role in forecasting applications are also discussed. Finally, the paper presents a case study on forecasting of stock earnings for 49 U.S. companies.

1. Introduction

The subject of forecasting has occupied an important role in the theory of sto-chastic processes and time-series analysis. The earliest work on the subject is that of Kolmogorov [25] for discrete-time stationary stochastic processes and that of Wiener [55] for continuous-time processes. Kolmogorov [25] uses a representation suggested by Wold [58] and Wiener reduces the prediction problem to the solution of a Wiener-Hopf integral equation. Simplified readable accounts of the two approaches can be found in Papoulis [42], Whittle [54] and Davenport and Root [7].

Kalman [22] and Kalman and Bucy [24] extend the Kolmogorov-Wiener results to nonstationary processes and finite observation intervals. However, for the case of no process noise, the work of Swerling [53] predates that of Kalman and Bucy. Similarly, Stratonovich [52] worked on the scalar continuous-time case before Kal-man and Bucy. Using the Bayesian decision theory approach, Raiffa and Schlaifer [45] also derive recurrence relations that are similar to the Kalman filter recursions [see Bryson and Ho [4] for the relationships].

The full generality of Kalman's results [23], the state vector formulation, and the ease of implementation on the digital computer have been the main factors for the popularity of the Kalman filter in numerous applications such as aerospace problems [4,5,17,30,40], power systems [26,52], process control [2,40] and fore-casting [15,38]. The experience gained through the applications has led to further developments of the theory and to certain practical guidelines for the design of Kalman filters.

The purpose of this paper is to review the various aspects of Kalman filters and discuss a case study of their application to the forecasting of stock earnings for 49 companies. First presented is a review of the Bayesian decision analysis approach, which provides a unified framework not only for the derivation and understanding of Kalman filters, but also for the design of forecasting systems involving different decison makers and subjective information. Next state space models are introduced, and the Kalman filter equations are derived, after which statistical and numerical properties of Kalman filters are discussed. The next section deals with practical Kalman filter design and tests of validation, and is followed by a discussion of adaptive Kalman filters than can detect and compensate for changes in system behavior. Next, a case study of forecasting stock earnings for 49 companies is presented, and finally the conclusions and future prospects are briefly discussed.

2. Bayesian decison analysis approach

In the language of Bayesian decision analysis, forecasting is a decision process regarding the future values of a given random process. The basic elements of a decision theory formulation for forecasting are:

1. unknown state of the world denoted by a state vector $x(t)$, for $t = 0, 1, 2, 3,...$ or in abbreviated notation by $\{x(t)\}$

2. prior knowledge regarding the process $\{x(t)\}$ in the form of prior probabilities and evolution equations that result in a prior probability specification $p(\{x(t)\})$

3. a vector of observations $\{y(t)\}$ related to the true state $\{x(t)\}$ according to a known probability law $p(\{y(t)\} | \{x(t)\}, \theta)$, which may depend on a set of parameters, θ

4. a loss function $l[\{x(t)\}, \{\hat{x}(t)\}]$ that expresses the loss to the decision maker of choosing forecasts $\{\hat{x}(t)\}$ when the true values are $x(t)$. The forecast $\hat{x}(t)$ is a function of all the observations available at time t.

The optimal decision strategy is to choose $\{\hat{x}(t)\}$ so as to minimize the expected value of the loss function, where the expectation is taken with respect to all the random variables in the loss function. It may be shown [44] that an efficient way to obtain optimal decision is to compute recursively in time the posterior distributions of the state $\{\hat{x}(t)\}$ and perform expectations of the loss function with respect to these distributions. The main computational burden, therefore, in applying Bayesian decision analysis is in the calculation of posterior probabilities, and that is exactly where a Kalman filter becomes useful. In the next section, we discuss specific models for this abstract Bayesian formulation and state the conditions under which a Kalman filter recursion is obtained.

3. State space models

State space models of random processes are based on the Markov property that, in simple terms, implies the independence of the future of the process from its past, given the present state. In other words, the state of a Markov process summarizes all the information from the past that is necessary to predict its future. For obvious reasons, only the case in which the state vector is of finite dimension is of practical interest. A general state vector model is typically specified in terms of the following five quantities: 1) three vectors of input $u(t)$, output $y(t)$, and internal state variables $x(t)$, 2) a rule for transformation of the state vector from one time instant to the next, 3) a relationship between the input-output and state variables, 4) initial state $x(0)$; and 5) joint statistics of all random variables. Figure 1 illustrates the state vector model. Mathematically,

$$x(t + 1) = f[x(t), u(t), \theta, t] + w(t), \tag{1}$$

$$y(t) = h[x(t), u(t), \theta, t] + v(t), \tag{2}$$

$$t = 0, 1, 2, ...,$$

where $x(t)$ is $n \times 1$ state vector, $u(t)$ is $r \times 1$ input vector, $w(t)$ is $q \times 1$ process noise vector, θ is $m \times 1$ parameter vector, $y(t)$ is $p \times 1$ output vector, and $\dot{w}(t)$ and $v(t)$ are assumed to be uncorrelated white noise sequences with known distributions. Similarly, the distribution of $x(0)$ is assumed known.

All mathematical models including the state vector model are only approximations to reality. It will be shown here that a number of models used in forecasting can be written in the form of equations (1) and (2). If the model is physical or conceptual, the state $x(t)$ has a physical meaning. In black-box or time-series models,

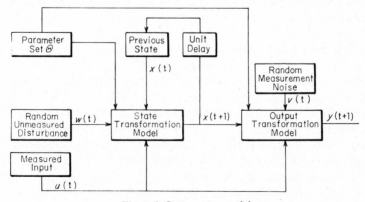

Figure 1. State vector model.

the state need not have a physical meaning. However, it still possesses the abstract mathematical meaning stated above for a Markov process.

When equations (1) and (2) are linear, the model is known as a Gauss–Markov model. It is of special significance and is written as

$$x(t + 1) = \phi x(t) + Gu(t) + \Gamma w(t), \tag{3}$$

$$y(t) = Hx(t) + v(t) \tag{4}$$

$$t = 0, 1, 2, ...,$$

where $w(t)$ and $v(t)$ are assumed to be Gaussian white noise (GWN) sequences with zero mean and covariances Q and R. The initial state $x(0)$ is normally distributed with mean $\hat{x}_0$ and covariance P_0. The matrices ϕ, G, H. Γ, Q, R, and P_0 are deterministic but may be time varying. The main advantage of the representation (3) and (4) is that the mean, covariance, and correlation functions for $x(t)$ and $y(t)$ can be computed recursively by solving a set of first-order vector difference equations [4]. Furthermore, the posterior distribution $p[x(t)|y(t), y(t-1), ..., y(1)]$ turns out to be Gaussian, and its first two moments are computed recursively by the Kalman filter. This subject will be discussed further in the next section. The role of various terms in the model (3) and (4) can best be shown by giving examples.

3.1. Process and measurement noise

The state vector model (3) and (4) contains two white noise terms – process noise $w(t)$ and measurement noise $v(t)$ – which have quite different interpretations and effects. The errors inherent in observing the true state of the system $x(t)$ are represented by $v(t)$, whereas $w(t)$ represents random shocks during the evolution of $x(t)$. If one neglects $v(t)$ and assumes for the time being that all the state variables can be observed – that is, $y(t) = x(t)$ – and all matrices are time invariant, equation (3) may be written as

$$y(t + 1) = \phi y(t) + Gu(t) + \Gamma w(t). \tag{5}$$

Equation (5) represents a first-order autoregressive process with observed input or exegeneous variable, $u(t)$ and random errors $w(t)$ [5]. Chow [6] and Mehra [33] show how econometric simultaneous equation models may be written in the form of equation (5).

Consider now, the case in which there is no process noise, that is $w(t) = 0$, and the initial state $x(0)$ is known perfectly. Then, given $\{u(t)\}$, the $\{x(t)\}$ process is deterministic and equation (4) represents a signal plus noise model. The prediction problem, in this case, consists essentially of separating the signal from noise. Notice that this nice interpreatation may be lost if $x(t) = y(t) - v(t)$ is substituted into equation (3), yielding

$$y(t+1) = \boldsymbol{\Phi} y(t) + \boldsymbol{G}u(t) + [v(t+1) - \boldsymbol{\Phi}v(t)]. \tag{6}$$

Equation (6) corresponds to a vector first-order autoregressive moving average (ARMA) model [54]. The same type of model is obtained even if the $w(t)$ term is kept in the model.

Three more examples will show the modeling flexibility of the state vector form:

3.1.1. Time-varying regression model.

A time-varying regression model with $d(t)$ as the dependent variable and $z_1(t)$, ..., $z_m(t)$ as the independent variables can be given as

$$d(t) = \sum_{i=1}^{m} a_i(t) z_i(t) + \eta(t). \tag{7}$$

If one assumes that the time variation of each of the regression coefficients can be described by a first-order scalar model with random shocks $\xi_i(t)$, then

$$a_i(t+1) = \alpha_i a_i(t) + \xi_i(t), \tag{8}$$

$$i = 1, ..., m.$$

Equation (7) and (8) may be expressed in the form of equation (3) and (4) by defining

$$y(t) = d(t), \qquad \eta(t) = v(t),$$

$$x^T(t) = [a_1(t), ..., a_m(t)], \qquad G = 0, \ \Gamma = I,$$

$$H(t) = [z_1(t), ..., z_m(t)],$$

$$\boldsymbol{\Phi} = \begin{bmatrix} \alpha_1 & & 0 \\ & \alpha_2 & \\ & & \ddots \\ 0 & & \alpha_m \end{bmatrix}, \qquad w(t) = \begin{bmatrix} \xi_1(t) \\ \vdots \\ \xi_n(t) \end{bmatrix}.$$

3.1.2. Error-in-variable model (EVM with correlated independent variables [35])

If in equation (7), the independent variables $z_i(t)$ can only be observed as $b_i(t)$ with errors $e_i(t)$, then

$$b_i(t) = z_i(t) + e_i(t), \tag{9}$$

$$i = 1, ..., m.$$

If one supposes further that $z_i(t)$ may be modeled as a first-order scalar Markov process, then

$$z_i(t+1) = \phi_i z_i(t) + \zeta_i(t). \tag{10}$$

The model of equation (7), (9) and (10) may be written in the linear state vector form of equations (3) and (4) for the constant coefficient case and in the nonlinear form of equations (1) and (2) for the time-varying case. The state vector in the latter case consists of $[z_i(t), ..., z_m(t), a_1(t), ..., a_m(t)]$. The resulting evolution equation (1) is linear in both cases, but the output equation (2) in the time-varying case involves products of states. See [35] for further details.

3.1.3. Stochastic S-curve model
A number of product sales curves have a mean history that follows an S-curve described by the relationship

$$S_t = a \exp[br^t], \tag{11}$$

where S_t denotes sales at time t, and a, b, and r are model parameters with $0 < r < 1$. Equation (11) may also be written as

$$S_{t+1} = a^{1-r} S_t^r, \tag{12}$$

$$S_0 = ae^b. \tag{13}$$

A stochastic version of the above model would involve random shocks in equation (12) to express deviations from the mean S-curve, that is

$$S_{t+1} = a^{1-r} S_T^r + w_t, \tag{14}$$

$$y_t = S_t + v_t,$$

a nonlinear state equation model and linear measurement equation. The unknown parameters a and r may be modeled as additional state variables if they are time dependent.

4. Recursive state estimation and Kalman filter equations

Considering the model of equations (1) and (2) with θ and $p[x(o)]$ specified, one can derive recursive equations to propagate conditional densities as follows, starting from $p[x(0)]$:

$$p[x(t)|Y_t] \rightarrow p[x(t+1)|Y_t] \rightarrow p[x(t+1)|Y_{t+1}],$$
$$\quad \text{(prediction)} \qquad \text{(update)}$$

where $Y_t = [y(t), y(t-1), ..., y(1)]$ denotes the set of all observations available at time t

One-step-ahead prediction is done by using the state equation as follows:

$$p[x(t+1)|Y_t] = \int p[x(t+1), x(t)|Y_t]\, dx(t)$$

$$= \int p[x(t+1)|x(t),\, Y_t]\, p[x(t)|Y_t]\, dx(t)$$

$$= \int p_{w(t)}\, \{x(t+1) - f[x(t),\, u(t),\, \theta,\, t]\}$$

$$p[x(t)|Y_t]\, dx(t), \tag{15}$$

where $p_{w(t)}(\cdot)$ denotes the probability distribution of $w(t)$ and the integration is carried over the sample space of $x(t)$.

Measurement update is done by using Bayes rule as follows:

$$p[x(t+1)|Y_{t+1}] = p[x(t+1)|Y_t, y(t+1)]$$

$$= \frac{p[y(t+1)|x(t+1)]\, p[x(t+1)|Y_t]}{\int p[y(t+1)|x(t+1)]\, p[x(t+1)|Y_t]\, dx(t+1)}. \tag{16}$$

Notice that

$$p[y(t+1)|x(t+1)] = p_{v(t+1)}[y(t+1) - h(x(t+1),\, u(t+1),\, \theta,\, (t+1)],$$

where $p_{v(t+1)}$ denotes the probability distribution of $v(t+1)$. Also, equation (15) may be used repeatedly for prediction more than one step ahead.

The actual forecasts are obtained by minimizing the loss function averaged with respect to the prediction densities. For example, if the loss function is mean square forecast error one step ahead, then the mean of $p[x(t+1)|Y_t]$ is chosen as the best forecast. Other attributes of a density function commonly used in practice are the median and the mode, the former minimizing the absolute forecast error and the latter selecting the most probable value of the random variable. For details, see Degroot [8] and Bryson and Ho [4].

The computation of equations (15) and (16) is quite cumbersome because of the multidimensional integrations and the nonparametric specification of the density functions. By using the special case of the linear Gauss-Markov model — equations (3) and (4) — elegantly simple results are obtained for the following reason:

1. Linear transformations of Gaussian random variables are also Gaussian.
2. The Gaussian family has the conjugate property that for Gaussian priors and Gaussian likelihood functions, the posterior distributions are also Gaussian.
3. Gaussian distributions are completely specified by their first two moments — mean and covariance.

A justification for using the Gaussian assumption comes from the central limit theorem. According to this theorem , the limiting sums of non-Gaussian independent random variables, under certain regularity conditions, have Gaussian distributions.

4.1. Kalman filter equations

One can let the mean and the covariance of the Gaussian density function $p[x(t + 1)|Y_t)$ be denoted by $\hat{x}(t + 1|t)$ and $P(t + 1|t)$ respectively. These relationships can also be denoted as respectively.

$$p[x(t + 1)|Y_t] \sim N[\hat{x}(t + 1|t), P(t + 1|t)],$$

$$p[x(t)|Y_t] \sim N[\hat{x}(t|t), P(t|t)].$$

Equation (15) leads to the following two equations:

4.2. Prediction equations

$$\hat{x}(t + 1|t) = \boldsymbol{\phi}(t)\hat{x}(t|t) + G(t)u(t), \tag{17}$$

$$P(t + 1|t) = \boldsymbol{\phi}(t)P(t|t)\boldsymbol{\phi}^T(t) + \boldsymbol{\Gamma}(t)Q(t)\boldsymbol{\Gamma}^T(t). \tag{18}$$

Equation (16) leads to the following equations:

4.3. Update equations

$$\hat{x}(t + 1|t + 1) = \hat{x}(t + 1|t) + K(t + 1)\upsilon(t + 1), \tag{19}$$

$$\upsilon(t + 1) = y(t + 1) - H(t + 1)\hat{x}(t + 1|t), \tag{20}$$

$$K(t + 1) = P(t + 1|t)H^T(t + 1)\Sigma^{-1}(t + 1), \tag{21}$$

$$\Sigma(t + 1) = H(t + 1)P(t + 1|t)H^T(t + 1) + R(t + 1), \tag{22}$$

$$P(t + 1|t + 1) = (I - K(t + 1)H(t + 1))P(t + 1|t). \tag{23}$$

4.4. Initial conditions for equations (17) through (23)

$$\hat{x}(0|0) = x_0, \tag{24}$$

$$P(0|0) = P_0. \tag{25}$$

Equations (17) through (23) constitute the basic Kalman filtering equations and they are solved recursively starting from the initial conditions of equations (24) and (25) in the sequence (17), (18), (20), (22), (21), (19) and (23). For predictions more than one step into the future, only equations (17) and (18) are used recursively. Since for Gaussian density functions, the mean, mode, and median are the same, the k-step-ahead forecast $\hat{x}(t + k|t)$, will be optimal for a whole class of symmetric loss functions — even functions of estimation error [8]. The covariance matrix $P(t + k|t)$ provides confidence limits for the forecasts $\hat{x}(t + k|t)$.

5. Properties of Kalman filters

In addition to the optimality properties stated above in the Bayesian decision theory sense, the Kalman filters have a number of other interesting properties of practical significance. These properties are mentioned here without detailed proofs.

5.1. Innovation property

The one-step-ahead prediction error sequence $v(t) = y(t) - H\hat{x}(t|t - 1)$ is known as the innovation sequence, since it represents new information brought by observations $y(t)$ in addition to the information contained in the past observation history Y_{t-1}. The sequence $v(t)$ has the interesting property that for an optimal filter it is a zero mean Gaussian white noise sequence with covariance $\Sigma(t)$. It will be shown later how this property may be used to test the optimality of Kalman filters, to detect changes in process model, and to build adaptive and robust Kalman filters. Kailath [20] has shown that the innovation property follows directly from the orthogonality principal of linear least squares estimation and that this property may be used as a starting point for the derivation of the Kalman filter. Furthermore, since $\{v(t)\}$ may be obtained from $\{y(t)\}$ by a causal and a causally invertible transformation, the innovation sequence contains as much information as the original observation sequence.

5.2. Stability

It has been shown by Kalman [23] and others that the Kalman filter possesses the property of global asymptotic stability for a completely controllable and observable system. The last two properties of the system are of central importance in modern system theory and relate to the structure of the system matrices ϕ, Γ, and H. For time-invariant systems, necessary and sufficient conditions for the system of equations (3) and (4) to be completely controllable and observable are that the rank for the following two matrices be n, where n is the dimension of the state vector, that is,,

$$\text{Rank}[\Gamma, \phi\Gamma, \phi^2\Gamma, ..., \phi^{n-1}\Gamma] = n, \tag{26}$$

$$\text{Rank}[H^T, \boldsymbol{\phi}^T H^T, ..., (\boldsymbol{\phi}^{n-1})^T H^T] = n. \tag{27}$$

The physical interpretation of the observability property is that for a noise-free observable system, the initial state $x(0)$ can be reconstructed uniquely from the noise-free measurements at n time instants, that is $[y(1), ..., y(n)]$. The controllability property implies the existence of a control sequence transferring the system from a given initial state to any other state in finite time and with finite control energy.

The practical significance of the controllability and observability conditions are that for time-invariant systems, the filter covariance matrices $[P(t + 1|t), P(t|t)]$ and Kalman gain $K(t)$ reach constant steady-state values, independent of the initial conditions. Furthermore, since these matrices can be precomputed, without having observations $\{y(t)\}$, the real-time Kalman filter computations can be reduced to equations (17), (19) and (20). In many applications, the assumption of constant Kalman filter gain does not degrade filter performance by very much but yields significant computational savings. Wiener filtering [55] for stationary processes corresponds to the case of a constant Kalman gain.

5.3. Numerical properties

The Kalman filter equations (17 through (23) can be written in different forms with different numerical properties. Unfortunately, equations (17) through (23), known as the covariance form of the Kalman filter, though physically easiest to comprehend, are not best suited for numerical computation. In systems with widely separated eigenvalues of the filter covariance matrices, round-off errors can lead to nonnegative definite covariance matrices. A solution to the problem is obtained by using Cholesky square roots of the covariance matrices by equations of the type

$$P(t|t) = S(t|t)S^T(t|t). \tag{28}$$

Recursive equations are developed for $S(t|t)$ and equation (28) is used to compute $P(t|t)$. Another advantage of this approach is improved accuracy on finite bit machines, since the condition number of $S(t|t)$ is half that of $P(t|t)$. In particular, the accuracy of single-precision square-root Kalman filters is comparable to that of double-precision covariance Kalman filters. The triangular factorization of $P(t|t)$ offers several other advantages, which are discussed in a recent book by Bierman [1].

Kalman filter equations can also be written in terms of the information matrices, which are defined as the inverses of the covariance matrices (see Schweppe [50]). The information form has the nice property that the prior information P_0^{-1} can be set to zero without any numerical difficulties. The information form also plays a role in square-root filtering and in systems with Fisher-unknown inputs (Schweppe

[50], Mehra [34]). In the latter case, the limit $Q \rightarrow \infty I$ is considered to model input-forcing functions that are deterministic but completely unknown — that is, there is no prior information on $\{w(t)\}$.

Cases in which the measurement noise is correlated or some of the measurements are noise free have been considered by Bryson and Henrickson [3]. It is possible to reduce the size of the Kalman filter in these cases. Other techniques for reducing the dimension of Kalman filters are discussed by Galdos and Gustafson [12].

6. Kalman filter design and testing

Certain guidelines, based on the previous discussion, can be developed for the design of Kalman filters. These are categorized here as model selection, parameter specification, algorithm selection, sensitivity analysis, validation and testing. For specific case studies, the reader is referred to Schweppe [51], Gelb [13] and Mehra and Wells [40].

6.1. Model selection

Selecting the model is perhaps the most important step in Kalman filter design, since the model ultimately determines the usefulness, accuracy, and computational requirements if the filter. It is recommended that the state variables of the model have physical significance and that the model not be overly complex unless great confidence can be placed in it. In several socioeconomic and business applications, there may be so little a priori modeling information that it would be better to identify the state vector model directly from the historical data. A solution to this problem is discussed in the paper by Mehra and Cameron [37], that describes a general technique for identifying state vector model from historical data. It is a good strategy to consider multiple models when models can be developed on theoretical as well as on empirical bases. A technique for designing Kalman filters based on multiple models will be discussed later. Another application of multiple models arises when the model of the system may be expected to change suddenly in time, but the exact time of abrupt change is not known beforehand. In such cases, hypothesis-testing techniques based on multiple Kalman filters may be devised to detect these changes. Harrison and Stevens [21] claim this to be a key ingredient of real-life forecasting applications.

6.2. Parameter specification

Once a model of the form of equations (3) and (4) has been selected, Kalman filter design requires specification of matrices ϕ, G, Γ, H, Q, R, $\hat{x}_0$ and P_0. For theoretically based models, most of this information comes from the physical understanding of the process. For black-box models, special canonical forms have to be

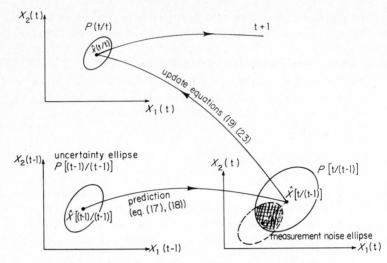

Figure 2. A discrete-time Kalman filter in two dimensions.

assumed so that the parameters can be identified uniquely from the historical input-output data [37]. Maximum likelihood, Bayesian, and other techniques have also been developed for estimating unknown parameters in theoretical models by using past historical data. These will be discussed more fully in the next section.

However, there are several applications when very little or no historical information is available to specify the above matrices. Indeed, one advantage of the Kalman filter is that it may be started with very little objective information and adapted as data become available. For example, if the initial state $x(0)$ is known poorly, the Kalman filter is started with large diagonal elements in the covariance matrix P_0. Similarly if the matrices ϕ, G, and Γ are known poorly, the process noise covariance matrix Q is assumed to be large. Both of these choices have the relative effect of increasing the filter covariance matrix $P(t|t-1)$ and the Kalman gain matrix $K(t)$, thereby allowing the filter to weight new information (or innovations) more heavily in equation (19).

The Kalman filter (KF) may be thought of as a device for combining two types of informations — model information and observations. For example, at time $(t+1)$, the KF first estimates $x(t+1)$ based on the previous state estimate $\hat{x}(t|t)$ and the state equation (3) [see equation (17)]. It then updates $\hat{x}(t+1|t)$, based on the observation $y(t+1)$ and the relative covariances of the errors. A graphical representation of this process in two dimensions is shown in fig. 2.

The implication of the above interpretation for Kalman filter design is that the forecaster can use his judgment regarding the relative accuracy of the model and the observations to select appropriate values for the noise covariance matrices Q and R.

He can then examine the actual operation of the filter and adjust these values if the situation changes at a later time. In doing so, he can use certain statistical tests described later to check the optimality of the Kalman filter by performing whiteness and chi-square tests on the innovation sequence.

An important consideration in parameter specification is the sensitivity of the Kalman filter to parameter misspecifications. This topic is discussed below.

6.3. Sensitivity analysis

The effect of modeling and parameter errors on the performance of the Kalman filter can be determined through sensitivity analysis. It is only necessary to solve the covariance equations to study the effect of errors, but the covariance equations for the suboptimal Kalman filter must be derived first. A number of authors have investigated this problem [11,16,28,41,43,48]. In general a $2n \times 2n$ linear matrix equation has to be solved to study the large-scale sensitivity of the Kalman filter. It is shown in ref. [28] that the KF has extreme sensitivity to the underestimation of the measurement noise variance. Underestimation of the process noise covariance matrix can cause a similar problem of filter divergence [11,43,49].

6.4. Validation and testing

As stated earlier, an optimal Kalman filter has the property that the innovation sequence is zero mean and white with covariance Σ. Statistical tests for checking the whiteness property are
1. correlation tests for testing local linear dependence [29].
2. integrated spectrum test for periodic linear dependence [19] and
3. run tests for linear and nonlinear dependence (Fama [10])
The sample mean and covariance of the normalized innovation sequence $\Sigma^{-1/2}(t)\mathfrak{v}(t)$ computed as follows also provide useful information for tuning the Kalman filter:

$$\hat{b} = \frac{1}{N} \sum_{t=1}^{N} \Sigma^{-1/2}(t)\mathfrak{v}(t), \tag{29}$$

$$\hat{C}(0) = \frac{1}{N} \sum_{t=1}^{N} \Sigma^{-1/2}(t)\mathfrak{v}(t)\mathfrak{v}^T(t)\Sigma^{-1/2}(t) \tag{30}$$

where N is chosen large enough to provide statistically significant estimates of $\hat{b}$ and $\hat{C}(0)$. For an optimal filter, $\hat{b}$ and $\hat{C}(0)$ should not differ significantly from zero and the identity matrix respectively. One may use t-statistics and chi-square tests or employ hypothesis-testing techniques for the above verifications.

7. Adaptive Kalman filters

Four different approaches may be used for adapting Kalman filters when there are large uncertainties regarding the parameter value or the structure of the model. Listed in decreasing order of accuracy and computational requirements, these methods are 1) Bayesian, 2) maximum likelihood (ML), 3) correlation or least squares, and 4) covariance-matching.

Bayesian methods compute the posterior probabilities of the parameter set $\boldsymbol{\theta}$, $p(\boldsymbol{\theta}|Y_t)$, and of the state given the parameters, $p[z(t)|Y_t, \boldsymbol{\theta}]$.

In the maximum likelihood technique, $\boldsymbol{\theta}$ is estimated by maximizing the likelihood function $\log p(Y_N|\boldsymbol{\theta})$ with respect to $\boldsymbol{\theta}$. It is easily shown [14,32] that

$$\log p(Y_N|\boldsymbol{\theta}) = \frac{1}{2} \sum_{t=1}^{N} [\boldsymbol{\upsilon}^T(t, \boldsymbol{\theta}) \boldsymbol{\Sigma}^{-1}(t, \boldsymbol{\theta}) \boldsymbol{\upsilon}(t, \boldsymbol{\theta}) + \log |\boldsymbol{\Sigma}(t, \boldsymbol{\theta})|] \qquad (31)$$

The correlation or least squares techniques apply only to time-invariant systems under stationary conditions. It is shown in ref. [32,30] how the canonical parameters in equations (3) and (4) may be estimated from the sample correlation function of the output observations $\{y(t)\}$ or the innovation sequence $\{\upsilon(t)\}$. The covariance-matching techniques of Sage and Husa [47] and Jazwinski and Bailie [18] compare the theoretical covariance of the innovations, $\Sigma(t)$, with the sample covariance and adjust Q and R matrices to bring the two into agreement. Though computationally attractive, these techniques are not guaranteed to converge and may actually degrade filter performance.

Methods for the detection of changes and jumps in states and the parameters of the system are discussed in Willsky [56] and in a forthcoming paper by Mehra [36]. Two general approaches that have been used successfully in practice are 1) generalized likelihood ratio (GLR) tests and 2) Wald's sequential probability ratio tests (SPRT).

Another technique that has been used for on-line parameter estimation is extended Kalman filtering (Jazwinski [17]). This is an approximate technique for nonlinear filtering and can be derived from the basic equations (15) and (16) under special assumptions. This technique, though conceptually simple, has the following limitations for parameter estimation: 1) it cannot be used to estimate the noise covariances; 2) it can be very sensitive to initial conditions, in particular, to the initial parameter estimates and their prior covariance maxtrix; and 3) it can fail to converge to consistent parameter estimates [27,39]. Some of these difficulties can be alleviated by using more advanced nonlinear filters such as iterated sequential filter, second-order filter, and modified extended Kalman filter [27,31,54].

8. Forecasting of stock earnings using annual data

Estimation of stock earnings per share or growth in earnings per share is an important problem in finance. The forecasts are generally made by security analysts using fundamental analysis and are an important input to portfolio selection and cost of capital models. The mechanical forecasting of stock earnings using past earnings data has been considered by Elton and Gruber [9]. They used nine forecasting techniques and concluded that the best mechanical forecasts were produced by the exponentially weighted moving average method and these forecasts compared favorably with the analysts' projections.

Elton and Gruber [9] did not use any macroeconomic data for forecasting stock earnings. In a joint study undertaken for Baker Weeks, Inc., the author investigated the use of regression and Kalman filtering methods for 49 companies, using the following models:

8.1. Log-ratio model

$$\log \frac{E(t)}{E(t-1)} = \sum_{i=1}^{5} a_i(t) \log \frac{Z_i(t)}{Z_i(t-1)} + a_6(t) + v(t),$$

$$(34)$$

$$t = 1952, ..., 1970,$$

where $E(t)$ denotes pre tax earnings per share in year t, the independent variables $[Z_1(t), ..., Z_5(t)]$ being respectively GNP, GNP (actual)/GNP (potential), disposable personal income (DPI), corporate investments (CI), and housing starts (HS). For individual companies, a subset of the above independent variables were used based on prior economic judgment. The coefficients $a_i(t)$ may be interpreted as elasticities.

8.2. Log-level model

$$\log E(t) = \sum_{i=1}^{5} b_i(t) \log Z_i(t) + b_6(t) + v(t),$$

$$(35)$$

$$t = 1952, ..., 1970.$$

The performance of the models was tested over the period from 1966 to 1970 in terms of one-, two-, and three-year forecasts. The data from 1952 to 1966 was used to estimate the parameters.

The parameters $a_i(t)$ and $b_i(t)$ were assumed constant for the regression runs, but were made to follow a random walk model for the Kalman filtering runs. The state vector $x(t)$ thus consisted of at most six coefficients, that is, $a_i(t)$'s or $b_i(t)$'s.

The KF equations were set up in the information matrix form to allow for infinite initial covariance matrix. For the log-ratio model, the a priori statistics $\hat{x}_0$ and P_0 were specified as

$$\hat{x}_0 = \begin{bmatrix} \hat{a}_1(0) \\ \hat{a}_2(0) \\ \\ \hat{a}_6(0) \\ \\ \end{bmatrix} = \begin{bmatrix} 1.5 \\ 1.0 \\ 1.5 \\ 2.0 \\ 2.0 \\ 0.5 \end{bmatrix}, \qquad \Sigma(0) = \frac{1}{1.8225} \begin{bmatrix} 1 & & & & 0 \\ & 1 & & & \\ & & 1 & & \\ & & & 1 & \\ & & & & 1 \\ 0 & & & & & 4 \end{bmatrix}$$

The state equations may be written as

$$x(t+1) = x(t) + w(t), \tag{36}$$

$$y(t) = H(t)x(t) + v(t), \tag{37}$$

where $y(t) = \log [E(t)]/[E(t-1)]$, $H(t)$ is a row vector of independent variables, and $w(t)$ and $v(t)$ are Gaussian white noise sequences with covariances assumed to be of the following form:

$$Q(t) = \alpha^2 \begin{bmatrix} \hat{a}_1^2(t|t) & & 0 \\ & \ddots & \\ 0 & & \hat{a}_6^2(t|t) \end{bmatrix} \tag{38}$$

$$R(t) = [\beta y(t)]^2. \tag{39}$$

The above for $Q(t)$ and $R(t)$ involve only two tuning parameters, α and β. The α parameter represents percentage root mean square change in the coefficients over one time step, and β represents the signal to noise ratio for the observations. The restriction of a common parameter α for all the coefficients may be too severe, but since the parameters are to be estimated from sample sizes of 14 to 18, it almost seems to be mandatory. Of course, for some companies better results would be obtained by other structures for Q and R matrices, but the emphasis in this study was on the use of a common forecasting model for all the companies.

Table 1 shows the results based on the data of 49 companies for both the log-ratio and the log-level models. The maximum inprovement over regression is obtained for 3-year forecasts by using the log-ratio model. Table 1 reveals another interesting result. The performance of regression is very sensitive to model specification, since the errors for the log-level model are almost 50% higher than the errors

Table 1
Results based on actual data of 49 companies (1952–1970).

Method	% Mean Absolute Error in Earning Forecasts		
	1 Year	2 Years	3 Years
Log-ratio model Regression	19.9	28.1	35.5
Adaptive Kalman filter	18.7	25.4	28.9
Log-level model Regression	31.7	41.1	49.2
Adaptive Kalman filter	20.7	29.2	33.2

for the log-ratio model. The performance of the Kalman filter, on the other hand, is quite insensitive to model specification, since the errors with the log-level Kalman filter are only slightly higher than the errors with the log-ratio Kalman filter. Intuitively speaking, the Kalman filter is able to compensate for the model specification errors by allowing the coefficients to change over time. It is also interesting to note that the performance of the KF is rather insensitive to a wide range of α and β values and that on a 10-company sample the best results are obtained for $\alpha = 1$ and $\beta = 2$. (See table 2 for the 10-company results.)

Another advantage of using the Kalman filtering approach with time-varying regression models, pointed out by Rosenberg [16], is that the confidence limits will be more realistic than those produced by regression. In fact, regression would generally underestimate the total uncertainty in the forecasts, since it neglects the random variation in the parameters. The effect of such underestimation can be quite serious when the confidence limits are used in the decision-making process.

Table 2
Results for 10 companies.

α	β	Average % Mean Deviation in Forecasts		
		1 Year	2 Years	3 Years
← Regression →		20.34	31.50	41.38
1	1	18.88	30.48	29.34
2	2	18.84	30.41	29.14
1	2	18.38	28.20	29.77
1	4	18.90	28.35	30.53

Verification of the above statement and results with other models are currently under investigation. The complete results of this study will be published in the near future.

9. Conclusion

Kalman filtering based on state space models is rapidly emerging as a general approach to forecasting. Although continuing studies can be expected to improve the technique for practical application, it is already clear that KF offers a number of advantages. Among these are:
(1) It is a flexible approach to obtain optimal forecasts for a large number of different models for linear, nonlinear and time varying processes.
(2) It extends classical single series methods such as exponential smoothing, Wiener filtering and polynomial filtering.
(3) It provides complete probability distributions on forecasts so that confidence limits and expected values of loss functions can be evaluated explicitly.
(4) Kalman filters can be used to detect significant changes in the time series. Furthermore, they can be made to adapt to these changes.

References

[1] G.J. Bierman, Factorization Methods for Discrete Sequential Estimation (Academic Press, New York, 1976).
[2] T. Bohlin, Four cases of identification of changing systems from discrete time series, in: R.K. Mehra and D.G. Laintootis, eds., System Identification, Advances and Case Studies (Academic Press, New York, 1976).
[3] A.E. Bryson and L.J. Henrickson, Estimation using sampled data containing sequentially correlated noise, Journal of Spacecraft and Rockets 6 (1968) 662–665.
[4] A.E. Bryson and Y.C. Ho, Optimal Programming, Estimation and Control (Blasdell, New York, 1968).
[5] R.S. Bucy and P.D. Joseph, Filtering for Stochastic Processes with Applications to Guiddance (Wiley–Interscience, New York, 1968).
[6] G. Chow, Analysis and Control of Dynamic Economic Systems (Wiley, New York, 1975).
[7] W.B. Davenport, Jr., and W.L. Root, An Introduction to the Theory of Random Signals and Noise (McGraw-Hill, New York, 1958).
[8] M. Degroot, Optimal Statistical Decisions (McGraw-Hill, New York, 1970).
[9] E.J. Elton and M.J. Gruber, Earnings estimates and the accuracy of expectational data, Management Science 8 (1972).
[10] E. Fama, The behaviour of stock-market prices, The Journal of Business of the University of Chicago, January, 1965.
[11] R.J. Fitzegerald, Error divergence in optimal filtering problems, paper presented at the 2nd IFAC Symp. Automatic Control in Space, Vienna, Austria, 1967.
[12] J.I. Galdos and D.E. Gustafson, Information and distortion in reduced-order filter design, IEEE T-IT, 1977 (in press).

[13] A. Gelb, ed., 1974, Applied Optimal Estimation (M.I.T. Press, Cambridge, Massachusetts, 1974).
[14] N.K. Gupta and R.K. Mehra, Computational aspects of maximum likelihood estimation and reduction in sensitivity function calculations, IEEE Trans. on Automat. Contr., Special Issue on System Identification and Time Series Analysis, December, 1974.
[15] P.J. Harrison and C.F. Stevens, Bayesian forecasting, Royal Statistical Society (1975) 205–247.
[16] H. Heffes, The effect of erroneous models on the Kalman filter response, IEEE Trans. Automat. Contr., AC-11 (1966) 541–543.
[17] A.H. Jazwinski, Stochastic Processes and Filtering Theory (Academic Press, New York, 1970).
[18] A.H. Jazwinski and A.E. Bailie, Adaptive filtering, Analytical Mechanics Associates, Inc., Rep. (1967) 67-6.
[19] G.M. Jenkins and D.G. Watts, Spectral Analysis and Its Applications, (Holden-Day, San Francisco, 1968).
[20] T. Kailath, An innovations approach to least-squares estimation, Part I: Linear filtering in additive white noise, IEEE Trans. Autom. Contr., AC-13 (1968) 646–655.
[21] T. Kailath, Some new algorithms for recursive estimation in constant linear systems, IEEE Trans. on Information Theory, IT-19(6), 750–760, November 1973.
[22] R.E. Kalman, A new approach to linear filtering and prediction problems, J. Basic Eng. 82 (1960) 340–345.
[23] R.E. Kalman, New methods in Wiener filtering theory, in: G.L. Bogdanoff and J. Kozin, eds., Proceedings of First Symp on Eng. Appl. of Random Function Theory and Probability (Wiley, New York, 1963).
[24] R.E. Kalman and R.S. Bucy, New results in linear filtering and prediction theory, Trans. ASME, Ser. D., Journal of Basic Eng. 83 (1961) 95–107.
[25] A.N. Kolmogorov, Interpolation and extrapolation of stationary random sequences, Bull. Moscow University, URRS. Ser. Math. 5 (1941).
[26] R.E, Larson, W.F. Tinney and J. Peschon, State estimation in power systems – Parts I and II, IEEE T-PAS, vol. PAS-89 (1970) 345–363.
[27] L. Ljung, The extended-Kalman filter as a parameter estimator for linear systems, Report LiTH-ISY-I-0154, Univ. of Linköping, Sweden, 1977).
[28] R.K. Mehra, On optimal and suboptimal linear smoothing, Proceedings of the National Electronics Conference, December 1968.
[29] R.K. Mehra, Identification of variances and adaptive Kalman filtering, IEEE Trans. on Automat. Contr., February 1970.
[30] R.K. Mehra, Identification of linear dynamic systems, AIAA Journal, January 1971.
[31] R.K. Mehra, A comparison of several nonlinear filters for reentry vehicle tracking, IEEE Trans. on Automat. Control., August 1971.
[32] R.K. Mehra, Approaches to adaptive filtering, IEEE Trans. on Automatic Control, October 1972.
[33] R.K. Mehra, Identification and control and econometric systems, similarities and differences, Annals of Economic and Social Measurements, January 1974.
[34] R.K. Mehra, Sequential estimation for dynamic systems with unknown deterministic inputs and duality with singular control, IEEE Trans. on Autom. Contr., October 1975.
[35] R.K. Mehra, Identification and estimation of the error-in-variables model (EVM) in structural form, in: Proceedings of Symposium on Stochastic Systems, June (North-Holland, Amsterdam, 1976).
[36] R.K. Mehra, Fault detection, diagnosis and compensation in dynamic systems, unpublished, 1976.
[37] R.K. Mehra and A.V. Cameron, State space forecasting for single and multiple time series, unpublished. (presented at 1976 ORSA Fall Meeting)

[38] R.K. Mehra and P.S. Krishnaprasad, A unified approach to the structural estimation of distributed lags and stochastic differential equations, paper presented at the 3d NBER Conference on Stochastic Control, Washington, D.C., 1974.

[39] R.K. Mehra and J.S. Tyler, Case studies in aircraft parameter identification, paper presented at the 3d IFAC Conference on Identification and System Parameter Estimation, Hague, Netherlands, June 1973.

[40] R.K. Mehra and C.H. Wells, Dynamic modeling and estimation of Carbon in a basic oxygen furnace, paper presented at the 3d International IFAC/IFIP Conference Helsinki, June 2–5, 1971.

[41] T. Nishimura, Error bounds of continuous Kalman filters and the application to orbit determination problems,IEEE Trans. Automat. Contr., AC-12 (1967) 268–275.

[42] A. Papoulus, Probability Random Variables and Stochastic Processes (McGraw-Hill, New York, 1965).

[43] C.F. Price, An analysis of the divergence problem in the Kalman filter, IEEE Trans. Autom. Contr., AC-13 (1968) 699–702.

[44] H. Raiffa, Decision Analysis (Addison-Wesley, Reading, 1970).

[45] H. Raiffa and R. Schlaifer, Applied statistical Decision theory (Division of Research, Graduate School of Business Administration, Harvard University, Boston, 1961).

[46] B.M. Rosenberg, A survey of stochastic parameter regression, Annals of Economic and Social Measurements 2 (1973) 381–397.

[47] A.P. Sage and G.W. Husa, Adaptive filtering with unknown prior statistics, in: Proc. Joint Automatic Control Conf., (1969) 760–769.

[48] F.H. Schlee, C.J. Standish and N.F. Toda, Divergence in the Kalman filter, AIAA J. 5 (1967) 114–1120.

[49] S.F. Schmidt, Computational techniques in Kalman filtering, in: Theory and application of Kalman filtering, NATO Advisory Group for Aero-Space Research and Development, AGARDograph 139, Technical Editing and Reproductions Limuted, Harford House, London, February 1970.

[50] F.C. Schweppe, Uncertain dynamic systems (Prentice-Hall, New York, 1974).

[51] F. Schweppe et al., Power system – Static state estimation, Parts I, II and III, IEEE-T-PAS, PAS89 (1970) 120–135.

[52] Stratonovich, Topics in the theory of random noise (Addison-Wesley, Reading, 1963). (The Russian publication of one of the papers in the book is around 1957.)

[53] P. Swerling, First order error propagation in a stagewise smoothing procedure for satellite observations, J. Astronaut. Sci. 6 (1959) 46–52.

[54] P. Whittle, Prediction and Regulation (Van Nostrand, Princeton, 1963).

[55] N. Wiener, The Extrapolation, Interpolation and Smoothing of Stationary Time Series with Engineering Applications (Wiley, New York, 1949).

[56] A.W. Willsky, A survey of design methods for failure detection in dynamic systems, Automatica, November 1976.

[57] R.P. Wishner, R.E. Larson, R.K. Mehra and M. Athans, Filters of varying complexity for radar target tracking, Proc. Joint Automatic Control Conferences, St. Louis, August 1971.

[58] H. Wold, A Study in the Analysis of Stationary Time Series (Almquist and Wiksell, Uppsala, Sweden, 1938).

TIMS Studies in the Management Sciences 12 (1979) 95–111
© North-Holland Publishing Company

AN ECONOMETRIC APPROACH TO FORECASTING DEMAND AND FIRM BEHAVIOR: CANADIAN TELECOMMUNICATIONS *

Vittorio CORBO

*Concordia University, Montreal, and
National Bureau of Economic Research*

and

Robert S. PINDYCK

Massachusetts Institute of Technology

1. Introduction

Econometric approaches to forecasting have played an increasingly important role in both public and private managerial decision-making. Managers have begun to recognize that explicit quantitative models in which individual relationships have been empirically tested often provide a more reliable means for forecasting than do intuitive or subjective methods of implicit modeling. Also, the usefulness of a forecast is increased when it is accompanied by a statistical measure of confidence. The use of econometric models to generate forecasts usually means that forecast confidence intervals can be computed (and interpreted) in a straightforward manner — either by directly calculating standard errors of forecast in the case of a simple regression or time-series model, or through Monte Carlo simulation in the case of a multi-equation simulation model. [1]

Our objectives in this paper are twofold: to provide an introduction to the construction, use, and limitations of econometric modeling for those less familiar with this forecasting tool, and to present some new econometric approaches to forecasting and regulatory policy analysis in the Canadian telecommunications industry.

---

* The authors wish to thank Jose Vrljičak for his efficient research assistance, and two referees for their comments and criticisms.

[1] Decision-makers who use forecasts seem to have come to recognize three main advantages in the use of explicit *models* instead of intuitive (implicit) relationships, and of econometric models in particular. First, explicit model building itself is more likely to force one to account for most or all of the important interrelationships involved in a problem. Second, it is important that individual relationships be tested empirically or validated in some way, and this is an integral part of econometric modeling. Finally, the use of purely intuitive methods, as well as certain simulation techniques, often precludes any quantitative measure of confidence in the resulting forecast.

Our approach is to develop two related examples of the construction and application of econometric models for forecasting and analysis. Both examples deal with forecasting problems in a regulated industry, but the point of view of each is rather different, as is the nature of the model constructed. The first problem deals with forecasting the demand for telephone services, and takes the point of view of the company that must make medium-term decisions about needed capacity. The model developed in this case is a single-equation demand model estimated from pooled time-series and cross-section data. The second problem deals with the effect of rate of return regulation on the factor input choices of the company, and takes the point of view of the regulatory agency that must determine the trade-off between captured monopoly profits and increased costs resulting from regulation-induced inefficiencies. The model developed here is a multi-equation model that describes the production behavior of the firm and determines the extent to which regulation results in over-capitalization (i.e., the Averch—Johnson effect).

We begin with a brief overview of econometric forecasting methods, intended for those readers who have less familarity with econometric approaches to forecasting; it will prevent them from mistakenly concluding that the two models presented here exhaust the spectrum of econometric techniques. In section 3 we present a model of the demand for interprovincial flows of telephone services in Canada and apply it to the generation of demand forecasts and forecasts confidence intervals. In section 4 we develop a model of the production behavior of Bell Cananda and use it to determine the effect of regulation on the factor input mix. In the last section we offer come concluding comments on econometric forecasting and its limitations.

2. Econometric approaches to forecasting

It seems useful to divide econometric forecasting models into three general classes: single-equation regression models, multi-equation models, and time-series models. Each involves a different degree of model complexity and structural explanation, and a different level of comprehension of the real world processes that are being modeled.

Probably the most widely used forecasting tool today is the single-equation regression model, in which the variable of interest is related to a single function of explanatory variables and an implicit additive error term (that accounts for the unexplained variance in the dependent variable). This function need not be linear in the variables themselves, but if it is linear in the unknown parameters, least-squares estimation is usually straightforward, and standard errors of the estimated parameters and the implicit additive error terms can easily be calculated and used as a basis for significance and hypothesis testing. In addition, the parameter estimates will be unbiased, consistent, and efficient (minimum variance) within the class of linear unbiased estimators as along as the implicit error terms in the equation are of constant variance, and uncorrelated with each other and with the explanatory variables.

The least-squares criterion (choose parameter values to minimize the sum of squared differences between the actual and estimated values of dependent variable) is the most widely used in applied econometric modeling, but it is certainly not the only criterion available. Other criteria (e.g., minimize the sum of absolute values of the differences) can be and are used for some estimation problems, but statistical tests become much more complicated. In addition, the least-squares criterion has the optimality property that it provides minimum variance estimates for the linear regression model.

If the error terms are also normally distributed, the least-squares estimator is absolutely efficient (i.e., the variance of the estimator achieves the Cramer–Rao lower bound). Often one or more of the conditions for the error terms do not hold, and the bulk of econometric method deals with alternatives to or modifications of ordinary least-squares estimation that would in this case still yield estimators with one or more of the properties of consistency, unbiasedness, and efficiency.

The forecasts generated from a single-equation regression model will have an associated error than can come about from each of four distinct sources. First, in making a forecast we assume that the implicit additive error will equal zero (its expected value), but the *realized* values of this error will differ from zero. Second, the estimated parameter values are random variables which are unlikely to be exactly equal to the true parameter values. Third, the forecast is often conditional on the future values of explanatory variables, and forecasts of these future values are likely to be in error themselves. Finally, errors will be introduced if the model specification (i.e., the functional form of the equation) is not a correct representation of the true real world process. It is not difficult to compute a standard error of forecast for a regression model that takes into account the first three of these sources of error, as we demonstrate in the demand model that follows. [2] Accounting for specification error is more problematical; no simple technique exists, although sensitivity studies can be performed to determine the effects of alternative model specification on the value of the forecast.

If a regression model is not linear in its unknown parameters, estimation may still be feasible, although computationally costly. A number of algorithms for nonlinear estimation exist, but all are based on maximum likelihood estimation and take one of two basic alternative computational approaches. The first is *direct optimization,* where parameter estimates are obtained by differentiating directly the sum-of-squared errors function with respect to each coefficient, setting the derivatives equal to zero (thus defining a minimum), and solving the resulting set of nonlinear equations. The second approach is based on iterative linearization, where the

---

[2] For the calculation of the standard error of forecast (i.e., the standard deviation of the forecast error), see Pindyck and Rubinfeld [27, Chapter 6].

nonlinear equation is linearized around some initial set of parameter values, least squares estimates of the parameters are obtained, the nonlinear equation is relinearized around these new parameter values, and the process is repeated until convergence occurs. [3]

A number of problems exist with both approaches. First, there is no guarantee of convergence, and some nonlinear estimation problems simply do not yield a solution. Second, if a solution is reached, there is no guarantee that it represents a global, and not local, minimum of the sum of squares. Third, and perhaps most important, the estimated parameters and estimated value of the error term variance no longer follow standard distributions, so that the statistical tests usually used to evaluate the fit of a linear regression and perform hypothesis tests are no longer strictly applicable. In practice, significance and hypothesis tests are often based on a linearization of the regression equation. Furthermore, the proper calculation of standard errors of forecasts requires the use of Monte Carlo simulation, which is computationally expensive.

A limitation of the single-equation regression model is its failure to explain the interdependencies that may exist among the explanatory variables themselves, or the relationships of these variables to other variables. In addition, it explains causality in only one direction, as there is no feedback relationshp between the dependent variable and the explanatory variables. Multi-equation models, on the other hand, provide a greater degree of structural explanation by accounting simultaneously for interrelationships among a set of variables.

While a multi-equation model may lead to greater forecast accuracy, the main motivation for its construction is usually a desire for increased structural explanation in order to better assess the impact of alternative policy measures and changes in other exogenous factors. However, the benefit of this structural explanation must be weighed against the higher cost of model construction. There are a number of methodological issues in multi-equation model construction that make it a more involved process than simply constructing and combining a set of individual regression equations. For example, there is always a question of whether individual equations in the model can be identified (i.e., whether the model's structure permits the parameter values to be inferred from the data), alternatives to ordinary least squares must be used for consistent and efficient parameter estimation (and if the sample set is small, the choice of estimator is not clear), and an analysis of the model requires studying the characteristics of the entire system of difference equations. [4]

---

[3] The most commonly used variation of the first approach is the *steepest-descent* method, and is described in detail in Draper and Smith [15]. For a discussion of the second approach, see Eisner and Pindyck [16]. This approach is also the basis for Marquardt's method; see Marquardt [24]. For a general discussion of nonlinear estimation methods, see Goldfeld and Quandt [18].

[4] For an introduction to the analysis of a model's dynamic structure, see Pindyck and Rubinfeld [27, Chapters 9–12] and Chow [10].

In addition, model validation and evaluation is more difficult, since a set of individual regression equations that was intended to comprise a model might fit the data and forecast well when the equations are considered individually, but when they are combined they might yield unstable or otherwise unrealistic forecasts. The reason is that the model explains not only individual causal relationships, but also the dynamic structure of an overall system, and explaining the latter well may be difficult. Thus standard statistics for individual equations will not suffice as an evaluation of the model as a whole; additional criteria must be used, and usually these involve statistics that describe the model's simulation and forecasting performance under different conditions. On the other hand, in some cases (such as the model of Bell Canada in section 4 of this paper) this overall system structure is crucial to the generation of useful forecasts, and the effort involved in constructing a multi-equation model is justified.

We also consider pure time-series models as a class of econometric forecasting models, although they are different in nature from the models described above. A pure time-series model contains no explanatory variables and generates predictions based solely on the past behavior of the variable of interest. A time-series model is often the preferred means of forecasting when the desired forecast is short-term, when it is difficult or impossible to explain to movement of a variable through the use of a structural model, or when a structural model is not useful for forecasting because explanatory variables in the model cannot themselves be forecasted.

Recent work initiated by Zellner and Palm [29] has extended the pure time-series model to include additional explanatory variables with their own time-series structure, and to allow for estimation of simultaneous systems of time-series equations. However most of the current applied work in time-series analysis make use of the pure models described above. For an up-to-date and comprehensive treatment of time-series analysis, see Granger and Newbold [19].

The linear time-series models of the type introduced by Box and Jenkins [6] have found the widest application to economic and business forecasting. These models can be constructed for time series that are stationary or homogenous non-stationary (i.e., transformable into a stationary series by differencing one or more times). Statistical tests are available to determine whether or not the model is correctly specified, and it is straightforward to compute standard errors and confidence intervals for the model's forecasts.

The most basic linear time-series model is the mixed autoregressive moving average (*ARMA*) model, which is represented by the following equation:

$$y_t = \phi_1 y_{t-1} + \phi_2 y_{t-2} + \dots + \phi_p y_{t-p} + \delta + \epsilon_t - \theta_1 \epsilon_{t-1} - \dots - \theta_q \epsilon_{t-q},$$

where $y_{t-1}, \dots, y_{t-p}$ are the autoregressive terms, δ defines the mean value of the series, and the remaining terms represent a moving average error process. The estimation of the parameters of this equation involves the use of a nonlinear estimation process, but if a computer and the appropriate software are available, estimation does not impose any particular problem. This equation can only be applied to a time-series that is stationary (i.e., the mean and moments of the series are the same at any point in time), but many nonstationary series can be differenced one or more times to yield a stationary series to which the equation can be applied. [5]

A promising application of time-series models is in combination with a regression model. The idea is first to use a regression model to obtain the best structural explanation possible for a particular variable, and then to construct a time-series model to explain movements in the implicit additive error term of the regression; i.e. to explain (and forecast) the unexplained variation in the dependent variable. Often the combined model provides better forecasts than a regression model or time-series model alone. For example, suppose that the structural model to explain a variable $\ddot{y}$ is given by the equation

$$y_t = a_0 + a_1 x_{1t} + a_2 x_{2t} + \epsilon_t,$$

where x_{1t} and x_{2t} are explanatory variables, and ϵ_t is the random error. After estimating this equation, a time-series model of the residuals is used to explain the error process ϵ_t. Alternatively, the parameters of the time-series model and the structural model can be estimated simultaneously. (This produces more efficient estimates, but is much more computationally costly.) [6]

We now turn to the development and use of two specific econometric models for forecasting and policy analysis. The first is a single-equation model of telephone service demand in Canada, and the second is a multi-equation model that predicts the factor input mix used in the production of telecommunication services by Bell Canada. These models should help illustrate the use of some of the methods described above.

3. Forecasting the demand for interprovincial flows of telephone services in Canada [7]

We begin with a set of single-equation structural models designed to forecast on a quarterly basis the flow of interprovincial telephone services in Canada. The purpose of these models is to assist the company in determining intermediate-term needs for telephone equipment. [8] The models will predict the traffic originating in

[5] For an introduction to the construction and use of time-series models, see [27] and Nelson [26].

[6] For examples of this approach see [27], sections 17.4 and 17.5.

[7] This section is based on a larger study by Vittorio Corbo entitled Interprovincial Flows of Telephone Services, and done under a grant from the Department of Communications of the Canadian government.

[8] To forecast capital needs, revenues, and costs, a model that integrates the functioning of the company with its environment is needed, and this is usually a structural multi-equation model, where some of the equations might be technological relationships. Such a model is pres-

the provinces of Ontario and Quebec (served by Bell Canada) and destined to each Canadian province. The models allow for differences in the directions of calls, since calls from, say, Ontario to Quebec are regarded as different from calls from Quebec to Ontario.

Our model is of the habit formation type often used in demand estimation, and is based on the assumption that the demand for telephone service q_t is a function of expected income y_t^e, expected price p_t^e, and a state variable s_t proportional to last period's demand, and representing the stock of telephone habits:

$$q_t = \alpha_0 + \alpha_1 y_t^e + \alpha_2 p_t^e + \alpha_3 s_t, \quad \text{with} \quad s_t = \theta q_{t-1}.$$

Next, we represent expected price and income by a two-period moving average of their actual values. [9] Letting $Q_{ij,k}(t)$ represent telephone service in thousands of calls for sector k (k = production, service, government, public, and household) originating in province i (Ontario or Quebec) and destined to province j in period t, $CRPP_{ij}(t)$ a composite of real provincial product in provinces i and j in period t (formed from a weighted average of real product of the province where the call originates (3/4) and the province where the call is received (1/4)), PT(t) a price index for Trans-Canada long distance telephone calls, and $CIP_{ij}(t)$ a composite price index (a weighted average of the retail price index of the province where the calls originate and the retail price index of the province where the calls are received, with weights equal to each province's relative share of the total product of the two provinces), we obtain the following estimating equation:

$$Q_{ij,k}(t) = \gamma_0 + \gamma_1 [CRPP_{ij}(t) + CRPP_{ij}(t-1)]$$

$$+ \gamma_2 \left[\frac{PT(t)}{CIP_{ij}(t)} + \frac{PT(t-1)}{CIP_{ij}(t-1)} \right] + \gamma_3 Q_{ij,k}(t-1). \tag{1}$$

A priori, we expect $\gamma_1 > 0$, $\gamma_2 < 0$ and $1 > \gamma_3 > 0$. Due to the presence of a lagged endogenous variable on the right-hand side of the equation, ordinary least squares would yield inconsistent estimates if the disturbances are autocorrelated. We therefore begin by assuming a first-order autoregressive process for the disturbances, and use the Hildreth-Lu procedure to estimate simultaneously the coeffi-

---

ented in the next section. Here we assume that management is interested only in forecasts of individual exogenous variables (e.g., business long distance traffic, Sunday household traffic, etc.), so that either a structural model or a time-series model can be used. Since our main interest is identifying the economic determinants of demand and forecasting their individual impacts, a structural model is more useful.

[9] Other representations of expected price and income are certainly possible, such as more flexible distributed lag structures.

Table 1
Production sector: habit formation model. [a]

A. Ontario origin

Ontario to:	γ_0	γ_1	γ_2	γ_3	ρ	R^2
British Columbia	−61.162	0.006	5.005	0.707	−0.20	0.982
	(−1.011)	(2.858)	(0.168)	(4.870)	(−0.957)	
Alberta	−61.971	0.006	4.582	0.690	−0.00	0.978
	(−0.854)	(2.408)	(0.133)	(4.773)	(−0.00)	
Saskatchewan	−7.266	0.002	−6.098	0.342	−0.10	0.913
	(−0.219)	(1.996)	(−0.399)	(1.735)	(−0.471)	
Manitoba	−49.280	0.008	−5.713	0.545	−0.30	0.966
	(−0.627)	(2.957)	(−0.149)	(3.441)	(−1.475)	
Ontario	2041.403	0.872	−4246.410	−0.516	0.60	0.960
	(0.247)	(4.083)	(−1.096)	(−3.243)	(3.518)	
Quebec	3765.521	0.035	−2317.543	−0.413	0.80	0.939
	(2.558)	(1.052)	(−2.915)	(−2.343)	(6.254)	
New Brunswick	−14.234	0.003	−6.202	0.475	−0.20	0.968
	(−0.498)	(2.788)	(−0.459)	(2.857)	(−0.957)	
Maritimes	−17.529	0.005	−11.944	0.461	0.20	0.973
	(−0.351)	(2.489)	(−0.506)	(2.590)	(0.957)	
Newfoundland	−14.690	0.001	3.165	0.750	−0.40	0.952
	(−1.167)	(2.130)	(0.565)	(4.832)	(−2.047)	

B. Quebec origin

Quebec to:	γ_0	γ_1	γ_2	γ_3	ρ	R^2
British Columbia	37.039	0.002	−29.772	0.488	−0.10	0.953
	(1.100)	(1.533)	(−1.824)	(3.172)	(−0.471)	
Alberta	70.658	0.0004	−43.897	0.439	0.30	0.978
	(2.608)	(0.390)	(−2.961)	(2.647)	(1.475)	
Saskatchewan	27.959	−0.0002	−16.219	0.284	0.30	0.929
	(2.476)	(−0.482)	(−2.792)	(1.397)	(1.475)	
Manitoba	63.023	0.002	−42.036	0.344	0.10	0.935
	(1.851)	(0.957)	(−2.545)	(2.238)	(0.471)	
Ontario	5083.258	−0.017	−2914.161	−0.255	0.80	0.952
	(5.048)	(−0.705)	(−4.909)	(−1.228)	(6.254)	
Quebec	12731.469	0.307	−8119.633	−0.604	0.80	0.840
	(3.227)	(2.502)	(−3.281)	(−3.097)	(6.254)	
New Brunswick	105.881	0.0009	−64.643	0.436	0.20	0.956
	(2.504)	(0.422)	(−3.090)	(3.083)	(0.957)	
Maritimes	95.449	−0.0005	−54.510	0.514	−0.20	0.951
	(2.775)	(−0.283)	(−3.313)	(3.924)	(−0.957)	
Newfoundland	100.227	0.001	−65.964	−0.042	0.70	0.964
	(4.014)	(1.094)	(−4.317)	(−0.207)	(4.598)	

[a] *t*-statistics are in parentheses.

cient of the autogressive process and the coefficients of the equation. [10] All of these regressions were estimated using data from the fourth quarter of 1967 to the first quarter of 1973. Due to space limitations we reproduce here in table 1 only the results relating to the production sector. [11]

Observe that our a priori expectation regarding the sign pattern of the coefficients is satisfied in most of the cases. For calls originating in Ontario, income is highly significant but price often is not, while just the reverse is true for calls originating in Quebec. The results for prices are not surprising — establishments in Quebec are generally smaller in scale than in Ontario, and therefore are more liekly to be price-sensitive. The lack of significant positive income effect in Quebec, however, is harder to explain. [12] The habit formation process as represented by the lagged dependent variable is generally significant and of the expected sign (even after the correction for serial correlation in the disturbance). Finally, note that the large variation in parameter values (particularly for the price variable) results from differences in the sizes of the dependent variables.

Forecasts of interprovincial telephone services are presented in table 2. [13]

[10] Assuming the Hildreth–Lu procedure converges on the global minimum of the residual sum of squares, the resulting parameter estimates are consistent and, if the corrected disturbances are identically and independently normally distributed, are equivalent to the maximum likelihood estimates. In addition, the estimates are equivalent to the generalized least squares estimates that would result if the first observation were dropped.

[11] In the larger study from which this section draws, five sectors are distinguished and separate demand equations and forecasts are made for each one. These sectors are production, service, government, public and household. Furthermore, three different theoretical formulations are used for the specification of a single-equation structural demand model: a simple demand model in which the quantity demanded of telephone services is expressed as a function of overall economic activity (usually the variable chosen is Gross Provincial Product) and relative prices, and discrete and continuous versions of the habit formation model. (For an introduction to these models, see Houthakker and Taylor [21]). The best results were obtained for the discrete version of the habit formation model, and consequently that is presented here.

[12] The income effect in Quebec was insignificant for the other models forms tested as well.

[13] To generate forecasts from this model, it was first necesary to forecast the explanatory variables themselves. There are two such variables, real provincial product (RPP) and the relative price of telephone services (PT/CIP). RPP might have been forecasted using a regional macro-model, but since one was not available to us, we simply used an extended autoregressive equation:

$$\text{RPP}_i(t) = \delta_0 + \delta_1 D_1(t) + \delta_2 D_2(t) + \delta_3 D_3(t) + \delta_4 t + \delta_5 \text{RPP}_i(t-1),$$

where $\text{RPP}_i(t)$ is real provincial product in province i in period t, $D_1(t)$, $D_2(t)$, and $D_3(t)$ are seasonal dummy variables, equal to one in the first, second, and third calendar quarters respectively and zero otherwise, and t is time in quarters ($t = 1$ in the first quarter of 1966). To forecast the relative price variable we used a first-order autoregressive process with a time trend. Note that we might have used a more general time-series model to forecast these explanatory variables.

Table 2
Production sector telephone services, Ontario origin.

Quarter	To British Columbia (thousands of calls)		To Alberta (thousands of calls)	
	Forecast	± 2 S.E.	Forecast	± 2 S.E.
1973.4 (Actual)	78.05	–	76.08	–
1973.2	82.13	5.80	80.08	6.17
1973.3	87.35	5.78	84.64	6.33
1973.4	91.05	6.11	87.91	6.51
1974.1	92.87	6.50	89.32	6.94
1974.2	95.33	6.38	91.50	6.87
1974.3	99.43	6.21	95.44	6.72
1974.4	102.82	6.48	98.65	6.99
1975.1	104.60	6.95	100.22	7.54
1975.2	107.15	6.81	102.63	7.46
1975.3	111.39	6.61	106.80	7.26
1975.4	114.91	6.95	110.21	7.57
1976.1	116.82	7.47	111.95	8.91
1976.2	119.48	7.36	114.49	8.09
1976.3	123.81	7.15	118.75	7.88
1976.4	127.41	7.53	122.25	8.22

Because of space limitations, we present here only the forecasts for telephone flows of the production sector originating in Ontario and with destination British Columbia and Alberta. These forecasts were made using the information on the autocorrelation of the implicit error term in (1), and this information was also used to compute standard errors of the forecasts. [14] The 95% confidence intervals (±2 standard errors) for the forecasts are also shown in table 2. Finally, the forecasts and confidence bands are shown graphically in figs. 1 and 2. Note that these standard errors are based on the assumption that (1) is the correct specification for demand (as explained in section 2, we cannot compute a standard error of forecast that accounts for the possibility of misspecification). Given this assumption, we see that the probability is 95% that after three years, the true value of demand will be within ±7% of our forecasted value. [15]

[14] The formulas used for the forecasts and for the computation of the standard errors are from Theil [28], pp. 281–282. However, these standard errors do not account for errors in the forecasts of the explanatory variables.

[15] Sometime forecast errors, especially for nonstationary variables, are presented in terms of forecasted changes in the variables, and are compared to the predicted change in the variable. This would, of course, yield a much greater percent error.

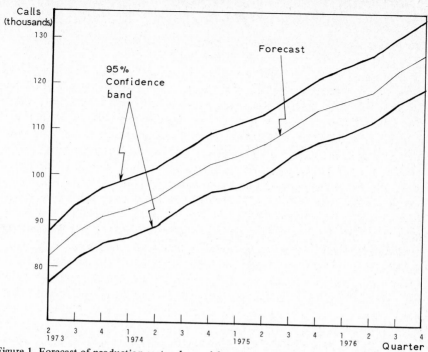

Figure 1. Forecast of production sector demand for telephone services: Ontario to British Columbia.

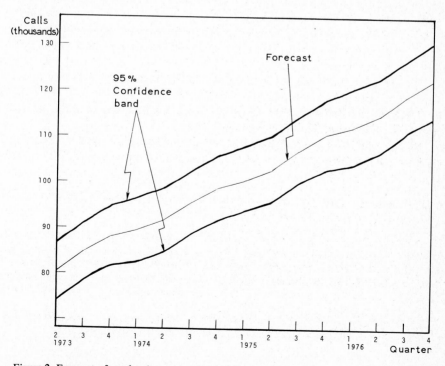

Figure 2. Forecast of production sector demand for telephone services: Ontario to Alberta.

4. Analyzing the effects of regulation: a model of Bell Canada

We turn next to a model that determines the effect of rate of return regulation on the factor input mix of Bell Canada. [16] In the early sixties, Averch and Johnson [1] developed the proposition that a monopolist subject to rate of return regulation will not be efficient in choosing factor proportions; in particular, more capital per unit of labor would be used than that needed to minimize the cost of production. For the next ten years a substantial amount of theoretical discussion on the validity of this proposition, as well as some extensions of it, followed [3,2,23]. These developments in the theory of regulation have opened up an interest on the part of the regulatory authorities and the CRTC in particular in having a quantitative measure of the economic side effects of rate of return regulation. [17] Here an econometric model of the firm can be used to determine the effects of regulation. Such a model must take into account the interrelationships among variables such a revenue, output, labor input, capital input, cost of capital services, cost of labor services, allowable rate of return, etc. These variables are interrelated through behavioral relations (e.g., demand equations, equilibrium relations for input choice by firms), technological relations (e.g., production functions), and institutional relations (e.g., the specific form of the regulatory constraints, tax relations, etc.).

Our model is of the Averch–Johnson type and based on three main assumptions: (i) the firm seeks to maximize profits; (ii) the decision process is constrained by the available technology and by the imposition of an upper limit on the rate of return that it can ern on its capital (this rate of return is the "allowed rate of return", and is assumed to be greater than the firm's cost of capital but lower than the rate of return that the firm would achieve if it were an unregulated monopoly); and (iii) no regulatory lags exist.

If this model is an approriate description of the behavior of a regulated firm then the following two main propositions follow (E. Bailey [2]):

1. At the output level selected by the regulated firm, the capital/labor ratio chosen is *greater than* that which minimizes cost.

2. The output of the regulated firm would not rise above that of the unregulated profit-maximizing firm, except in the unusual circumstance in which capital is

---

[16] Regulatory bodies have been entrusted with the task of providing a framework for the functioning of companies under their jurisdiction. In the regulation of the telecommunications industry in Canada, and of Bell Canada in particular, one of the main concerns of the regulatory authority (until recently the Canadian Transport Commission (CTC) and now the Canadian Radio-Television and Telecommunications Commission (CRTC)) has been rate-of-return regulation. The main objective of regulation has been to prevent the carriers from capturing large monopoly profits, particularly through price discrimination. Only lately have some additional elements like the quality of the service and the rate structure begun to be considered as integral elements of a rate case.

[17] In a rate case of 1974 before the CTC, for the first time the issue of over-capitalization in Bell Canada was raised. Canadian Transport Commission case T-2/74 Ottawa, 1974.

an inferior input (i.e., when an increase in output is accompanied by a decrease in capital used). [18]

We now lay out the complete model in analytical form, as derived from maximizing a strictly concave revenue function subject to rate of return regulation. Letting $F(L, K)$ be a production function of labor and capital, $D(Q, Y)$ an inverse demand function, Q output, Y income, P_K and w the prices of capital and labor services respectively, s the allowed price of capital services, and λ the Lagrange multiplier associated with the rate of return constraint, we have the following five equations in the unknowns $Q, L, K, P,$ and λ (see [3]):

$$Q = F(L, K), \tag{2}$$

$$P = D(Q, Y), \tag{3}$$

$$\frac{\partial (Q \cdot P)}{\partial L} = w, \tag{4}$$

$$\frac{\partial (Q \cdot P)}{\partial K} = \frac{P_K - \lambda s}{1 - \lambda}, \tag{5}$$

$$Q \cdot P = wL + sK. \tag{6}$$

After estimating this model, it could be used to simulate or forecast all of the five endogenous variables. Our focus here, however, is more restricted; we are concerned with the effect of regulation on the firm's capital/labor ratio K/L. Therefore we work with a transformation of this model that does not require estimation of the demand relation (3) so long as demand is assumed to be isoelastic in price.

We begin with the production function. We reviewed existing estimates of production functions for Bell Canada, i.e., Dobell et al. [14] and Millen [25], and concluded that there is no clear-cut evidence as to the appropriate specification of technology. It is thus attractive to assume a general form of production function. We use the transcendental logarithmic production function (translog) due to Christense et al. [8,9], which reduces to a Cobb—Douglas form as a special case. We

[18] The following propositions can also be shown to hold: (3) the regulated firm has an incentive to expand in competitive markets even if marginal revenues fall below marginal costs in those markets, with the difference more than compensated for by increased net revenues allowed through rate increases in the regulated market; (4) the capital/labor ratio will increase rather than decrease as the allowable rate of return is lowered towards the market cost of capital; and (5) the over capitalization discussed in (1) above does not, in general, imply "goldplating," or purchase of plant solely to be held idle, but simply means that the firm seeks to obtain whatever additional revenue is obtainable through over-capitalization. As long as the objective is to maximize profits, subject to a rate of return constraint, an "entirely productive use of capital is always preferable to one entailing waste" [23, p. 90]).

estimated a general translog production function and tested both for constant returns to scale and then for complete global separability (Berndt and Christensen [5]). We cannot reject either hypothesis, and thus the final production function is [19]

$$\ln(Q_t/L_t) = \begin{matrix} -0.330 \\ (-9.356) \end{matrix} + \begin{matrix} 0.391 \ln(K_t/L_t) + \\ (6.486) \end{matrix} \begin{matrix} 1.136\, D_t \\ (11.826) \end{matrix}$$

$$R^2 = 0.9984, \quad \hat{\rho} = 0.391, \quad \text{SSR} = 0.007050, \quad \text{D.W.} = 1.83,$$

Years: 1953–1972,

where Q is total value added, measured as value of output (including uncollectibles) minus indirect taxes and raw materials in millions of 1967 dollars, rescaled to make the average equal to one during the sample period, L is weighted man-hours (where the weights are the relative hourly wage rates of different labor categories) rescaled as above, K is net capital stock in millions of 1967 dollars and D_t is percentage of calls direct distance dialed (an indicator of changes in technology). [20]

Since the production function exhibits constant returns to scale, and since we assume isoelastic demand, we can further simplify the first-order conditions (4) and (5) to study the behavior of the capital/labor ratio. We can write (4) as

$$P(1 + 1/\eta)\beta_L \frac{Q}{L} = w, \tag{4'}$$

and we can write (5) as:

$$P(1 + 1/\eta)\beta_K \frac{Q}{K} = \frac{P_K - \lambda s}{1 - \lambda}. \tag{5'}$$

Here η is the price elasticity of demand, and β_L and β_K are the labor and capital elasticities of the production function ($\beta_L + \beta_K = 1$). Now dividing (4') by (5'), and using the estimated values $\beta_K = 0.391$ and $\beta_L = 1 - 0.391 = 0.609$ from the production function, we have

$$K/L = 0.642 \frac{w(1 - \lambda)}{P_K - \lambda s}. \tag{7}$$

This equation can be used to determine the effect of λ on K/L. For $\lambda = 0$ we have the pure monopoly case, and if the regulatory constraint is binding, λ must be

---

[19] Ordinary least squares estimation is used, since with 20 observations it is not clear that a simultaneous equation estimator has any real advantage. See, for example, Fair [17]. Here $\hat{\rho}$ is the estimated coefficient of a first order autoregressive process on the random errors of the equation, SSR is the sum of squares of the residuals, and D.W, is the Durbin–Watson statistic. The figures in parenthesis are t-ratios. For details of these tests see Corbo [13].

[20] Rescaling of the variables is done so that the estimated translog production function can be used not only as a production function by itself, but also as a second-order approximation to any production function (see [9]).

between 0 and 1. We determine the value of λ for the sample period by estimating a transformed version of $(5')$ and treating λ as a parameter:

$$\frac{P_K K}{PQ} = (1 - \lambda)\mu + \lambda\frac{sK}{PQ}, \tag{8}$$

where $\mu = (1 + 1/\eta)\beta_K$. This equation is nonlinear in the parameters λ and μ and must be estimated using a nonlinear estimation procedure. Using maximum likelihood estimation, we obtain the estimated average value of $\lambda, \hat{\lambda} = 0.715$, with an approximated standard error of 0.095.

Now we use (7) to solve for K/L with regulation ($\hat{\lambda} = 0.715$) and without regulation ($\lambda = 0$). As a means of validating the model, we first solve (7) for $\hat{\lambda} = 0.715$ and the average values of w, P_K, and s during the sample period (1952–1972), obtaining $K/L = 34.4$. The actual average value of K/L during the sample period is 33.44. Next we use (7) to simulate the effect on K/L of eliminating the regulatory constraint. For this purpose we make $\lambda = 0$ in (7), obtaining $K/L = 16.9$.

We can now compute the dollar value of this over-capitalization. Using the average employment figures, and the capital/labor ratio computed above, we find that it is on the order of 941.1 million 1967 dollars, almost half of the average capital stock over the whole period. Therefore, we conclude that there is strong evidence of over-capitalization in Bell Canada. [21]

A few words are in order regarding the limitations of our approach. We constructed a multi-equation model of Bell Canada and used it to quantify the possible over-capitalization effects of rate of return regulation. The results show that, through the effect on the price of factor inputs, rate of return regulation creates a substantial over-capitalization. Of course, we have not quantified the benefits that the regulatory process can provide to consumers through lower prices and/or by forcing firms to operate at a greater output level. Thus, to evaluate the whole regulatory process, one should compare the cost created by inefficient production with benefits to consumers. [22]

[21] Note that (7) (which is effectively a reduced form for K/L) can also be used to simulate the effects on factor proportions of changes in the wage rate, the cost of capital, depreciation rate, corporate income tax, etc.

[22] There can be other costs of regulation which we have not studied here. First the regulated firm may lose much of its incentive for technological improvements and efficiency increases. If the firm can always earn profits up to the allowed ceiling by increasing prices for those services with a smaller elasticity of demand, then there is no financial reward for cost saving. Second, if there is some measure of vertical integration in the industry, and the rate base is computed in terms of replacement costs, then transfer pricing may be encouraged. (The new capital acquired from its suppliers at inflated prices will not decrease the firm's allowed profits, while at the same time the replacement of older machines by more expensive ones will actually increase the rate base.) And third, destructive price cutting by the monopolist may occur for those services which are supplied in competitive markets. Any losses which the firm may incur in such markets can be made good (up to the allowed rate of return) by price increases in its inelastic demand services, and once competitors have been driven out of the competitive market by predatory pricing, the monopoly can invest further in this area in order to expand its rate base.

5. Concluding remarks

We began this paper with a brief overview of econometric forecasting models, and we explained that the choice of model often involves trade-offs between the cost of model construction and the degree of structural explanation, so that in many cases it is not clear which type of model is most appropriate. In modeling the demand for Canadian telephone services it was not necessary to formulate a full simultaneous-equation model, since demand can only affect price very slowly through the regulatory process, so that for intermediate term forecasting price and income can be taken as exogenous. Thus a single-equation regression model was judged to be an appropriate means of forecasting the demand for telephone services. Of course a time-series model might have been used as an alternative, but then we would not have gained information about price and income effects. In analyzing the long-term economic inefficiency cost of rate of return regulation, on the other hand, a multi-equation model was needed since production, price, factor input quantities, and the resulting realized rate of return are all interrelated.

Two advantages of the econometric approach stressed in this paper are the fact that it is straightforward to generate statistics for significance and hypothesis testing (and thus model validation), and the fact that we can usually compute confidence intervals for the forecasts generated by our models. However, lest we appear overly sanguine, we should emphasize that an important limitation of these statistical tests and confidence intervals is their inability to deal with possible (probable?) specification error. The 95% confidence bands in figs. 1 and 2 have meaning only if the model used to predict demand is the correct specification; since there is some probability that it is not correct, the true confidence bands should be significantly larger. Users of econometric forecasts often fail to keep this in mind. In addition, confidence intervals are usually not generated for forecasts based on multi-equation models, since doing so requires the use of Monte Carlo simulation, which may be computationally expensive. Despite these limitations, econometric models are useful for a variety of forecasting and analysis problems.

References

[1] H. Averch and L.L. Johnson, Behavior of the firm under regulatory constraint, American Economic Review 52, part II.
[2] E. Bailey, Economic Theory of Regulatory Constraint (D.C. Heath, Lexington, Mass., 1973).
[3] W. Baumol and A. Klevorick, Input choices and rate-of-return regulation: an overview of the discussion, Bell Journal of Economics 1, No. 2 (Autumn 1970).
[4] Bell Canada, Rate Hearings, Exhibits No. B-73-61 and B-73-62.
[5] E.R. Berndt and L.R. Christensen, The translog function and the substitution of equipment structures, and Labor U.S. manufacturing 1929–1968, Journal of Econometrics 1, No. 1 (March 1973).

[6] G.E.P. Box and G.M. Jenkins, Time Series Analysis, Forecasting and Control (Holden-Day, San Francisco, 1970).

[7] Canadian Transport Commission, Case T-2/1974, Ottawa, 1974.

[8] L. Christensen, D. Jorgenseon and L. Lau, Conjugate duality and the transcendental logarithmic production function, Econometrica 39, 1971, No. 4.

[9] L. Christensen, D. Jorgenson and L. Lau, Transcendental logarithmic production frontiers, The Review of Economics and Statistics, May 1973.

[10] G.C. Chow, Analysis and Control of Dynamic Economic Systems (Wiley, New York, 1976).

[11] G.C. Chow, Tests of equality between sets of coefficients in two linear regressions, Econometrica 28 (1960) 561−605

[12] V. Corbo, Interprovincial flows of telephone services, Report to the Department of Communications, Ottawa, 1974.

[13] V. Corbo, The effect of regulation on factor proportions: the case of Bell Canada (Mimeo) 1977.

[14] R. Dobell, L.D.Taylor, L. Waverman, T.H. Liu and M.D.G. Copeland, Telephone communication in Canada: demand production and investment decisions, The Bell Journal of Economics and Management Science 3 (Spring 1972).

[15] N. Draper and H. Smith, Applied Regression Analysis (Wiley, New York, 1966), pp. 270−272.

[16] M. Eisner and R.S. Pindyck, A generalized approach to estimation as implemented in the TROLL/1 system, Annals of Economic and Social Measurement 2, No. 1 (1973).

[17] R.C. Fair, A comparison of alternative estimators of macroeconomic models, International Economic Review 14 (1973) 261−277.

[18] S.M. Goldfeld and R.E. Quandt, Nonlinear Methods in Econometrics (North-Holland, Amsterdam, 1972).

[19] C.W.J. Granger and P. Newbold, Forecasting Economic Time Series (Academic Press, New York, 1977).

[20] R.E. Hall and D.W. Jorgenson, Application of the theory of optimum capital accumulation, in Tax Incentives and Capital Spending, Chapter II, edited by G. Fromm (The Brookings Institution, Washington, 1971).

[21] M. Houthakker and L.D. Taylor, Consumer demand in the United States, 1929−1970, Analysis and Projections (Harvard University Press, Cambridge, Mas., 1970).

[22] Institute of Applied Economic Research (I.A.E.R.), Rate Adjustment Guidelines for Regulated Industries, A Study made for the Department of Communications, Ottawa, May 1976.

[23] L.L. Johnson, Behavior of the firm under regulations constraint: a reassessment, American Economic Review (May 1973).

[24] D.W. Marquardt, An algorithm for least squares estimation of nonlinear parameters, Journal of the Society of Industrial and Applied Mathematics 2 (1963) 431.

[25] R. Millen, Automatic rate adjustments and short term productivity objectives for Bell Canada, unpublished Ph.D. thesis, Concordia University, 1974.

[26] C.R. Nelson, Applied Time Series Analysis for Managerial Forecasting (Holden-Day, San Francisco, 1973).

[27] R.S. Pindyck and D.L. Rubinfeld, Econometric Models and Economic Forecasts (McGraw-Hill, New York, 1976).

[28] H. Theil, Principles of Econometrics (Wiley, New York, 1971).

[29] A. Zellner and F. Palm, Time series analysis and simultaneous equation econometric models, Journal of Econometrics 2 (1974) 17−54.

TIMS Studies in the Management Sciences 12 (1979) 113–139
© North-Holland Publishing Company

INPUT-OUTPUT METHODS IN FORECASTING

J.M. BLIN, E.A. STOHR and B. BAGAMERY *

Graduate School of Management, Northwestern University

1. Introduction

Forecasts are more easily produced than they can be reconciled. The number of forecasting techniques available is only exceeded by the number of possible levels and time spans for which forecasts are sought. Forecasts range from very broad macro forecasts of variables such as GNP, inflation rate and gross investment, to product line sales, and material requirements forecasts within a corporation. Choosing the right forecasting technique involves trade-offs between costs (e.g., system development and computational costs), lead time and accuracy. Simple rules of thumb are sometimes offered suggesting, for instance, the use of 1) low-cost time-series methods for tracking many disaggregated corporate series; 2) more sophisticated time-series models for broader-based series calling for increased accuracy; and 3) full-fledged econometric models for a corporation (or a division thereof), an industry or the national economy. Table 1 summarizes the links between the various forecasting requirements and available models.

Referring to this table the following observations can be made. In general time-series models have been found useful to track a large number of highly disaggregated series – e.g. inventories – in situations where the causal links are stable enough to allow one to extrapolate safely from past observations on that series. When more aggregate series are involved, the impact of a wider range of contributing factors must be allowed for. Econometric techniques are well suited for this purpose. But in this case forecasting requires the knowledge – or the prediction – of exogenous explanatory variables. This additional information requirement makes the resulting forecast conditional; on the other hand, it allows more opportunities for sensitivity analysis. As is well known, econometric model specification is a difficul art. Existing macroeconomic theories and corporate planning models are helpful

* The authors wish to acknowledge the suggestions of Clopper Almon, University of Maryland, Philip Ritz and Albert Walderhaug, U.S. Department of Commerce, Bureau of Economic Analysis. Also, Don Eldridge, U.S. Department of Commerce, Jack Faucett, David Goettee, U.S. Department of Transportation, Ron Kutscher, Bureau of Labor Statistics, and Bob Wilson, Federal Preparedness Agency, GSA, all provided numerous data, documentation and advice, without which many of the illustrations given in the paper would have been impossible.

Table 1
Hierarchy of forecasts.

Level	Typical uses	Link to ensure forecast consistency	Usual techniques	Examples
Aggregate economic forecasts Example: macroeconometric models	1. National and/or international economic policy formulation 2. Results become exogenous inputs for industry and corporate models	Integration of national macromodels (e.g. project LINK) and input-output systems (e.g. INFORUM, LINK [41])	General simultaneous equation econometric	[19]
Industry forecasts	1. Formulation and testing of alternate economic policies; e.g., (de)regulation of certain industries 2. Results also used as exogenous inputs to corporate models	National input-output systems	Input-output simultaneous equation model integrating all interrelations between industries Industry-specific econometric models	[4] [48]
Corporate forecasts	1. Strategic policy projection of income statements and balance sheets for corporate planning 2. Results serve as inputs to lower divisional and departmental models	"Market share" models Corporate input-output systems	Corporation specific econometric models and Time-series techniques	[44]
Product line inventory item forecasts			Time-series techniques	

in this task. However, linking macro and micro models is no simple matter. For instance, saying that real GNP will grow at a rate of 5.5% over the next twelve months hides many varied fortunes and misfortunes for different industries. Corporations are vitally interested in knowing about these divergent fates as they bear on their growth and/or diversification plans. When it comes to taking account of the full array of interconnections between all industries and the potential impacts they have on each other, no comprehensive econometric model can be specified without some broad theoretical framework to help the econometrician. Input-output tables provide such a framework. At the corporate level input-output analysis (IO) allows corporations to get a detailed, coherent, and comprehensive view of their position among other industries and final markets and even, if properly interpreted, within their industry. By quantifying the network of technical interdependence linking all industries within a given geographical area (metropolis, region, or more commonly nation), IO analysis enables the corporation to understand the repercussions of changing conditions among its vendors and its clients — and their respective vendors and clients etc. By specifying and measuring the degree of interrelatedness between industries, and firms within these industries, IO analysis is capable of translating broad macro forecasts into the precise industry specific forecasts they imply.

In this paper, we explain the use of the IO methodology in forecasting. Since its inception, a number of articles have reported on the usefulness of IO techniques for sales forecasting [1,43] and financial decision making [45]. Similar uses are, of course, suggested and sketched in Leontief's original exposition of the method [31, 32,33]. Following the introduction of the static input-output model by Leontief some 40 years ago, theoretical and applied research on IO has grown steadily, exploring 1) the formal properties of Leontief matrices [22,29]; 2) their relationships with linear programming and general optimization problems [18,30]; 3) their application to management problems [44]; and 4) their extensions to regional [29,37,38,50] or metropolitan economic forecasting [26], integrated IO international trade flows forecasting [41], and dynamic systems [34]. Paralleling this growth in research, public and private research and consulting organizations have estimated actual input-output tables and integrated them with forecasting models of varying degrees of complexity. Federal agencies such as the Bureau of Economic Analysis, U.S. Department of Commerce [12], the Bureau of Labor Statistics [15], the Federal Preparedness Agency, and the U.S. Department of Transportation, all have developed IO tables and related series at various levels of industry disaggregation. Universities and research institutes have also developed and/or used their own IO systems; examples include the University of Maryland INFORUM model [4,5], and the Battelle Memorial Laboratory PREVIEWS model [8]. Finally, IO models and forecasts are currently marketed by various corporations and consulting firms such as Arthur D. Little [35], Data Resources Inc. [20], Wharton [42], Chase Econometrics [28], the General Electric Corporation [36], and the Econoscope Group, Inc. [21]. Such widespread use and growing interest in IO techniques for corporate forecasting and planning underscores the need for an up-to-date exposition and numerical illustration of 1) the links between the input-output model and both macro and micro economic models and 2) traditional and new ways of using input-output methods for managerial planning and forecasting. These are discussed in sections 3 and 4 respectively. To make this paper self-contained, a brief tutorial on the fundamentals of IO analysis is given in section 2. We remark on the limitations and likely future improvements in IO methods in the conclusion.

2. Fundamentals of input-output analysis

This section gives a self-contained presentation of 1) the derivation of an input-output table from national and business accounting data and 2) the interpretation of such tables from a production function or market share standpoint. Also, some of the key IO identities, which hold exactly only if the assumptions discussed throughout this section are met, are summarized for convenient reference. Departure from these key assumptions and the resulting adjustments required are also briefly described to give the reader some feel for the adequacy of the model and the reliability of existing tables.

2.1. The accounting framework

Consider the summary income statement of some firm as given in table 2. A simple modification for inventory changes yields the firm production statement as

Table 2
Income statement of firm X.

Expenditures	Receipts
1. Purchases from other firms (intermediate purchases)	1. Sales to industrial users (other firms and industries)
2. Value added	1.1. Company No. 1
	1.2. Company No. 2
1. Employee compensation (wages and salaries)	1.3. Company No. 3
2. Indirect business taxes	2. Sales to final users
3. Property-type income	
	2.1. Consumers
3.1. Proprietor's income	2.2. Business on capital account (investment)
3.2. Rental income	
3.3. Corporate profits and inventory valuation adjustment	2.3. Government
	. Federal
3.4. Net interest	. State and local
3.5. Depreciation (Capital consumption allowances)	2.4. Rest of the world
Total current expenses	Total current receipts

Table 3
Production statement of firm X.

Allocations	Receipts
Total current expenses	Inventory change
Allocation of total value of production	Total value of production

Table 4

Transaction table, millions of dollars 1967.

Sales purchases	Intermediate demands					Final demand				Total final demand	Total gross output (sales)
	Construction	Durables	Non-durables	Services	Total Inter-mediate Sales	Consump-tion	Invest-ment	Net Exports	Govern-ment		
Construction	30	1793	2290	13583	17696	0	59258	0	26325	85534	103280
Durables	34652	113586	44626	31747	224610	115896	97578	6994	27142	247611	472222
Nondurables	10992	55682	141500	33440	241615	131551	2970	−248	13304	147578	389193
Services	12017	61953	58300	103960	236230	143724	0	760	80737	225220	461450
Total interme-diate purchases	57690	233014	246717	182731	720153	391171	159808	7506	147509	705992	
Wages	27002	141677	84385	165078	418142	} GNP					
Property-type income	14562	76407	45509	82097	225505						
Indirect business	4026	21124	12582	24613	62613						
Total value added	45590	239208	142475	278718							
Total gross output (purchases)	103280	74222	389193	461450							1425145

given in table 3. With these accounting data for all firms in an economy, it is theoretically straightforward to construct an IO matrix. Specifically, if each company produces a homogeneous type of output we can group companies into (say) n industries and record for each such industry the dollar value of sales to all others over a given accounting period. These sales profiles form the n rows of the IO transactions matrix $[x_{ij}]$. A moment's thought will also convince us that the purchases from other firms' (item 1) in the income statement need not be separately recorded, as it is obtained by labeling the columns of the table with the same industry breakdown as for the rows. The resulting table is thus a square matrix with the same industries (products) over its rows and columns. To balance the system we can also record to the right of the IO table the final sales (item 2) classified as in table 2. This yields the $(n \times z)$ matrix, $F = [f_{ik}]$ showing the industrial composition of final sales. Similarly, we can record the various incomes originating in this firm (value added) by adding them to the bottom of each industry column, thus obtaining a $(s \times n)$ matrix, $V = [v_{hj}]$ of 'primary' inputs to production. Table 4 summarizes the overall accounting scheme for a very aggregated four-industry version of the actual U.S. 1967 IO table [12].

The IO transactions table is in the upper left-hand corner of table 4. As can be seen from this table, IO data expand the general national income and product accounts by focusing on intermediate transactions (sales/purchases) between industries which are normally excluded from GNP computations to avoid "double-counting."

2.2 Implementing an IO system

Practical implementation of the above framework requires certain assumptions and compromises to process existing data. First, the question of the *industry grouping* raises the same problems as the setting up of a Standard Industrial Classification system SIC. Very few firms are so specialized as to produce a single product. The SIC classification is used (with some regroupings) to process the quinquennial U.S. Census of Manufactures data which serve as the basic data source for the U.S. tables. [1] The most disaggregated table is at the four-digit SIC level, comprising 484 industries. Aggregated tables for 365 and 81 industries are also made available by the U.S. Department of Commerce. Other organizations have used different aggregation levels to meet their special needs — ranging from about 200 to 35 industries. As explained later, the grouping scheme bears upon the forecast accuracy of an IO system and raises some important theoretical issues [9,10]. To deal with multi-product firms, the data are collected at the "establishment" [47] level. The primary product of that establishment is recorded in the corresponding industry row and

---

[1] Benchmark IO tables exist for 1947 [13], 1958 [24], 1963 [14] and 1967 [12]. The 1972 table is about to be published. Summary annual updates have also been obtained up to 1976 for the Federal Preparedness Agency.

column; any other output — secondary product — is considered to be part of the output of some other appropriate industry and allocated accordingly. Secondly, *imports* for which comparable domestic substitutes are available are similarly allocated, while nonsubstitutable imports are treated as primary inputs and included in a separate row at the bottom of the table. Thirdly, a few *dummy industries* have to be set up to record such diverse items as business travel and entertainment — a fitting reminder of the pervasive expense account phenomenon! — and small office supplies. To the extent that these allocations can never be made unambiguously, the resulting data contain some unavoidable noise, analogous to the measurement error in any econometric work. [2] A final word of caution about the *prices* used in the U.S. IO tables should be given. Producers' prices as opposed to purchasers' prices are used, and the trade, insurance, and transporatation margins, which make up the difference between these two, are recorded separately as transactions with three other industries — 'trade,' 'insurance,' and 'transportation.'

2.3. IO assumptions and relationships

2.3.1. IO Projections from exogenous demand

The transactions data thus recorded are not yet usable for forecasting purposes without some basic assumptions to explain these observed transactions amounts. Traditionally, a fixed coefficient production function assumption is made to explain the *columns* of the $n \times n$ transactions matrix $[x_{ij}]$. Specifically, it is assumed that, for example, the amount of steel (i) per automobile (j) is fixed in the short run so that any change in automobile output will require a proportionate change in steel input. Each industry production process is thus described by n input coefficients, a_{ij}, $i = 1, 2, ..., n$:

$$a_{ij} = x_{ij}/x_j,$$ (1)

where $x_j = \Sigma_j x_{ij} + \Sigma_k f_{ik}$ and f_{ik} is the final sale of i to the kth final demand category.

In theory these a_{ij} coefficients could be computed in physical units, e.g., so many pounds of steel or square feet of sheet metal per automobile of a given kind. The huge product breakdown which such a method entails has precluded its implementation so far. Practically, the coefficients are derived in dollar terms (dollar worth of steel per dollar worth of auto output). The resulting n column vectors with n entries (including possibly some 0's) are the production functions of the n

---

[2] The extent of the model specification error — if any — on the other hand depends, among other things, on the adequacy of the fixed coefficient production function assumption as discussed later.

Table 5
Direct coefficients matrix, 1967.

	Construction	Durables	Nondurables	Services
Construction	0.0002	0.0037	0.0058	0.0294
Durables	0.3355	0.2405	0.1146	0.0687
Nondurables	0.1064	0.1179	0.3635	0.0724
Services	0.1163	0.1311	0.1497	0.2252

industries. Together they form the *input coefficient matrix, A,* as shown in table 5 above. This table represents an aggregation into four industries of the actual U.S. input-output tables for 1967 (81 industry level).

Although in the sequel only value IO coefficients will be used, we note that the relation between the physical, $\tilde{a}_{ij}$, and the value coefficient a_{ij} is

$$a_{ij} = P_i/P_j\,\tilde{a}_{ij} \quad \text{or} \quad A = \langle P \rangle \tilde{A} \langle P \rangle^{-1}, \tag{1'}$$

where $\langle P \rangle$ is a diagonal matrix with P_{ii} = price of ith product.

Letting e be a vector of ones and taking the final matrix, F, as exogenous for the moment, we obtain the basic 'open' IO model:

$$\text{Total Output} = \text{Intermediate Sales} + \text{Final Sales (for each industry).} \tag{2}$$

$$X = AX + Fe. \tag{2'}$$

$$(I - A)X = Fe, \tag{2''}$$

where I is the $n \times n$ identity matrix. Under certain conditions on A [25,39,46], which are obviously met by actual tables, the system is workable in the sense that $(I - A)$ is nonsingular so that we can solve for X.

$$X = (I - A)^{-1}(Fe). \tag{3}$$

Note that the coefficients of the inverse $(L = (I - A)^{-1})$ are nonnegative and no less than the corresponding entries in A. Each entry of L is readily interpreted as the total direct and indirect — i.e., including all second-round, third-round etc. — derived input demand for input i per dollar of final sales of product j. These coefficients can also be shown to be a comprehensive measure of overall interrelatedness between industries (i) and (j) [11]. Table 6 illustrates the *Leontief inverse matrix, L,* for our previous example.

The difference between the indirect and direct requirements for each industry can be quite large. For instance, the primary aluminum industry has no direct sales to

Table 6
Direct and indirect requirements, L.

	Construction	Durables	Nondurables	Services
Construction	1.0127	0.0157	0.0220	0.0419
Durables	0.5196	1.3949	0.2964	0.1713
Nondurables	0.2995	0.2947	1.6728	0.1940
Services	0.2980	0.2955	0.3769	1.3636

the mobile home construction industry, yet it "is among the leaders in total sales generated by mobile home production" [53]. Not all components of final demand need to be assumed exogenous; some can be made endogenous by computing input coefficients for this new industry and assuming their short-run stability for forecasting purposes. For instance, the household sector can be endogenized by treating personal consumption expenditures in this fashion. Correspondingly, the wages and other household income flows (dividends, etc.) are treated as intermediate inputs; in effect, the household industry is removed from the margin and added as a row and column in the IO matrix. Investment in producer's durables is another obvious case which leads to the computation of a capital coefficient matrix — so much worth of steel per dollar worth of output of a given kind of producers' equipment. Completing this endogenization process for all final demands and corresponding primary inputs elements leads to the 'closed' IO system

$$X - AX = 0, \tag{4}$$

where X and 0 are $(n + z) \times 1$; A is $(n + z) \times (n + z)$. Clearly, solutions to a fully closed system are uninteresting for forecasting purposes since there are no exogenous factors. However, the theoretical properties of such a system are useful in a variety of applications [22].

Returning to the 'open' IO system, note that $(2')$ and (3) correspond respectively to the 'structural form' and the 'reduced form', of a simultaneous equation econometric model. A possible model specification error would result from 1) erroneously assuming fixed input coefficients or 2) adopting a sectoring plan — industry grouping — which does not exactly reflect the types of material inputs considered by firms. As explained later, discriminating between these two causes for explaining and correcting IO forecast errors is made difficult by the fact that historically observed coefficient changes can arise from any one of three factors: 1) *product mix* changes in a given industry; 2) *relative input price* changes; and 3) *actual technological* changes in the industry — for instance, as a result of (2) (see [16,17]). Yet the basic interpretation of an open IO system remains: dollar sales for each industry (endogenous variables) are explained (hence, can be forecast) as a linear combination of the prespecified (exogenous) set of industry-specific final demands; the coefficients in this combination being the corresponding industry row vector in the Leontief inverse matrix. This forecast equation contrasts with the standard regression estimation techniques for stochastic simultaneous equation models. Here the reduced form coefficients (entries of the Leontief inverse l_{ij}) are computed from an estimated base year transactions matrix and the forecast is derived as explained. Forecast errors result from 1) variations in the coefficients and 2) incorrect final demand assumptions. This latter source of error is, of course, present in any econometric forecasting equation; even with known coefficients, the forecast is only as accurate as our estimates of the exogenous inputs. Formulas for the model-specific forecast errors are explicitly computed for the empirical example given in section 4.

3.3.2. IO projections from primary inputs

A less well known view of IO relationships can be developed by considering output coefficients as introduced in [6] and [23]. In this case we define the output coefficient b_{ij} as the share of industry i sales to j in industry i total sales:

$$b_{ij} = x_{ij}/x_i. \tag{5}$$

We note the relationships between b_{ij}'s and a_{ij}'s: $b_{ij} = a_{ij} \cdot (x_j/x_i)$. Thus, if the a's are assumed stable over time, the b's cannot be, and conversely. The balance condition for the whole system requires that each industry's total sales just exhaust its total outlays on intermediate and primary inputs:

$$x_j = \sum_{i=1}^{n} b_{ij}x_i + \sum_{h=1}^{s} v_{hj}, \tag{6}$$

where v_{hj} is the dollar value of the hth type primary input (e.g., the wage bill) in industry j. Equivalently, we can write

$$B'X + V'e = X, \tag{6'}$$

where B' is the transpose of the $(n \times n)$ *output coefficient matrix;* and V' is the transpose of the $(s \times n)$ primary inputs matrix. Under the same workability conditions as before (3) , we can solve for total sales of each industry:

$$(I - B')X = V'e, \quad \text{and} \tag{6''}$$

$$X = (I - B')^{-1}(V'e). \tag{7}$$

The output coefficient matrix and the $M = (I - B')$ inverse are illustrated for our example in tables 7 and 8.

Table 7
Output coefficient matric, B.

	Construction	Durables	Nondurables	Services
Construction	0.0002	0.0173	0.0221	0.1315
Durables	0.0733	0.2405	0.0945	0.0672
Nondurables	0.0282	0.1430	0.3635	0.0859
Services	0.0260	0.1342	0.1263	0.2252

Table 8
$M = (I - B')^{-1}$

	Construction	Durables	Nondurables	Services
Construction	1.0127	0.1136	0.0795	0.0667
Durables	0.0719	1.3949	0.3576	0.3024
Nondurables	0.0831	0.2443	1.6728	0.3179
Services	0.1874	0.1674	0.2300	1.3636

Interpretation of the M matrix is quite simple. It enables us to explain (predict) total sales of each industry (endogenous variables) by a linear combination of the total dollar value of primary inputs available (or allocated by, for instance, skill-specific job considerations), in every industry. The (reduced form) coefficients in this combination, yielding our industry sales forecast, are the entries of each row of the M matrix. Each such entry measures the dollar value of industry i output attainable with primary inputs given by the value added matrix V. Also, we can usefully contrast the two views (input vs. output) of industry sales forecast as given by (3) and (7). A final demand-driven model leads to the usual Leontief inverse L, while a primary input-driven model leads to the M matrix. If final demand and primary inputs are both taken to be exogenous, the two sales forecasts X_F from (3) and X_V from (7) will be equal only if industry sales have changed by a scale factor, say λ. In this case $X^{(t)} = \lambda X^{(0)}$ so that the proportions $x_i^t/x_j^t = x_i^0/x_j^0$ for all pairs of indus-

Table 9
Matrix Q, 1967.

	Construction	Durables	Nondurables	Services
Construction	0.9581	−0.1026	−0.0567	−0.0116
Durables	0.2942	0.9772	−0.0651	−0.0814
Nondurables	0.0814	0.0189	0.9884	−0.0659
Services	0.0370	0.1078	0.1254	1.0227

tries (i, j) – or equivalently $(Fe)^{(t)} = (Fe)^{(0)}$. In this case, clearly $b_{ij}^{(t)} = a_{ij}x_j^{(t)}/x_j^{(t)} = b_{ij}^{(0)}$. Whereas if $X^{(t)} = TX^{(0)}$, where T is a general linear transformation, then the ratios $b_{ij}^{(0)} = x_{ij}^{(0)}/x_i^{(0)}$ change to $b_{ij}^{(t)} = x_{ij}^{(t)}/x_i^{(t)} \neq x_{ij}^{(0)}/x_i^{(0)}$. Of course, for a given year, if all IO relations are measured exactly the system will balance, yielding a relationship explaining income flows (value added) by final demand. Presumably, some adjustment process needs to be specified through a macro model to provide the link with F that yields a consistent sales forecast. In any case, the following condition, obtained by combining (3) and (7), must be satisfied, *ex-post*:

$$(V'e) = (I - B')(I - A)^{-1}(Fe) \quad \text{or} \tag{8}$$

$$V'e = Q(Fe). \tag{8'}$$

The matrix, Q, for the sample data is shown in table 9.

For forecasting from a base period into the future, if we adopt the input view of the model and take the a_{ij}'s as constant, the translation of an X_F forecast into a $(V'e)$ forecast can be done by using a simple diagonal matrix $\langle (V'e)_i/x_i \rangle$ to premultiply $(I - A)^{-1}(Fe)$, since it is easily shown that assuming $[a_{ij}]$ constant is equivalent to assuming constant $(V'e)/x_i$. This "specialized Leontief inverse" $[\langle (V'e)_i/x_i \rangle \cdot L]$ is used in [52] and [19]. On the other hand, if we take the output view, we assume the fixity of the b_{ij}'s, then the a_{ij}'s – and, hence, the l_{ij} coefficients of the inverse – have the change so that (8') holds with unchanged b_{ij}'s. With either assumption – fixed a's or fixed b's – (8') acts as a constraint that holds ex post and thus can be used to compute the updated b or a coefficients.

3. The interface between IO methods and macro and micro forecasts

Having thus described the fundamental IO assumptions and algebra, we are now in a position to specify how the IO model serves as a link between macro forecasts and micro (corporate) forecasting. Actually, this can be done in many ways. Here we do not intend to cover all the conceivable ways of integrating IO in a hierarchy of forecasts. Rather we intend to discuss some of the key submodels needed to close the system. Relevant assumptions bearing on forecast accuracy are also specified. In this manner, the reader will be able to judge for himself how the many existing macroeconometric models can be related to corporate forecasting systems via IO.

3.1 The macro-IO interface

At the most aggregate level, a very simple way of translating (say) a GNP forecast into an industry sales forecast is to use the basic open IO relation given in (3):

$$X = (I - A)^{-1}(Fe). \tag{3}$$

We only need to allocate GNP into its industry components to obtain the final demand vector (*Fe*). A simple assumption is to consider that the allocation of GNP by industry for some base year will remain unchanged for the forecast year. The percent breakdown coeffcients thus obtained are one instance of what are commonly called 'bridge coefficients.' Clearly, the assumption underlying (3) is that final demand (*Fe*) is entirely exogenous to the system. Such demand-dominated models, popularized in textbook expositions of elementary Keynesian economics, are, or course, one-sided.

At the other end of the spectrum, one can consider pure supply-dominated models in the spirit of Ricardian economics. There, a basic variable to be explained is the income distribution − globally and by industry. To illustrate, supoose for a moment that we are given the total amount of all primary inputs available − say, for instance, labor measured in man-hours − then the demand for primary inputs by industry is simply given as a function of gross industry output as in (6″):

$$(V'e) = (I - B')X. \tag{6″}$$

And, of course, if X is itself explained by some other exogenous variable − for example, final demand − we can write as in (8′):

$$(V'e) = Q(Fe). \tag{8′}$$

One step beyond this would make the primary inputs themselves endogenous as implied by (7). This is done, for instance, for capital in the dynamic Leontief IO system, where account is taken of the fact that one component of final demand, gross investment, determines the capital stock over time. Another alternative is to make the drastic Malthusian assumption of an endogenous labor force via feedback effects of starvation wages on population.

These extensions, however, point the way to a much broader integration of the IO 'marginals' (*V* and *F*) − and components thereof − of the IO table to close the macro system. An obvious method has already been mentioned in the context of the closed IO system. Consider each final demand component as an industry and compute consumption, investment, government and exports input coefficients for each such industry. For instance, the household industry production function consists of the percent breakdown of aggregate consumption by product (industry). This, of course, assumes stable product shares in a typical consumer budget − which may be less realistic than the assumption of fixed IO coefficients for manufacturing industries. Paralleling this endogenization of the right-hand side (F) marfinal of IO, a similar process is applied to the bottom marginal, *V*. If, for instance, households' income consists of, say, wages only, then the wage row in *V* when divided through by the total output of the column industry describes the labor input coefficient per unit of output of each industry. The resulting system is the closed Leontief system:

$$AX = X \quad \text{or} \quad (I - A)X = 0, \tag{4}$$

which has only the trivial (0) or indeterminate solutions – one of the x's, say x_i, must be set in order to determine the others. The extreme solution represented by the closed IO system suggests more general and useful feedback mechanisms to integrated IO within a macro system, thus opening the way to a consistent translation of macro forecasts into industry and corporate forecasts. In all cases 'bridge' models are required. Two broad classes of models can be used.

3.1.1. Constant 'bridge' coefficient tables

In constructing a bridge for V it can be assumed, for instance, that in each industry the labor/output ratio is constant for any level of output, but possibly different across industries. Similarly, for other primary inputs the same fixed coefficient assumption can be made. Alternatively other 'bridges' can be defined for V and F; e.g., the wage bill in industry j/total factor payment in j; or consumption of product i/total consumption, etc. In all such cases the choice of a particular type of bridge coefficient is guided by 1) what data are assumed known (exogenous), for instance, given by an outside source (model, expert judgment, etc.); and 2) if alternative data (disaggregated or aggregated) are equally available, which bridge coefficients can be more safely assumed to be stable. An example of this is given by GNP vs. components of GNP (consumption, investment, government, rest of the world) forecasts. Clearly, the more disaggregated the exogenous data are, the greater the amount of information required to compute the chosen "bridge" coefficients and then prepare the forecast. Also, as noted earlier, assuming certain coefficients to be stable rules out the constancy of other coefficients (e.g. a's vs. b's) so that consistency among assumptions must always be checked. Table 10 below summarizes the variety of industry level forecasts obtainable from alternative assumptions about which variables are taken to be exogenous and which bridge coefficients are used. By and large, many of the published and commercially developed industry sales forecasts correspond to the first two rows (*I.A* and *I.B*) of this table. An obvious way to extend the bridge coefficients approach short of a full integration within a macroeconometric [40] model is to track their time path and adjust them accordingly [4,51]. We illustrate the use of these methods with empirical results in the next section.

3.1.2. Fully integrated variable bridge coefficients models.

In this class we find many large-scale macroeconometric models which attempt to disaggregate their forecasts at the industry level. Well known examples include the Brookings model [19], and C. Almon's INFORUM model [3,4,5]. The logic of this type of integration is best illustrated in fig. 1, wherein some typical exogenous variables are specified and the most common linkages used to (partly) close the model are shown. As in any simultaneous equation econometric model such linkages can be of the exact nonstochastic type (identities) or they can be assumed behavioral relations – e.g. consumption functions or investment functions, etc. These stochastic behavioral relations are estimated using standard econometric pro-

Table 10

Queries	Structural assumptions	Exogenous input	Computations		Residual model error covariance
			"Bridge" coefficients	Forecasting equation	
(I) Industry sales forecast (final demand approach) from GNP.	1. Stability of input coefficients (a_{ij}) over time.	A. Aggregate GNP level.	$B_F = \dfrac{1}{e'Fe} \cdot Fe$	$\hat{X}_F = LB_F e'Fe$	
	2. Stability of proportions of final demand in GNP (only necessary for A and B).	B. GNP by major final demand categories (e.g., consumption, investment).	$B_F = \dfrac{1}{e'Fe} \cdot F$	$\hat{X}_F = LB_F(e'F)$	
		C. GNP by industry		$\hat{X}_F = LFe$	$\Sigma \hat{X}_F = LE[\epsilon_{Fe} \cdot \epsilon Fe]L'$
		D. GNP by industry and final demand category.		$\hat{X}_F = L\hat{F}e$	
(II) Industry sales forecast (primary inputs availability approach) from NI.	1. Stability of output coefficients (b_{ij}) over time.	A. Aggregate national income NI (value added) level.	$B_V = \dfrac{1}{e'Ve} V'e$	$\hat{X}_V = MB_V ve'Ve$	
	2. Stability of proportions of factor payments in NI (only necessary for A and B).	B. NI by major type of factor payments (e.g., wages, profit, rent, interest, indirect business taxes).	$B_V = \dfrac{1}{e'Ve} \cdot V'$	$\hat{X}_V = MB_V Ve$	$\Sigma \hat{X}_F = ME[\xi_e'\hat{V} \cdot \epsilon e'\hat{V}]M'$
		C. NI by industry		$\hat{X}_V = MV'e$	
		D. NI by industry and type of factor payments.		$\hat{X}_V = Me'\hat{V}$	

Table 10 (continued)

Queries	Structural assumption	Exogenous input	Computations — "Bridge" coefficients	Computations — Forecasting equation	Residual model error covariance
(III) Components of value added e.g., corporate profits from final demand).	1. Stability of input coefficients (a_{ij}) over time.	A. GNP at any level of disaggregation (see IA, B, C, D, above).	Bridge for $\hat{F}e$ constructed as in I above	$v'e = Q\hat{F}e$	
	2. Stability of proportions of factor payments in NI and possibly:		$\tilde{B}_V = V\langle e'V\rangle^{-1}$	$\hat{V} = \tilde{B}_V\langle \hat{V}'e\rangle$	$\Sigma_{e'V} = QE[\epsilon\hat{F}e\epsilon\hat{F}e]Q'$
	3. Stability of proportions of final demand in GNP (depending upon level of disaggregation).				
(IV) Components of final demand from available primary inputs.	1. Stability of input coefficients (a_{ij}) over time;	A. National income at any level of disaggregation (see IIA, B, C, S, above).	Bridge for constructed as in II above.	$\hat{F}e = Q^{-1}(\hat{V}'e)$	
	2. Stability of proportions of final demand in GNP and possibly:		$\tilde{B}_F = \langle Fe\rangle^{-1} \cdot F$	$\hat{F} = \langle \hat{F}e\rangle\tilde{B}_F$	$\Sigma_{Fe} = Q^{-1}E[\epsilon_e'\tilde{v}\epsilon_e'\tilde{v}I]Q'^{-1}$
	3. Stability of proportions of factor payments in NI (depending upon the level of disaggregation of NI forecast).				

Legend:
^ refers to a forecast value.
⟨ ⟩ Diagonal matrix.
E Expectation operator.

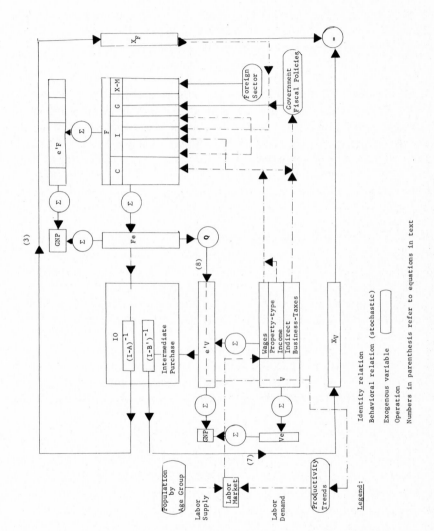

Figure 1. Summary of IO-macro interface.

cedures: single equation or, preferably, simultaneous equation procedures.

Fig. 1 summarizes the basic relations required to go beyond the fixed, or more generally time-trended, bridge coefficient model. We note the following points:

(i) Only the general scheme is shown here and a variety of functions can be postulated depending upon the level of disaggregation of the macro model. For instance, consumption functions can be estimated globally or at the level of specific personal consumption expenditures (PCE) industry categories, as in the INFORUM model. For consumption, typical explanatory variables are, say, income and relative prices for which elasticity estimates are computed. Investment functions can be of the desired capital-output ratio type — with discrete adjustments over time to reach this level. Government expenditures can be assumed all exogenous — a component of the fiscal policy package — or partly endogenous. For instance, at the state and local level, education expenses may be related to the population by age group distribution (INFORUM [4]). Imports can be made endogenous by estimating global or sectoral import functions (Brookings) [19]. On the primary inputs side labor demand by industry can be obtained at various levels of sophistication — e.g., different constant or time-trended labor/output, labor/value added or even total value added/output coefficients for each industry (Brookings).

(ii) The role of IO relations is clear. They ensure *consistency* of the forecast by translating, for instance, the final demand by industry into the gross product-originating (value-added) by industry, which then leads to industry sales forecasts, demand for primary inputs (e.g., employment) forecasts, etc. IO relations allow us to achieve industry-by-industry, PCE category-by-industry and a host of other such consistent mappings between specific components of V and F. This point is highlighted by the fact that (8) $- V'e = (I - B')(I - A)^{-1}(Fe)$ — acts as a constraint on changes in the b or a coefficients to guarantee such consistency. A direct consequence of that consistency condition is the well-known scalar equality $e'Fe = e'Ve = e'(I - B')(I - A)^{-1}(Fe) = e'QFe$, namely, the sum of value added by all industry — Gross Product originating — equals the sum of final demand by industry equals GNP.

(iii) The IO-macro interface in fig. 1 ignores some important links involving goods and inputs prices, and the financial sector. This simplification is for brevity only and should not be construed as implying that IO is incapable of accommodating such extensions; models such as Brookings integrate these other factors.

(iv) The user of IO forecasting models can use any number of existing macro models as exogenous inputs or design his own model. In any case he can operate at various levels of industry, final demand categories and value-added components disaggregation depending upon the purpose of his forecasts.

Once these forecasts are obtained, they can be used more or less directly as inputs to corporate forecasts and planning rather than using the common approximation of specifying simple single equation models relating, say, corporate sales to GNP, unemployment, relative prices, etc. This widely used method entails an unnecessary model specification error resulting in systematic forecast errors.

3.2. The corporate micro IO interface

A basic difficulty often encountered by the line manager is to translate corporate economic assumptions into product forecasts. So far the IO model coupled with a macro model — or at least driven by some broad macro forecast, e.g., GNP growth rate translated into final demand by some bridge coefficients — only provides total dollar sales forecast for the industries that make up the sectoring plan of the IO tables. To date, existing tables are still too aggregated to be directly usable by a corporation, or, even less so, by a division of a corporation. As IO usage has grown among large corporations, the problem has been faced and some good approximate solutions have been devised. Let us consider, for instance, the case of a division of a corporation [3] whose sales are in refractories, minerals, foundry equipment, and industrial and residential glass as described in [43] and [44]. In refractories alone 24 varieties of separate products can be identified ranging from fireclay brick (No. 1) to bonding mortars (No. 20). Markets for these products comprise 19 different industries ranging from open-hearth melting (No. 12) to chemicals (No. 13). Even if we use the finest IO table, 484 industries at the SIC four-digit level, we are still left with a three-digit gap to reach the 24-product breakdown — at the seven-digit level. This means that the direct input coefficient of the Stone and Clay Products industry (IO No. 36) per dollar of sales of, say, Primary Iron and Steel Manufacturing (IO No. 37), $a_{36;37} = 0.00355$, is a weighted average of many different "mini" coefficients — one for each product market combination in this pair of IO industries (36;37). Further this product-mix/market (or output)-mix may not accurately reflect the weighted average coefficient for this company as market shares differ among vendors to the primary steel industry. [4] Blind application of this coefficient, or the corresponding inverse matrix entry l_{ij}, would hardly help the line manager translate a broad economic guideline — e.g., "assume a 10% increase in steel imports next year and a 5% increase in new construction" — into product-specific forecasts. As more disaggregated up-to-date IO tables become available, the problem will be attenuated. For now, a good approximate solution is to build a detailed products-by-consuming-industry sales matrix ($[\chi_{ij}]$) for the company (an "Almon's skirt" [4]); where ι ranges over all the firm's products classified within an IO industry row, and j corresponds to the IO purchasing industry. This information is easily accessible from product sales data. Coefficients $\alpha_{ij} = \chi_{ij}/x_j$, of product use per dollar (or ton) of output of each market (e.g., Primary Iron and Steel) can be derived from interviews with technical experts, trade association data or any other source. Grouping these micro-input coefficients into a matrix allows the company readily to translate client-industry sales forecasts $\hat{x}_j$ into product-specific direct

---

[3] Combustion Engineering, Cermatec.

[4] As mentioned in section 2 above, variations in relative prices between these many product-market pairs will also affect the value coefficient even without any change in physical coefficients.

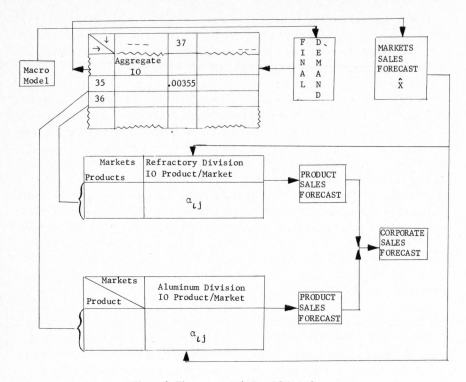

Figure 2. The corporate/micro IO interface.

sales forecasts, as shown in fig. 2. IO-based energy studies offer a timely example of this type of product/market breakdown. Energy-producing sectors are refined into various types of fuel consuming industrial and final markets [27]. Clearly, this type of product-market breakdown can also be related to the other basic IO matrices. Using the classic Leontief inverse L, for instance, the impact of, say, a predicted sharp drop in auto sales (IO No. 59) on the company sales of fireclay brick will be given by:

$$\sum_j \alpha_{\iota j} \cdot l_{j59} \cdot \Delta(Fe)_{59},$$

where ι denotes the fireclay brick product category and j ranges over all IO industry markets for fireclay brick.

The approximation involved in this type of calculation stems from ignoring the upstream effect (and feedbacks) of an increase in output of each refractory product on the refractory division's vendors. The smaller the proportion of this firm's pro-

duct in the entire IO industry to which it belongs, the better the approximation. [5]
For most large diversified firms the method gives a good approximation as reported
in [43] and [44].

Two final points should be noted. First the accuracy of the coefficients in the
Product/Market technology matrix must be checked periodically, as results are particularly sensitive to changes therein. Time trend studies are often used in practice,
e.g., logistic curve fittings as commonly used in technological forecasting [4]; technical information from industry experts is also useful for those adjustments. Second, another type of IO corporate interface deserves mentioning, as it can easily
complement the previous model for large technologically integrated multi-division
corporations with many inter-division transactions. A corporate IO table can be set
up with divisions, or portions thereof, corresponding to the industries and sales to
and purchases from other companies corresponding to final demand and primary
inputs respectively [45]. All IO techniques described so far readily apply to this
corporate IO table.

4. Empirical results

4.1. Data sources, computations and results

In this section we describe the forecasts obtained with the IO methodology
described in the previous section. The 1967 U.S. matrix was used, at the 81, 42 and
four-industry level. Data on the marginals F and V were obtained from 1) various
BEA publications [12], and 2) U.S. Department of Commerce National Income and
Product Accounts Time Series. To ensure consistency between SIC-based and
IO-based industry data, the original IO matrix was aggregated to a 42-industry
breakdown, and the corresponding A, L, M and Q matrices were computed. All data
were deflated to 1967 dollars through GNP price deflators. To keep the calculations
manageable, we purposely did not attempt to drive our IO forecasts via some larger
macro model as described in section 3.1.2 above; thus we focused exclusively on the
simple bridge coefficient approach of section 3.1.1 above, with the bridges $B_F =$
$(1/e'Fe)$. Fe and $B_v = (1/e'Ve).V'$ calculated for the base year 1967. An ex-post
static simulation was also carried-out using the actual marginals V and F thus
enabling us to gauge the extent of the model-specific error when compared to the
results obtained with bridge coefficients.

Table 11 summarizes the results for the period 1967 through 1971 for six
leading industries, measured in terms of their sales in total GNP. Table 12 summarizes the aggregate forecast error in terms of the percent Root Mean Square Error

---

[5] To include such effects would in effect disaggregate the whole IO matrix to the division
product detail level, which is clearly impractical and too expensive in most cases.

Table 11
Percent deviation of four gross output estimates and Theil's optimal linear correction for six slected industries.

	X_F	$X_F C$	$X_F B$	$X_F BC$	X_V	$X_V C$	$X_V B$	$X_V BC$
1967								
AFF	0.6	0.5	0.6	0.5	−0.4	−0.3	−0.5	−0.3
CC	0.0	−0.1	−0.0	−0.1	0.3	−0.2	−0.3	−0.2
F&K	0.1	0.1	0.1	0.1	0.2	0.3	0.2	0.3
PM	0.0	−0.1	0.0	−0.1	−3.4	−3.3	−3.4	−3.3
MXE	−0.0	−0.1	−0.1	−0.5	0.3	0.3	0.5	−0.3
MVE	−0.0	−0.1	−0.0	−0.1	−1.0	−0.8	−1.0	−0.8
1971								
AFF	3.0	3.8	8.9	11.4	12.8	8.2	7.8	10.4
CC	−2.0	−1.2	−5.9	−3.8	6.6	2.4	−6.3	−3.9
F&K	0.4	1.2	8.7	11.1	17.9	13.2	8.7	11.4
PM	7.6	8.4	15.8	18.4	37.5	31.9	11.8	14.6
MXE	3.1	3.9	17.1	19.7	20.1	12.3	16.5	19.4
MVE	4.1	4.9	−6.8	−4.8	7.6	3.3	−7.7	−5.4

Legend
AFF = Agriculture forestry and fisheries.
CC   = Contract construction.
F&K = Food and kindred products.
PM   = Primary metals.
MXE = Machinery except electrical.
MVE = Motor vehicles and equipment.

X_F: X forecast using actual F and (3).
$X_F B$: X forecast using bridge-derived F and (3).
X_V: X forecast using actual V and (7).
$X_V B$: X forecast using bridge-derived V and (7).
$X_F C, X_F BC, X_V C, X_V BC$: corresponding corrected forecast using Theil's optimal linear correction [49].

Table 12
Aggregate forecast errors.

% RMS error	67	68	69	70	71
X_F	0.2	2.9	2.4	3.2	3.8
$X_F C$	0.2	2.8	2.3	3.1	4.0
$X_F B$	0.2	5.0	5.0	8.1	12.3
$X_F BC$	0.2	4.9	4.7	8.3	12.6
X_V	0.9	5.7	7.8	13.4	14.9
$X_V C$	0.9	4.4	5.7	10.2	11.8
$X_B B$	0.9	5.0	4.7	8.0	12.2
$X_V BC$	0.9	5.0	4.7	7.8	12.0

(% RMSE) for the same years, over all industries. [6] Consistent with other empirical studies, the results show a high degree of accuracy. Comparison of the forecast obtained with the actual F (or V) values for a year and the forecasts derived from estimates of F (and V) using bridge coefficients enable us to assess the extent of the IO specific forecast error. Updating of the bridge and IO coefficients for the years 1968 through 1971 would further reduce the error. It is also worth noting that a simple test of the degree of stability of the a vs. the b coefficients over time is the relative errors in X_F vs. X_V forecasts. The clear superiority of X_F vs. X_V — when using actual F and V — would imply the greater stability of the a coefficients. Yet as we move to bridge-derived F and V this superiority vanishes. Finally this type of comparison is limited by the fact that the a's are in dollar terms whereas the b's are straight proportions as the price terms cancel out in $b_{ij} = p_i \tilde{x}_{ij}/p_i \tilde{x}_i$.

4.2. Forecast errors, sources and corrections

4.2.1. Sources of error

It is important to distinguish between three sources of errors in IO forecasts: 1) errors in the IO coefficients; 2) errors arising from the bridge procedure; 3) errors in forecasts of the exogenous variables. Only (1) is attributable to the IO methodology per se. As explained earlier, specification errors — e.g., variable rather than fixed coefficient industry production functions — and/or measurement errors — e.g., a suboptimal sectoring plan or changes in prices, product mix or technology — all lead to inaccurate coefficients. Much research has been done to measure the relative importance of each source of coefficient error in actual tables and correct it. Without attempting to cover all these approaches it should be noted that optimal sectoring plans — i.e., forecast-error-minimizing industry groupings — have been studied and tested [9,10], and a number of coefficient adjustment methods have been proposed, e.g., time trend studies, industry expert surveys, and the bi-proportional ('RAS') method. This last method attempts to adjust the base year IO coefficients by a least-squares criterion so that the resulting IO tables for later years are consistent with the recorded marginals F and V for these years [2]. Existing integrated IO systems often use a combination of these approaches to adjust the coefficients.

As regards errors from the use of bridge coefficients, it should be noted that, as shown in table 10, there are many types of bridge coefficients. They can be computed from total final demand (GNP) or for each component (consumption, investment, etc.) when individual forecasts of these components are known. Further, whichever coefficients are used, they can be adjusted in two ways: by tracking their time trends, or by linking them with a full-fledged macro model. In the latter case,

---

[6] Theoretically X_V should equal X_F for the base year, 1967. The difference must be attributed to residual statistical errors in estimating V.

Table 13
Error covariance matrices for 1967 data.

$E[\epsilon_{Fe} \cdot \epsilon'_{Fe}]$				Σ_X				$\Sigma_{V'e}$			
88	−17	−10	−63	85	27	11	−41	90	−4	−12	−94
−17	154	87	168	27	463	402	528	−4	114	62	140
−10	87	77	124	11	402	412	525	−12	62	63	121
−63	168	124	275	−41	528	525	769	−94	140	121	357

the bridge coefficients become functionally dependent upon the level of activity. For instance, consumption by industry can depend on the level of after-tax income [4]. Such procedures invariably result in appreciable error reduction.

Finally, as regards forecast errors in exogenous variables, the same prescription for reducing them applies as in any simultaneous equation model. Better outside models are needed to limit this source of error. Here again, this may involve more or less sophisticated macro models, e.g., econometric models for simultaneous time series analysis.

4.2.2. Residual model error covariance

Suppose appropriate adjustments have been made to the bridge coefficients and the IO coefficients, and a model has been built to provide forecasts for the exogenous variables. The computed residuals, ϵ (deviations from predicted values), for the forecast variables can be linearly translated into errors in the endogenous variables. For example, if we fit a forecasting model to each industry final demand and compute the residual variance-covariance matrix $E[\epsilon_{Fe} \cdot \epsilon'_{Fe}]$, the variance-covariance matrix of $V'e(\Sigma_{V'e})$ and of $X(\Sigma_X)$ are given by:

$$\Sigma_{V'e} = QE[\epsilon_{Fe} \cdot \epsilon'_{Fe}]Q' \quad \text{and} \quad \Sigma_X = LE[\epsilon_{Fe} \cdot \epsilon'_{Fe}]L' \tag{9}$$

where $E[\ ]$ represents the expectation operator. For the four-industry example, table 13 summarizes variance-covariance matrices of X and $V'e$ given the residual variance-covariance matrix obtained after a linear time trend model has been fitted to Fe, for quarterly data from 1946 to 1976.

5. Conclusion

The previous discussion has shown the potential of IO-based forecasts. Current limitations stem mostly from the extensive data requirements of IO. The cost of obtaining frequent updates on interindustry transactions is aggravated when further disaggregation is sought. Yet such disaggregation is the key to large-scale routine use of IO by corporations. The corporate/IO interface sketches a partial answer to this problem. New corporate information systems and reporting requirements are likely to provide easier and more frequent access to IO usable data. This may also be the key for compiling enough price information on disaggregated product lines to allow the calculation of physical IO tables. On a more theoretical level, the implications of the distribution of the model-specific errors for certain key issues in industrial organization and corporate finance [7] hold out the promise of a better understanding of widely divergent trends in different industries.

References

[1] American Chemical Society Symposium on The Use of IO as a Marketing and Economic Tool (Chicago, Ill. 1967).

[2] R.J.G. Allen and W.F. Gossling, eds., Estimating and Projecting Input-Output Coefficients (I.O. Publishing Co., London, 1975).

[3] Clopper A. Almon, The American Economy to 1975 (Harper and Row, N.Y., 1966).

[4] Clopper A. Almon et al., 1985: Industry Forecasts of the American Economy (D.C. Health, Lexington, Mass.).

[5] Clopper A. Almon et al., 1973–1985 in Figures (D.C. Health, Lexington, Mass., 1974).

[6] M. Augustinovics, Methods of international and intertemporal comparison of structure, in Contributions to IO Analysis, A.P. Carter and A. Brody, eds. (North-Holland, 1972, 249–269).

[7] B.D. Bagamery, On the use of IO analysis in assessing the interrelatedness of firm's returns, Northwestern University Ph.D. dissertation (in progress).

[8] Battelle Memorial Labs, Inc., Preview 85, Battell Memorial Labs, Inc., Columbus, Ohio.

[9] J.M. Blin and C. Cohen, Technological similarity and aggregation in IO systems: a cluster analytic approach, Review of Economics and Statistics 59 (1977).

[10] J.M. Blin and C. Cohen, Clustering and aggregation in IO systems, IEEE Proceedings (1976).

[11] J.M. Blin and F.H. Murphy, On measuring economic interrelatedness, Review of Economic Studies 41 (1974).

[12] Bureau of Economic Analysis, The IO structure of the U.,S. economy: 1967, Survey of Current Business 54, Nc. 2 (1974) 25–57.

[13] Bureau of Economic Analysis, IO structure of the U.S. economy: 1947, mimeo, 1970.

[14] Bureau of Economic Analysis, IO structure of the U.S. economy: 1963, Survey of Current Business, 49, No. 11 (1969) 16–47.

[15] Bureau of Labor Statistics, The Structure of the U.S. Economy in 1980 and 1985, Bulletin 1831, 1975.

[16] A. Carter, Structural Change in the American Economy (Harvard University Press, 1970).

[17] A. Carter, Changes in the structure of the American economy, Review of Economics and Statistics 49 (1969).

[18] R. Dorfman, P.A. Samuelson and R. Solow, Linear Programming and Economic Analysis, McGraw-Hill, N.Y., 1958).

[19] J.S. Duesenberry et al. (eds.), The Brookings Quarterly Econometric Model of the United States: Some Further Results (Rand-McNally, Chicago, 1969).

[20] O. Eckstein, E.W. Green and A. Sinai, The Data Resources Model: Uses, Structure and Analysis of the U.S. Economy, DRI, Lexington, Mass., 1974.

[21] ECONOSCOPE, The Econoscope Beta System, Econoscope Group, Inc. Warren, N.J.

[22] D. Gale, The Theory of Linear Economic Models (McGra-Hill, N.Y., 1960).

[23] A. Ghosh, Input-output approach in an allocation system, Economica 25, No. 97 (1958) 58–64.
[24] M.R. Goldman, M.L. Marimont and B.N. Vaccara, The interindustry structure of the U.S., Survey of Current Business 44, No. 11 (1964) 10–16.
[25] D. Hawkins and H.A. Simon, Some conditions of macroeconomic stability, Econometrica 17, No. 3 (1949).
[26] Werner Hirsch, Interindustrial-relation of a metropolitan area, Review of Economics and Statistics 41 (1959).
[27] K.C. Hoffman and D.W. Jorgenson, Economic and technological models for evaluation of energy policy, The Bell Journal of Economics 8, No. 2 (1977) 444–466.
[28] L.M. Horowitz, A Quarterly Input-Output Model of the United States (Chase Econometrics, Inc., Bala Cynwyd, Pa., 1974).
[29] Walter Isard, Interregional and regional IO analysis: a model of a space economy, Review of Economics and Statistics 33 (1951).
[30] G.J. Koehler, A.B. Whinston and G.P. Wright, Optimization over Leontief substitution systems (North-Holland, Amsterdam, 1975).
[31] W. Leontief, The Structure of the American Economy, 1919–1939, 2nd ed. (Oxford University Press, N.Y., 1951).
[32] W. Leontief et al., Studies in the Structure of the American Economy (Oxford University Press, N.Y., 1953).
[33] W. Leontief, Input-Output Economics (Oxford University Press, N.Y., 1966).
[34] W. Leontief, The Leontief dynamic inverse, in Contributions to IO Analysis, A.P. Carter and A. Brody, eds. (North-Holland, Amsterdam, 1972).
[35] D. Little, Inc., A Technical User's Guide to the ADL Input-Output Model, Arthur D. Little, Inc.
[36] MAPCAST, The General Electric Co., MAP Services, Rockvillem Maryland.
[37] L.N. Moses, A General equilibrium model of production, interregional trade and location of industry, Review of Economics and Statistics 42 (1960).
[38] L.N. Moses, The stability of interregional trading patterns and IO analysis, American Economic Review 43 (1955).
[39] H. Nikaido, Convex Structures and Economic Theory (Academic Press, N.Y., 1968).
[40] M. Nerlove, A tabular survey of macroeconometric models 7, No. 2 (1966) 127–175.
[41] D. Nyhus and C. Almon, The INFORUM international system of IO models and bilateral trade flows, INFORUM Research Report No. 21, U. of Maryland (Sept. 1977).
[42] R.S. Preston, The Wharton long term model: Input-output within the context of a macro forecasting model, IER 16, No. 1 (1975) 3–19.
[43] E.D. Ranard, Use of IO concepts in sales forecasting, Journal of Marketing Research 9 (1972).
[44] E.D. Ranard, IO concepts in corporate planning, Internal Report, Combustion Engineering Inc. (1972).
[45] J.A. Russo, Input-output analysis for financial decision-making, Management Accounting 57, No. 9 (1976) 22–24.
[46] R. Solow, On the structure of linear models, Econometrica 20 (1952).
[47] Standard Industrial Classification Reference Manual, U.S. Govt. Printing Office, 1967 (revised 1972).
[48] J.L. Steele, The Use of Econometric Models by Federal Regulatory Agencies, (Heath Lexington, Lexington, Mass., 1971).
[49] H. Theil, Applied Economic Forecasting (North Holland, 1975).
[50] Charles M. Tiebout, Regional and Interegional IO Models: An Appraisal, the Southern Economic Journal 24 (1957).

[51] B.N. Vaccara, An input-output method for long-range projections, Survey of Current Business 51, No. 7 (1971) 47–56.

[52] A.J. Walderhaug, The composition of value added in the 1963 input-poutput study, Survey of Current Business 53, No. 4 (1973) 34–44.

[53] A.H. Young and C.M. Ball, Industrial impacts of residential construction and mobile home production, Survey of Current Business 50, No. 10 (1970) 14–17 and 38.

TIMS Studies in the Management Sciences 12 (1979) 141–147
© North-Holland Publishing Company

THE UTILITY OF LONG-TERM FORECASTING

Olaf HELMER

University of Southern California

Forecasts are an essential ingredient of the planning process. Although frequently of necessity inaccurate, they can nevertheless be of considerable utility, for they should not be judged by the degree of uncertainty they convey but by the degree to which they permit differentiation between genuine and avoidable uncertainty.

The utility of forecasts is further enhanced if they result from a coherent body of theory, because then the planner is provided with helpful explanations regarding causal relationships. In a typical, multidisciplinary planning context such a theoretical basis is generally not available, but cross-impact analysis may on occasion serve as an expedient substitute.

1. Futures research and long-term forecasting

Futures research as an identifiable intellectual activity received much of its early impetus from the long-range forecasting studies conducted under Rand and TRW auspices in the middle sixties and their subsequent emulations by numerous other organizations. Recently a slight disenchantment with long-range forecasting seems to have set in in some circles, probably caused largely by the realization that predictions about the future more than a few years hence have been quite inaccurate. This inaccuracy may have been caused either by altogether wrong prophecies, especially in economics, or by a failure to foresee important developments, for example, the OPEC oil embargo, which triggered a sudden awareness of the energy crisis among the oil-importing countries. This disenchantment may be based on some misconceptions, having to do largely with the role of uncertainty. While the task of the forecaster surely includes the removal of as much uncertainty about the future as can legitimately be accomplished, it is equally important to bring genuine uncertainty, caused by deficiencies in currently available information, to the attention of planners. Futures research, and long-range forecasting in particular, should not be judged by the degree of uncertainty it conveys but by the degree to which it is capable of differentiating between unnecessary and unavoidable uncertainty.

Futures research may be defined as that part of operations research which is concerned with the support of planning activities relating to a future sufficiently far distant that the operating environment at the time the plans are implemented differs substantially from the operating environment at the time the plans are being made. An essential aspect of futures research, therefore, is the forecasting (not the prediction!) of such changes in operating conditions. [1]

For example, someone preparing to publish a new newspaper may safely rely on a survey of present preferences among the newspaper-reading public in order to decide what emphasis to give to various features. The operating environment is not likely to change very fast, and no futures research is required. On the other hand, someone growing trees for profit and having to decide between lumber, wood pulp, and other uses of his product decades hence must be concerned over the continuing demand for wooden houses and newsprint at that time. Here, futures research may be of help, both by deriving relevant probabilistic forecasts and by establishing planning procedures that properly account for the expected changes and the uncertainties implied by such forecasts.

2. The role of conditional forecasts

In addition to providing nonconditional forecasts of exogenous developments that will constitute the setting against which plans for the long-term future have to be made, it is equally important, if not more so, for futures research to furnish certain conditional forecasts, specifically, estimates of the probable implications of various alternative policies and of alternative action programs for implementing a given policy; furthermore, these conditional forecasts should take into consideration the previously established forecasts of external operating conditions. Such conditional forecasts are clearly needed when the planner operates in what is called the exploratory mode — that is, when a selective decision among competing policies or action programs has to be made — for it is by their implications that they will be judged. Conditional forecasts also play a role, though a somewhat different one, in the so-called normative planning mode. Here the planner operates in reverse: he starts with what he considers a preferred end condition and then, if indeed he acts as a planner and not just a utopian dreamer, searches for ways and means of implementing the "policy" of attaining the wished-for state. In this case, a conditional forecasting analysis will serve to ascertain which implementation plan may be expected to come closest to achieving the desired end.

3. Intuitive and theory-based forecasts

Thus, from a planner's point of view, the desirability of having both absolute and conditional long-term forecasts seems to be quite evident and, if none are supplied, it is inevitable that, in fact, the planner merely relies on his own, perhaps

---

[1] In the terminology generally accepted by now, *forecasts* as distinct from *predictions* are stated in probabilistic terms.

not even articulated, forecasts. One should note in passing that even forecasts based merely on purely intuitive insight rather than on established theory are of some value here, provided there is reason to have some trust in their reliability. If a forecast does happen to be theory-based, in the sense of being an instance of general law that derives explanatory force from being part of a coherent theory of the phenomena in question, that will be of additional utility to the planner; it will not only enable him to choose the best among given alternative strategies but, because of its explanatory character, it will help him design strategies that are apt to influence the future in a desired direction. Since forecasts frequently fail to be explanatory in this sense, the burden of constructing candidate strategies tends to fall upon the inventive imagination of the planner – a creative aspect of planning that is often given inadequate attention.

In view of the planner's need for forecasts and their added utility to him when they incorporate explanations, the two principal questions that remain are 1) whether it is possible to obtain forecasts of sufficient reliability and precision to improve the planning process over what it would be if the planner were left to rely solely on his own intuitive expectations, and 2) whether, in addition, such forecasts can be made within the framework of an explanatory theory.

4. Reliability and precision of forecasts

With regard to the first question, a number of comments are appropriate. First of all, it is important to keep in mind that perfection in planning, while a laudable ideal, is not a necessary criterion of the utility of forecasts to the planning process. Even if, statistically speaking, the systematic use of forecasts produces only a slight improvement in the expected results of planning, such forecasts may well be worthwhile.

Secondly, experience has shown that long-range forecasts obtained from professional experts can in fact be quite accurate. A survey conducted at the Institute for the Future a few years ago [1], examined Delphi-generated forecasts made years earlier. The survey showed that of the events that had been given a probability, say, of 60 percent of occurring by the time the survey was made, about 60 percent had in fact occurred by that time.

Thirdly, it may be objected by some that, even if exactly 60 percent of all events forecasted with a probability of 60 percent to occur by a certain date did occur by that date, the uncertainty implied by this information would still be so great as to render the forecast useless to the planner. In response to this objection it must be pointed out that it would be a delusion to think that planning does not proceed in an atmosphere of uncertainty. A probabilistic forecast, as opposed to a precise prediction, imposes a realistic awareness of the uncertainty of the future. This awareness compels the planner to incorporate provisions for contingencies in his plans; without such provisions he might be courting disaster.

Fourthly, and finally, it has been said quite correctly that it is the mark of a good executive to display sufficient acumen in discerning likely future contingencies to be able to make the right decisions without having to resort to outside advice in the form of forecasts. However, this phenomenon does not testify to the existence of some form of divination but more likely points to the presence of a relatively superior intelligence that enables the executive to judge the reliability of all sorts of signals he receives from the environment and thereby to form, implicitly or explicitly, his own set of forecasts. He is, in other words, himself the kind of professional expert whose forecasting talents one might wish to use beyond his own decision-making sphere.

5. Availability of an explanatory theory

Let us now consider the second question raised earlier, which concerns the feasibility of making forecasts that are supported by the explanatory framework of a coherent theory. The ideal case here is represented by astronomical forecasts — which virtually amount to predictions — such as that of the next reappearance of Halley's comet. What makes this such a high-probability forecast is its being based on well-understood and well-confirmed physical laws, plus the fact that deliberate intervention in the occurrence of this event is not a practical possibility. Most of our planning, of course, takes place in a sphere that lacks this high degree of certainty, and the kind of long-range forecasts on which we would like to rely inevitably involve some aspect of human affairs, either in the sense that the subject matter itself if societal in nature or that the probability of occurrence of the event being forecasted is affected by the degree of human intervention.

Typical examples are economic and technological forecasts. The occurrence, say, of another worldwide economic depression clearly concerns, and is affected by, human events. And even a purely technical forecast, say, of a breakthrough in solar-to-electric energy conversion obviously is influenced by the amount of research and development effort devoted to it. In cases of these kinds, the theoretical structures on which the forecasts are based are neither well understood nor well confirmed, which is typical of a context that is multidisciplinary and lies at least partly within the social sciences (cf. [4]). Intuitive insight therefore plays at least as large a part as reasoned arguments in obtaining such forecasts.

Thus the answer to the question under discussion cannot be wholly in the affirmative: not all forecasts of interest in typical planning situations may be expected to occur within the explanatory framework of a coherent theory. Yet, while the reasons for a long-range forecast containing societal elements are apt to be largely intuitive, there are generally some law-like regularities, having a limited but nonnegligible degree of confirmation, which at least lend some support to purely intuitive insight. Thus there tends to be an explanatory element present that may carry enough weight to permit the planner to identify measures that have more than a random chance of influencing events in the desired direction. For example, a government planner, wishing to bring about a reduction in the consumption of motor fuel, may propose a doubling of the gasoline tax, in the exceptation that the demand will be somewhat elastic and will respond to the resultant price rise. The implied forecast here is based on a law of economics which, though known to have exceptions, provides a certain amount of guidance for economic behavior. Moreover, reliance on past time series, in this case, will furnish some clues as to how much of a reduction in gasoline demand might be expected as a result of the proposed tax increase.

While in the field of economics such mildly confirmed regularities abound, often even in quantified form, that is rarely the case in other social sciences and occurs even less often in multidisciplinary situations. It is here that the cross-impact approach offers, if not a complete remedy, at least a better-than-nothing substitute for law-like regularities.

6. Cross-impact analysis as a theory substitute

The cross-impact concept was invented in the first place to enrich the results of sets of intuitive forecasts, such as a series of technological forecasts that might be obtained through a Delphi survey of expert opinions. Instead of merely requiring estimates of the probabilities of occurrence of potential future events considered in isolation from one another, a cross-impact analysis also inquires into the effects the occurrence of any one of the events included in the survey would have on the probability of occurrence of the remaining events. Intuitive numerical estimates of these effects, called cross impacts, are recorded in a square matrix, (x_{ij}), where x_{ij} is a measure of the impact which the occurrence of the ith event, E_i, has on the probability of occurrence of the jth event, E_j. Thus, the cross-impact matrix represents a set of estimates of the causal relationships among the events under consideration. The quantities x_{ij} as a rule have to be obtained through intuitive estimation by experts and do not in themselves convey any information that would explain the reasons for the causal relationships they indicate. However, if the x_{ij} are generated through some kind of Delphi procedure, the respondents, in justifying a nonzero assignment to a particular x_{ij}, may provide an intuitive argument for, and thus a possible explanation of, the claimed causal relationship. Moreover, while the x_{ij} individually and aside from any incidental explication given by their estimators are not explanatory in nature, the matrix (x_{ij}) as a whole represents a coherent pattern of causality assertions and may be regarded as the next best thing to a theory of the phenomena under consideration.

Possible scenarios of the future, which a planner may be considering, are formulated in terms not only of events – such as technological breakthroughs, acts of legislation, earthquakes, and elections – that take place at specific times, but also of trends representing gradual developments – such as population growth,

GNP, and degree of pollution. Cross-impact analysis has been extended to include trends as well as events, essentially by interpreting as an event a trend's deviation from its anticipated value [3]. The estimation of causal connections, or cross impacts, can thus be extended to all of the elements that make up a scenario of the future.

7. Application to multidisciplinary planning

The utility, to a planner of a long-range forecasting study augmented by a cross-impact analysis, becomes very apparent when the subject area in which plans are to be made is essentially multidisciplinary, because conventional extrapolative analyses almost certainly will fail to provide the kind of explanatory information from which a sound strategy can be constructed. A good example is a recently conducted study in the area of long-range transportation planning [2]. Here the planning agency was confronted with the need to forecast not only developments in transportation technology but also in its future operating environment, that is, in communication technology, demography, economic conditions, land-use policies, energy availability, people's changing values, and so on. In a planning situation of this kind where there are no well-confirmed regularities covering the different areas of concern and, especially, their interconnections, the planner can attempt to put together his own surrogate theory in the form of a cross-impact analysis. Thus he can build a foundation upon which to design strategies that have at least a slightly better chance of coping with future contingencies than those arrived at without the benefit of this kind of systematic underpinning.

The procedural steps he would have to follow in such an undertaking might be described very briefly as follows:

1. Identify potential future developments, either events or trends, whose occurrence or whose deviation from expected values would have a significant effect on the future operating environment of the planner's subject area.

2. Obtain forecasts, through Delphi or other methods, regarding these developments.

3. Estimate the cross impacts among these developments.

4. Use cross-impact analysis [2,3], to establish the relative sensitivity of the developments to one another.

5. Estimate the degree to which the event probabilities or the trend values can be influenced by deliberate intervention on the part of the decisionmaker or decision-making agency on whose behalf plans are being made. In doing so, separate the developments that are not influenced easily from those that are. The former establish the spectrum of exogenous, uncontrollable characteristics of the future environment for which plans are being made. The latter are the operative developments through the manipulation of which the planner can hope to influence the course of future events in a desired direction.

6. Establish the resource constraints that prospective plans must be designed to accommodate.

7. Using the sensitivities ascertained earlier and the developments identified as operative, select or invent alternative action programs within the stated resource constraints that seem to be promising candidates for attaining desired objectives.

8. Use cross-impact analysis to determine the relative merits of these alternative action programs in terms of expected results and their dispersion, and thus select one or several of the most promising alternatives.

For many obvious reasons — the surrogate character of the cross-impact analysis as a theory substitute: the possibly inadequate selection of developments for inclusion in the analysis; the relative unreliability of the forecasts as well as of the cross-impact estimates, even if obtained from experts; the possibly incomplete selection of action programs included in the comparative analysis — the outcome of this approach may not, in fact, be the optimal strategy. Yet the procedure represents a selection process which, if carried out judiciously and conscientiously, may yield a set of strategies from which, through a process of further analysis, a satisfactory close-to-optimal strategy can be distilled.

8. Summary

The points made here may be summarized as follows: forecasts, whether explicit or merely implicit, are an essential ingredient of the planning process. In the case of long-range planning, the planner needs two kinds of long-range forecasts: those concerning the expected, changed operating environment and those concerning the consequences of contemplated policies. The utility of such forecasts depends on their precision and reliability and is further enhanced if they are developed within an explanatory setting that enables the planner to understand any causal relationships and to use them to design appropriate strategies. Forecasts are rarely very precise, especially if they concern societal and multidisciplinary matters, but their precision as well as their reliability can be at least slightly enhanced if they are obtained through a systematic solicitation of expert opinions, such as might be provided by a Delphi survey. An explanatory setting for forecasts in the form of a well-confirmed theory is generally absent; however, a substitute having some, though limited, utility can be constructed through the vehicle of a cross-impact analysis.

References

[1] R. Ament, Comparison of Delphi forecasting studies in 1964 and 1969, Futures 2 (1970).
[2] P. Gray and O. Helmer, The California transportation system, Report by the Centre for Futures Research, University of Southern California, November 1974.
[3] O. Helmer, Problems in futures research — Delphi and causal cross-impact analysis, Futures 9 (1977).
[4] O. Helmer and N. Rescher, On the epistemology of the inexact sciences, Management Science 6 (1959).

TIMS Studies in the Management Sciences 12 (1979) 149–165
© North-Holland Publishing Company

FORECASTING AND WHITENING FILTER ESTIMATION *

Emanuel PARZEN

Texas A&M University

An approach to time series modeling and forecasting is described in which the identification
stage is not accomplished chiefly by graphical inspection of the time series and of computed
auxiliary sample functions such as the autocorrelation function, partial autocorrelation function, and spectrum. Rather the transfer function g_∞ of the whitening filter is directly estimated
and parsimoniously parameterized by using a criterion called CAT for determining the order of
approximating autoregressive schemes. Ideas are stated for how to obtain time series models
that can be interpreted as providing decompositions of time series into trend and seasonal components, as well as optimal forecasts of the future evolution of the time series.

1. Introduction: statistical modeling without scientific theory

Can one model and forecast a time series without any technical expertise about
the real events of which the time series is the numerical record? In other words, can
one model without theory? Clearly it is better to model with theory. But when
theory about the events being observed is unavailable, or is unreliable, or one would
like to check it, it seems preferable to consider the models that are generated solely
by their statistical fit to the data. An example of such a model is the ever-present
alternative hypothesis of pure randomness.

The view that statistical model fitting is a valid approach to answering scientific
questions underlies the approach presented in this paper. Scientific questions about
real events can often be translated into statistical questions about the statistical
nature of time series. A time series can be defined as measurements or numbers
ordered in time that represent real events. It should be pointed out that the measurements may have errors that distort reality; then the model describes only the
behavior of the measured process and not the real process.

One can list some general statistical questions about a time series that should be
investigated.

1. Change of probability law—nonstationarity. Determine if the statistical distribution of the time series is changing significantly over time. For example, does a

* Research for this paper was supported by the Office of Naval Research under contract
N00014-72-C-508 (NR 042-234).

model that fits the time series up to a time t_0 fail to fit the time series values after t_0.

2. Trend. Determine if a trend is present in the time series.

3. Seasonal adjustment. Determine if seasonal components are present in the time series that should be eliminated to better discern the trend.

4. Spectral analysis. Determine the frequency content of the time series or its representation as a continuous superposition of cyclic components.

5. Forecast. Predict future values of the time series.

Among these questions, spectral analysis and forecasting play a special role. In addition to being scientific questions of primary interest, they provide essential tools for modeling the statistical nature of a time series, since the criteria for the goodness of fit of a model are a) that the model have a smooth spectral density that is a likely smoothing of the highly wiggly raw spectral density or periodogram of the observed time series, and 2) that the model yield one-step-ahead predictors whose prediction errors constitute as closely as possible a white noise time series. [1]

In this paper the aim is to describe an approach to time series analysis that provides simultaneously:

a model — which is defined as a transformation to white noise

a spectral analysis

a decomposition into trend and seasonal components

forecasting procedures, which are often most desired.

A time series is denoted here as $Y(t)$, $t = 0, \pm 1, ...$, which represents observations at a series of equally-spaced times of a variable Y.

2. Averaging and whitening operators

A time-series decomposition means a representation of $Y(t)$ as the sum of two components, which are denoted $Y^\mu(t)$ and $Y^\nu(t)$:

$$Y(t) = Y^\mu(t) + Y^\nu(t), \tag{1}$$

where $Y^\mu(t)$ is the explained part of $Y(t)$, $Y^\nu(t)$ is the error, or unexplained, part of $Y(t)$.

The explained part $Y^\mu(t)$ is usually a linear function of explanatory variables $X_1(t), X_2(t), ...$ with coefficients denoted as $\beta_1, \beta_2, ...$; explicitly,

$$Y^\mu(t) = \beta_1 X_1(t) + ... + \beta_j X_j(t) + ... + \beta_k X_k(t) + ... \tag{2}$$

The sum is written as infinite series because in theory there are an infinite number

---

[1] A time series is called white noise, often denoted $\epsilon(t)$, if it consists of independent zero mean constant variance random variables.

of possible explanatory variables. However, only a finite number of explanatory variables X_j are expected to have coefficients β_j sufficiently different from zero that the benefit, in mean square error terms, of estimating β_j is preferred to the cost of considering β_j equal to 0, and thus omitting X_j from the model.

The error term $Y^\mu(t)$ is best regarded as the residual $Y(t) - Y^\mu(t)$ after constructing $Y^\mu(t)$ to explain as much as possible of the value of $Y(t)$.

The Greek letter nu is used as a superscript to indicate that $Y^\nu(t)$ represents what is new or transiting in $Y(t)$ after explaining as much of its value as possible by the best available explanatory variables $X_1(t), ..., X_k(t)$. The Greek letter mu is used as a superscript because it connotes a mean, and $Y^\mu(t)$ connotes an average or smooth value about which $Y(t)$ fluctuates.

It is customary to denote the error term by $\epsilon(t)$, and write the model for $Y(t)$ as a regression model

$$Y(t) = \beta_1 X_1(t) + ... + \beta_k X_k(t) + \epsilon(t), \qquad t = 1, 2, ..., T. \tag{3}$$

Given a finite sample $Y = [Y(t), t = 1, ..., T]$, one forms estimators $\hat\beta_1, ..., \hat\beta_k$ of the regression coefficients $\beta_1, ..., \beta_k$, which are functions of the regression functions $X_1, ..., X_k$ and the sample Y. The vector $Y^\mu = [Y^\mu(t), t = 1, ..., T]$, $Y^\mu(t) = \hat\beta_1 X_1(t) + .. + \hat\beta_k X_k(t)$, can be represented

$$Y^\mu = AY, \tag{4}$$

where A is a suitable matrix, or operator. A is called the averaging operator. $I - A$ is called the whitening operator, since the vector Y^ν of errors $Y^\nu(t) = Y(t) - Y^\mu(t)$ can be represented as

$$Y^\nu = (I - A)Y. \tag{5}$$

In regression analysis a variety of estimation approaches are available – ridge regression, subset regression, Bayesian regression, and so on. With each estimator one can define an averaging operator A. Recent research by Wahba [8] gives a criterion that can be used to choose the optimal parameter estimator, and thus the optimal regression model. Wahba defines a cross-validation criterion

$$CV(A) = \|(I - A)Y\|^2 / [\text{Trace}(I - A)]^2. \tag{6}$$

Let $\hat A$ be the matrix minimizing $CV(A)$ over the family of averaging matrices being considered. The optimum smoother of the data Y is $Y^\mu = \hat A Y$. The justification of this criterion is beyond the scope of this paper; it is mentioned only to note that the approach described here toward finding criteria for selecting a time-series model – and thus a forecasting procedure – is philosophically quite general.

When modeling and forecasting a single time series $Y(t)$ is the aim, past values

$Y(t-1)$, $Y(t-2)$, ... are taken as the explanatory variables. One assumes $Y(t)$ to consist of normally distributed random variables and defines $Y^\mu(t)$ to be the best predictor of $Y(t)$ from past values, in the sense of minimum mean square error prediction:

$$Y^\mu(t) = E[Y(t)| Y(t-1), Y(t-2), ...]. \qquad (7)$$

$Y^v(t) = Y(t) - Y^\mu(t)$ is called the innovation at time t. The innovation series $Y^v(t)$ has two characterizing properties: 1) $Y^v(\cdot)$ is a white noise series, 2) $Y(s)$ and $Y^v(t)$ are independent for all $s < t$.

The operator by which the series $\dot{Y}^\mu(\cdot)$ is obtained from $Y(\cdot)$ is denoted A to indicate that it is an averaging operator, which can be written explicitly as

$$-Y^\mu(t) = -AY(t) = \alpha_\infty(1)Y(t-1) + ... + \alpha_\infty(m)Y(t-m) + ... \qquad (8)$$

Then $I - A$ is the operator transforming $Y(\cdot)$ to $Y^v(\cdot)$, and

$$Y^v(t) = (I-A)Y(t) = Y(t) + \alpha_\infty(1)Y(t-1) + ... + \alpha_\infty(m)Y(t-m) + ... \qquad (9)$$

$I - A$ is called the whitening operator.

The foregoing discussion may be summarized as follows. To model a time series, find the whitening operator $I - A$. To forecast a time series, find the averaging operator A. The two problems are clearly equivalent.

3. Stationary time series

To develop a rigorous theory of time-series prediction one starts with the case of a zero mean stationary normal time series $Y(t)$. Unfortunately the notation of time-series analysis is not standard, and one naturally prefers ones' own notation (see Parzen [5,6,7])

covariance function $R(v) = E[Y(t) Y(t+v)]$, $v = 0, \pm 1, ...$;

correlation function $\rho(v) = \text{Corr}[Y(t), Y(t+v)] = R(v)/R(0)$;

spectral density function $f(u) = \sum_{v=-\infty}^{\infty} R(v)\exp(-2\pi iuv)$, $0 \leqslant u \leqslant 1$.

The argument u of the spectral density function is usually taken in the range $-0.5 \leqslant u \leqslant 0.5$. Since $f(u)$ is an even periodic function satisfying $f(u) = f(-u)$, $f(u+1) = f(u)$, one can take the range 0 to 1, which is convenient for the current research on time-series theoretic methods for nonparametric statistical inference.

The innovation $Y^\nu(\cdot)$ of a stationary time series $Y(\cdot)$ can be represented

$$Y^\nu(t) = g_\infty(L)\,Y(t) \tag{10}$$

in terms of a function

$$g_\infty(z) = 1 + \alpha_\infty(1)z + \dots + \alpha_\infty(m)z^m + \dots$$

and an operator L, called the lag operator, defined by

$$LY(t) = Y(t-1), \quad L^m\,Y(t) = Y(t-m).$$

This lag operator is denoted as B by Box and Jenkins [1]. The term $g_\infty(z)$ is called the autoregressive transfer function, abbreviated ARTF. The problem of estimating the whitening filter $I-A$ becomes the problem of estimating $g_\infty(z)$. Next one reviews how a knowledge of g_∞ helps to provide both the spectral density of the time series and forecasting formulas.

The relation $Y^\nu(t) = g_\infty(L)Y(t)$ implies that the spectral densities $f(u)$ of $Y(\cdot)$ and $f_{Y\nu}(u)$ of $Y^\nu(\cdot)$ satisfy the relation

$$f(u)\,|g_\infty[\exp(2\pi i u)]|^2 = f_{Y\nu}(u). \tag{11}$$

Now $Y^\nu(\cdot)$ is white noise with variance $\sigma_\infty^2 R(0)$, defining

$$\sigma_\infty^2 = E[|Y^\nu(t)|^2]/E[|Y(t)|^2], \tag{12}$$

called the normalized infinite memory one-step-ahead mean square prediction error. Its spectral density is a constant:

$$f_{Y\nu}(u) = \sigma_\infty^2 R(0), \qquad 0 \leqslant u \leqslant 1. \tag{13}$$

Finally we obtain a basic formula for $f(u)$:

$$f(u) = \sigma_\infty^2 R(0)\,|g_\infty[\exp(2\pi i u)]|^{-2} \tag{14}$$

Consequently estimators $\hat{\sigma}_\infty^2$ and $\hat{g}_\infty$ of the innovation variance and ARTF respectively yield an estimator $\hat{f}(u)$ given by

$$\hat{f}(u) = \hat{R}(0)\hat{\sigma}_\infty^2\,|\hat{g}_\infty[\exp(2\pi i u)]|^{-2}. \tag{15}$$

The optimum (minimum mean square error) predictor of $Y(t+k)$, given $Y(t)$, $Y(t-1)$, ..., is denoted $Y^\mu(t+k|t)$; its mean square prediction error is denoted

$$\sigma_{\infty,k}^2 = E[|Y^\mu(t+k|t) - Y(t+k)|^2]. \tag{16}$$

Note $Y^\mu(t+1|t)$ is also denoted $Y^\mu(t+1)$, and $\sigma^2_{\infty,1} = \sigma^2_\infty$. Given the coefficients $\alpha_\infty(\,\cdot\,)$, one can recursively generate $Y^\mu(t+k|t)$ by the relation

$$-Y^\mu(t+k|t) = \alpha_\infty(1)\,Y^\mu(t+k-1|t) + \ldots$$

$$+ \alpha_\infty(k-1)\,Y^\mu(t+1|t) + \alpha_\infty(k)\,Y(t) \tag{17}$$

$$+ \alpha_\infty(k+1)\,Y(t-1) + \ldots .$$

Formula 17 implies that one can generate forecasts of the entire future evolution of time series given its past, and that the various forecast values are linked rather than being derived by separate forecasting formulas.

The general nonparametric formula for $g_\infty(z)$ involves an infinite number of parameters. The parametric approach to estimation of g_∞ assumes a finite parametric model for g_∞ — that is, a representation for g_∞ as a function of a finite number of parameters. To assume that the time series obeys an ARMA (autoregressive moving average) scheme of specified orders is equivalent to assuming a finite parametric representation for g_∞. The difficult problem is to estimate the orders; this is called identifying the model.

In the approach proposed here, one uses finite order AR (autoregressive) schemes as approximations to the true model, which are then used to generate estimators of σ^2_∞ and g_∞.

A stationary zero mean stationary time series $Y(\,\cdot\,)$ is said to obey an $AR(p)$, or autoregressive scheme of order p, if $Y(\,\cdot\,)$ satisfies

$$g_p(L)\,Y(t) = \dot{\epsilon}(t) \tag{18}$$

for some white noise $\epsilon(\cdot)$ and polynomial

$$g_p(z) = 1 + \alpha_p(1)z + \ldots + \alpha_p(p)z^p, \tag{19}$$

all of whose roots in the complex z-plane lie outside the unit circle. An equivalent characterization of an $AR(p)$ is that the infinite memory one-step-ahead predictor $Y^\mu(t)$ of $Y(t)$, given past values $Y(t-1)$, $Y(t-2)$, ..., coincides with the finite memory p one-step-ahead predictor.

The finite memory m one-step-ahead predictor $Y^{\mu,m}(t)$ is the conditional expectation

$$Y^{\mu,m}(t) = E[Y(t)|Y(t-1), \ldots, Y(t-m)]. \tag{20}$$

For a zero mean normal stationary time series it can be represented

$$-Y^{\mu,m}(t) = \alpha_m(1)\,Y(t-1) + \ldots + \alpha_m(m)\,Y(t-m). \tag{21}$$

The prediction error $Y^{v,m}(t) = Y(t) - Y^{\mu,m}(t)$ can be represented

$$Y^{v,m}(t) = g_m(L)Y(t), \tag{22}$$

defining

$$g_m(z) = 1 + \alpha_m(1)z + \dots + \alpha_m(m)z^m. \tag{23}$$

The normalized finite memory m one-step-ahead mean square prediction error, measured as a fraction of the variance of $Y(t)$ is denoted

$$\sigma_m^2 = E[|Y^{v,m}(t)|^2]/E[|Y(t)|^2]. \tag{24}$$

From prediction theory, it follows that the autoregressive coefficients $\alpha_m(1), \dots, \alpha_m(m)$ are determined by orthogonality conditions

$$E[Y^{v,m}(t)Y(t-v)] = 0, \qquad v = 1, \dots, m, \tag{25}$$

which yield the normal equations: for $v = 1, \dots, m,$

$$\rho(-v) + \alpha_m(1)\rho(1-v) + \dots + \alpha_m(m)\rho(m-v) = 0. \tag{26}$$

Finally σ_m^2 is given by

$$\sigma_m^2 = E[Y^{v,m}(t)Y(t)]/R(0) = 1 + \alpha_m(1)\rho(1) + \dots + \alpha_m(m)\rho(m). \tag{27}$$

Given a sample $[Y(t), t = 1, \dots, T]$ of a zero mean normal stationary time series, one estimates the correlation function $\rho(v)$ by

$$\hat{\rho}(v) = \sum_{t=1}^{T-v} Y(t)Y(t+v) \div \sum_{t=1}^{T} Y^2(t). \tag{28}$$

A currently popular approach to time-series model identification, owing to Box and Jenkins [1], is to graphically inspect $\hat{\rho}(v)$ and its partial autocorrelation function with the aim of discerning the type of ARMA scheme to be fitted. After estimating the parameters of the model type guessed, one performs a diagnostic check of the model fit by testing the residuals for closeness to white noise. After all this work, what one has essentially accomplished is an estimator of the ARTF g_∞.

The approach proposed here is to estimate g_∞ nonparametrically by using approximating AR schemes. In a sense, only AR schemes are used in modeling stationary time series. That seems reasonable, and indeed, ARMA schemes are useful and desirable only for modeling nonstationary time series.

The Yule–Walker equations are used to form estimators $\hat{\sigma}_m^2, \hat{\alpha}_{1,m}, \dots, \hat{\alpha}_{m,m}$ of the parameters of an AR scheme of order m: for $v = 1, ..., m$,

$$\hat{\rho}(-v) + \hat{\alpha}_{1,m}\hat{\rho}(1 - v) + ... + \hat{\alpha}_{m,m}\hat{\rho}(m - v) = 0. \tag{29}$$

$$\hat{\sigma}_m = \hat{\rho}(0) + \hat{\alpha}_{1,m}\hat{\rho}(1) + ... + \hat{\alpha}_{m,m}\hat{\rho}(m). \tag{30}$$

It seems plausible that there is a value of m, denoted $\hat{m}$, such that

$$\hat{g}_m(z) = 1 + \hat{\alpha}_{1,m}z + ... + \hat{\alpha}_{m,m}z^m, \tag{31}$$

with $m = \hat{m}$ is an optimal estimator of g_∞; in symbols,

$$\hat{g}_\infty(z) = \hat{g}_{\hat{m}}(z). \tag{32}$$

One can show that approximately the overall mean square percentage error of any $\hat{g}_m$ as an estimator of g_∞ satisfies

$$\frac{1}{2\pi} \int_{-\pi}^{\pi} E \left| \frac{\hat{\sigma}_m^{-2}\hat{g}_m[\exp(i\omega)] - \sigma_\infty^{-2}g_\infty[\exp(i\omega)]}{\sigma_\infty^{-2}g_\infty[\exp(i\omega)]} \right|^2 d\omega$$

$$= \frac{1}{T}\sum_{j=1}^{m} \sigma_j^{-2} + \sigma_\infty^{-2} - \sigma_m^{-2} \tag{33}$$

where T is the sample size and σ_j^2 is the memory j one-step-ahead mean square prediction error. Therefore in practice $\hat{m}$ is chosen to minimize a criterion function $CAT(m)$, defined as follows:

$$CAT(m) = -(1 + 1/T)$$

$$CAT(m) = \frac{1}{T}\sum_{j=1}^{m} \hat{\sigma}_j^{-2} - \hat{\sigma}_m^{-2}, \tag{34}$$

where $\hat{\sigma}_m^2$ is an unbiased estimator of σ_m^2 defined by

$$\hat{\sigma}_m^2 = (1 - m/T)^{-1}\hat{\sigma}_m^2. \tag{35}$$

When $\hat{m} = 0$, the hypothesis that the observed time series is white noise is accepted.

Having determined the maximum order $\hat{m}$ of the approximating autoregression transfer function $\hat{g}_{\hat{m}}(z)$, one next uses subset regression techniques to determine the significantly nonzero autoregressive coefficients in the transfer function. As an example, on monthly data if one determined that $\hat{m} = 13$, it would be of interest to determine whether $\hat{g}_{13}(z)$ were approximately of the form

$$\hat{g}_{13}(z) = (1 - \theta_1 z)(1 - \theta_{12} z^{12}). \tag{36}$$

Subset autoregression is discussed by McClave [3.]

The foregoing approach has the advantage that time-series model identification becomes more automated; its disadvantage is that it may require more parameters to model the generating process and more computing.

4. Nonstationary time series modeling

To predict a time series $Y(t)$ one can often suggest a naive predictor of the form

$$Y^{\text{naive}}(t) = Y(t - \lambda_1) + Y(t - \lambda_2) - Y(t - \lambda_1 - \lambda_2), \tag{37}$$

for suitable lags λ_1 and λ_2. Often $\lambda_1 = 1, \lambda_2 = 12$ for monthly data. The prediction error of this predictor is given by

$$\tilde{Y}(t) = Y(t) - Y^{\text{naive}}(t) = Y(t) - Y(t - \lambda_1) - Y(t - \lambda_2)$$

$$+ Y(t - \lambda_1 - \lambda_2) = (I - L^{\lambda_1})(I - L^{\lambda_2})Y(t) = \nabla_{\lambda_1} \nabla_{\lambda_2} Y(t). \tag{38}$$

In words, taking λ_1th and λ_2th differences is equivalent to forming the naive prediction errors.

A time series $Y(t)$ is considered to be nonstationary if it is predictable in the sense that there exists a predictor whose prediction error time series $\tilde{Y}(t)$ satisfies the criterion that the ratio of the average square of $\tilde{Y}(t)$ to the average square of $Y(t)$ is of the order of $1/T$.

Ad hoc differencing could be used to find whether $\tilde{Y}(t)$ satisfies this criterion. However the types of differencing that are appropriate can be discerned by using CAT to find an autoregressive predictor of optimal order. The closeness to zero of the corresponding residual variance $\hat{\sigma}_m^2$ is used as a diagnostic of whether the series $Y(t)$ is stationary or not. In practice, the following criterion has proven useful: when $\hat{\sigma}_m^2 < 8/T$, the time series is considered to be nonstationary and the autoregressive predictor that has been found is interpreted as a naive predictor. When $\tilde{Y}(t)$ is stationary (nonpredictable) it can be modeled by an approximate autoregressive scheme,

$$\hat{g}_{\hat{m}}(L)\tilde{Y}(t) = \epsilon_t, \tag{39}$$

which can be used to form $\tilde{Y}^\mu(t)$, the best one-step-ahead predictor of $\tilde{Y}(t)$. The best one-step-ahead predictor of $Y(t)$ is given by

$$Y^\mu(t) = Y^{\text{naive}}(t) + \tilde{Y}^\mu(t). \tag{40}$$

To prove this relationship, note the identity

$$Y(t) = Y^{\text{naive}}(t) + \tilde{Y}(t)$$

and form the conditional expectation of both sides of this identity with respect to $Y(t-1), Y(t-2), \ldots$.

A remarkable fact is the equality of the prediction errors of $Y(t)$ and $\tilde{Y}(t)$:

$$Y^\nu(t) = Y(t) - Y^\mu(t) = \tilde{Y}(t) - \tilde{Y}^\mu(t) = \tilde{Y}^\nu(t). \tag{41}$$

It follows that to find the whitening filter

$$Y(t) -\boxed{}- \epsilon_t$$

for a nonstationary time series $Y(t)$ — which includes almost all time series with seasonal components — it suffices to apply any one-sided filter whose output $Y(t)$ is stationary. In practice this determination can either be suggested by an ad hoc deseasonalizing procedure or found by applying the CAT method and discovering that $\hat{\sigma}_{\hat{m}}^2$ is less than $8/T$. The series filter

$$Y(t) -\boxed{}- \tilde{Y}(t) -\boxed{}- \tilde{Y}^\nu(t) = \epsilon_t$$

then yields the whitening filter. While the filter leading to $\tilde{Y}(t)$ is not unique, the overall filter leading to ϵ_t is unique.

For a nonstationary time series, the modeling problem is not only to find the whitening filter, which transforms $[Y(t)]$ to $[Y^\nu(t)]$, but to interpret it as several filters in series:

D_0: a detrending filter that in the spectral domain eliminates the low frequency components corresponding to trend,

D_λ: a deseasonal filter that in the spectral domain eliminates periodic components with period λ or components corresponding to the harmonics with frequencies that are multiples of $2\pi/\lambda$,

g_∞ or Π: an innovations filter that transforms to white noise the series $Y^{(\text{stat})}(t) = D_0 D_\lambda Y(t)$ representing a transformation of $Y(t)$ to a stationary series.

The time-series modeling problem is thus to find the filter representation

	detrend	deseasonal		innovations	
$Y(t) -$	D_0	D_{λ_1}	$\cdots$	D_{λ_k}	g_∞	$- \epsilon_t = Y^\nu(t)$

where the possibility of several different periods λ_1, ..., λ_k is admitted. For example, in monthly data λ values are often 12 and 3; in daily data λ values are often 7 and 365; in hourly data λ values are often 24 and 168.

Given the above decomposition, one can form various derived series:

$$
\begin{aligned}
Y^{(0)}(t) \quad &= D_0 Y(t), \quad \text{the detrended series,} \\
Y^{(\lambda)}(t) \quad &= D_\lambda Y(t), \quad \text{the seasonally adjusted series,} \\
Y^{(0,\lambda)}(t) &= Y^{(\text{stat})}(t) = D_0 D_\lambda Y(t) = D_\lambda D_0 Y(t), \quad \text{the detrended sea-} \\
&\qquad \text{sonally adjusted series,} \\
Y^\nu(t) \quad &= Y^{(\text{white})}(t) = g_\infty D_0 D_\lambda Y(t), \quad \text{the innovations series.}
\end{aligned}
$$

A parsimonious parametrization of a whitening filter has as few parameters as possible; an example might be the ARMA $(1, 1)$ scheme $(I + \alpha L)Y(t) = (I + \beta L)\epsilon(t)$. In the analysis of seasonal series with period λ, parsimony is sought through multiplicative or factored models of the form

$$
g(L)G(L^\lambda)\nabla^d \nabla_\lambda^D Y(t) = h(L)H(L^\lambda)\epsilon(t), \tag{42}
$$

where $\nabla_\lambda = I - L^\lambda$, G is a polynomial of degree P, and H is a polynomial of degree Q. The above model is called an ARIMA $(p, d, q) \times (P, D, Q)_\lambda$ model.

It is not always obvious what the important seasonal periods are. Thus, for monthly economic data, both quarterly, $\lambda = 3$, and annual, $\lambda = 12$, periods may be present, as in the AR model

$$
[I + \alpha(3)L^3 + \alpha(12)L^{12} + \alpha(15)L^{15}] Y(t) = \epsilon(t). \tag{43}
$$

When one encounters a parametrization of this kind, one should check whether it can be written

$$
[I + \alpha(3)L^3][I + \alpha(12)L^{12}] Y(t) = \epsilon(t), \tag{44}
$$

which is equivalent to $\alpha(15) = \alpha(3)\alpha(12)$. Such factorizations often arise in empirical time-series analysis of economic and social time series. However, they should not be routinely assumed; rather, one should routinely test for their presence. Thus an ARMA model, even though parsimonious, makes assumptions that may not hold true.

The question remains of how to find in practice the detrending and deseasonal filters. For ease of exposition, the one-parameter family of filter are mainly considered here:

$$
D_\lambda(\theta) = (I - L^\lambda)/(I - \theta L^\lambda), \tag{45}
$$

where the parameter θ is chosen (usually by an estimation procedure) between 0 and 1. When $\theta = 0$ the filter is ∇_λ, the λth difference.

To understand the role of the filter $D_\lambda(\theta)$, denote it for brevity by D and rewrite it as follows: if $I - L^\lambda = I - \theta L^\lambda - (1 - \theta)L^\lambda$, then

$$D = I - [(1 - \theta)L^\lambda]/(I - \theta L^\lambda)$$

$$= I - [(1 - \theta)(L^\lambda + \theta L^{2\lambda} + \theta^2 L^{3\lambda} + ...)].$$

Then the output $Y^{(D)}(t) = DY(t)$ of a filter D with input $Y(t)$ can be written $Y^{(D)}(t) = Y(t) - (1 - \theta)[Y(t - \lambda) + ...]$ In words, $Y^{(D)}(t)$ is the result of subtracting from $Y(t)$ the exponentially weighted average of $Y(t - \lambda)$, $Y(t - 2\lambda)$, ...

It seems open to investigation whether the filter D of mixed autoregressive moving average type is superior to the approximately equivalent autogressive filter

$$D' = (I - L^\lambda)(I + \theta L^\lambda) = I - (1 - \theta)L^\lambda - \theta L^{2\lambda},$$

whose output $Y^{(D')}(t) = Y(t) - (1 - \theta)Y(t - \lambda) - \theta Y(t - 2\lambda)$.

It appears that the role of moving averages in Box–Jenkins ARIMA models is to build filters of the type $D_\lambda(\theta)$. Thus the ARIMA model

$$(I - L)(I - L^{12})Y(t) = (I - \theta_1 L)(I - \theta_{12} L^{12})\epsilon_t \tag{46}$$

should be viewed as the whitening filter

$$D_1(\theta_1)D_{12}(\theta_{12})Y(t) =$$

$$[(I - L)/(I - \theta_1 L)][(I - L^{12})/(I - \theta_{12} L^{12})] Y(t) = \epsilon_t. \tag{47}$$

The following conclusions can be drawn from these considerations. To find a transformation of a nonstationary time series to stationarity one could apply pure differencing operators, such as $I - L$ or $I - L^{12}$, that are suggested by an initial autoregressive approximation. The whitening filter that transforms the residuals after differencing to the innovations series should be expressed if possible in terms of factors corresponding to filters such as $I - \theta_1 L$ and $I - \theta_{12} L^{12}$, since such factors will make it possible to interpret the overall whitening filter

$$Y(t) - \boxed{\begin{array}{c} \text{whitening} \\ \text{filter} \end{array}} - \epsilon_t$$

as a series of filters

$$Y(t) - \boxed{\begin{array}{c|c|c} \text{detrend} & \text{deseasonal} & \text{innovations} \\ \text{filter} & \text{filter} & \text{filter} \end{array}} - \epsilon_t.$$

5. Illustrative example: the airline model

The airline model from Box and Jenkins [1] can illustrate the use of the methods just described. Let $Y(t)$ denote the time series (given in Box and Jenkins [1, p. 305 of monthly passenger totals in international air travel from 1949 through 1960; let $Z(t)$ denote its logarithms.

The model fitted by Box and Jenkins to the airline data is of the form

$$\nabla_{12}\nabla_1 Z(t) = (1 - \theta_1 L)(1 - \theta_{12}L^{12})\epsilon(t). \tag{48}$$

This model type is often called the *airline model* by researchers who find it as a model for their own data. The airline model takes first and twelfth differences to transform a series to a stationary time series, which is then modeled as a multiplicative moving average. Experience indicates that when twelfth differencing is applied, one does not need and should not apply first differencing because it will destroy and hide any long-term cycles, such as the possible sunspot cycle in air polution time series.

The aim here is not to criticize the validity of the airline model for the airline data on which it was first developed. Rather the aim is to show how one would derive it using the approach described above.

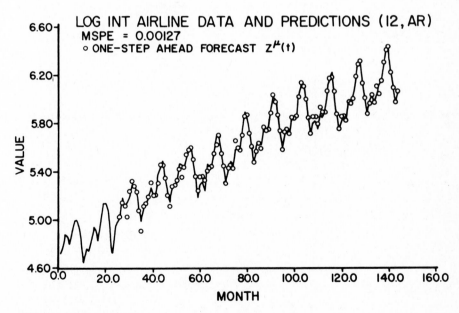

Figure 1. Graph of log airline time series $Z(t)$ and one-step-ahead forecasts $Z^\mu(t)$, using the model $\nabla_{12}Z(t)$ is an AR(13).

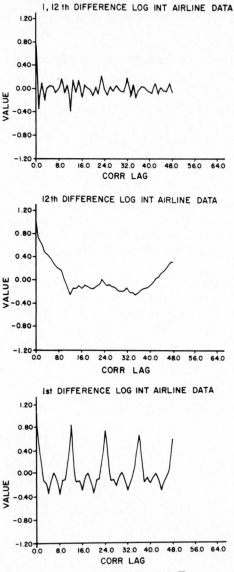

Figure 2. Correlation functions of $\nabla_1\nabla_{12}Z(t)$, $\nabla_1 Z(t)$, and $\nabla_{12}Z(t)$.

The parameters of the airline model for the airline data were estimated by Box and Jenkins to be $\theta_1 = 0.4$, $\theta_{12} = 0.6$, $\sigma_\epsilon^2 = 0.0013$. The series length is $T = 144$. The model fitted to the airline data can be written in the notation developed here are

$$D_1(0.4)D_{12}(0.6)Z(t) = \epsilon(t), \qquad \sigma_\epsilon^2 = 0.0013. \tag{49}$$

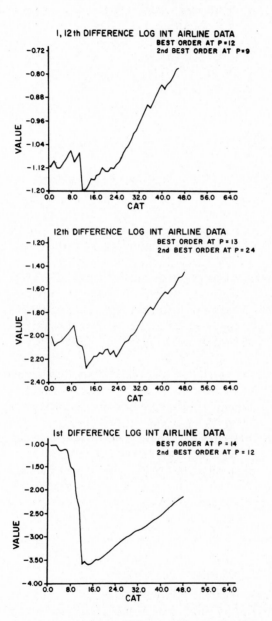

Figure 3. Graph of CAT for $\nabla_1 \nabla_{12} Z(t)$, $\nabla_1 Z(t)$, and $\nabla_{12} Z(t)$.

To determine suitable transformations to change from a nonstationary time series Z to a stationary time series $\tilde{Z}$, one examines a best approximating autoregressive scheme whose order $\hat{m}$ is determined by CAT and whose parsimonious form is determined by subset autoregression.

One finds that the beast approximating autoregressive scheme to $Z(t)$ with order $\hat{m}$ determined by CAT has $\hat{m} = 13$, with coefficients

$$\begin{array}{ll} \alpha_1 = -1.00 & \alpha_8 = 0.08 \\ \alpha_2 = 0.09 & \alpha_9 = -0.11 \\ \alpha_3 = -0.03 & \alpha_{10} = 0.02 \\ \alpha_4 = 0.03 & \alpha_{11} = 0.07 \\ \alpha_5 = -0.02 & \alpha_{12} = -0.45 \\ \alpha_6 = 1.00 & \alpha_{13} = 0.48 \\ \alpha_7 = 0.02 & \end{array}$$

The normalized variance is 0.06; it just about equals the threshold $8/T$ below which we consider a residual indicates predictability and nonstationarity. Here $T = 131$ for the residual series, and $8/T = 0.06$. Having determined $\hat{m}$, one then uses subset autoregression to determine a more parsimonious AR scheme of order $\hat{m}$ that includes only autoregressive coefficients significantly different from zero. In the present case, one would find only lag 1 significant with coefficient 0.95; therefore as a $\tilde{Z}$ series representing a transformation of Z from nonstationarity to stationarity one might choose first differences: $\tilde{Z}(t) = Z(t) - Z(t-1)$, which has residual variance 0.01.

However experience shows that when $\hat{m}$ is greater than a natural period λ, it is preferable to take λth differences. Here $\hat{m} = 13$ and $\lambda = 12$, so twelfth differences are taken: $\tilde{Z}(t) = Z(t) - Z(t-12)$, which has residual variances 0.0038. To find the innovation series $Z^v(t)$ of $Z(\,\cdot\,)$, the innovation series $\tilde{Z}^v(\,\cdot\,)$ of $\tilde{Z}(\,\cdot\,)$ is found by fitting to $\tilde{Z}(\,\cdot\,)$ an autoregressive scheme whose order is now denoted by $\tilde{m}\hat{}$. One obtains $\tilde{m}\hat{} = 13$ by using CAT, with residual variance 0.00127. A comparable variance of 0.00134 is obtained by Box and Jenkins. Using subset autoregression on $\tilde{Z}$, one discovers lag 1, 12, and 13 have significant coefficients; therefore the residuals, with residual variance 0.0015, are formed as

$$\tilde{Z}^v(t) = \tilde{Z}(t) - 0.74\,\tilde{Z}(t-1) + 0.38\,\tilde{Z}(t-12) - 0.31\,\tilde{Z}(t-13)$$

$$\doteq (I - 0.74\,L)(I + 0.38\,L^{12})\tilde{Z}(t). \tag{50}$$

The model obtained by fitting a parsimonious autoregressive scheme to twelfth differences is

$$(I - 0.74\,L)(I + 0.38\,L^{12})(I - L^{12})Z(t) = \epsilon(t). \tag{51}$$

It can be written approximately

$$[(I - L)/(I - 0.26\,L)][(I - L^{12})/(I - 0.38\,L^{12})]\,Z(t) = \epsilon(t), \qquad (52)$$

which is similar to the model found by Box and Jenkins. The preferred notation is

$$D_1(0.26)\,D_{12}(0.38)\,Z(t) = \epsilon(t). \qquad (53)$$

It seems to be true that not all monthly airline time series obey the airline model (see Montgomery and Johnson [4, p. 235]); with the approach shown here, a monthly airline time series can be optimally forecast by taking twelfth differences to transform it into a stationary time series, which is then modeled by an AR(13) scheme.

The advantage of pursuing further the approach described in this paper is that the identification process currently used in ARIMA modeling, which is based on visual inspection of autocorrelation and partial autocorrelation functions (see Makridakis [2]), can be replaced by objective criteria based on estimating the transfer function in the frequency domain of the infinite autoregressive whitening filter.

As asserted earlier, the ideal whitening filter transforming a nonstationary time series $Y(\cdot)$ to its innovations $Y^v(\cdot)$ is unique, but its decompositions for purposes of interpretation are not unique. In practice, one may appear to be able to identify several different approximate whitening filters; additional experience in case studies is required to determine how to measure differences and equivalences of whitening filters.

References

[1] G.E.P. Box and G.M. Jenkins, Time Series Analysis: Forecasting and Control (Holden Day, San Francisco, 1070).

[2] S. Makridakis, A survey of time series, International Statistical Review 44 (1976) 29–70.

[3] J. McClave, Subset autoregression, Technometrics 17 (1975) 213–220.

[4] D.C. Montgomery and L.A. Johnson, Forecasting and Time Series Analysis (McGraw-Hill, New York, 1976).

[5] E. Parzen, Some recent advances in time series modeling IEEE Transcations on automatic control. AC-19 (1974) 723–730.

[6] E. Parzen, Some solutions to the time series modeling and prediction problem, in: D. Owen, ed., The Search for Oil (Marcel Dekker, New York, 1975, 1–16).

[7] E. Parzen, Multiple time series: Determining the order of approximating autoregressive schemes, in: ed. P. Krishnaiah, Multivariate Analysis–IV (North-Holland, Amsterdam, 1977) 283–295.

[8] G. Wahba, A survey of some smoothing problems and the method of generalized cross-validation for solving them, in: P. Krishnaiah, ed., Symposium on Applications of Statistics (North-Holland, Amsterdam, 1977), 507–523.

TIMS Studies in the Management Sciences 12 (1979) 167–187

AN ARIMA-BASED METHODOLOGY FOR FORECASTING IN A MULTI-ITEM ENVIRONMENT

Bert M. STEECE *

University of Oregon

and

Steven D. WOOD

Arizona State University

The objective of this study is to develop a methodology for predicting individual item demand for classified inventory. As an alternative to orthodox methodology, the authors suggest 1) expressing individual item demand as a fraction of the contemporaneous aggregate classification demand, 2) developing a sophisticated (ARIMA) time-series model for aggregate classification demand, 3) modeling each fractional series with simple smoothing models, and 4) generating individual item demand forecasts by multiplying the aggregate and fractional demand forecasts. To minimize forecast error costs, reductions generated by the product formulation are adjusted through asymmetric error cost functions. Each adjusted prediction is expressed as a fractile of the conditional distribution for the contemporaneous product of the two series characterized by ARIMA models. An actual hospital pharmacy inventory problem is used to demonstrate the methodology.

1. Introduction

This paper presents a forecasting methodology for a multi-item inventory system that achieves efficiency through classifying items into meaningful and predictable aggregates. An actual hospital pharmacy inventory problem is used to demonstrate the methodology.

An orthodox approach for predicting demand in a multi-item inventory system develops a separate forecasting model for each item. The exponential smoothing model [9] is the most frequently employed for predicting demand in such a system. If more accurate forecasts are desired, more complex forecasting models can be used. However, when the number of items in the system is large, the forecast error reduction gained from more complex models may not justify the additional costs of analysis, maintenance, and computation.

A forecasting methodology that substantially reduces the forecast errors and

* All correspondence should be directed to: Professor Bert M. Steece, College of Business Administration, University of Oregon Eugene, Oregon 97403.

requires but one complex forecasting model offers a desirable alternative to this orthodox approach. With the methodology presented here, items are classified into meaningful and predictable aggregates. The idea of classifying items for the purpose of reducing the magnitude of an inventory forecasting problem is not original. For example, Dickie [6] proposes a scheme in which items are classified with respect to cost. Essentially, Dickie's methodology translates Pareto's law [11] into a relevant characterization of a multi-item inventory system. Other common schemes include classifying by item characteristic and by customer characteristic. However, for the purpose of forecasting demand when there are many items, classifying items into predictable aggregates appears to be most appropriate.

This methodology requires: 1) developing an accurate and potentially complex forecasting model of the aggregate demand series, 2) deriving a fractional series for each item by dividing each item demand series by the contemporaneous aggregate demand series, 3) modeling each fractional series with a simple, perhaps adaptive, exponential smoothing model, and 4) generating each item forecast by combining the contemporaneous aggregate demand forecast and the fractional demand forecast. Since a linear asymmetric cost function frequently approximates the disutilities of over- and under-forecasting item demand, an expression that minimizes the expected cost associated with forecast errors is derived. This expression requires the fractiles of the conditional distribution of the contemporaneous product of the two time series — that is, the distribution of the product of two noncentral Gaussian random variables. Mellin transforms are used to numerically derive this conditional distribution. To the knowledge of the authors, this numerical derivation of the conditional distribution with Mellin transforms is unique.

The success of the methodology depends, of course, upon the successful characterization of the aggregate and fractional demand, the continuance of previously identified demand patterns, and the degree of correlation between the aggregate and fractional demand series. As the correlation increases, the fractional demand series stabilizes at a particular fractional level. Therefore, the fractional demand series is amenable to simple smoothing models. Furthermore, the correlation between the aggregate and fractional demand series tends toward zero. That justifies excluding the covariance term in the prediction equations and simplifies the evaluation of the conditional distribution of the contemporaneous product of the two series. An overview of the model structure will give the reader a clear perspective from which to view this methodology.

2. Time-series model structure

Although the methodology is relevant to many time-series structures, the integrated autoregressive-moving average (ARIMA) models of Box and Jenkins [3] are used throughout this presentation. The general form of the ARIMA structure is

$$\phi_p(B)\phi_P'(B^s)(1-B)^d(1-B^s)^{d'} Z_t = \theta_0 + \theta_q(B)\theta_Q'(B^s)a_t, \tag{1}$$

where

$$B = \text{backshift operator} \quad (BZ_t = Z_{t-1});$$

$$\phi_p(B) = \text{regular autoregressive parameters}$$

$$(1 - \phi_1 B - \phi_2 B^2 - \ldots - \phi_p B^p);$$

$$\phi_P'(B^s) = \text{seasonal autoregressive parameters}$$

$$(1 - \phi_1' B^s - \phi_2' B^{2s} - \ldots - \phi_P' B^{Ps});$$

$$(1 - B)^d = \text{difference term of order d};$$

$$(1 - B^s)^{d'} = \text{seasonal difference term of order d'};$$

$$\theta_0 = \text{deterministic trend constant};$$

$$\theta_q(B) = \text{regular moving average term}$$

$$(1 - \theta_1 B - \theta_2 B^2 - \ldots - \theta_q B^q);$$

$$\theta_Q'(B^s) = \text{seasonal moving average terms}$$

$$(1 - \theta_1' B^s - \theta_2' B^{2s} - \ldots - \theta_Q' B^{Qs});$$

$$a_t = \text{independent random variables distributed as } N(0, \sigma_a^2);$$

$$Z_t = \text{the value of the series at time } t.$$

Developing an accurate but parsimonious ARIMA model of this general form requires a three-stage iterative process: 1) model subclass identification, 2) parameter estimation, and 3) diagonistic checking [3, 17–20].

Within this framework and with the history of the series to time t, the conditional distribution of Z_{t+l} — the value of the series at time $t + l$ — is Gaussian with mean $\hat{Z}_t(l)$ and variance

$$(1 + \sum_{j=1}^{l-1} \psi_j^2) \sigma_a^2,$$

where $\hat{Z}_t(l)$ is the minimum mean square error forecast of Z_{t+l}, and the ψ_j values are weights applied to current and previous a_t's. The ψ_j values are calculated by equating powers of B from the general model structure $\phi_p(B)\phi_P'(B^s)(1 - B)^{d}$-$(1 - B^s)^{d'}\psi(B) = \theta_q(B)\theta_Q'(B^s)$ [3, 132]. The variance σ_a^2 is usually estimated from the residual variance of the fitted model, S_a^2.

3. The conditional expectation, variance, and conditional distribution of the product of two separately attained time series

The methodology requires developing a notational framework for the fractional and aggregate demand series. One can define Z_{1t} as a Gaussian random variable denoting the value of the fractional series at time t and Z_{2t} as a Gaussian random variable denoting the value of the aggregate demand series at time t. It is assumed that the random variables Z_{it} ($i = 1$, 2) form a jointly stationary Gaussian series, and Z_{it+l} ($i = 1$, 2) is defined as the value at time $(t + l)$ of Z_{it}. Given the history of the series to time t, H_{it}, the conditional distribution of Z_{it+l} ($i = 1$, 2) is Gaussian with mean $\hat{Z}_{it}(l)$ and variance

$$(1 + \sum_{j=1}^{l-1} \psi_{ij}^2)\, \sigma_{a_i}^2,$$

where the ARIMA structure is used.

Similarly, a notational framework is developed for the individual item demand series generated by multiplying the fractional and aggregate demand series. One can define X_t as a random variable denoting the value of the individual item demand series at time t, and it is assumed that X_t forms a stationary series. Then X_{t+l} is defined as the value at time $(t + l)$ of X_t.

Next, the conditional expectation and variance of X_{t+l} and the conditional distribution of X_{t+l} can be derived. The latter is then employed to derive a forecast that minimizes the expected cost of forecast errors when a linear asymmetric error cost function is appropriate.

3.1. The conditional expectation and variance

The conditional expectation of X_{t+l} is

$$E(X_{t+l}|H_{1t}, H_{2t}) = E(Z_{1t+l}|H_{1t})E(Z_{2t+l}|H_{2t})$$

$$+ C(Z_{1t+l}, Z_{2t+l}|H_{1t}, H_{2t}), \qquad (2)$$

where $C(Z_{1t+l}, Z_{2t+l}|H_{1t}, H_{2t})$ is the partial covariance. Alternatively, one can express the expectation as

$$E(X_{t+l}|H_{1t}, H_{2t}) = \hat{Z}_{1t}(l)\hat{Z}_{2t}(l) + C(Z_{1t+l}, Z_{2t+l}|H_{1t}, H_{2t}). \qquad (3)$$

A result from Bohrnstedt and Goldberger [2] is used to obtain the conditional variance of X_{t+l},

$$
\begin{aligned}
V(X_{t+l}|H_{1t}, H_{2t}) = {}& \hat{Z}_{1t}^2(l)\, V(Z_{2t+l}|H_{2t}) + \hat{Z}_{2t}^2(l)\, V(Z_{1t+l}|H_{1t}) \\
& + 2\hat{Z}_{1t}^2(l)\, \hat{Z}_{2t}(l)\, C(Z_{1+l}, Z_{2t+l}|H_{1t}, H_{2t}) \\
& + V(Z_{1t+l}|H_{1t})\, V(Z_{2t+l}|H_{2t}) + C^2(Z_{1t+l}, Z_{2t+l}|H_{1t}, H_{2t}).
\end{aligned}
$$

(4)

If one assumes that Z_{1t+l} and Z_{2t+l} are not correlated (conditionally independent) then equation (3) reduces to

$$
\dot{E}(X_{t+l}|H_{1t}, H_{2t}) = \hat{Z}_{1t}(l)\hat{Z}_{1t}(l)\hat{Z}_{2t}(l),
$$

(5)

and equation (4) reduces to

$$
\begin{aligned}
V(X_{t+l}|H_{1t}, H_{2t}) = {}& \hat{Z}_{1t}^2(l)\, V(Z_{2t+l}|H_{2t}) + \hat{Z}_{2t}^2(l)\, V(Z_{1t+l}|H_{1t}) \\
& + V(Z_{1t+l}|H_{1t})\, V(Z_{2t+l}|H_{2t}),
\end{aligned}
$$

(6)

since the covariance terms are zero.

Employing the ARIMA structure, one can express the conditional variance of X_{t+l} as

$$
\begin{aligned}
V(X_{t+l}|H_{1t}, H_{2t}) = {}& \hat{Z}_{1t}^2(l)\,(1 + \sum_{j=1}^{l-1} \psi_{2j}^2)\, \sigma_{a_2}^2 + \hat{Z}_{2t}^2(l)(1 + \sum_{j=1}^{l-1} \psi_{1j}^2)\, \sigma_{a_1}^2 \\
& + (1 + \sum_{j=1}^{l-1} \psi_{1j}^2)\, \sigma_{a_1}^2 (1 + \sum_{j=1}^{l-1} \psi_{2j}^2)\, \sigma_{a_2}^2.
\end{aligned}
$$

(7)

Since $\sigma_{a_1}^2$, $\sigma_{a_2}^2$ and ψ_{ij} in equation (7) are typically not known, these parameters must be estimated with the residual variances, $S_{a_1}^2$ and $S_{a_2}^2$, and estimated weights $\hat{\psi}_{ij}$. By substituting $S_{a_1}^2$, and $S_{a_2}^2$ and estimated weight $\hat{\psi}_{ij}$, into equation (7), one obtains the estimated conditional variance of X_{t+l},

$$
\begin{aligned}
S^2(X_{t+l}|H_{1t}, H_{2t}) = {}& \hat{Z}_{1t}^2(l)(1 + \sum_{j=1}^{l-1} \hat{\psi}_{2j}^2)\, S_{a_2}^2 + \hat{Z}_{2t}^2(l)(1 + \sum_{j=1}^{l-1} \hat{\psi}_{1j}^2)\, S_{a_1}^2 \\
& + (1 + \sum_{j=1}^{l-1} \hat{\psi}_{1j}^2)\, S_{a_1}^2 (1 + \sum_{j=1}^{l-1} \hat{\psi}_{2j}^2)\, S_{a_2}^2.
\end{aligned}
$$

(8)

3.2. The conditional distribution of X_{t+l}

The methodology also requires the fractiles of the conditional distribution of X_{t+l}. The assumption that the aggregate and fractional series are conditionally independent simplifies the calculation of the fractiles, and the conditional distribution of X_{t+l} is the product of two independent noncentral Gaussian random variables. The parameters of this distribution are ξ_1 and ξ_2, the reciprocals of the coefficients of variation for the two random variables. Although Craig [5] derives an expression for the distribution function of X_{t+l}, this expression is not computationally tractable. However, if X_{t+l} is standardized with respect to the mean and variance as

$$W = \frac{X_{t+l} - E(X_{t+l}|H_{1t}, H_{2t})}{\sqrt{\{V(X_{t+l}|H_{1t}, H_{2t})\}}}, \qquad (9)$$

Aroian [1] demonstrates that W is asymptotically Gaussian with mean zero and variance one as $[\max(\xi_1, \xi_2)]$ becomes large. Unfortunately the literature does not answer the question of how large $[\max(\xi_1, \xi_2)]$ should be before a Gaussian approximation is appropriate.

To address this question, one can employ the Mellin transform to numerically

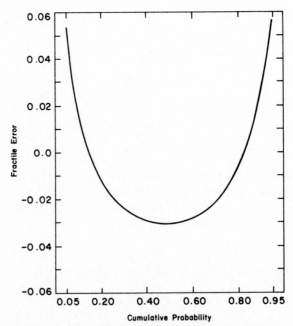

Figure 1. Fractile error resulting from a Gaussian approximation for $W(\xi_1 = \xi_2 = 10)$.

Table 1
Fractiles of the distribution for W

$\alpha = 0.05$

ξ_1	ξ_2						
	0.0	2.0	4.0	6.0	8.0	10.0	12.0
0.0	−1.595 (−1.262)	−1.650	−1.642	−1.641	−1.642	−1.643	−1.644
2.0	(−1.261)	−1.310 (−1.258)	−1.470	−1.554	−1.577	−1.599	−1.620
4.0	(−1.261)	(−1.256)	−1.487 (−1.251)	−1.529	−1.555	−1.579	−1.602
6.0	(−1.260)	(−1.253)	(−1.247)	−1.541 (−1.240)	−1.558	−1.576	−1.592
8.0	(−1.259)	(−1.252)	(−1.243)	(−1.232)	−1.570 (−1.216)	−1.582	−1.593
10.0	(−1.267)	(−1.258)	(−1.248)	(−1.238)	(−1.191)	−1.587 (−1.124)	−1.593
12.0	(−1.276)	(−1.271)	(−1.266)	(−1.260)	(−1.239)	(−1.176)	−1.594 (−1.034)

$\alpha = 0.10$

ξ_1	12.0	10.0	8.0	6.0	4.0	2.0	0.0

ξ_2	12.0	10.0	8.0	6.0	4.0	2.0	0.0

Table 1 (continued)

$\alpha = 0.20$

ξ_1 \ ξ_2	0.0	2.0	4.0	6.0	8.0	10.0	12.0
0.0	−0.517 (−0.544)	−0.680	−0.786	−0.815	−0.821	−0.828	−0.834
2.0	(−0.544)	−0.848 (−0.546)	−0.838	−0.837	−0.837	−0.837	−0.838
4.0	(−0.544)	(−0.548)	−0.857 (−0.553)	−0.854	−0.851	−0.848	−0.845
6.0	(−0.544)	(−0.550)	(−0.557)	−0.856 (−0.565)	−0.853	−0.851	−0.848
8.0	(−0.543)	(−0.548)	(−0.557)	(−0.566)	−0.852 (−0.581)	−0.853	−0.849
10.0	(−0.548)	(−0.537)	(−0.543)	(−0.549)	(−0.571)	−0.852 (−0.613)	−0.850
12.0	(−0.530)	(−0.515)	(−0.510)	(−0.505)	(−0.480)	(−0.377)	−0.850 (−0.250)

$\alpha = 0.30$

ξ_1	ξ_2
12.0	0.0
10.0	2.0
8.0	4.0
6.0	6.0
4.0	8.0
2.0	10.0
0.0	12.0

$\alpha = 0.40$

ξ_1 \ ξ_2	0.0	2.0	4.0	6.0	8.0	10.0	12.0
0.0	-0.089 (-0.029)	-0.158	-0.228	-0.242	-0.245	-0.247	-0.250
2.0	(-0.030)	-0.387 (-0.031)	-0.328	-0.279	-0.274	-0.268	-0.263
4.0	(-0.030)	(-0.031)	-0.331 (-0.033)	-0.310	-0.297	-0.285	-0.273
6.0	(-0.030)	(-0.324)	(-0.035)	-0.306 (-0.038)	-0.297	-0.288	-0.280
8.0	(-0.024)	(-0.363)	(-0.049)	(-0.063)	-0.291 (-0.085)	-0.286	-0.280
10.0	(-0.014)	(-0.025)	(-0.036)	(-0.048)	(-0.087)	-0.283 (-0.154)	-0.280
12.0	(-0.000)	(-0.000)	(-0.000)	(-0.000)	(-0.000)	(-0.000)	-0.279 (-0.000)

$\alpha = 0.50$

ξ_1 \ ξ_2	0.0	2.0	4.0	6.0	8.0	10.0	12.0
12.0	0.0						

Table 1 (continued)

α = 0.60

ξ_1	ξ_2 0.0	2.0	4.0	6.0	8.0	10.0	12.0	ξ_2
0.0	0.089 (0.503)	0.158	0.228	0.242	0.245	0.247	0.250	
2.0	(0.503)	0.099 (0.500)	0.164	0.203	0.214	0.226	0.238	12.0
4.0	(0.503)	(0.498)	0.171 (0.493)	0.192	0.203	0.214	0.225	10.0
6.0	(0.502)	(0.495)	(0.488)	0.198 (0.481)	0.207	0.216	0.224	8.0
8.0	(0.502)	(0.495)	(0.488)	(0.474)	0.213 (0.457)	0.219	0.225	6.0
10.0	(0.495)	(0.488)	(0.481)	(0.479)	(0.447)	0.222 (0.393)	0.225	4.0
12.0	(0.510)	(0.500)	(0.490)	(0.505)	(0.480)	(0.377)	0.225 (0.250)	2.0

α = 0.70

ξ_2	12.0	10.0	8.0	6.0	4.0	2.0	0.0	ξ

α = 0.80

ξ₁ \ ξ₂	0.0	2.0	4.0	6.0	8.0	10.0	12.0
0.0	0.517 (1.299)	0.680	0.786	0.815	0.821	0.828	0.834
2.0	(1.299)	0.767 (1.300)	0.798	0.813	0.819	0.825	0.831
4.0	(1.299)	(1.302)	0.810 (1.305)	0.817	0.821	0.826	0.830
6.0	(1.299)	(1.303)	(1.309)	0.822 (1.314)	0.825	0.827	0.830
8.0	(1.298)	(1.303)	(1.307)	(1.315)	0.827 (1.326)	0.829	0.831
10.0	(1.293)	(1.300)	(1.294)	(1.299)	(1.317)	0.830 (1.341)	0.832
12.0	(1.285)	(1.289)	(1.266)	(1.260)	(1.239)	(1.176)	0.833 (1.034)
	(1.276)	(1.271)					

α = 0.90

ξ₁ \ ξ₂	0.0	2.0	4.0	6.0	8.0	10.0	12.0

Table 1 (continued)

α = 0.95

ξ₁ \ ξ₂	0.0	2.0	4.0	6.0	8.0	10.0	12.0
0.0	1.595	1.650	1.642	1.641	1.642	1.643	1.644
2.0	–	1.863	1.776	1.719	1.701	1.683	1.666
4.0	–	–	1.778	1.745	1.724	1.703	1.684
6.0	–	–	–	1.738	1.723	1.709	1.694
8.0	–	–	–	–	1.713	1.703	1.694
10.0	–	–	–	–	–	1.699	1.693
12.0	–	–	–	–	–	–	1.692

Note: Values shown in parentheses correspond to the fractiles given beneath the table.

evaluate the distribution of W. The reader who is not conversant with Mellin transforms should consult Epstein and Springer [10] for further information. Table 1 reports the fractiles for W. Clearly, as $[\max(\xi_1, \xi_2)]$ becomes large, the fractiles of W approach the fractiles of the standard Gaussian distribution. Fig. 1 reflects the fractile errors for a Gaussian approximation when $\xi_1 = \xi_2 = 10$. In the authors' opinion, the Gaussian approximation is usually appropriate for general forecasting problems.

4. The optimal forecast with a linear asymmetric cost function

If a linear asymmetric error cost function appropriately reflects the costs of over- and under-forecasting X_{t+l}, a result from Granger [8] can be used to express the optimal forecast of X_{t+l} by the fractile, α_l, of the conditional distribution of X_{t+l}. Thus,

$$F(\alpha_l) = k_u/(k_u + k_o), \tag{10}$$

where k_o is the cost per unit of an over-forecast and k_u is the cost per unit of an under-forecast. Since the conditional distribution of X_{t+l} can be approximated with a Gaussian distribution, the optimal forecast is

$$\alpha_l = \hat{X}_t^*(l) = E(X_{t+l}|H_{1t}, H_{2t}) + c_l\sqrt{\{V(X_{t+l}|H_{1t}, H_{2t})\}}, \tag{11}$$

where c_l is the appropriate fractile of the standard Gaussian distribution.

5. An application

An actually observed hospital pharmacy inventory problem will demonstrate the practicality of the methodology. The pharmacy manager wishes to predict demand for 810 drug items that are particularly important to the operation of the pharmacy. Since these items are classified into pharmacological categories, there is a natural framework for predictable aggregates. Typical categories include antibiotics, antiinflammatories, antihypertensives, analgesics, and antihistamines.

The prediction of demand for three types of antihistamines — Dimetapp, Chlortrimetron, and Ornade Spansule — will illustrate the use of the methodology. Observations are taken weekly to reflect aggregate demand for antihistamines and demand for each of these three types. It should be emphasized that these three drugs do not constitute the entire set of antihistamines available in the pharmacy. Furthermore, the methodology does not require that all subaggregate elements be involved.

First, a fractional demand series is created for each of the three antihistamines.

Since the empirical work shows that each fractional series is appropriately and satisfactorily characterized by uncomplicated forecasting models, each fractional series can be characterized by a simple exponential smoothing model. Next, the aggregate demand series for antihistamines is characterized by an appropriate ARIMA model. Then forecasts for each of the three antihistamines are generated by combining the aggregate and fractional forecasts.

5.1. The data investigated

In this application, 132 consecutive weekly observations of aggregate demand for antihistamines and item demand for Dimetapp, Chlortrimetron, and Ornade Spansule are used. These observations for the first two years are used to establish parameters for 1) the ARIMA model of aggregate demand for antihistamines and 2) the first-order exponential smoothing models for the three fractional series. The last 28 observations are used to evaluate the methodology.

5.2. Decision regarding the covariance terms

To determine if the aggregate and fractional demand series are conditionally independent, one calculates the zero-lag cross-correlation coefficient and performs a t-test to determine if the coefficient is significantly different from zero. The zero-lag cross-correlation coefficient is appropriate because the two series are generated by contemporaneous time series. The results are reported in table 2. They show no significant correlation between the series, which indicates that the series are conditionally independent and that the covariance terms can be excluded.

5.3. Linear asymmetric error cost function

The cost structure for over- and under-forecasting antihistamine demand can be approximated with a linear symmetric cost function. For under-forecasting demand the costs are 1) the loss of potential revenue, 2) the loss of physician and outpatient goodwill, and 3) the cost of unscheduled orders. The costs for over-forecasting demand are holding costs, which are apportioned uniformly among the various pharmaceutical items maintained in inventory.

Table 2
Zero-lag cross-correlation between aggregate antihistamine demand and fractional demand.

Fractional series	Zero-lag cross-correlation	t-Statistic
Dimetapp	0.031	0.313
Chlortrimetron	0.042	0.424
Ornade Spansule	0.044	0.444

The relevant per unit costs for over- and under-forecasting antihistamine demand are reported in table 3. The judgmental estimates of the hospital administration are used to measure the cost of the loss of physician and outpatient goodwill. The other reported costs reflect historical accounting data. Although k_u and k_o are here developed from an aggregation of the cost elements for over- and under-forecasting demand, clearly, direct estimates of the ratio k_u/k_o, which might be more easily obtained from practitioners, are equally applicable to the methodology.

5.4. Model statistics

To develop an accurate but parsimonious model for the aggregate demand series, the three-stage iterative procedure of Box and Jenkins [3, 17–20] is used. This procedure gives the following model for aggregate antihistamine demand:

$$(1 - B)(1 - \hat{\phi}_1 B)Z_t = (1 - \theta_1 B - \theta_2 B^2) \quad (1 - \theta'_{52}B^{52})a_t, \qquad (12)$$

where $\hat{\phi} = 0.64, \hat{\theta}_1 = 0.42$, $\hat{\theta}_2 = 0.27$ and $\hat{\theta}'_{52} = 0.26$. The estimated residual standard error for aggregate demand, S_a is 64.738. The mean value for the aggregate demand series over the model-fitting horizon is 6670.

For the three fractional demand series, one obtains the following first-order exponential smoothing model — that is, IMA (0, 1, 1):

$$(1 - B)Z_t = (1 - \hat{\theta}_1 B)a_t, \qquad (13)$$

where $\hat{\theta}_1 = 0.73$ for the Dimetapp series, $\hat{\theta}_1 = 0.59$ for the Chlortrimetron series, and $\hat{\theta}_1 = 0.54$ for the Ornade Spansule series. The estimated residual standard errors, S_a, are 0.037, 0.019, and 0.017 respectively. The mean values for the three series over the fitting horizon are 0.258, 0.168, and 0.098 respectively.

Employing the estimated residual standard errors and $\hat{\psi}_j$ values yields the estimated standard errors of the forecasts as reported in table 4.

Table 3
The costs per unit associated with over- and under-forecasting antihistamine demand.

Cost	Dimetapp	Chlortrimetron	Ornade Spansule
Revenue loss	0.039	0.034	0.049
Goodwill loss	0.008	0.008	0.008
Unscheduled order	0.010	0.010	0.010
k_u	0.057	0.052	0.067
k_0	0.014	0.014	0.014

Table 4
Estimated standard errors for various forecast lead times.

Model	Lead time			
	1	2	3	4
Aggregate demand	64.738	66.287	68.702	69.671
Fractional demand				
Dimetapp	0.037	0.038	0.040	0.041
Chlortrimetron	0.019	0.021	0.022	0.023
Ornade Spansule	0.017	0.019	0.021	0.023

5.5. The forecast model

Since the forecast for a particular antihistamine is the product of aggregate anti-histamine demand forecast and the corresponding fractional demand forecast, equation (3) is used, and the forecast is expressed as

$$\hat{D}_{it}(l) = \hat{T}_t(l)\,\widehat{DF}_{it}(l) + \hat{C}(T_{t+l}, DF_{it+l}|H_{1t}, H_{2t}), \tag{14}$$

where $\hat{D}_{it}(l)$ is the conditional forecast for drug i at time t for l periods ahead; $\hat{T}_t(l)$ is the conditional forecast for aggregate antihistamine demand for the same time frame; $\widehat{DF}_{it}(l)$ is the conditional forecast for the fractional series for item i for the same time frame, and $\hat{C}(T_{t+l}, DF_{it+l})$ is the estimated partial covariance between the two series. Since the results reported in table 2 indicate no significant associa-tion between the aggregate demand series and the three fractional series, one can exclude the partial covariance term from the model.

Employing equation (8) and the estimates in table 4, one gets the conditional standard errors of the forecasts for various lead times. For example, the estimated standard errors for 1- and 4-weeek forecasts for Dimetapp are

$$S(D_{1t+1}|H_{1t}, H_{2t}) = \{\hat{T}_t^2(1) \cdot (0.037)^2 + [\widehat{DF}_{1t}(1)]^2 \cdot (64.738)^2$$

$$+ (64.738)^2 \cdot (0.037)^2\}^{1/2},$$

and

$$S(D_{1t+4}|H_{1t}, H_{2t}) = \{\hat{T}_t^2(4) \cdot (0.041)^2 + [\widehat{DF}_{1t}(4)]^2 \cdot (67.022)^2$$

$$+ (67.022)^2 \cdot (0.041)^2\}^{1/2}.$$

Since the costs of forecast errors can be approximated with a linear asymmetric cost function, equation (11) is used to express the optimal forecast as

$$D_{it}^*(l) = \hat{T}_t(L)\widehat{DF}_{it}(l) + c_l S(D_{it+l}|H_{1t}, H_{2t}),$$ (15)

where c_l is the appropriate fractile of the standardized conditional distribution of
the product of the two time series. Note that the fractiles of the conditional distribution can be approximated by the fractiles of the standardized Gaussian distribution. For example, if the average cost per unit of overforecasting is $k_o = \$\,0.014$,
and the average cost per unit of under-forecasting is $k_u = \$\,0.057$; the appropriate
fractile is 0.832, and the fractile for the Gaussian approximation is 0.842.

5.6. Model evaluation

To evaluate the methodology (model 1), 1- and 4-week forecasts for the last 28
weeks were generated and compared with the observed values. These forecasts were
generated with both the symmetric [equation (14)] and asymmetric [equation
(15)] error cost formulations for the model. A 1- and 4-week forecast horizon was
chosen because this range represents the typical short-term prediction horizon for
hospital pharmacy inventories.

To assess the relative forecasting capabilities of our proposed formulation, three
alternative formulations are considered: a deseasonalized (65 period − annual) first-
order exponential smoothing model for each individual antihistamine demand series
(model 2); a deseasonalized (52 period − annual) first-order exponential smoothing
model for the aggregate antihistamine series with first-order exponential smoothing
models for each subaggregate fractional series (model 3), and intuitive forecasts of
the pharmacy manager (model 4). Model 2 is an attempt to replicate, in objective
terms, the intuitive methodology employed by the pharmacy manager. This exponential smoothing formulation is the most frequently employed model for predicting demand in a multi-item inventory system. Model 3 represents a basis for
assessing the value of the complex aggregate model formulation. Model 4 is provided
only as a basis for assessing the potential benefits of an objective formulation over a
subjective formulation. For purposes of simplifying the narrative, each formulation
is referred to as follows:

  model 1 − ARIMA model aggregate series; first-order exponential smoothing
             model each fractional series
  model 2 − deseasonalized first-order exponential smoothing model antihista-
             mine series
  model 3 − deseasonalized first-order exponential smoothing model aggregate
             series; first-order exponential smoothing model each fractional series
  model 4 − intuitive estimates

To determine the comparative forecast accuracy of the three objective model formulations, a symmetric error cost function and an asymmetric error cost function
are applied to models 1, 2, and 3.

Table 5

Forecast errors and their costs for various models.

	Model 1		Model 2		Model 3		Model 4	
	Symmetric cost	Asymmetric cost	Symmetric cost	Asymmetric cost	Symmetric cost	Asymmetric cost	Symmetric cost	Asymmetric cost
				Dimetapp				
Mean absolute error (MAE) Lead time (weeks):								
1	86	340	226	287	259	299		415
4	95	361	270	432	301	447		463
Forecast error costs ($) Lead time (weeks):								
1	–	42	–	97	–	134		211
4	–	51	–	119	–	160		241

Chlortrimetron

Mean absolute error (MAE)							
Lead time (weeks):							
1	43	116	88	173	106	185	196
4	48	131	102	189	130	199	214
Forecast error costs ($)							
Lead time (weeks):							
1	–	23	–	61	–	81	117
4	–	27	–	70	–	89	129

Ornade Spansule

Mean absolute error (MAE)							
Lead time (weeks):							
1	39	101	110	168	132	196	221
4	45	128	136	191	160	220	254
Forecast error costs ($)							
Lead time (weeks):							
1	–	20	–	69	–	82	130
4	–	25	–	86	–	104	148

The comparative forecast accuracy of the four models is reported in table 5. The mean absolute errors (MAE) are computed from the 28 comparisons of forecasts with actual data. Clearly, model 1 is superior with respect to MAE over the forecast horizon for both linear symmetric and linear asymmetric error cost functions. Furthermore, model 2 is consistently preferred to model 3 and 4. The poor relative performance of model 3 emphasizes the importance of the ARIMA model formulation for the aggregate series. The deseasonalized exponential smoothing model provides a relatively poor characterization of the aggregate series which, in turn, causes substantial forecast errors when the fractional series and aggregate series forecasts are combined.

To focus on the cost benefits of the methodology, the 28 weekly forecast errors are used to compute the total forecast error cost over the forecast horzion. Table 5 reports the total forecast error cost for the asymmetric error cost and intuitive formulations. The symmetric error cost formulation is inferior to the asymmetric formulation for all models. Clearly, the product methodology (model 1) has the lowest total forecast error costs. These costs for model 1 are less than one-half the costs for models 2, 3, and 4. This superiority in reducing total forecast error cost is due to an increased ability to characterize the data history.

With respect to the model development costs for models 1, 2, and 3, it should be emphasized that these costs are relatively insignificant. By employing the authors' interactive ARIMA model development program, the aggregate ARIMA model for model 1 is obtained in 20 minutes. The aggregate exponential smoothing model for model 3 requires approximately 5 minutes. The individual exponential smoothing models for model 2 require approximately 3 minutes per model. The fractional exponential smoothing models for models 1 and 3 require approximately 2 minutes per model. For a general comparison of the cost and effort for developing models of the type considered here, the reader should consult Chamber, Mullick, and Smith [4].

5. Conclusions

Classifying inventory items into meaningful and predictable aggregates enables a forecaster to substantially reduce error without creating a complex forecasting model for each item. Essentially, the methodology presented here for classified inventories requires but one complex model. If the costs of over- and under-forecasting item demand can be approximated with a linear asymmetric error cost function, the proposed methodology minimizes the expected forecast error cost. Otherwise, the methodology expresses a forecast as the product of the mean square error forecasts for the aggregate and fractional demand series.

The numerical results (see table 1) provide guidelines for the use of the Gaussian distribution as an approximation for the distribution of the product of two independent noncentral Gaussian random variables. These guidelines and the fractiles reported in table 1 will be useful for other problems in which the distribution of the product is relevant — for example, the Jaedicke-Robichek cost-volume-profit model.

References

[1] L.A. Aroian, The Probability function of a product of two normally distributed variables, The Annals of Mathematical Statistics 18 (1947) 265–271.

[2] G.W. Bohrnstedt and A.S. Goldberger, On the exact covariance of products of random variables, Journal of the American Statistical Association 64 (1969) 1439–1442.

[3] G.E.P. Box and G.M. Jenkins, Time series analysis: Forecasting and control (Holden-Day, San Francisco, 1970).

[4] J.C. Chambers, S.K. Mullick and D.D. Smith, How to choose the right forecasting technique, Harvard Business Review 9 (1967) 45–74.

[5] C.C. Craig, On the frequency function of xy, The Annals of Mathematical Statistics 7 (1936) 1–15.

[6] H.D. Dickie, The *abc*'s of inventory analysis, Factory Management and Maintenance 109 (1951) 92–94.

[7] B. Epstein, Some applications of the Mellin transform in statistics, The Annals of Mathematical Statistics 19 (1948) 370–379.

[8] C.W.J. Granger, Prediction with a generalized cost of error function, Operational Research Quarterly 20 (1969) 199–207.

[9] R.M. Kirby, A comparison of short and medium range statistical forecasting methods, Management Science 13 (1967) B-202–210.

[10] M.E. Springer, The algebra of random variables (Wiley, New York, 1979).

[11] A. Zellner, An introduction to Bayesian inference in econometrics (Wiley, New York, 1971).

TIMS Studies in the Management Sciences 12 (1979) 189–201
© North-Holland Publishing Company

TIME-SERIES ANALYSIS AND FORECASTING WITH AN ABSOLUTE ERROR CRITERION *

Kenneth O. COGGER

University of Kansas

This paper considers time-series analysis and forecasting using parameter estimates obtained by a minimum absolute deviation criterion. Empirically, ex-post comparisons are made between least squares and absolute deviation forecasts, based on small to moderate sample sizes and using a number of real and artificially generated time series. Such comparisons indicate that absolute deviation approaches to the estimation of ARIMA time-series models should receive further attention in practice. Since the asymptotic sampling theory of such an approach has not been developed, suggestions are made about this aspect of the problem. Finally, preliminary identification procedures, analogous to those based on autocorrelation and partial autocorrelation functions, are proposed that should help to achieve parsimonious parameterization of ARIMA models when an absolute deviation criterion is employed.

1. Introduction

Minimum absolute deviation, or MAD, regression estimators have been studied by many investigators. Charnes and his coauthors [6] first demonstrated that such estimators are easily computed with linear programming. Wagner [19], further eased computational burdens by considering the associated dual linear programming problem. These developments were followed by the important empirical study of Meyer and Glauber [13], which revealed that regression equations for investment estimated by MAD were generally superior to those estimated by least squares, or LS, when interest was focused upon ex-post forecasting accuracy. Further support for MAD is provided by the Monte Carlo studies of Blattberg and Sargent [4], Glahe and Hunt [8], and Oveson [14], which compare LS and MAD sampling properties when errors are generated by a variety of distributions. Such studies suggest that the empirical performance of MAD estimators is superior in the presence of heavy tailed distributions.

These results encourage the study of MAD in other contexts. The present paper

* This research was supported by grant No. 3298-5038, University of Kansas General Research Fund.

The author wishes to thank the referees for their helpful comments.

reports on the use of MAD in time-series analysis, using models developed by Box and Jenkins [5]. Empirical comparisons are made between LS and MAD forcasts and theoretical issues are briefly discussed.

2. MAD time-series analysis

The estimation of parameters of the general ARIMA (p, d, q) time-series model, as described in Box and Jenkins [5], generally uses a least squares algorithm. When a moving average component seems necessary, based on preliminary identification procedures, a nonlinear least squares algorithm such as that of Marquardt [12] is employed. Treatment of such models with a MAD estimation criterion uses mathematical programming algorithms. [1] In this paper attention is focused upon pure autoregressive models for reasons of brevity.

To introduce notation, let the time series of interest be described by the ARIMA $(p, 0, 0)$ model

$$X(t) = \sum_{j=1}^{p} X(t - j)\beta_j + \beta_0 + \epsilon(t); \qquad t = ..., -1, 0, 1, ..., \qquad (1)$$

where the β_j are fixed but unknown parameters and the $\epsilon(t)$ are random equation errors. [2] The MAD estimation problem is to obtain estimates for the β_j based on a sequence of observations $X(1), X(2), ..., X(T)$ such that

$$D = \sum_{t=p+1}^{T} \left| X(t) - \sum_{j} X(t - j)\beta_j - \beta_0 \right| \qquad (2)$$

is minimized. Since the results of Charnes et al. [6] are immediately applicable to this problem, the equivalent linear program

$$\text{minimize} \quad \sum_{j}(e_{t+} + e_{t-}) \qquad (3)$$

$$\text{such that} \quad \sum_{j} X(t - j)\beta_j + \beta_0 + e_{t+} - e_{t-} = X(t);$$

$$p + 1 \leqslant t \leqslant T,$$

$$\text{where} \quad e_{t+} \geqslant 0, \qquad e_t \geqslant 0$$

[1] For ARIMA (p, d, o), or autoregressive models, standard linear programming algorithms may be used. For ARIMA (o, d, q), or moving average models, nonlinear programming may be used. Alternatively, direct search procedures may be used, such as in Schlossmacher [17].

[2] It is assumed that an appropriate degree of differencing has been employed to arrive at this representation.

may be solved. From a computational viewpoint, as well as for its subsequent insight into sampling theory, the dual of (3) is of some interest. As Wagner [19] first noted, in the context of multiple regression, the dual can be expressed in the form

$$\text{maximize} \quad \sum_t X(t)\lambda_t \tag{4}$$

$$\text{such that} \quad \sum_t \lambda_t = 0,$$

$$\sum_t X(t-j)\lambda_t = 0; \qquad 1 \leqslant j \leqslant p,$$

$$\text{where} \quad -1 \leqslant \lambda_t \leqslant 1.$$

The latter problem has fewer variables than (3) and, when using bounded variable algorithms, has fewer constraints, thus it is important from a computational viewpoint. However, the correspondence between the primal (3) and dual (4) problems, which is of greater interest in the present study, is embodied in complementary slackness conditions. The theorem of complementary slackness states that in corresponding optimal solutions of the primal and dual problems, either a nonnegative primal variable will be zero or else the corresponding dual constraint will be satisfied as an equality. For the present problems (3) and (4), this implies that either $e_{t+} = 0$ or $\lambda_t = 1$ and thet $e_{t-} = 0$ or $\lambda_t = -1$. By the definitions of e_{t+} and e_{t-}, this results in λ_t being essentially the algebraic sign of the residual. [3]

Before empirical testing of models estimated from problems (3) and (4), it is interesting to note the analogies between LS and MAD estimation of model (1). For LS estimation, estimates b_j must satisfy the normal equations

$$\sum_t \left[X(t) - \sum_j X(t-j)b_j - b_0 \right] = 0, \tag{5}$$

$$\sum_t \left[X(t) - \sum_j X(t-j)b_j - b_0 \right] X(t-j) = 0; \qquad 1 \leqslant j \leqslant p.$$

Clearly, one analogy between MAD estimation and LS estimation is that with the former, weighted sums of the signs of the residuals must be zero, while with the latter, weighted sums of the residuals themselves must be zero. Another link between LS and MAD procedures is that the weighted sums in both equations (4) and (5) are, for a fixed sequence of observations, the partial derivatives of the criterion, total deviation or total squared deviation, with respect to β_0 and the β_j. [4] Such

---

[3] $e_{t+} > 0$ requires $\lambda_t = 1$, while $e_{t-} > 0$ requires $\lambda_t = -1$.
[4] In the case of MAD, these partial derivatives are not continuous, which prevents the application of calculus in a tractable manner.

analogies between MAD and LS suggest appropriate procedures for studying sampling properties and for developing preliminary identification tools for MAD, these topics are considered in later sections of this paper.

3. Empirical support for MAD

While the asymptotic sampling theory of MAD parameter estimates may be of considerable interest, such a theory is of small comfort when small to moderate sample sizes are encountered in practice. The same applies, of course, to least squares estimates. In many practical situations the forecasting performance of the estimated model is more important than the sampling behavior of the parameter estimates themselves. In this section, therefore, results on the relative forecasting performance of models estimated by LS and MAD are presented. Although of secondary concern, results for the actual parameter estimates obtained from each procedure are also tabulated, which allows minimum sample size rules to be suggested.

Seven time series are studied. Four of these series are artificially generated, based on sequences of independent normal random errors $\epsilon(t)$ in equation (1). Series I is a first-order autoregressive process with $\beta_0 = 4.5$ and $\beta_1 = -0.5$. Series II, III, and IV are second-order processes originally generated by Wold [20] and are tabulated in Anderson [1] Each of these three series is characterized by $\beta_2 = \beta_1^2$ with β_1 equal to 0.25, 0.70, and 0.90 respectively. Since Wold originally generated each series with a mean of zero, and small sample properties of the estimator of β_0 may be of interest, nonzero values of this parameter were achieved by adding 2.00 to all values of series II and III, and 3.00 to all values of series IV.

The above series, of course, are generated in such a way that least squares estimators should be asymptotically efficient. They therefore constitute a worst-case situation for the forecasting performance of MAD relative to least squares. [5] In practice, the generating mechanism of a time series cannot be safely assumed to be normal, and three additional series were studied for which normality could not be assured. These series – *B, D,* and *E* from Box and Jenkins – were chosen because of their extensive analysis by those authors, their large sample identification as autoregressive processes, and the variety of physical, industrial, and economic contexts for application they represent. [6]

It should be noted that this section is mainly concerned with relative forecasting performance of MAD and LS. In order to avoid confounding the effects of parameter estimation error upon forecast error and the effects that might arise from misspecification of the underlying model, the time series chosen for study were limited

---

[5] Asymptotically, LS estimates will result in minimum forecast error variance. Alternative estimators such as MAD will be, at best, no better.

[6] Series B was identified as ARIMA (0, 1, 1) but an ARIMA (2, 0, 0) is an entirely adequate approximation for the purposes of the present study.

Table 1
Series I. $\beta_0 = 4.5$ $\beta_1 = -0.5$

T	Criterion	S	D	P	RP	U	b_0	b_1
10	LS	1.55	1.34	−62.3	286.4	0.242	3.66	−0.266
	MAD	1.78	1.59	−82.1	422.7	0.276	2.98	0.030
15	LS	1.17	0.86	−50.3	252.8	0.197	4.22	−0.473
	MAD	1.40	1.18	−74.1	360.5	0.239	3.06	−0.047
20	LS	0.82	0.61	−20.5	235.2	0.144	4.26	−0.488
	MAD	0.89	0.72	−5.6	210.8	0.162	4.44	−0.652
25	LS	0.76	0.56	−3.5	165.3	0.132	4.12	−0.489
	MAD	0.83	0.66	3.1	158.7	0.147	4.44	−0.652
30	LS	0.71	0.52	−19.4	161.2	0.122	4.16	−0.467
	MAD	0.67	0.48	−14.0	153.4	0.119	4.09	−0.486
35	LS	0.65	0.46	−0.5	69.9	0.113	4.15	−0.480
	MAD	0.66	0.46	2.4	67.8	0.117	4.09	−0.486

to those with known structures or with structures identified in large samples.

Estimation and forecasting results are presented for six different sample sizes for each of the seven time series. Various suggestions have been made for minimum adequate sample sizes when LS estimation is employed without a priori knowledge of the form of the ARIMA model. Box and Jenkins [5, p. 33], for example, suggest a minimum of 50 observations if preliminary identification is required. In the

Table 2
Series II.
$\beta_0 = 1.63$ $\quad$ $\beta_1 = 0.25$ $\quad$ $\beta_2 = -0.0625$

T	Criterion	S	D	P	RP	U	b_0	b_1	b_2
10	LS	1.26	1.19	−83.9	340.6	0.275	3.35	0.091	−0.371
	MAD	1.46	1.39	−77.7	318.1	0.313	3.13	0.685	−0.817
15	LS	1.12	1.03	−86.2	164.6	0.277	2.63	0.073	−0.165
	MAD	1.31	1.25	−102.0	177.9	0.309	3.21	−0.131	−0.237
20	LS	0.79	0.66	−49.0	226.7	0.210	1.66	0.256	−0.025
	MAD	0.68	0.57	−28.6	178.0	0.193	1.71	0.201	−0.186
25	LS	0.68	0.52	−21.0	219.5	0.176	1.23	0.307	0.069
	MAD	0.60	0.48	−6.9	182.6	0.162	1.45	0.320	−0.183
30	LS	0.95	0.66	−4.9	126.5	0.211	1.39	0.294	0.004
	MAD	1.01	0.63	11.3	93.8	0.240	1.75	0.217	−0.220
35	LS	1.26	0.98	−47.5	691.7	0.262	1.43	0.291	−0.028
	MAD	1.32	1.05	−17.0	525.9	0.294	1.84	0.189	−0.246

Table 3
Series III.
$\beta_0 = 1.58 \qquad \beta_1 = 0.7 \qquad \beta_2 = -0.49$

T	Criterion	S	D	P	RP	U	b_0	b_1	b_2
10	LS	0.88	0.81	−63.0	266.2	0.202	2.28	0.550	−0.434
	MAD	1.10	1.02	−56.8	267.4	0.245	2.71	1.068	−1.13
15	LS	0.60	0.52	−39.9	102.6	0.167	1.61	0.546	−0.267
	MAD	0.78	0.56	23.8	89.9	0.287	−0.01	0.365	0.386
20	LS	0.62	0.52	−28.2	137.3	0.168	1.40	0.615	−0.281
	MAD	0.54	0.47	−19.9	99.0	0.151	1.86	0.530	−0.557
25	LS	0.58	0.47	−11.3	139.6	0.145	1.11	0.656	−0.225
	MAD	0.68	0.57	10.8	111.0	0.192	0.88	0.476	−0.128
30	LS	0.77	0.53	−2.0	93.6	0.168	1.30	0.631	−0.293
	MAD	0.78	0.47	10.5	76.6	0.178	1.62	0.633	−0.530
35	LS	1.03	0.78	−11.1	306.9	0.218	1.36	0.622	−0.324
	MAD	1.02	0.81	9.2	229.5	0.226	1.85	0.536	−0.563

present study, the order of the autoregressive model is known or has been determined from previous studies, which suggests that far fewer observations might be
reasonable. Since no previous studies have examined MAD in the present context,
minimum sample size guidelines were developed by employing sample sizes of $T =$
10 to $T = 35$ in increments of five. The small to moderate sample sizes considered

Table 4
Series IV.
$\beta_0 = 2.73 \qquad \beta_1 = 0.9 \qquad \beta_2 = -0.81$

T	Criterion	S	D	P	RP	U	b_0	b_1	b_2
10	LS	0.35	0.28	−2.3	40.5	0.061	2.93	0.763	−0.839
	MAD	0.57	0.39	−10.6	59.8	0.096	3.62	0.913	−1.174
15	LS	0.43	0.37	−0.4	88.7	0.080	2.49	0.727	−0.683
	MAD	0.54	0.44	0.1	109.3	0.100	2.49	0.453	−0.432
20	LS	0.48	0.40	−5.3	95.8	0.083	2.53	0.740	−0.677
	MAD	0.53	0.42	−8.4	114.1	0.093	2.24	0.595	−0.408
25	LS	0.47	0.34	−2.0	84.0	0.087	2.55	0.807	−0.762
	MAD	0.46	0.35	0.3	78.0	0.086	2.20	0.793	−0.638
30	LS	0.56	0.40	−3.3	85.4	0.100	2.54	0.767	−0.707
	MAD	0.66	0.49	−7.9	87.5	0.116	2.22	0.681	−0.508
35	LS	0.58	0.47	9.3	57.0	0.092	2.48	0.758	−0.688
	MAD	0.65	0.57	4.7	66.9	0.104	2.22	0.681	−0.508

Table 5
Series B.
$\beta_0 \approx 4.0$ $\beta_1 \approx 1.09$ $\beta_2 \approx -0.098$

T	Criterion	S	D	P	RP	U	b_0	b_1	b_2
10	LS	14.07	12.58	2.6	4.9	0.0145	220.6	1.442	−0.915
	MAD	5.34	4.35	0.3	3.7	0.0054	75.3	0.744	0.100
15	LS	5.84	4.39	−0.5	2.5	0.0060	54.0	1.214	−0.323
	MAD	6.32	5.56	−0.8	3.8	0.0065	33.3	0.836	0.100
20	LS	3.76	3.29	−0.6	1.8	0.0039	72.9	1.076	−0.225
	MAD	4.09	3.57	−0.6	1.9	0.0043	68.0	1.103	−0.241
25	LS	3.28	2.69	−0.4	1.9	0.0034	80.9	1.100	−0.266
	MAD	2.71	2.26	−0.3	1.6	0.0028	71.5	0.899	−0.047
30	LS	1.76	1.44	−0.3	0.8	0.0018	79.7	1.055	−0.220
	MAD	1.89	1.67	−0.3	0.7	0.0020	71.3	0.753	0.100
35	LS	3.59	2.23	−0.4	2.5	0.0038	79.0	1.059	−0.223
	MAD	3.49	2.19	−0.4	2.6	0.0037	59.2	0.892	−0.015

here are often encountered in practice, and although larger sample sizes were not explicitly considered, there is evidence [5, p. 400) that once stability of estimates has been achieved, as in the present study, larger sample sizes will produce only slight changes in forecasting performance measures.

Table 6
Series D.
$\beta_0 \approx 1.17$ $\beta_1 \approx 0.87$

T	Criterion [a]	S	D	P	RP	U	b_0	b_1
10	LS	0.246	0.207	1.9	8.5	0.0148	5.13	0.369
	MAD	0.268	0.240	2.3	8.2	0.0162	4.00	0.500
15	LS	0.330	0.311	3.6	3.7	0.0196	5.49	0.327
	MAD	0.301	0.280	3.2	3.7	0.0178	5.47	0.333
20	LS	0.362	0.291	2.2	13.4	0.0209	3.72	0.552
	MAD	0.356	0.287	1.9	14.0	0.0205	2.73	0.667
25	LS	0.327	0.250	0.3	14.1	0.0191	2.89	0.656
	MAD	0.361	0.240	−0.6	16.0	0.0210	0.00	1.000
30	LS	0.300	0.234	1.5	9.1	0.0175	2.85	0.663
	MAD	0.224	0.180	1.3	5.6	0.0130	0.00	1.000
35	LS	0.312	0.241	2.0	9.2	0.0177	2.80	0.667
	MAD	0.300	0.240	0.4	11.0	0.0169	0.00	1.000

[a] The appearance of identical MAD estimates for $T = 30$ and $T = 35$ reflects the fact that additional observations occasionally do not require revision of a basis in the simplex procedure.

Table 7
Series E.

$\beta_0 \approx 14.4 \qquad \beta_1 \approx 1.42 \qquad \beta_2 \approx -0.73$

T	Criterion	S	D	P	RP	U	b_0	b_1	b_2
10	LS	29.73	22.43	−14.4	351	0.196	51.3	1.223	−1.096
	MAD	45.30	33.24	−19.5	472	0.297	73.5	1.184	−1.423
15	LS	15.03	12.29	7.91	53	0.091	32.2	1.216	−0.740
	MAD	24.22	16.75	15.33	67	0.155	17.9	0.845	−0.250
20	LS	20.52	18.07	−186	683	0.214	35.8	1.276	−0.800
	MAD	21.48	17.84	−199	689	0.214	36.2	1.396	−0.839
25	LS	23.01	21.61	−212	622	0.303	34.0	1.272	−0.764
	MAD	21.67	20.28	−188	513	0.287	29.7	1.475	−0.838
30	LS	14.57	12.76	−176	1200	0.195	22.5	1.345	−0.723
	MAD	8.43	7.10	−87	703	0.127	10.7	1.224	−0.497
35	LS	15.79	15.26	[a]	[a]	0.332	19.4	1.337	−0.686
	MAD	8.75	7.89	[a]	[a]	0.212	10.2	1.227	−0.496

[a] Data are not available.

Tables 1 through 7 present LS and MAD results for each of the time series. The true generating model or the model estimated by least squares in large samples is described in each table.

As these tables show, for $T \geqslant 25$ drastic changes in the coefficient estimates do not often occur. Such stability suggests a minimum adequate sample size of $T = 25$ for both LS and MAD, when a priori knowledge of the underlying autoregressive order is available. Thus, at least for the kinds of series examined here, heuristic sample size rules for LS are reasonable for MAD as well. These tables also provide preliminary evidence of the extent of MAD sampling error in the case of series 1 through IV, since there the true coefficient values are known.

Some additional comments of practical interest can be made about estimation. The linear programming algorithm used was a simple modification of LINPRO, which is written in the BASIC language. As such, computational efficiency was quite low because compilation was required before each analysis. In spite of these deficiencies, the total cost of each MAD analysis was only about 30% higher than that of the corresponding LS analysis. The LS analyses used BMDP2R, a relatively sophisticated program that did not require compilation, being loaded in object form. [7] From the limited experience of the present study, it appears that for moderate sample sizes computational cost differentials between LS and MAD estimation are not significant.

[7] Unused options may have contributed to the low cost differential, but execution times also differed by the same magnitude.

Table 8
Artificial series.
Average relative efficiencies, MAD : LS

T	S^2	D	RP	U
10	0.63	0.80	0.86	0.80
15	0.67	0.83	0.89	0.77
20	1.09	1.02	1.15	1.00
25	0.97	0.93	1.14	0.94
30	0.92	1.01	1.15	0.93
35	0.92	0.93	1.13	0.93

The ten observations immediately following each estimation period were used in evaluating the relative forecasting performance of the LS- and MAD-estimated models. In addition, various performance measures were calculated, including standard error, S, average absolute deviation, D, average percentage error, P, range of percentage errors, RP, and Theil's U-statistic. All forecasts made were one step ahead, and used the same fitted model. This method corresponds in practice to the continued use of an estimated model for ten time periods before considering model revision because of forecast error analyses. This length of time was felt to be a reasonable choice, because it is difficult to detect unusual error behavior in shorter periods of time and because of costs associated with more frequent revisions. In practice, these considerations might lead to more or less frequent revisions. [8] The ex-post forecasting procedure described, of course, should reveal whether the optimal properties of each estimation method are indeed reflected in periods beyond those which were used to estimate the model.

Based on the previously suggested minimum sample size rule, the forecasting results should be most reliable for samples of size $T \geqslant 25$. As tables 1 through 4 show, LS usually outperforms MAD when the underlying generating mechanism is normal. LS is not universally better, however, since on some measures, such as percentage error, MAD occasionally outperforms LS. With respect to series B, D, and E, tables 5 through 7 show that LS performed relatively poorly.

Tables 8 and 9 give a clearer picture of the performance of LS and MAD. Averaging across each of series I through IV and across series B, D, and E, relative efficiencies were computed by dividing the performance measures for LS by those for MAD in tables 1 through 7. Average relative efficiencies less than unity favor LS, while those exceeding unity favor MAD. These summary measures present rather

---

[8] If each model were to be used indefinitely, the eventual mean square error might be calculated as in Cogger [7], but such a measure does not seem to be meaningful in the present context. The use of ten observations in the holdout sample is similar to Meyer and Glauber [13]. Replication across seven series and numerous sample sizes reduces the risk that the reported results may be spurious.

Table 9
Series B, D, and E.
Average relative efficiencies, MAD : LS

T	S^2	D	RP	U
10	2.74	1.48	1.04	1.42
15	0.81	0.88	0.81	0.87
20	0.93	0.98	0.98	0.98
25	1.14	1.10	1.09	1.06
30	1.73	1.32	1.47	1.26
35	1.80	1.32	[a]	1.21

[a] Data are not available.

striking features. When LS is known to be optimal, as in table 8, the relative efficiency of MAD is fairly high, commonly exceeding 0.90. On the other hand, when
the generating mechanism is unknown, as in the cases of series B, D, and E, MAD
performs much better than LS. Only for samples of size 15 and 20 did LS reflect its
optimal properties, and these sample sizes are probably too small for strong conclusions to be made. Summarizing across all series studied, forecasts based on MAD-
estimated models achieve relative efficiencies of at least 0.90 for all accuracy measures and are uniformly larger than unity when the underlying probability distribution of errors cannot be assumed normal, at least for the moderate sample sizes $T \geqslant$
25 employed in this study.

In explaining these results and in considering their generality, the sequences of
normal errors that generated series I through IV and the fluctuations that were observed in series B, D, and E were examined. [9] The results support several conclusions that are consistent with previous empirical comparisons of MAD and LS from
multiple regression models. In small samples, $T \leqslant 20$, LS was generally better than
MAD as long as outliers, extreme values, or unusual patterns did not occur with any
frequency in the observed time series. In the presence of such conditions, MAD
generally outperformed LS although in the case of normally generated series, differences were not pronounced. In larger samples, where stronger conclusions are possible, MAD had high relative efficiencies with normally generated series. However,
when extreme values in the normal variates occurred with any frequency, and
when the generating process was nonnormal, MAD was highly preferable to LS.

These results encourage the consideration of MAD for forecasting purposes.
Optimal conditions for LS are seldom demonstrable with any degree of certainty in

---

[9] Theil's U-statistic was also decomposed into mean, variance, and covariance components,
but did not contribute additional insights.

practice and, even when such conditions exist, evidence indicates that MAD performs extremely well. [10]

4. Sampling theory

The empirical results reported here encourage future study of the sampling properties of MAD time-series estimation. Although definitive results are not yet available, tentative conclusions suggest potentially fruitful directions of research.

Bassett and Koenker [3], Rosenberg and Carlson [16], and Taylor [18] have considered the sampling properties of MAD estimators in multiple regression models. These studies suggest that the large sample distribution of such estimators is approximately normal with covariance matrix $(X'X)^{-1}/4f^2(0)$, where X is the matrix of nonstochastic independent variables and $f(\cdot)$ is the error density function. Of particular interest in these studies is the lack of assumptions concerning the mean and variance of the equation errors, which may explain some of the empirical results reported with MAD estimation.

In estimating autoregressive time series such as equation (1), the relevant X matrix is stochastic, and the procedures and results of the above studies require modification. Preliminary research by the author along the lines of Mann and Wald [11] suggests that a satisfactory modification is the replacement of $X'X$ by its stochastic limit in the above expression. Future efforts along the lines the authors mentioned above have explored may also be useful. If distributional assumptions for MAD time-series estimation are less stringent than those of LS, that may partially explain the empirical results reported here, given the concern expressed in the literature about the existence of error distributions with large variances. [11]

5. Preliminary identification

The present study presumed the adequacy of the models estimated for each of seven series. In practice, the preliminary identification of such models is normally based on autocorrelations and partial autocorrelations and uses approximate tests developed by Bartlett [2] and Quennouille [19]. Although such procedures may be used even if MAD estimation is employed, alternative statistics were found during the course of the present investigation that are analogous to correlations, arise more

---

[10] Forecast performance measures used in this study are only proxies for the costs of forecasting error in managerial practice. The broad range of measures suggests, however, that MAD would perform well in general. Linear programming is also capable of handling general cost functions if they are approximated by piecewise linear functions. Alternatively, direct search procedures may be used.

[11] See Granger and Orr [9] for potential alternatives to MAD in such situations, and Mandelbrot [10] for a discussion of such distributions.

naturally in the context of MAD, and appear to be useful in preliminary identification.

In LS estimation, autocorrelations may be obtained by estimating (1) with $\beta_j = 0$ for $j \geqslant 1$, obtaining $\hat{\beta}_0$ as the sample average $\overline{X}$, and then computing and suitably normalizing $\Sigma_t e_t X(t-j)$ where $e_t = X(t) - \overline{X}$ is the estimated residual. An analogous approach in MAD is obtained by fitting (1) under identical conditions, giving $\hat{\beta}_0$ as the sample median of the $X(t)$, and computing $\Sigma_t \hat{\lambda}_t X(t-j)$ where $\hat{\lambda}_t$ is the solution to the dual (4) and, under these conditions, is the algebraic sign of the residual $X(t) - \hat{\beta}_0$. Given the distinction between LS and MAD estimation – that residuals in the former have counterparts in the signs of the residuals in the latter – $\Sigma_t e_t X(t-j)$ and $\Sigma_t \hat{\lambda}_t X(t-j)$ are quite analogous. During the course of the investigations, these two statistics produced quite similar fluctuations and results suggest that the latter statistic may be useful in identifying moving average processes.

Also in LS estimation, partial autocorrelations of lag k may be obtained by fitting equation (1) with $p = k - 1$ and then computing and suitably normalizing $\Sigma_t e_t X(t-k)$ where, again, e_t is the estimated residual. The analogy with MAD is to compute $\Sigma_t \hat{\lambda}_t X(t-k)$ under the same conditions. The latter statistic was found to exhibit fluctuations similar to those of the partial autocorrelation function for each of the seven series in the present study, and is therefore suggested as a potentially useful tool in identifying autoregressive processes.

While a definitive sampling theory has not been developed for these statistics, they may be of importance in practice, since they implicitly depend on the signs of errors rather than the errors themselves. This characteristic may offer a greater degree of protection against model misspecification when there are outliers and extreme observations.

6. Summary

The empirical results presented here suggest that time-series models estimated by a minimum absolute deviation approach will often be superior to those estimated with a least squares approach when forecasting error is of primary concern. Computationally, such an estimation procedure is not significantly more complex. Although sampling theory and preliminary identification procedures need to be further developed, several suggestions appear to offer a good starting point for future efforts. Naturally occurring statistics have been proposed for aiding in the preliminary identification of suitable time-series models when a minimum deviation approach is taken, and the form of these statistics lends additional support to the generality of the empirical results.

The present state of knowledge concerning MAD estimation in time-series analysis is similar to the situation 35 years ago for least squares estimation. Further empirical investigation seems justified by the results of the present limited study, and theoretical work along the lines of the classic study by Mann and Wald [11] would be of great importance.

References

[1] T.W. Anderson, The statistical analysis of time series and stochastic processes (Wiley, New York, 1971).

[2] M.S. Bartlett, On the theoretical specification of sampling properties of autocorrelated time series, Journal of the Royal Satistical Society B8 (1946) 27–41.

[3] G.W. Bassett and R. Koenker, Generalized quantile estimators for the linear model, paper presented at the San Francisco Meeting of the Econometric Society, 1974.

[4] R. Blattberg and T. Sargent, Regression with non-Gaussian stable disturbances: some sampling results, Econometrica 39 (1971) 501–510.

[5] G.E.P. Box and G.M. Jenkins, Time series analysis, forecasting and control (Holden-Day, San Francisco, 1970).

[6] A. Charnes, W.W. Cooper and R.O. Ferguson, Optimal estimation of executive compensation by linear programming, Management Science 1 (1955) 138–151.

[7] K.O. Cogger, Specification analysis, Journal of the American Statistical Association 68 (1973) 899–905.

[8] F.R. Glahe and J.G. Hunt, The small sample properties of simultaneous equation least absolute estimators vis à vis least squares estimators, Econometrica 38 (1970) 742–753.

[9] C.W.J. Granger and D. Orr, Infinite variance and research strategy in time series analysis, Journal of the American Statistical Association 67 (1972) 275–285.

[10] B. Mandelbrot, 1963. New methods in statistical economics, Journal of Political Economy 71 (1963) 421–440.

[11] H.B. Mann and A. Wald, On the statistical treatment of linear stochastic difference equations, Econometrica 11 (1943) 173–220.

[12] D.W. Marquardt, An algorithm for least squares estimation of non linear parameters, Journal of the Society for Industrial and Applied Mathematics 11 (1963) 431–441.

[13] J.R. Meyer and R.R. Glauber, Investment decisions, economic forecasting, and public policy (Harvard Business School Press, Cambridge, Mass., 1964).

[14] R.M. Oveson, Regression parameter estimation by minimizing the sum of absolute errors, Ph.D. dissertation, Harvard University, 1968.

[15] M.H. Quennouille, Approximate tests of correlation in time series, Journal of the Royal Statistical Society B11 (1949) 68–84.

[16] B. Rosenberg and D. Carlson, The sampling distribution of least absolute residuals regression estimates, Working Paper IP-64, Institute of Business and Economic Research, University of California, Berkeley, 1971.

[17] E.J. Schlossmacher, An iterative technique for absolute deviation curve fitting, Journal of the American Statistical Association 68 (1973) 857–859.

[18] L.D. Taylor, Estimation by minimizing the sum of absolute errors, in: P. Zerembka, ed., Frontiers in econometrics (Academic Press, New York, 1973, 169–190).

[19] H.M. Wagner, Linear programming techniques for regression analysis, Journal of the American Statistical Association 54 (1959) 206–212.

[20] H.O.A. Wold, Bibliography on time series and stochastic processes (Oliver and Boyd, Edinburgh, 1965).

TIMS Studies in the Management Sciences 12 (1979) 203–211

A MULTIDETERMINISTIC APPROACH TO FORECASTING

James E. REINMUTH
University of Oregon

and

Michael D. GEURTS
Brigham Young University

This article suggest the use of a recursive regression algorithm for two or more forecasts and creating a multideterministic forecast model. Empirical results involving three different data sets suggest that the regression combination procedure provides substantial improvement over that obtained by using a unideterministic forecast model. Primarily because of its ease of use and interpretation, the recursive regression combination procedure is recommended instead of the "best" Bates and Granger combination procedure, even though the performance levels of the methodologies are nearly the same.

1. Introduction

When developing a forecasting model, most analysts examine several different forecasting techniques, finally choosing the one generating the most satisfactory measure of forecast accuracy. Naturally, the final selection depends upon the accuracy criteria used in the analysis, but the most common statistics employed to measure forecast accuracy are the sum of squared errors, Theil's U coefficient and the portmanteau test proposed by Box and Jenkins [3]. The principal objective of this unideterminant approach to forecasting is to identify that forecasting model among the competing models which best fits the underlying time series and generates the most accurate projections of future process values.

Bates and Granger [1] have concluded that the forecasting accuracy of the best single forecasting model can usually be improved by combining the forecasts generated by two competing forecasting models. This multideterminant approach to forecasting is based upon the premise that a discarded forecast almost surely contains some useful information independent of that supplied by the chosen model. As the quantity of information supplied by an estimator is inversely related to its variance, the multideterminant approach should return forecasts with smaller error variances than the forecasts of either component model.

Bates and Granger [1] and later Newbold and Granger [8] have proposed a complicated set of weights that might be used for combining forecasts in a multideterminant forecasting model. This paper offers a simplified procedure for combining forecasts by letting the separate forecasts assume the role of independent variables in a general linear regression equation.

This approach also permit combining more than two separate forecasting models, and provides for the capture of a maximum amount of independent information related to future realizations of a time series.

2. The combination of forecasts

Bates and Granger first proposed the idea that forecasting accuracy can be improved by combining the forecasts resulting from different forecast models. Their studies involved combining forecasts from the application of exponential smoothing and Box–Jenkins type models to airline traffic data. In most cases, they found the combination of forecasts to have a smaller residual variance than the best single forecast model.

The motive for combining forecasts is to reduce the forecast residual variance. It is assumed that each single forecast model explains a certain portion of the variation in the underlying time series but that the information content supplied by the various models is not identical. Thus, a second or third forecast model reduces the amount of variation unexplained by an original forecast model and, in turn, reduces the size of the forecast errors.

2.1. Combining two forecasts

Bates and Granger [1] shows explicitly that their proposed data mining approach does, in fact, reduce the forecast residual variance. If $\hat{y}_{1t}$ and $\hat{y}_{2t}$ are forecasts generated by two separate models for time period t and σ_1^2, σ_2^2 are their respective residual variances, then the variance of errors in the combined forecast is

$$\sigma_c^2 = k^2\sigma_1^2 + (1-k)^2\sigma_2^2 + 2\rho k\sigma_1(1-k)\sigma_2,$$

where k is the weight assigned to the first set of forecasts, $(1-k)$ is the weight assigned to the second set, and ρ is the correlation between the two residual sets. It can be shown that σ_c^2 is minimized by the choice of

$$k = \frac{\sigma_2^2 - \rho\sigma_1\sigma_2}{\sigma_1^2 + \sigma_2^2 - 2\rho\sigma_1\sigma_2}$$

if both forecasts are unbiased. The variance of the combined forecast errors then becomes [1]

$$\sigma_c^2 = \frac{\sigma_1^2\sigma_2^2(1-\rho^2)}{\sigma_1^2 + \sigma_2^2 - 2\rho\sigma_1\sigma_2}$$

Then, it can be shown (contrary to the finding of Bates and Granger) that

$$\sigma_c^2 - \sigma_1^2 = \frac{-\sigma_1^2(\sigma_1 - \rho\sigma_2)^2}{(\sigma_1 - \rho\sigma_2)^2 + \sigma_2^2(1 - \rho^2)} \leqslant 0.$$

Therefore, $\sigma_c^2 < \sigma_1^2$ and, by symmetry, $\sigma_c^2 < \sigma_2^2$.

Bates and Granger have identified three desirable properties for the weighting constants for the combination of forecasts in a multideterministic model. The weights should:

1. converge toward their optimum values (even though these limits are unknown) as the size of the time series increases.
2. be adaptive, changing as new process information becomes available.
3. exhibit a small variance around their optimum values.

Five methods for the estimation of k were studied by Bates and Granger for the combination of two forecast models. The method that provided the best results in their empirical studies is

$$k_{1,n} = \frac{\sum_t (e_{2,t})^2}{\sum_t (e_{1,t})^2 + \sum_t (e_{2,t})^2}, \qquad k_{2,n} = 1 - k_{1,n},$$

where $e_{1,t}$ and $e_{2,t}$ are the forecast errors recorded during time period t for the two forecast models involved in the combination. Thic choice of weight is appealing, since it provides an empirical approximation to the optimal weight assuming the two forecast series are uncorrelated ($\rho = 0$). It is interesting to note that the weight assuming $\rho = 0$ consistently outperformed one allowing for the inclusion of an estimate of the covariance between the two series in their studies [1]. Although it is uncertain whether the Bates–Granger weight satisfies the convergence criterion, there is little question that criteria (2) and (3) are satisfied by this choice.

2.2. Combining two or more forecasts

The multideterminant approach can be extended to the combination of several forecasts (see Reid [9]). The optimal vector of weighting constants for combining p-forecasts for time period n,

$$k_n' = (k_{1,n}, k_{2,n}, ..., k_{p,n}),$$

can be found to be a function of the separate forecast model error variances σ_1^2, σ_2^2, ..., σ_p^2 and their pairwise correlations (see Newbold and Granger [8]). Since in practice, the true variances and correlations are seldom known, many approximating procedures have been proposed both by Bates and Granger and by Newbold and Granger. The latter have even suggested a Bayesian approach, where k_{in} is a subjective probability indicating one's belief that the ith forecast model best monitors the underlying time series during time period n.

An approach for estimating the weighting coefficients that satisfies the Bates and Granger criteria, but was not considered by them, is employing a recursive regression algorithm. Reinmuth and Wittink [11] show that for the general linear model

$$y_n = x'_n + \epsilon_n,$$

relating to y to $\mathbf{x}$: $(p \times 1)$ based upon all data accumulated over the n-consecutive time periods $t = 1, 2, ..., n$, the best linear unbiased estimator (BLUE) for the parameter vector may be written in recursive form as

$$\hat{\boldsymbol{\beta}}_n = \hat{\boldsymbol{\beta}}_{n-1} + M_n x_n (y_n - x'_n \hat{\boldsymbol{\beta}}_{n-1}),$$

where $M_n^{-1} = (X'_n X_n)$ is the matrix of sums of squares and cross-products (usually referred to as the information matrix in regression analysis) and $\hat{\boldsymbol{\beta}}_{n-1}$ is the BLUE based on data accumulated through $t = n - 1$. The recursive algorithm thus allows for the regression parameters to be updated with each new observation (y_t, x_t) without requiring several observations to be recorded.

Translating the notation of the general linear model to the specific notation of our study, y_t is the actual value of the time series at time period t and

$$x'_t = (\hat{y}_{1,t}, \hat{y}_{2,t}, ..., \hat{y}_{p,t})$$

is the vector of forecasts of y_t obtained from p separate forecasting models. The parameter vector estimate $\hat{\ }_n$ is k_n, the vector of weighting constants to use in the multideterministic forecast equation. Reinmuth [10] shows that the parameter vector estimate converges to the true vector when using recursive regression if k_t is deterministic; thus, the first Bates and Granger criterion is satisfied. Their second criterion is satisfied, since the recursive regression algorithm requires that the parameter vector be estimated anew after each new observation. By the Gauss–Markov theorem, regression parameter estimates are BLUE, satisfying the third criterion.

The combination of forecasts using regression was first proposed by Crane and Crotty [8] who combined a regression forecast with an exponential smoothing forecast. However, their objective was to capture the benefits of the auxiliary information provided by a regression forecast with the pattern fitting characteristics provided by exponential smoothing when using data with a distinct seasonal component. The Crane and Crotty objective is not necessarily consistent with the data mining objective first sought by Bates and Granger. It is the latter that is of interest in our study.

3. Some illustrative examples

The following examples demonstrate the usefulness of the recursive regression approach for combining forecasts. As a measure of forecast accuracy, we shall use Theil's forecast accuracy coefficient [2],

$$ U = \frac{[\sum_t (y_t - \hat{y}_t)^2]^{1/2}}{(\sum_t y_t^2)^{1/2}}, $$

a measure that is proportional to the forecast error variance. [1]

3.1. The Geurts–Ibrahim example

In an attempt to examine the efficacy of Box–Jenkins forecasting procedures, Geurts and Ibrahim [7] compared the ability of a $(0, 1, 1)(1, 1, 1)$ Box–Jenkins model with that of a second-order seasonally adjusted exponential smoothing model ($\alpha = 0.1$) to forecast the monthly Hawaii tourist traffic. Monthly data for the period 1952 through 1971 were available, with 1971 held back for purposes of testing and comparing the two chosen models. The authors used each model to separately forecast the monthly tourist traffic with a one-month lead period over the 1971 holdback period and obtained quite satisfactory results. However, if a multideterministic approach is used and the weights k_{1t} and k_{2t} are determined by the recursive regression algorithm, the one-month lead forecasts are drastically improved.

Table 1 shows the actual monthly tourist traffic listed by Geurts and Ibrahim, their one-month lead forecasts as determined by the second-order exponential smoothing model, the one-month lead $(0, 1, 1)(1, 1, 1)$ Box–Jenkins forecasts, and the multideterminant, recursive regression one-month lead forecasts. For purposes of comparison, the table also shows the one-month lead forecast generated by the best Bates–Granger model (listed earlier) for combining two forecasts generated by Geurts and Ibrahim. Notice that this model also provides forecasts that are drastic improvements over those generated by the unideterministic models.

As table 1 shows the recursive regression multideterministic model provides a 59.2% improvement in forecast accuracy (reduction in U) over that provided by the second-order exponential smoothing model and a 60.8% improvement over that provided by the $(0, 1, 1)(1, 1, 1)$ Box–Jenkins mode. The Bates–Granger approach slightly outperforms the recursive regression approach; however, one is never cer-

---

[1] One interesting aspect of the U-statistic is that if $U > 1$, the naive model $\hat{y}_t = y_{t-1}$ (today's forecast equals the last period's outcome) will outperform the forecast model under investigation.

Table 1
Comparison of forecasts for Hawaii tourist traffic data (in 1,000 s).

Month t	Actual y_t	Exponential smoothing $\hat{y}_{1,t}$	Box-Jenkins $\hat{y}_{2,t}$	Recursive regression $\hat{y}_{R,t}$	Bates-Granger $\hat{y}_{BG,t}$
January	18.024	15.395	17.332	16.079	16.303
February	18.806	17.109	20.069	19.150	18.814
March	21.707	19.162	25.976	23.259	23.144
April	13.463	13.424	13.512	13.643	13.464
May	14.930	15.844	13.961	14.908	14.988
June	12.287	13.618	11.046	12.499	12.448
July	16.248	15.583	16.664	16.124	16.079
August	11.466	13.944	9.287	11.738	11.795
September	12.672	15.979	10.291	13.029	13.273
October	13.630	16.394	9.769	12.790	13.029
November	14.422	14.479	14.262	14.449	14.376
December	14.441	13.660	15.043	14.473	14.317
U = statistic	–	0.125	0.130	0.051	0.046

tain whether the Bates–Granger weights satisfy the convergence criterion or not. Since the recursive regression approach does satisfy all three criteria and since the forecast error reduction is comparable when using the recursive regression or the Bates–Granger weights, the position taken in this paper is that recursive regression should be the preferred multideterministic model.

3.2. National Surface Coating sales

The monthly gross sales volume for the National Surface Coating (NSC) Company — a firm dealing in paint and varnish — for the years 1972 and 1973 were used to develop a number of different forecasting models. An econometric model using new housing starts, private and public new construction, and consumer installment credit extended for repairs and modernization as independent variables was used to generate one-month lead forecasts of NSC gross sales for the twelve months of 1974. Also used as one-month lead forecast models for 1974 were three first-order, three second-order, and three third-order exponential smoothing models ($\alpha = 0.1, 0.2, 0.3$) and several Box–Jenkins type models. [2]

Table 2 lists the 21 forecast models involved in the analysis with their associated Theil U coefficients measuring each model's ability to forecast the 1974 monthly gross sales of NSC. A multideterministic approach was then used for forecasting

---

[2] The Box–Jenkins models used are those that are not screened out in the model identification and diagnostic checking stages of the Box–Jenkins procedure.

Table 2
U = statistics for models used to forecast NSC monthly sales.

Model	*U* statistic	Model	*U* statistic
Econometric	0.1425	Box-Jenkins	
Exponential Smoothing [a]		(1, 1, 0) (1, 1, 0)	0.0415
Single, α = 0.1	0.1261	(1, 1, 0) (0, 1, 1)	0.0489
Single, α = 0.2	0.0934	(2, 1, 0) (1, 1, 0)	0.0516
Single, α = 0.3	0.0797	(2, 1, 1) (1, 1, 1)	0.0534
Double, α = 0.1	0.0728	(2, 1, 0) (0, 1, 1)	0.0571
Double, α = 0.2	0.0618	(1, 0, 1) (1, 1, 1)	0.0649
Double, α = 0.3	0.0613	(2, 1, 0) (1, 1, 0)	0.0675
Triple, α = 0.1	0.0656	(2, 1, 1) (1, 1, 0)	0.0942
Triple, α = 0.2	0.0598	(1, 0, 0) (1, 1, 1)	0.1302
Triple, α = 0.3	0.0677	(0, 1, 1) (0, 1, 1)	0.1447
Multideterministic	0.0068	(0, 1, 1) (1, 1, 1)	0.1690

[a] Single, double, and triple exponential smoothing refer to the first-order, second-order, and third-order multiple exponential smoothing models, respectively [4].

1974 sales by using recursive regression methods to separately combine each of the 210 pairs of models and compute the forecasts generated by each pair. The combination with the most accurate forecast of 1974 sales involved the econometric model and the (2, 1, 0) (1, 1, 0) Box—Jenkins model. Its measure of forecast accuracy for the 1974 sales data was U = 0.006768, an 83.7% improvement over the U-value for the best individual forecast model, the (1, 1, 0) (1, 1, 0) Box—Jenkins model.

It is interesting to note that the best pair of forecast models does not involve either of the two best individual forecast models. This is due to the fact that the two series BJ (1, 1, 0) (1, 1, 0) and BJ (1, 1, 0) (0, 1, 1) are not independent; there thus exists a commonality of information supplied by the two forecast models.

3.3. Salt Lake City retail sales

The gross monthly sales from the retail establishments of Salt Lake City (SLC) were recorded for 1973 and 1974 and used to develop an econometric forecasting model and a number of different exponential smoothing and Box—Jenkins type forecasting models. These models were used to generate one-month lead forecasts for the SLC retail sales for the first six months of 1975. The five unideterminant models generating the greatest measure of forecast accuracy are shown in table 3.

As noted earlier, the regression approach for the combination of individual forecast models lends itself well to the combination of any number of unideterministic models. Table 4 lists the U-statistic, as a measure of forecast accuracy, for five different combinations of the best individual models listed in table 3. Note that the

Table 3
Comparison of five unideterministic forecast models: Salt Lake City retail sales.

Unideterministic model	U-statistic
Second-order exponential smoothing (α = 0.1)	0.0434
Third-order exponential smoothing (α = 0.1)	0.0943
Box–Jenkins (1, 1, 0) (1, 1, 1)	0.0836
Box–Jenkins (1, 1, 0) (1, 1, 0)	0.0822
Econometric	0.0310
Multideterministic	0.0035

best combination provides an 88% improvement in forecast accuracy over the best individual model (U = 0.0035 vs. U = 0.0310). It is also interesting to note that all multideterministic models involving the combination of three or more individual forecasts outperform the one involving the combination of only two forecasts. Thus, one might conclude that the inclusion of additional auxiliary information into an existing multideterministic model cannot decrease its measure of forecast accuracy. But that is not surprising because it is a natural result of an increase in the number of independent variables in a general linear regression model. One must, however, be cautioned against the usual problems of interpretation in a regression analysis that occur when the number of independent variables is increased while the sample size is held constant

Table 4
Comparison of five multideterministic forecast models: Salt Lake City retail sales.

Multideterministic model	U-statistic
Second-order exponential smoothing (α = 0.1) Third-order exponential smoothing (α = 0.1) Box–Jenkins (1, 1, 0) (1, 1, 1) Box–Jenkins (1, 1, 0) (1, 1, 0)	U = 0.0057
Second-order exponential smoothing (α = 0.1) Box–Jenkins (1, 1, 0) (1, 1, 0)	U = 0.0125
Box–Jenkins (1, 1, 0) (1, 1, 1) Box–Jenkins (1, 1, 0) (1, 1, 0) Econometric	U = 0.0094
Second-order exponential smoothing (α = 0.1) Third-order exponential smoothing (α = 0.1) Econometric	U = 0.0046
Second-order exponential smoothing (α = 0.1) Box–Jenkins (1, 1, 0) (1, 1, 0) Econometric	U = 0.0035

4. Conclusion

Examination of the utility of using regression analysis for the conbination of two or more forecasts indicate that the multideterministic forecast model is virtually assured of outperforming any individual unideterministic model. These findings are similar to those reported by Bates and Granger [1] and Newbold and Granger [8].

Bates and Granger [1] have offered a number of different procedures for combining two forecasts and Reid [9] offers a method for combining any number of forecasts. The position taken in this paper is that the recursive regression combination procedure is preferred to the combination procedures offered by other authors since 1) it provides a common method for the combination of any number of forecasts, 2) it is easy to apply and provides results that are easy to interpret, and 3) it satisfies the three Bates and Granger optimality criteria.

The authors are conducting further studies to investigate the sensitivity of the performance of the recursive regression multideterministic forecast model to collinear relationships between individual forecast series and the forecast lead time.

References

[1] J.M. Bates and C.W.J. Granger, The combination of forecasts, Operational Research Quarterly 20 (1969) 451–568.
[2] F. Bliemel, Theil's forecasting accuracy coefficient: A clarification, Journal of Marketing Research 10 (1973) 444–446.
[3] G.E.P. Box and G.M. Jenkins, Time Series Analysis: Forecasting and Control (Holden-Day, San Francisco, 1970).
[4] R.G. Brown, Smoothing, Forecasting and Prediction of Discrete Time Series (Prentice-Hall, Englewood Cliffs, N.J., 1963).
[5] R.L. Brown, J. Durbin and J.M. Evans, Techniques for testing the constancy of regression relationships over time, Journal of the Royal Statistical Society, Ser. A, 138 (1975) 149–163.
[6] D.B. Crane and J.R. Crotty, Two stage forecasting model: Exponential smoothing and multiple regression, Management Science 13 (1967) B501–507.
[7] M.D. Geurts and I.B. Ibrahim, Comparing the Box–Jenkins approach with the exponentially smoothed forecasting model: Application to Hawaii tourists, Journal of Marketing Research 12 (1975) 182–188.
[8] P. Newbold and C.W.J. Granger, Experience with forecasting univariate time series and the combination of forecasts, Journal of the Royal Statistical Society, Ser. A, 137 (1974) 131–164.
[9] D.J. Reid, A comparative study of time series prediction techniques on economic data, Ph.D. dissertation, University of Nottingham, Nottingham, England.
[10] J.E. Reinmuth, Recursive estimation, Australian Journal of Statistics 18 (1976) 62–72.
[11] J.E. Reinmuth and D.R. Wittink, Recursive models for forecasting seasonal processes, Journal of Financial and Quantitative Analysis, 9 (1972) 659–684.

TIMS Studies in the Management Sciences 12 (1979) 213–225
© North-Holland Publishing Company

INFLATION'S TURN *

Geoffrey H. MOORE

National Bureau of Economic Research and Hoover Institution, Stanford University

A chronology of the rate of inflation, based upon the consumer price index, reveals seven upswings and eight downswings in inflation between 1947 and 1976. Each of the downswings has been associated with a business cycle recession or slowdown, while the upswings have always accompanied the intervening economic recoveries. It is shown that the magnitude of these inflationary episodes, in both wages and prices, has been more closely associated with the percentage of the population employed than with the unemployment rate. The use of the inflation chronology to develop and analyze leading, coincident and lagging indicators of the rate of inflation is illustrated. The fact that economic forecasts have turned out to be a lagging indicator prompts a recommendation that more research effort be devoted to this approach to forecasting inflation.

The month of May 1977 was the twenty-sixth month of a business cycle expansion. There is nothing controversial about that statement. Most economists accept the finding of the National Bureau of Economic Research (NBER) that the bottom was reached in March 1975, and most would agree that the expansion continued through May 1977 and beyond. But here is a more controversial statement: the month of May 1977 was the thirteenth month of an upswing in the rate of inflation; April 1976 was the bottom.

What does this statement mean? It means that just as one can construct a chronology of the business cycle, as the National Bureau has done for many years, so also one can construct a chronology of the rate of inflation. Just as the business cycle chronology pinpoints the dates when recessions begin and end, so an inflation chronology pinpoints the dates when the waves of inflation reach their crests and troughs. The two chronologies are not the same, though they are related. Just as leading indicators of the business cycle can be developed and analyzed to anticipate the next turning point in the economy, so leading indicators of inflation can be developed and analyzed to anticipate the next turning point in the rate of inflation. Not much of this latter work has been done, but now is a good time to make a

---

* This paper represents the views of the author and is not an official report of the National Bureau. It is based upon an address given before the Conference on the Management of Funds, held by The Conference Board, New York City, May 11, 1977. It draws also upon: An inflation chronology, NBER Reporter (June 1977). No attempt has been made to bring up to date the figures used at the time these pieces were prepared.

start. In fact, if the April 1976 data for the inflation upturn is correct, the analysis should have begun a year ago. But last year at this time economists were basking in the euphoria of a declining inflation rate. They didn't know the rate had hit bottom.

In this paper the rate of inflation is taken to be the rate of change in the consumer price index (CPI) over a six-month interval, after adjustment for seasonal variation. This rate is computed every month by the Bureau of Labor Statistics, together with rates of change over the preceding month, over three months, and over twelve months. The six-month rate has the advantage of being less erratic than the shorter rates and more up to date than the twelve-month rate. The six-month rate does not, however, really apply to the month for which it is calculated. The convention is to center it in the middle of the six-month interval. Hence the rate calculated for the six months from December to June is dated March, the rate for January to July is dated April, and so on. It can be thought of as an approximation to the underlying trend of inflation in the middle month of the six-month period. One learns what the rate actually is at the end of the period.

It turns out that the rate centered on April 1976, 4.7 percent, was the lowest rate in a downswing that began in July 1974, when the rate was 12.6 percent. All the six-month rates of increase since April 1976 have been higher than 4.7 percent. The latest one at this writing, centering on January 1977 and covering the six months from October 1976 to April 1977, was 8.0 percent. The rate has come a long way from the bottom. In fact, it has covered more than a third of the distance back up the downhill road that it traveled from July 1974 to March 1976.

This does not mean that the current upswing will move the inflation rate all the way back to the unseemly double-digit levels of 1974. It may or may not. What it does mean is that an upswing in the inflation rate has been under way for some time, that it is of significant size, and that the latest figure is the highest yet.

Upturns of the April 1976 variety do not happen often. Since 1948, according to the chronology given in Table 1, there have been seven of them. The current upturn is the eighth. Sometimes the upswings have petered out rather quickly — one lasted only eight months, one only twelve — but most have lasted two or three years. The smallest and shortest upswings have raised the CPI rate a little more than 2 percentage points, and the current upswing has already exceeded that minimum. But most have raised the rate by 4, 6 or even more percentage points. Where any given upswing will stop is highly conjectural. Past experience indicates that an upswing is not likely to stop until there are signs that a new business recession or slowdown is getting under way.

Comparison of the inflation chronology with the business cycle chronology yields some simple but important truths, based upon experience since 1948. One is that for every business downturn there has been a matching downturn in the inflation rate and for every business upturn there has been a matching upturn in the inflation rate (see Table A-1 in the appendix). This pattern has recurred twelve times in a row. On two occasions (1950 and 1966) a downturn in inflation occurred

Table 1
A chronology of peaks and troughs in the rate of inflation.

Date		Peak rate (%)	Trough rate (%)	Percentage point change		Length (in months)	
Peak	Trough			Down-swing	Upswing	Down-swing	Upswing
Oct. 1947	–	13.5	–	–	–	–	–
–	Nov. 1948	–	–4.2	–17.7	–	13	–
Nov. 1950	–	14.0	–	–	18.2	–	24
–	Nov. 1952	–	–0.6	–14.6	–	24	–
July 1953	–	2.1	–	–	2.7	–	8
–	Sept. 1954 [a]	–	–1.4	–3.5	–	14	–
July 1956	–	4.3	–	–	5.7	–	22
–	July 1958	–	–0.2	–4.5	–	24	–
July 1959	–	2.4	–	–	2.6	–	12
–	Mar. 1961	–	0.1	–2.3	–	20	–
Jan. 1966	–	4.0	–	–	3.9	–	58
–	Jan. 1967	–	1.3	–2.7	–	12	–
Jan. 1970 [a]	–	6.6	–	–	5.3	–	36
–	Oct. 1971	–	2.8	–3.8	–	21	–
July 1974	–	12.6	–	–	9.8	–	33
–	Apr. 1976 [b]	–	4.7	–7.9	–	21	–
Average 1947–76		7.4	0.3	–7.1	6.9	19	28

Note: The chronology is based upon the rate of change in the consumer price index, seasonally adjusted, computed over six-month periods and expressed at an annual rate. The rates are dated in the middle month of the six-month period. For example, the rate for April 1976 (4.7 percent) is the change from January to July 1976, annualized. Except as noted, the dates through 1970 are as given in Moore [6]. See pp. 4–5 for a discussion of the relative merits of different price indexes and alternative measures of their rates of change for this purpose.

[a] These dates were revised because of a change in seasonal adjustment. Prior to revision the dates were August 1954 and February 1970 (Moore [6]).

[b] The selection of this date is tentative.

without a business recession, but in both instances there was a near recession, that is, a marked slowdown in the rate of growth (to around 3 percent in real GNP at annual rate). In other words, a marked slowdown or absolute decline in economic activity has been both necessary and sufficient to bring about a downswing in the rate of inflation, while an economic expansion has always been accompanied by a rise in the rate of inflation. That is one reason why one can be fairly confident that the April 1976 trough in the inflation chronology is a genuine one, comparable with the preceding seven. It followed the business upturn by a year, which is an unusually long lag. If it isn't genuine, it will be the first exception in 60 years. [1]

Another implication of the relationship between the business cycle and inflation chronologies is that since the inflation rate has always reached its lowest ebb in the vicinity of a business cycle trough, inflation must have begun to accelerate when economic activity was quite depressed, well before it fully recovered from recession. At such times unemployment is still high, often close to its peak, and many plants have plenty of excess capacity. Neither a high unemployment rate nor a low utilization rate have been sufficient to stop inflation from accelerating if a business expansion was under way. When demand is rising, prices tend to rise faster.

April 1976, the date after which the inflation rate began to rise, is a good example of this situation. The unemployment rate was 7.5 percent then, and it stayed around or above that level through the summer, fall and winter. In April 1977 it was still 7 percent. The capacity utilization rate in manufacturing, according to the Federal Reserve Board, was 80 percent in the second quarter of 1976 and remained close to that level during the ensuing year. Neither the high unemployment rate nor the low utilization rate prevented the inflation rate from starting its upswing, and moving up from 4.7 percent to 8.0 percent during the next twelve months. Of course, that is only one example, but a look at the record will reveal that it is the rule, not an exception. Arthur Burns [4] said it well, more than a quarter of a century ago: "Inflation does not wait for full employment." Burns' responsibilities as Chairman of the Federal Reserve Board have not caused him to forget the rule, as his recent testimony before Congress has revealed. [2]

What does appear to make a difference in the inflation rate, however, is the rate of economic growth, that is, the speed with which employment and output rise. Slow growth during the first two years or so of a business recovery has been quite consistently associated with modest increases or even some temporary decline in the rate of inflation. Recoveries characterized by rapid growth have been associated with larger increases in the rate of inflation. The record of containing inflation has been better when the growth rate was moderate than when it was rapid. [3]

A moderate growth rate does not mean stagnation. In recent months a relatively high percentage of the population of working age has been employed. In April 1977, the twenty-fifth month of the present recovery, the percentage employed reached 57 percent, higher than in the twenty-fifth month of any of the preceding five recoveries. That is to say, even though the unemployment rate was high, an exceptionally large proportion of the working age population had jobs, a situation more associated with boom than stagnation. Moreover, even if the percentage em-

---

[1] The consumer price index is available monthly back to 1913. Each of the eight business cycle recoveries between 1914 and 1948 was accompanied by an upswing in the CPI rate of change measured in the manner described in the text, and the like was true of the five recoveries since 1948.

[2] See especially Burns' testimony before the Committee on the Budget, United States Senate, March 22, 1977.

[3] Evidence on this point can be found in Moore [8].

ployed were to remain constant from here on, that would mean increasing the number employed by about 1.500,000 each year, or 1.7 percent, just to keep pace with population growth. Output could, of course, grow faster than that, depending on the rate of productivity growth.

Figs. 1 and 2 show how important it is to keep track of the employment per-

HOURLY COMPENSATION, UNEMPLOYMENT RATE,
AND PERCENTAGE OF POPULATION EMPLOYED, 1948–1976

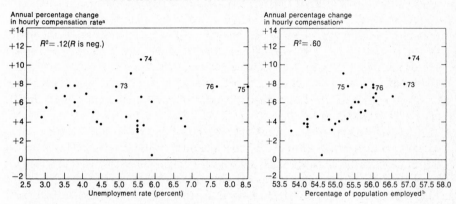

Note: The correlation (R^2) is based on data ending with 1974.
[a] Fourth quarter of preceding year to fourth quarter of current year, private nonfarm sector.
[b] Civilian employment as percent of noninstitutional population sixteen years of age and over.
Source: U.S. Department of Labor, Bureau of Labor Statistics.

Figure 1

CONSUMER PRICE INDEX, UNEMPLOYMENT RATE,
AND PERCENTAGE OF POPULATION EMPLOYED, 1948–1976

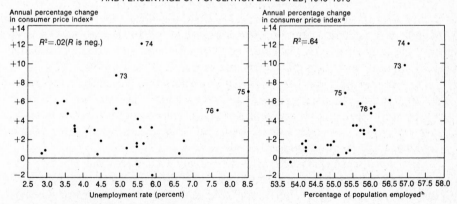

Note: The correlation (R^2) is based on data ending with 1974.
[a] December of preceding year to December of current year.
[b] Civilian employment as percent of noninstitutional population sixteen years of age and over.
Source: U.S. Department of Labor, Bureau of Labor Statistics.

Figure 2

centage. The left-hand panels show the unemployment rate and the rates of change in wages and in prices, from which there appears to be little or no relationship between unemployment and the rate of wages or between unemployment and the rate of change in prices. The Phillips curve is not a curve, but a cloud. A high rate of unemployment has not consistently held down wages or prices.

The right-hand panels relate the percentage of the population employed to the rate of change in wages (fig. 1) and in prices (fig. 2). Clearly, high employment percentages have been associated with high rates of increase in wages and in prices.

It is also clear that the employment percentage in 1976, 56 percent, was better than in most of the years since 1948. Only five exceeded it. Moreover, the monthly figures in 1977 have been even higher. The April figure, 57 percent, was never exceeded during the entire period since 1948 except for a few months in 1973 and 1974. Since those years are in the upper right-hand corner of the figure, the choice of the April level as an illustrative figure to stabilize at, in the preceding example, can hardly be called conservative.

To explain why the rate of wage and price inflation is more closely related to the employment percentage than to the unemployment rate is not a simple matter. It has to do with the changing trade-off between employment and unemployment in recent decades. An increase in employment does not bring about the same reduction in unemployment as it used to. After the first 25 months of the current recovery the economy was providing jobs for nearly 6 million more persons than when the recovery began, but unemployment was reduced by only 1 million. Nearly six additional jobs had to be created to take one person off the unemployment rolls. In the 1950s and early 1960s the ratio during similar two-year periods ranged from one-to-one to three-to-one. The creation of jobs at a faster rate than the rate of population growth and the hiring of people to fill these jobs causes a tighter labor market, with pressure on wages and unit labor costs. In addition employers see a bigger demand for their products and buyers are willing – and able, because of their higher earnings – to pay higher prices. These conditions can, and did, occur without much effect on unemployment, but they do affect the rate of inflation. For additional analysis of these factors see Green [3]; Moore and Shiskin [12].

Another significant use of an inflation chronology is to help identify and analyze leading, coincident, and lagging indicators of inflation. Such indicators, supported by an economic rationale and careful study on their record of performance, may prove helpful in monitoring the process of inflation and appraising the near-term outlook. The following examples illustrate the point.

The rate of change in whole sale prices of crude materials – line 2 on fig. 3 – is an instance of a leading indicator. It has led the inflation rate at every turn but one since 1947, a score of 15 out of 16 turns (see table A-2). The average lead was about six months. Its latest upturn preceded the upturn in consumer prices by 16 months, an unusually long interval. The most recent figure, the six month change from October 1976 to April 1977, was 14 percent at annual rate. Reports from purchasing agents confirm that materials have been rapidly getting more costly.

INFLATION INDICATORS

(annual percentage rates)

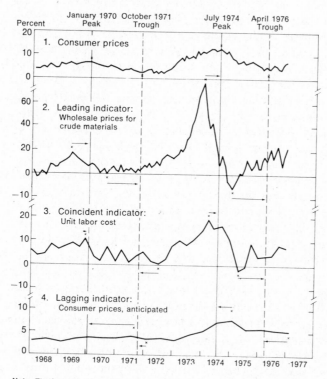

Note: The intervals covered by the rates are: Lines 1 and 2, six months; line 3, one quarter; line 4, eight months. The rates are entered within these intervals. The x's mark the peaks and troughs in the series and the arrows show the lead or lag with respect to the inflation rate (line 1).

Sources: Lines 1-3: U.S. Bureau of Labor Statistics. Crude materials prices exclude foods, feeds, and fibers. Unit labor cost is for nonfarm business sector. Line 4: John A. Carlson, "A Study of Price Forecasts," *Annals of Economic and Social Measurement,* National Bureau of Economic Research, vol. 6, no. 1 (Winter 1977), pp. 33-34.

Figure 3. Inflation indicators.

This index is a leading indicator because prices of materials like scrap steel, rubber, and hides respond more promptly to demand/supply conditions than many other prices. Moreover, materials represent a significant element in costs of production. Hence they exert, with a lag, an influence on the supply prices of the goods they enter into. Crude materials prices are also significantly influenced by international economic conditions. A concerted recovery in the major industrial countries is likely to produce upward pressures on materials prices, and that was no doubt a factor in their rise during 1976.

Another vital element in the cost of production is labor. The rate of change in unit labor cost can be regarded as a coincident indicator. Its turning points have matched those in the inflation chronology at every turn since 1947, and nine of the sixteen turns occurred within three months of each other (see Table A-3). There were as many leads as lags. Hence, although the level of unit labor cost is classified as a lagging indicator in the business cycle, its rate of change is roughly coincident with the inflation cycle. The rate has been moving upward since 1975, reaching about 7.5 percent per year early in 1977.

One should not quickly conclude that prices are accelerating because labor costs are. The relationship is more complex than that. Prices affect wages, too, and both are affected by other things. Rising demand for output can raise labor costs as well as prices, just as falling demand can bring on a search for ways to economize, greater efficiency, less overtime pay, lower labor costs and lower prices. For all these reasons the movements in the rates of change in labor costs and in prices are closely related to one another, in roughly coincident fashion. Neither one has gotten very far out of line with the other for very long.

Finally, to fill the position of lagging indicator of inflation are the forecasts of what the rate of inflation is going to be. These forecasts by economists are as nearly perfect a lagging indicator as one could expect to find. Almost always late, almost never early.

The records of price forecasts support this choice. One such record has been compiled since 1947 by Joseph Livingston of the *Philadelphia Inquirer.* He induces about 50 economists to respond to a survey twice a year and tell him their forecasts of the consumer price index, among other things. When the group's average forecast of the consumer price index for six months ahead is compared with the inflation chronology, which is also based upon the CPI, it turns out that only twelve of the sixteen turns were recognized by the forecasters at all. The forecasts were late at ten of the twelve (see Table A-4). The average lag was six months. [4] As fig. 3 shows, when the latest survey was taken in December 1976, the average forecast was still declining, at least a little, which is just what one would expect a lagging indicator to do in the face of an upturn in the inflation rate some eight months before.

Judging from the rather sorry record of price forecasting that this characterization suggests, it might be well if as much attention were devoted to the timely and systematic study of indicators of inflation as has been devoted to indicators of recession and recovery. One of the chief results of the latter type of analysis has been the development of better anticipatory indicators, promptly accessible to the public, with a well-documented record that reveals both their value and limitations. The inflation chronology may help toward that end, but much remains to be done. The factors usually considered in analyses of inflation, including the money supply, the volume of credit, interest rates, the Federal deficit, unemployment, capacity

---

[4] A similar finding based upon annual forecasts of the GNP implicit price deflator is documented by Moore [10].

utilization, inventory accumulation, profits, monopoly elements in labor and commodity markets, and international economic relations, all should be brought into the picture. But it seemed best to start with simpler matters, which is the limited purpose of this paper.

Appendix A
A record of leads and lags in inflation indicators

Tables A-1 through A-4 show the relationship in time between the turning points in the inflation chronology (the rate of change in the consumer price index) and 1) the business cycle, 2) the rate of change in wholesale prices of crude materials, 3) the rate of change in unit labor costs, and 4) a set of forecasts of the rate of change in the consumer price index. The methods by which the turning points are chosen

Table A-1
Relation between business cycle and inflation chronologies.

Business cycle		Inflation rate (CPI)		Lead (−) or lag (+) of inflation rate at business cycle (in months)	
Peak	Trough	Peak	Trough	Peak	Trough
Nov. 1948	–	Oct. 1947	–	−13	–
–	Oct. 1949	–	Nov. 1948	–	−11
a	–	Nov. 1950	–	a	–
–	a	–	Nov. 1952	–	a
July 1953	–	July 1953	–	0	–
–	May 1954	–	Sept. 1954	–	+4
Aug. 1957	–	July 1956	–	−13	–
–	Apr. 1958	–	July 1958	–	+3
Apr. 1960	–	July 1959	–	−9	–
–	Feb. 1961	–	Mar. 1961	–	+1
a	–	Jan. 1966	–	a	–
–	a	–	Jan. 1967	–	a
Dec. 1969	–	Jan. 1970	–	+1	–
–	Nov. 1970	–	Oct. 1971	–	+11
Nov. 1973	–	July 1974	–	+8	–
–	Mar. 1975	–	Apr. 1976	–	+13

Note: The business cycle chronology is published by the National Bureau of Economic Research, Inc. The inflation chronology is based upon the rate of change in the consumer price index, published by the Bureau of Labor Statistics. The rate is measured over a six-month interval, seasonally adjusted, centered in the middle month of the span.

a There was no corresponding business cycle turn.

Table A-2
A leading indicator of inflation: crude materials prices.

Inflation rate (CPI)		Rate of change in crude materials prices		Lead (−) or lag (+) of crude materials prices at inflation	
Peak	Trough	Peak	Trough	Peak	Trough
Oct. 1947	–	Aug. 1947	–	−2	–
–	Nov. 1948	–	Apr. 1949	–	+5
Nov. 1950	–	July 1950	–	−4	–
–	Nov. 1952	–	Aug. 1951	–	−15
July 1953	–	Apr. 1953	–	−3	–
–	Sept. 1954	–	Oct. 1953	–	−11
July 1956	–	Sept. 1955	–	−10	–
–	July 1958	–	Oct. 1957	–	−9
July 1959	–	July 1958	–	−12	–
–	Mar. 1961	–	Aug. 1960	–	−7
Jan. 1966	–	Dec. 1965	–	−1	–
–	Jan. 1967	–	Oct. 1966	–	−3
Jan. 1970	–	May. 1969	–	−8	–
–	Oct. 1971	–	Aug. 1970	–	−14
July 1974	–	Jan. 1974	–	−6	–
–	Apr, 1976	–	Dec. 1974	–	−16

		Average lead (−) or lag (+)	
At peaks		−6	–
At troughs		–	−9
At peak and troughs		−7	

Note: The crude materials price index is the wholesale price index for crude materials less foods, feeds, and fibers, and is published by the Bureau of Labor Statistics. Its rate of change is measured over a six-month interval, seasonally adjusted, centered in the middle month of the span. Between April 1961 and April 1962 there was a decline in the rate that was not matched by a corresponding decline in the inflation rate (CPI).

and matched with one another are those followed for many years by the National Bureau of Economic Research in its business cycle studies (see Burns and Mitchell [2, chapters 4 and 5]). In recent years the selection of turning points has been largely computerized (see Bry and Boschan [1]).

The classification of indicators as leading, roughly coincident, and lagging also follows procedures developed by the National Bureau over a long period. It is based chiefly on the consistency with which the turning points in the data series match those in the reference chronology and on the regularity with which the matched turns lead, roughly coincide with, or lag behind those in the reference chronology

Table A-3
A roughly coincident indicator of inflation: unit labor cost.

Inflation rate (CPI)		Rate of change in unit labor cost		Lead (−) or lag (+) of unit labor cost at inflation (in months)	
Peak	Trough	Peak	Trough	Peak	Trough
Oct. 1947	—	July 1947	—	−3	—
—	Nov. 1948	—	July 1949	—	+8
Nov. 1950	—	Jan. 1951	—	+2	—
—	Nov. 1952	—	July 1951	—	−16
July 1953	—	Oct. 1952	—	−9	—
—	Sept. 1954	—	July 1954	—	−2
July 1956	—	Jan. 1956	—	−6	—
—	July 1958	—	Oct. 1958	—	+3
July 1959	—	July 1959	—	0	—
—	Mar. 1961	—	Oct. 1961	—	+7
Jan. 1966	—	Apr. 1966	—	+3	—
—	Jan. 1967	—	Apr. 1967	—	+3
Jan. 1970	—	Jan. 1970	—	0	—
—	Oct. 1971	—	July 1972	—	+9
July 1974	—	Apr. 1974	—	−3	—
—	Apr. 1976	—	Apr. 1975	—	−12

				Average lead (−) or lag (+)	
At peaks				−2	—
At troughs				—	0
At peaks and troughs				−1	

Note: The unit labor cost index is for the nonfarm business sector and is published by the Bureau of Labor Statistics. Its rate of change is measured from quarter to quarter, seasonally adjusted, and centered in the first month of the later quarter; that is, the change from the first to second quarter is centered in April, from the second to third in July, and so on.

(see Moore [6, chapter 7], Moore and Shiskin [11, chapters 2 and 3]). Such a classification (with respect to the business cycle rather than to the inflation rate) is used by the Department of Commerce in its monthly publication, *Business Conditions Digest*. The method of classification is briefly described in the front pages of each issue. For a more detailed, recent description, see Zarnowitz and Boschan [14] November 1975.

Table A-4
A lagging indicator of inflation: CPI forecasts.

Inflation rate (CPI)		Eight-month forecast rate (CPI)				Lead (−) or lag (+) (+) of forecast rate at inflation	
Peak	Trough	Peak		Trough		Peak	Trough
		Date	(%)	Date	(%)		
Oct. 1947	–	Feb. 1948	2.8	–	–	+4	–
–	Nov. 1948	–	–	Aug. 1949	−6.7	+3	+9
Nov. 1950	–	Feb. 1951	3.6	–	–	–	–
–	Nov. 1952	–	–	a	–	a	a
July 1953	–	a	–	–	–	a	–
–	Sept. 1954	–	–	Feb. 1954	−1.2	–	−7
July 1956	–	Feb. 1957	1.4	–	–	+7	–
–	July 1958	–	–	Aug. 1959	0.1	–	+13
July 1959	–	Feb. 1960	1.0	–	–	+7	–
–	Mar. 1961	–	–	Feb. 1961	0.2	–	−1
Jan. 1966	–	a	–	–	–	a	a
–	Jan. 1967	–	–	a	–	–	a
Jan. 1970	–	Aug. 1971	3.9	–	–	+19	–
–	Oct. 1971	–	–	Feb. 1972	3.0	–	+4
July 1974	–	Feb. 1975	7.7	–	–	+7	–
–	Apr. 1976	–	–	Feb. 1977	5.1 b	–	+10 b

	Average lead (−) or lag (+)

	Peak	Trough
At peaks	+8	–
At troughs	–	+5
At peaks and troughs	+6	

Note: The forecast rates are from the Livingston survey as compiled by John A. Carlson, "A Study of Price Forecasts", *Annals of Economic and Social Measurement*, Winter 1977, pp. 33−34. They pertain to eight-month intervals centered on February or August. The surveys are made in the preceding December or June.

a There is no corresponding turn.

b The trough date is tentative. The latest survey figure, centered on February 1977, is the lowest to date.

References

[1] G. Bry and C. Boschan, Cyclical Analysis of Time Series: Selected Procedures and Computer Programs (National Bureau of Economic Research, New York, 1971).

[2] A.F. Burns and W.C. Mitchell, Measuring Business Cycles (National Bureau of Economic Research, New York, 1971).

[3] C. Green, The employment ratio as an indicator of aggregate demand pressure, Monthly Labor Review, April 1977.

[4] W.C. Mitchell, What Happens During Business Cycles (National Bureau of Economic Research, New York, 1951).

[5] G.H. Moore, Business Cycle Indicators (National Bureau of Economic Research, New York, 1961).

[6] G.H. Moore, The Cyclical Behavior of Prices, Bureau of Labor Statistics, Report 384, 1971).

[7] G.H. Moore, How Full is Full employment? (American Enterprise Institute, 1973).

[8] G.H. Moore, Slowdowns, recessions and inflation, Explorations in Economic Research, Vol. 2 (1975) No. 2.

[9] G.H. Moore, Employment, unemployment and the inflation-recession dilemma, in: Fellner, W. (ed.) Contemporary Economic Problems (American Enterprise Institute, 1976).

[10] G.H. Moore, The President's Economic Report: a Forecasting Record, NBER Reporter April 1977) 4–12.

[11] G.H. Moore and J. Shiskin, Indicators of business expansions and contractions, National Bureau of Economic Research, New York, 1967).

[12] J. Shiskin, Employment and unemployment: the doughnut or the hole? Monthly Labor Review, February, 1976.

[13] V. Zarnowitz and C. Boschan, Cyclical indicators: an evaluation and new leading indexes, Business Conditions Digest, May 1975.

[14] V. Zarnowitz and C. Boschan, New composite indexes of coincident and lagging indicators, Business Conditions Digest, November 1975.

TIMS Studies in the Management Sciences 12 (1979) 227–246
© North-Holland Publishing Company

LESSONS FROM THE TRACK RECORD OF MACROECONOMIC FORECASTS IN THE 1970s

Stephen K. McNEES *

Federeal Reserve Bank of Boston

1. Introduction

Economic forecasters have come under a barrage of criticism for their poor performance for the 1974–75 recession. Their record over the early 1970s shows that those errors were unprecedented in magnitude, far larger than those before or since. The record also shows that forecasting errors have fallen into fairly distinct patterns over different *forecast periods* (i.e., the chronological time period that the forecast is intended to anticipate). Recently forecasting errors have returned, at least temporarily, to more normal magnitudes.

Forecasts are often evaluated by comparing the latest actual data with the most recent forecast. This comparison encompasses a very short forecast horizon because forecasts are issued so frequently (typically quarterly or even monthly). Forecasts of such short horizons are largely irrelevant for planning decisions because the time lag between actions and their impact is usually significantly longer. This study deals with one-year-ahead forecasts. Given the conventional rule-of-thumb of six- to nine-month lags, this horizon is sufficiently long that policy actions can affect policy goals. It also minimizes certain technical problems such as seasonal adjustment.

This study is based on the forecasts of five of the most widely known and influential forecasters. [1] Because the objective is to describe the variation in errors over different forecast periods rather than among different forecasters, the individual forcecasts are treated anonymously, designating only the high, median, and low errors.

The analysis focuses on nine "episodes" during the first half of the 1970s. These episodes were selected (somewhat arbitrarily) as periods in which the pace of economic activity changed considerably and/or in which the outlook was particularly controversial due to a major exogenous shock. The nine episodes selected are:

1. The severity of the 1970 recession, 1970: I to 1971: I.

---

* Vice President and economist, Federal Reserve Bank of Boston.

[1] The forecasts selected are those by the Bureau of Economic Analysis of the U.S. Department of Commerce, Chase Econometric Associates, Inc., Data Resources, Inc., Wharton Econometric Forecasting Associates, Inc., and the median forecast from the Economic Research Survey by the American Statistical Association and the National Bureau of Economic Research.

2. The strength of the early recovery, 1970: IV to 1971: IV.

3. The impact of the New Economic Policies, 1971: III to 1972: III.

4. Sustained expansion, 1972: II to 1973: II.

5. Soft landing turned stagflation, 172: IV to 1973: IV.

6. The impact of the oil embargo, 1973: III to 1974: III.

7. The recession of 1974-75, 1974: I to 1975: I.

8. The first year of the recovery, 1974: IV to 1975: IV.

9. The pause of 1976, 1975: IV to 1976: IV.

Virtually all of the forecasts examined were based on the pre-benchmark version of the National Income and Product Accounts (NIPA) data. In early 1976, these data were revised incorporating additional source data, new estimating procedures, and changes in definitions and classifications. On the presumption that the revised data provide a more accurate portrayal of the history of economic activity and that forecasts should be judged against the best approximation of the "true" values, these data are used as the actual values in this investigation. More precisely, it is assumed that the *percentage changes of the major economic aggregates* — GNP, real GNP, and the implicit GNP price deflator — *are fairly comparable on a pre- and post-benchmark basis.* [2]

While "the postwar growth trend of the revised GNP is about the same as that of the previously published one" and "the pattern of short-term fluctuations in the revised GNP is also similar to that shown previously," [3] substantial differences arise in some of the following episodes. These differences are noted below.

2. The severity of the 1970 recession, 1970: I to 1971: I

In their forecasts based on the preliminary actual data for 1970: I, forecasters expected the recession to be very mild. They knew that the economy was in a recession according to the simple definition that two consecutive quarterly declines in real GNP constitute a recession. The unemployment rate was only 4.4 percent in March, but rising rapidly, reaching 5.0 percent in May.

In this recessionary environment, forecasters expected that real GNP would increase 2.2 to 3.6 percent over the next year and the unemployment rate would

---

[2] Comparability cannot be assumed for levels (as opposed to percentage changes) of the major aggregates or for the components of GNP which were affected by defintional and classificational changes. Those who are unhappy with the comparability assumption are referred to previous assessment which was based on the final version of the pre-benchmark estimates.

[3] The national income and product accounts of the united states: revised estimates, 1929–74, *Survey of Current Business* (January 1976), Part I, p. 1. For a fuller discussion, see also ibid. 24–27, and George Jaszi and Carol S. Carson, The benchmark revision of the national income and product accounts: new perspective on the U.S. economy, *Business Economics* (September 1976), 9–13.

Table 1
The 1970 recession: 1970 : I to 1971 : I

Growth rate of (percent)	Forecasts			Actual
	High	Median	Low	
Real GNP	3.6	2.5	2.2	2.0
GNP deflator	4.0	3.8	3.0	5.1
GNP	7.7	6.2	5.3	7.2
Unemployment rate [a]	5.2	4.6	4.2	5.9

[a] Level in final quarter.

remain below 5.2 percent. The economic slowdown was expected to reduce the rate of inflation (as measured by the implicit GNP price deflator) from the 5.0 percent rate registered in 1970: I to 3.0 to 4.0 percent.

The expectation of resumed real growth proved highly accurate; the actual rate was 2.0 percent compared with the median forecast of 2.5 percent.

The accompanying rise in the unemployment rate to 5.9 percent was substantially underestimated, however, due largely perhaps to the unexpectedly strong growth in the civilian labor force. Moreover, inflation did not decelerate as expected; the rate over the next year held near the 5.0 percent pace of 1970: I. The errors in the inflation forecasts (which ranged from 1 to 2 percent) must be considered large for those times, when the actual rate of inflation varied little between 4 and 6 percent. In summary, the forecasts fairly accurately gauged the mildness of the 1970 recession as measured by output, but were far too optimistic about the consequent "Phillips curve".

3. The strength of the early recovery, 1970: IV to 1971: IV

When the early 1971 forecasts were issued, it was known that real output had declined in 1970: IV and that the General Motors strike had ended in late November. The unemployment rate had risen steadily to 6.0 percent in December, and the GNP deflator was rising at an annual rate of just over 5.5 percent in 1970: IV. The relevant forecasting issues were the strength of the 1971 recovery and the path of inflation.

Forecasters expected GNP growth of 8.2 to 9.8 percent, although the median forecast was only 8.3 percent. The actual 9.5 percent figure exceeded all but the highest forecast by more than 1 percentage point. The expectation of a very moderate recovery was in fact realized — actual real growth was identical to the median forecast and the largest error was only 0.6 percentage points. Most forecasters cor-

Table 2
1971 recovery: 1970 : IV–1971 : IV

Growth rate of (percent)	Forecasts			Actual
	High	Median	Low	
Real GNP	5.2	4.6	4.3	4.6
GNP deflator	4.4	3.6	3.3	4.7
GNP	9.8	8.3	8.2	9.5
Unemployment rate [a]	6.2	5.8	5.5	6.0

[a] Level in final quarter.

rectly judged that the unemployment rate would hold essentially flat during the year. The actual 5.9 percent fourth-quarter figure was very close to the median forecast.

The inflation forecasts are more complex to evaluate. Over the first half of the year, inflation substantially exceeded the forecasted range. The imposition of wage and price controls brought the inflation rate in the second half of the year down to the forecasted range. Thus, for the year as a whole, the inflation rate was underestimated although, thanks to Phases I and II, by relatively minor amounts. [4]

4. The impact of the new economic policies, 1971: III to 1972: III

During 1971: II, real GNP rose at a 3.6 percent annual rate, the unemployment rate inched up to 6.0 percent and the rate of inflation declined to 4.2 percent, the lowest since mid-1968. Against this backdrop, forecasters expected a continued modest recovery, with the rate of inflation declining moderately and an unemployment rate between 5.2 and 6.0 percent in 1972: III. In retrospect, the median GNP forecast proved to be 1.1 percent too low, the real growth forecast was 1.1 percent too low, the unemployment rate forecast for 1972: III was 0.2 percent too high, and the inflation forecast was just right.

These forecasts were issued before the unforeseen announcement of the New Economic Policies (NEP) on August 15, 1971. In the first set of forecasts after the NEP, the median GNP forecast was raised 0.7 percent and the median real growth forecast by 2.1 percent. The GNP adjustment brought the forecasts closer to the actual outcome, but the real GNP adjustment proved excessive—overshooting the actual 6 percent outcome by a full percentage point.

[4] The pre-benchmark division of GNP growth between output and prices reversed these conclusions. On a pre-benchmark basis, the median inflation forecast was on the mark and real output growth was above the forecasted range.

Table 3a
Pre-new economic policies: 1971 : III–1972 : III

Growth rate of (percent)	Forecasts			Actual
	High	Median	Low	
Real GNP	6.4	4.9	4.5	6.0
GNP deflator	4.3	3.9	3.5	3.9
GNP	10.1	9.1	8.6	10.2
Unemployment rate [a]	6.0	5.8	5.2	5.6

[a] Level in final quarter.

Table 3b
Post-new economic policies: 1971 : III–1972 : III

Growth rate of (percent)	Forecasts			Actual
	High	Median	Low	
Real GNP	7.7	7.0	6.1	6.0
GNP deflator	3.2	2.5	2.1	3.9
GNP	10.5	9.8	9.0	10.2
Unemployment rate [a]	5.4	5.3	5.0	5.6

[a] Level in final quarter.

After the NEP, the inflation forecasts were lowered from a 3.5 to 4.3 percent to a 2.1 to 3.2 percent range. The unemployment rate forecasts were also lowered in accordance with the revised expectation of more rapid output growth. Both these adjustments proved, after the fact, to be unwarranted, as they took the forecast range away from the highly accurate pre-NEP forecasts. [5]

5. Sustained expansion, 1972: II to 1973: II

By mid-1972, there was no doubt that a strong economic recovery was under way. Real GNP in the second quarter grew at an 8.9 percent rate and employment was rising rapidly, although the unemployment rate held at a plateau just under 6.0 percent. Phase II held the rate of inflation to 2.1 percent in the second quarter,

[5] On the pre-benchmark basis, the real rate of growth was 6.8 percent, suggesting the post-NEP adjustments were highly useful. Similarly the lower inflation rate on a pre-benchmark basis indicated the post-NEP downward adjustment was appropriate.

Table 4
Sustained expansion: 1972 : II—1973 : II

Growth rate of (percent)	Forecasts			Actual
	High	Median	Low	
Real GNP	7.3	6.0	5.7	5.9
GNP deflator	3.7	3.6	3.0	5.2
GNP	10.5	9.8	9.5	11.4
Unemployment rate [a]	5.2	5.1	4.8	4.9

[a] Level in final quarter.

down from the 5.1 percent bulge which followed the end of Phase I.

The mid-1972 forecasts were exceptionally accurate indications of the path of real economic activity in late 1972 and early 1973. The median real growth forecast was extremely close to the actual 5.9 percent, and only one forecaster erred by more than 0.5 percentage points. Similarly, the *maximum* error among unemployment rate forecasts was a 0.3 percent overestimate. The forecast of nominal variables accompanying this excellent real-variable forecast was poor by the standards of the time. The medium inflation forecast was 1.6 percentage points too optimistic. The 5.2 percent rate of inflation was underestimated due to the inability to foresee the acceleration of inflation which occurred in the first half of 1973, after the Phase II controls had been relaxed and reformulated into Phase III (on January 11, 1973). The inflation errors swamped the negligible real growth errors, producing underestimates of GNP growth of from 0.9 to 1.9 percent.

6. Soft landing turned stagflation, 1972: IV to 1973: IV

In early 1973, forecasters knew that real GNP had grown at an 8.5 percent annual rate in 1972: IV, the unemployment rate had held at 5.2 percent in December, and the rate of inflation had been held under 3 percent for three consecutive quarters by the Phase II controls. Before the new forecasts were made, the Phase II controls had been replaced by the more voluntary Phase III system, but there had not been enough time to see how well the new program would work.

Forecasters anticipated that inflation in 1973 would exceed the 1972 rate, but even the most pessimistic far underestimated the actual 7.5 percent which was in store. Similarly, even the highest nominal GNP growth forecast was 1.9 percent below the actual 11.1 percent.

In contrast to the underestimates of nominal variables the consensus forecast of a "soft landing", with real growth decelerating in the first half and slowing more substantially to below-trend rates in the second half, was overly optimistic. Over the

Table 5
Soft landing turned stagflation: 1972 : IV–1973 : IV

Growth rate of (percent)	Forecasts			Actual
	High	Median	Low	
Real GNP	4.9	4.8	4.5	3.4
GNP deflator	4.5	3.8	3.5	7.5
GNP	9.2	8.9	8.6	11.1
Unemployment rate [a]	5.0	4.9	4.8	4.8

[a] Level in final quarter.

year as a whole, fourth quarter to fourth quarter, real growth forecasts ranged narrowly from 4.5 percent to 4.9 percent. The narrow soft landing consensus overestimated the actual 3.4 percent real growth which occurred. The corresponding unemployment rate forecasts for 1973: IV were once again highly accurate.

7. The impact of the oil embargo, 1973: III to 1974: III

As of late October 1973, the forecasters knew that real growth had slowed to about 3.5 percent in 1973: III, that the unemployment rate had held level in August and September at 4.8 percent, and that their previous forecasts had seriously underestimated the 6.7 percent increase in prices in 1973: III. More importantly perhaps, they knew that the Middle East War had erupted on October 6 and that the posted price of crude oil had been raised by 70 percent on October 16 before their forecasts were made. But they did not yet know that the price of imported oil would soon quadruple. It was not until the November round of forecasts that the "energy crisis" was regarded as a serious threat to the prevailing soft landing view.

The pre-embargo real growth forecasts for the period 1973: III to 1974: III ranged from 2.1 to 3.4 percent. None foresaw the 1.9 percent decline which was to occur. Inflation forecasts had been raised from the early 1973 levels, but only to about half of the actual 10.8 percent rate. Given an optimistic real growth outlook, the expectation of a modest rise in the unemployment rate by 1974: III to 5.2 to 5.5 percent somewhat surprisingly only slightly understated the 5.6 percent actual figure.

These misses — real growth was overestimated by 4.0 to 5.3 percent, and the inflation rate was underestimated by 5.4 to 6.4 percent — were unprecedented in magnitude. These forecasts provided a very poor indication of where the economy was headed.

One of the primary reasons, or at least rationales, for the extraordinarily large errors was the unanticipated oil embargo, announced on October 17, and the conse-

Table 6a
Pre-embargo: 1973 : III–1974 : III

Growth rate of (percent)	Forecasts			Actual
	High	Median	Low	
Real GNP	3.4	2.4	2.1	−1.9
GNP deflator	5.4	4.6	4.4	10.8
GNP	8.1	7.4	6.7	8.7
Unemployment [a]	5.5	5.2	5.2	5.6

[a] Level in final quarter.

quent energy crisis. This unique external supply-side shock provided a severe challenge to the conventional, demand-oriented forecasting techniques.

To examine how well the forecasts were adapted to the oil embargo, consider the post-embargo forecasts of the same "energy spasm" period. In contrast to the pre-embargo forecasts, these forecasts are *three*-quarter-ahead forecasts that combine embargo adjustments with the actual data for 1973: IV.

The post-embargo set of nominal GNP forecasts changed little from the pre-embargo set, slightly underestimating the actual rate of 8.7 percent. The price-output mix was somewhat improved but remained far off the mark. The January forecasts of real growth over this period were flat – the median forecast was 0.6 percent and the low −0.1 percent. These forecasts lent credence to the view that the economy was suffering from a short-lived energy spasm, which would be followed by a resumption of real growth. This mistaken prognosis set the stage for the subsequent disputes about whether the economy was in a recession in early 1974, when employment, industrial production, and new orders for capital goods were holding up fairly well. Due perhaps to labor hoarding based on the expectation of an upturn, employment held up well. Productivity unexpectedly collapsed. This short-lived

Table 6b
Post-embargo: 1973 : III–1974 : III

Growth rate of (percent)	Forecasts			Actual
	High	Median	Low	
Real GNP	1.8	0.6	−0.1	−1.9
GNP deflator	8.3	6.6	5.6	10.8
GNP	8.3	7.6	6.4	8.7
Unemployment rate [a]	6.2	5.9	5.7	5.6

[a] Level in final quarter.

surprising stability in the unemployment rate has been examined in [3]. Despite the substantial *overestimation* of real output, there was an *overestimation* of the unemployment rate in 1974: III. After the oil embargo, most forecasters raised their estimates of third-quarter unemployment from about 5.2 percent (compared to the actual of 5.6 percent) to about 6.0. The unexpected stability in employment produced a variety of novel theories, indicating the need for an entirely new approach to the short-term demand for employment.

But time showed that the new theories were not needed. The failure instead had been in the timing, or lag structure, in the simple output-unemployment relationship. The unemployment rate, which had drifted up 1 percentage point between the start of the second and start of the fourth quarters, rose another full percentage point in the last two months of the year. Thus, the same post-embargo forecasts, which had overestimated the unemployment rate for 1974: III, turned out to be extremely accurate for the fourth quarter of the year.

Just the opposite conclusion is true of the real GNP forecasts. All the post-embargo forecasts showed an economic recovery or rebound in the second half of the year. Projections of real growth in 1974: IV ranged from 2.5 to 5.9 percent, a far cry from the actual −6.8 percent figure. The inability to foresee the collapse in demand which was to occur in 1974: IV may overstate the misinformation in the forecasts. A fairer statement is that the forecasters were predicting a year (fourth quarter to fourth quarter) of essentially flat economic growth in contrast to the actual outcome of a 4.1 percent decline in real GNP. The resulting errors were several times larger than the average error of real GNP forecasts over the previous three years.

In sum, the first set of forecasts after the oil embargo were generally correct in leaving the nominal GNP forecasts unchanged from pre-embargo predictions. However, adjustments to show more inflation and lower levels of output, while in the right direction, were not nearly large enough. The upward pressure on prices and downward pressure on output were far stronger than the post-embargo forecasts anticipated.

8. The recession of 1974–75, 1974: I to 1975: I

The next episode is one of even greater forecasting failure. In the late April 1974 forecasts made after the embargo had ended, there was still no appreciation of the severity of the 1974–75 recession. It was known that in this first quarter real GNP had declined by 5.8 percent and inflation had moved into the double-digit area, 10.8 percent in 1974: I.

In a wave of post-embargo euphoria, the forecasters predicted real GNP growth over the next four-quarter period to be as large as 3.8 percent, and inflation to recede to as low as 6.6 percent. The unemployment rate was projected to level off between 5.7 and 6.1 percent in 1975: I. None of the figures proved to be even a remote representation of the future reality.

Table 7a
The recession: 1974 : I–1975 : I

Growth rate of (percent)	Forecasts			Actual
	High	Median	Low	
Real GNP	3.8	2.2	1.6	−5.6
GNP deflator	8.5	7.0	6.6	11.6
GNP	11.6	10.3	8.9	5.4
Unemployment rate [a]	6.1	5.9	5.7	8.1

[a] Level in final quarter.

Unlike the 1973–74 forecasts which were quite accurate for nominal GNP but missed the mix between prices and output, the April 1974 forecasts seriously overestimated the growth of nominal GNP. GNP forecasts ranged from 8.9 to 11.6 percent, which compared with the actual rate of 5.4 percent, produced the largest GNP errors in the first half of the 1970s. This overestimate occurred despite a sizable, but far from record, underestimate of the inflation rate – the median forecast underestimated the 11.6 percent rate of inflation by 4.6 percent; the minimum error was 3.1 percent.

Relative to past performances, the most serious error occurred in the underestimation of the rise in the unemployment rate. The closest one-year-ahead forecast put the unemployment rate 2.0 percentage points below the actual 8.1 percent figure for 1975; I, an error about six times larger than the average error in the previous four years. Much of this error stemmed from overestimation of real GNP. The most pessimistic real growth forecast in April 1974, 1.6 percent, gave no indication of the actual 5.6 percent decline.

Table 7b gives a detailed breakdown of the errors of the high, median and low real GNP forecasts of 1974–75 along with the percentage distribution of the total errors among components. [6] The error distributions are similar for each of the three forecasts. As expected, the errors are disproportionately concentrated in the cyclical components: the largest proportion, about one-third, was in the change in business inventory investment; the second largest, about one-quarter of the total, was in business fixed investment; the next largest, of roughly 20 to 25 percent, was in expenditures on consumer durables; and the other sizable error component was investment in residential structures. Net exports, government purchases of goods and services, and consumer purchases of nondurable goods and services were the only components that increased in real terms over this time span. Net exports were the only major demand component whose strength was generally underestimated, partially offsetting some of the large overestimates in other areas. The underesti-

---

[6] Table 7b and the analysis in this section are based upon pre-benchmark revision NIPA data.

Table 7b

Errors and error distribution low, median, and high real GNP forecasts, 1974 : I to 1975 : I

	Actual change (1)	Forecast errors			Percent of ΔGNP Actual (5)	Percent of GNP error		
		Low Billions, 1958 $ (2)	Median Billions, 1958 $ (3)	High Billions, 1958 $ (4)		Low (6)	Median (7)	High (8)
(1) Real GNP	-50.5	63.5	68.5	82.5	100.0	100.0	100.0	100.0
(2) Consumer expenditures	-8.2	21.2	19.3	25.4	16.2	33.4	28.2	30.8
(3) Durables	-10.0	15.8	12.7	15.3	19.8	24.9	18.5	18.5
(4) Nondurables and services	1.7	5.5	6.7	10.2	-3.4	8.7	9.8	12.4
(5) Fixed investment	-21.7	24.7	31.3	29.0	43.0	38.9	45.7	35.2
(6) Business	-12.5	16.7	16.6	19.5	24.8	26.3	24.2	23.6
(7) Residential	-9.1	8.0	14.7	9.5	18.0	12.6	21.5	11.5
(8) Inventory investment	-22.3	22.4	19.9	26.3	44.2	35.3	29.1	31.9
(9) Net exports	0.1	-5.4	-5.0	-2.4	-0.2	-8.5	-7.3	-2.9
(10) Government purchases	1.7	0.5	2.9	4.0	-3.4	0.8	4.2	4.8

Note: Components may not add to totals because of rounding.

mates of consumer purchases of nondurable goods and services and of government purchases of goods and services were of relatively minor importance.

It is impossible to analyze fully the causes of these errors. Although no final accounting can be given, it is possible to speculate about some of the factors underlying these errors.

Part of the explanation for the overestimation of inventory investment, i.e., the underestimation of the swing to inventory liquidation, arises from the fact that these forecasts were based on preliminary GNP estimates which were subsequently revised to show substantially more inventory investment. Even after the July 1974 National Income and Product Account historical revisions, however, "The forecasters were betting against a regularity of postwar history in expecting no inventory liquidation." [7] This inability to forecast real final sales, particularly the collapse which occurred in 1974: IV, centered around the gross auto product final sales. This failure, in turn, must be attributable to factors peculiar to the 1975 models such as the substantial price increases and the introduction of new pollution control and safety equipment, as well as to more usual factors such as the low level of real disposable income and the erosion of real household wealth positions. The resulting substantial overhang of auto dealers' inventories by the end of the year, which in turn resulted in heavy liquidation in 1975: I, accounted for about 45 percent of the total inventory liquidation for the quarter.

Aside from auto sales, the major error in forecasting final sales comes from the inaccuracy of forecasts of fixed investment. Explanation of the fixed investment error leads to the question of monetary policy assumptions in the April 1974 forecasts. Evaluation of the monetary policy assumptions behind the forecasting errors is particularly difficult because of the lack of general agreement on the appropriate targets and indicators of monetary policy, the lag structure of the impact of monetary policy, and the size of monetary policy multipliers. The first issue can be partially avoided by examining the behavior of both aggregates and interest rates. Table 7c shows April 1974 forecasts of two of the more commonly watched indicators of monetary policy; the growth in the narrowly defined money stock and the interest rate on 4- to 6-month commercial paper. [8] The rate of money growth over the entire period was significantly overestimated and the level of commercial paper rates was generally underestimated. Monotary policy was "tighter" (and/or the demand for money was stronger) than the forecasters anticipated in their April forecasts.

However, because of the lag between financial variables and their impact on spending, production, and employment, the long-term financial variable assump-

[7] Arthur M. Okun, A postmortem of the 1974 recession, *Brookings Papers on Economic Activity* 1 (1975), 220. The 1970–71 experience is an exception to this "regularity", as there was no inventory liquidation or inventory cycle.

[8] Only four of the five forecasts provide detailed financial-monetary information. Money and the commercial paper rate are the only two financial variables common to all four forecasts.

tions had a negligible impact in the forecast period. With the conventional six- to nine-month lag assumption, only the monetary policy assumptions for 1974: II and 1974: III would be relevant for the outcome through 1975: I. Over that period, money growth was 1.75 percent lower than the highest growth forecast but only about 0.5 percent lower than the median forecast. Growth in the second quarter was acutually higher than generally anticipated. Taking instead the commerical paper rate in the middle quarters of 1974, it was generally expected that rates would decline throughout the remainder of the period. However, the actual rate continued to climb, reaching a level of nearly 12 percent in mid-July, and did not fall below 10 percent again until October.

It would be interesting to conduct an ex post simulation of the forecast period to examine the impact of underestimating financial stringency on the forecast in this period. In the absence of such a test, one can only speculate on its importance. One guess is that significant underestimation of the declines would have occurred despite foreknowledge of the degree of financial stringency which was to prevail in the middle quarters of 1974 although forecasts of fixed investment, particularly in residential structures, would certainly have improved. For econometric forecasters, most models' coefficients for aggregates or rates are too small and the distributed lags too long to capture the severity and rapidity of the decline. For judgmental forecasters, the memory of shortages, capacity problems, and the need to restructure the capital stock in accordance with the new higher price of energy were too

Table 7c

Monetary and financial forecasts issued April 1974

Forecaster	Actual [a] 1974 : I	Forecast			
		1974 : II	1974 : III	1974 : IV	1975 : I
		Money stock growth			
A	5.8	7.4	7.3	7.5	7.5
B	5.6	3.4	5.9	7.1	6.9
C	5.8	6.9	5.3	6.3	6.6
D	5.8	6.0	6.0	6.3	6.2
Actual	5.8	7.3	3.9	3.7	1.4
		Yield on 4- to 6-month commercial paper			
A	9.73	9.7	10.0	9.5	8.9
B	9.73	9.2	7.3	6.6	6.7
C	9.73	9.2	8.5	7.8	7.3
D	10.13	10.1	10.0	9.7	9.4
Actual	8.3	10.5	11.5	9.1	6.6

[a] Actual money stock growth is latest published data available at time of forecast. Actual yield on 4- to 6-month commercial paper is level in week preceding issuing of forecast; all other figures are quarterly averages.

fresh in mind to anticipate the collapse which was in store. Only if appropriate assumptions on the degree of financial stringency had been combined with knowledge of the magnitude of excess inventory holding, the fourth-quarter collapse in consumer demand (especially in auto demand), and the consequent year-end inventory overhang, could the record errors for the period have been reduced to more normal magnitudes.

9. The strength of the first year of recovery, 1975: I to 1976: I

At the time of their spring forecasts, the forecasters were aware of the 10.4 percent first-quarter drop in real GNP and the rise in the unemployment rate to 8.7 percent in March. Inflation had dipped below the double-digit rate, to 8.0 percent, so that nominal GNP fell at a 3.2 percent annual rate.

Despite the five consecutive quarterly declines in output, there were reasons to believe the cyclical trough was near: (1) The Tax Reduction Act of 1975, which provided for about $ 23 billion of fiscal stimulus, was enacted in late March. (2) The precipitous first-quarter drop in production reflected inventory liquidation; final sales held flat in real terms.

Against this background, the forecasters uniformly expected a moderate "U-shaped" recovery, with real growth forecasts ranging about 1 percentage point on each side of the median 4.4 percent forecast. While the onset of the recovery phase was correctly anticipated, the 7.3 percent actual increase resulted in the largest *underestimate* of this period. With a single exception, the forecasters anticipated moderate increases in the unemployment rate wherras in fact the rate fell 0.5 percent over the following year, producing the largest overestimate of this forecast period.

While the forecasters were overly pessimistic about the real variables, they accurately anticipated the deceleration in the rate of inflation. The 5.8 percent median forecast was only slightly above the 5.4 percent actual. Thus, the underestimates of GNP were due entirely to the underestimates of real growth.

Table 8
The first year of recovery: 1975 : I–1976 : I

Growth rate of (percent)	Forecasts			Actual
	High	Median	Low	
Real GNP	5.3	4.4	3.4	7.3
GNP deflator	6.8	5.8	5.6	5.4
GNP	11.5	11.4	9.8	13.1
Unemployment rate [a]	8.4	8.3	7.7	7.6

[a] Level in final quarter.

10. The "pause" of 1976, 1975: IV to 1976: IV

Early 1976 was a difficult time for economic forecasters to determine exactly where the economy stood. Their previous forecasts and econometric relationships had been based on the National Income and Product Accounts data issued before the January benchmark revisions. The official estimates of 1975: IV (as well as the latest revised estimates of earlier periods) were available only on the post-bench mark basis. The post-benchmark data for the last quarter of 1975 showed GNP had risen 12.2 percent, real GNP 5.4 percent, and inflation 6.5 percent. The unemployment rate for the quarter averaged 8.4 percent. Two of the forecasters continued to issue their forecasts on the pre-benchmark basis; the other three issued their next forecast on the post-benchmark basis.

The forecasters expected inflation to decelerate in 1976 into the 5 to 6.2 percent range. The actual deceleration, to 4.6 percent, was somewhat larger due probably to unexpected stability in food prices and relatively small increases in energy prices. Excluding food and energy, inflation in 1976 ran at about a 6 percent annual rate, very close to the median forecast.

The forecasters uniformly expected a continued, moderate recovery with real growth estimates ranging only from 5.2 to 5.7 percent. This moderate growth was expected to accompany a reduction in the unemployment rate to the 7.2 to 7.8 percent range. In fact, each of these expectations was slightly optimistic. Following a booming first quarter, the economy entered into a "pause" or "lull" lowering real growth for the year to only 5 percent and the unemployment rate to 7.9 percent in the final quarter. Thus, even though the final outcome fell outside the range of forecasts, the forecasts succeeded in a fairly accurate qualitative description of the economy in 1976.

Table 9
The "pause" of 1976, 1975 : IV–1976 : IV

Growth rate of (percent)	Forecast			Actual
	High	Median	Low	
Real GNP	5.7	5.4	5.2	5.0
GNP deflator	6.2	5.9	5.0	4.6
GNP	11.9	11.7	10.7	9.8
Unemployment rate [a]	7.8	7.3	7.2	7.9

[a] Level in final quarter.

11. A summary of the record

Table 10 summarizes the accuracy of the median one-year-ahead forecasts in the early 1970 s. The errors fall into six fairly distinct patterns.

The early-1970 forecasts correctly foresaw that the 1970 recession would be one of the mildest in the post-World War II period. They were, however, overly optimistic about the rise in the unemployment rate and the deceleration of inflation that would accompany the recession.

The forecasts made from mid-1970 through 1971 gave a highly accurate picture

Table 10

Errors of median one-year-ahead forecasts 1971 : I–1977 : III
(based on five forecasters).

Four quarters ending in	Percent change in			Change in unemployment rate
	GNP	Real GNP	Deflator	
71 : I	−1.0	0.5	−1.3	−0.9
71 : II	−1.3	0.3	−1.6	−0.9
71 : III	−1.1	0.5	−1.6	−0.5
71 : IV	−1.2	−0.1	−1.1	−0.4
72 : I	−0.5	0.5	−0.7	−0.1
72 : II	−0.8	−0.8	0.1	0.2
72 : III	−0.6	0.2	−0.7	−0.1
72 : IV	−1.7	−1.2	−0.4	0.2
73 : I	−2.3	−1.4	−0.7	0.4
73 : II	−1.6	0.2	−1.6	0.0
73 : III	−2.1	0.9	−2.8	0.3
73 : IV	−2.2	1.4	−3.7	0.1
74 : I	−0.5	3.9	−4.3	−0.3
74 : II	−0.8	3.4	−4.2	0.0
74 : III	−1.3	4.1	−6.0	−0.3
74 : IV	0.5	4.9	−5.0	−0.5
75 : I	4.9	7.8	−4.6	−2.4
75 : II	3.6	5.3	−2.1	−2.8
75 : III	1.3	−0.2	0.8	−1.6
75 : IV	−0.9	−1.9	1.2	−0.1
76 : I	−1.7	−2.9	0.4	0.7
76 : II	0.5	0.1	0.3	0.6
76 : III	1.9	0.3	1.3	−0.1
76 : IV	1.9	0.4	1.3	−0.6
77 : I	2.1	1.1	0.7	−0.6
77 : II	0.9	0.7	0.2	−0.3
77 : III	0.0	0.2	0.0	0.2
Mean absolute error	1.4	1.7	1.8	0.6

of the future path of all major economic variables. This performance is particularly notable because of both the atypical profile of that recovery — sluggish in 1971 and exuberant in 1972 — and the dramatic, simultaneous major policy shifts which were embodied in the New Economic Policies. Forecasts in this period provided about as much information about future developments as decision makers can ever hope to obtain.

The forecasts issued in 1972 failed to foresee the acceleration in inflation which occurred in 1973. This was the major cause of the substantial underestimation of nominal GNP. Real variable forecasts, on the other hand, continued to be highly accurate: both the second-half slowdown and the leveling off in the unemployment rate were anticipated well in advance.

Underestimation of the acceleration of inflation in 1974 did not result in an underestimation of current dollar GNP as it had for 1973, however. The failure in the forecasts of 1974 was the inability to apportion GNP growth between price and output increases — the underestimation of inflation was accompanied by roughly equal overestimation of real growth. Despite this, however, the forecasts of unemployment remained on track.

The forecasts made in early 1974 produced by far the largest errors of the period for GNP, real GNP, and the unemployment rate—errors many times larger than the "normal" errors for the early 1970s. These forecasts failed miserably in warning of the severity of the impending recession. The sources of the errors in real GNP, discussed earlier, were spread fairly evenly among its cyclical components. Because of the failure to account for a combination of adverse economic forces, these forecasts contributed to the mistaken impression, so widely prevalent even in mid-1974, that inflation was the only major policy problem and that an upturn was imminent.

Starting in 1975 the economic forecasts became significantly more accurate. The moderate increases in real growth and the deceleration of inflation were both captured with an unusually high degree of accuracy. The uneven path of the unemployment rate continued to prove difficult to anticipate, although the forecasts were far more accurate than those issued in the previous year.

These observations are based on the median forecast of a group of five major forecasters. They implicitly assume that all forecasters' errors were about the same. That assumption can be examined by evaluating the accuracy of different forecasters and forecasting techniques.

Because perfection is an unattainable standard — to forecast is to err — forecasting ability must be judged comparatively. The only answer to the standard question, "How good was the forecast?" must be in the Socratic manner, "Compared to what?" Therefore, this evaluation will contrast three different approaches to forecasting: econometricians', economists', and statisticians'.

12. Pure model vs. judgmental

The first comparison to be made is between economists and econometricians, or more precisely, between *judgmental* and *mechanical* use of econometric models. Only two model-builders have allowed their models to speak for themselves, i.e., without subjective "constant adjustments" — the small models developed by Ray Fair of Yale and by the Federal Reserve Bank of St. Louis. When the GNP forecasting accuracy of these two models was compared, the Fair model proved superior by three different tests. [9] However, when the ex ante mechanical forecasts of the Fair model are compared with the forecasts of the major, well-known forecasters, the "pure-model" or "mechanical" forecasts are distinctly inferior, especially for output, prices, and residential structures. [10]

13. Judgmental vs. statistical

The second comparison to be made is between economists' forecasts and those generated by purely statistical rules. In the old days, these were usually "naive" forecasts, such as "no-change" or "same-change" rules, but now they take the mathematically complicated form of ARIMA or time series models. Numerous studies in the literature purport to show the superiority of purely statistical over economic forecasts, but most of these studies suffer from one or more of the following flaws:

(1) Most studies compare the statistical rules with the ex post forecasts of econometric models. However, ex post forecasts need not give a good guide to ex ante performance when judgmental adjustments are permitted.

(2) Most of the studies are sorely out of date in two ways. They are based on obsolete versions of the current stock of models. Most use the 1960s as the forecast period. The experience of the 1960s appears tranquil in comparison to what we have seen so far in the 1970s.

(3) Many of these studies were confined solely to one-quarter-ahead forecasts. This practice seems bizarre in view of the important differences between single and multi-period forecasts and the irrelevance of one-period forecasts for many economic decisions.

(4) Statistical rules suffer the inherent disadvantage that they can produce only an unconditional forecast and cannot be used to assess alternative policies or other "exogenous shocks".

[9] Stephen K. McNees, A comparison of the GNP forecasting accuracy of the Fair and St. Louis econometric models, *New England Economic Review*, Sept./Oct. (1973).

[10] Stephen K. McNees, An evaluation of economic forecasts, *New England Economic Review*, Nov./Dec. (1975).

Statistical rules do have a role in forecasting – they are quick and relatively inexpensive alternatives to modeling (and/or "judgment"?!). However, the complex methods used today do not share the virtue of simplicity with their predecessor "naive" rules. Despite these grounds for skepticism, the jury is still out on the relative accuracy of statistical rules.

14. Judgment with or without models?

The first comparison suggests that presently existing econometric *models* do not forecast as well as *economists*. But if models are not *sufficient* to produce the most accurate forecasts, are they even *necessary* to produce the most accurate forecasts? Strictly speaking, we may never know. A clean test would require puely judgmental forecasts to be made in complete isolation from forecasts based on econometric models. Since *all* judgmental forecasters are probably influenced to some degree by the model-based forecasts, one can only guess at the change in accuracy that results from access to econometric models. Ignoring for the moment the possible influence econometric models may have on judgmental forecasts, the available data do not support the idea that an econometric model is necessary to produce accurate forecasts. This statement is based on the record of two noneconometric sets of forecasts – the GE Mapcast and the median forecast from the ASA/NBER survey. The ASA forecasts were never worse than the median of comparable econometrically-based forecasts. Their exact ranking depends on the specific variable being forecasted. The ASA forecast has been the most accurate for nominal GNP, housing starts, and the unemployment rate. For real GNP and inflation, the ASA forecasts were about average. The GE forecasts also performed respectably relative to comparable econometrically-based forecasts. They did relatively poorly for the unemployment rate, net exports, and Federal purchases and the deficit, about average for real GNP, and residential structures, and well for inflation, nominal GNP, and consumer purchases. In short, the available data *cannot* be used to reject the idea that a formal, econometric model is *not necessary* to produce accurate forecasts.

These data, however, are admittedly imperfect. The ASA survey group is not representative of the pure noneconometric approach to forecasting; it contains several econometric forecasters and many more econometric forecast subscribers. It is also probable that none of the individual forecasts comprising the ASA median are as accurate as the median itself. In addition, these "noneconometric" forecasters often use individual econometric relationships even though they are not blended together into a formal model. Finally, forecast users and purely judgmental forecasters are well aware that a large econometric model has advantages other than accuracy. In terms of speed, consistency, number of variables, and the ability to simulate alternative scenarios, access to a large econometric model is indispensable.

The summary error statistics of the major forecasters, both econometric and noneconometric, can be used either as standards of comparison to evaluate other forecasts, or as clues as to which forecasts can be relied on more heavily. These data do not indicate that any one forecaster is "best", in the sense of dominating all others. This follows in part from the fact that the usefulness of a forecast depends on the needs of the forecast user. More importantly, all of these forecasts (and most other forecasts) are typically about the same. No forecasters consistently do much better or much worse than the major commercial forecasters. They cannot do much worse because they can see what the major forecasters are saying by subscribing to their services. With some small exceptions, they also cannot do systematically better. This is primarily because everyone has access to the same information and roughly the same intellectual framework at the same time. If there is an exception to this general rule, we can all look forward to its being rigorously documented.

References

[1] S.K. McNees, A comparison of the GNP forecasting of the Fair and St. Louis econometric models, New England Economic Review (September/October 1973).

[2] S.K. McNees, An evaluation of economic forecasts, New England Economic Review (November/December 1975).

[3] A. Okun, Unemployment and output in 1974, Brookings Papers on Economic Aactivity (1974) 502–503.

[4] A. Okun, A post mortem of the 1974 recession, Brookings Papers on Economic Activity (1975) 220.

TIMS Studies in the Management Sciences 12 (1979) 247–264
© North-Holland Publishing Company

FORECASTING CONSIDERATIONS IN A
RAPIDLY CHANGING ECONOMY

Alan R. BECKENSTEIN *

Colgate Darden Graduate School of Business, University of Virginia

This article analyzes the impact of inflation, recession and inventory cycles on forecasting methodology and performance. Regression analysis is employed intensively in the analysis, but the impact on other time-series methods is also studied. The results suggest that careful choice of variables and technique was even more important during rapid economic change than under stable conditions, when inadequate practices still produced reasonable accuracy. The sensitivity of model choice decisions to the stability of economic events is deduced from ana analysis of recent experience. Prescriptions for improving future forecasting performance are offered.

1. Introduction

Recent events in the world economy have presented practical and technical challenges to those who employ statistical techniques to forecast industry and firm performance. This article addresses three subjects related to these events.
1. The nature and magnitude of several key changes in the economic environment.
2. The impact of the changes in the environment on traditional forecasting tools.
3. Proposed changes in choice of technique and selection of variables that would improve forecasting performance in the rapidly changing environment.
The objective of this article is to identify those economic factors that must be considered and compensated for to achieve success in forecasting and to make recommendations for improving forecasting performance.

2. Changes in the economic environment

Table 1 displays some important economic statistics for the U.S. during the period from 1957 through 1975. Three types of interrelated changes in the U.S. economy took place during this period. First, the trend in the inflation rate [1] was

* The author thanks Steven Wheelwright, Spyros Makridakis, and two anonymous referees for comments that improved the paper. Support was provided by the Colgate Darden Graduate Business School Sponsors, University of Virginia. Carolyn Geiger provided valuiable editorial advice.
[1] The rate was measured by changes in the *GNP* Implicit Price Deflator.

Table 1
Selected economic statistics: 1957–1975

Year	Annual growth over preceding year		*GNP* implicit price deflator
	GNP	Real *GNP*	
1957	5.2	1.8	3.4
1958	1.4	−0.2	1.6
1959	8.4	6.0·	2.2
1960	4.0	2.3	1.7
1961	3.4	2.5	0.9
1962	7.7	5.8	1.8
1963	5.5	4.0	1.5
1964	6.9	5.3	1.6
1965	8.2	5.9	2.2
1966	9.4	5.9	3.3
1967	5.8	2.7	2.9
1968	9.1	4.4	4.5
1969	7.7	2.6	5.0
1970	5.0	−0.3	5.4
1971	8.2	3.0	5.1
1972	10.1	5.7	4.1
1973	11.6	5.5	5.8
1974	8.2	−1.7	10.0
1975	7.3	−1.8	9.3

Source: *Economic Indicators,* Dec. (1976).

upward over the period. During the 1973–1975 period, inflation hit double digit levels, thereby creating management and forecasting problems that had not been encountered previously.

Second, the rapid growth of the economy from 1971 to 1973 caused the limited capacity of manufacturing facilities to constrain further real growth of output. This factor was a major determinant [2] of the dramatic rise in the inflation rate. However, the inflation of basic commodity prices endogenously created incentives to build inventory of both raw materials and finished goods. It is difficult to establish whether the inventory buildup was the primary determinant of the tight capacity situation itself. Regardless, there was a buildup of sales for inventory purposes that was not sustainable. Since historical time-series data of sales, production, and profitability had not been affected previously by such sudden inventory behavior, a problem of comparability of economic measures among time periods arose. More will be said about this problem below.

Third, and related to the first two issues, the most severe recession since the

[2] The massive increase in energy prices was also a major factor.

1930's occurred during the period from 1973–IV through 1975–I. [3] Real GNP declined throughout that period. Since only minor recessions had occurred during the previous thirty years, forecasting models built by fitting historical time series were denied the experience of comparable economic events from which reliable predictions could be drawn. Furthermore, the need for reliable forecasts was never greater than when significant turning points were being encountered.

The one redeeming attribute of these events was that they presented a contrast to the previous periods when sustained growth allowed correlations to be drawn among measures of phenomena that were not really related physically, behaviorally, or otherwise. Two tasks arising from this situation must be dealt with. One, the impact of the changes on forecasting tools in various industries, must be understood; that is, inadequate practices must be recognized and dropped. Two, superior substitute practices must be proposed. Performing these tasks will serve two equally necessary functions. First, a better understanding of past corporate performance may be obtained, which would serve control and policy-setting objectives of forecasting analysis. Second, prediction of future events may be enhanced, enabling better planning to occur.

3. Impact on forecasting methodology

The impact of inflation, inventory adjustments, and recession on forecasting methodology can be classified into several categories:

1. Problems of focusing on the wrong variables and therefore missing important events.
2. Problems of predicting turning points instead of simply finding the best fit.
3. Discovery of inadequate performance of models that were either too simplistic or too complicated but lacking adequate theoretical rationale.
4. Problems of predicting the recovery back to previous historical patterns or, possibly, to new relationships.
5. Assessment of the differential impact of the economic events among industries. That applies both to assessing forecasting methodology for the industry in which one competes and for those industries to which one sells.

Table 2 presents a qualitative assessment of the impact of economic events on forecasting. The analytical framework described by Chambers, Mullick and Smith [2] has been employed. The table describes the impact of economic events on several factors that influence the costs of inaccuracy (and the benefits of accuracy) and the costs of forecasting. For example, economic events affect the costs of inaccuracy by increasing variability in observed data, creating changes in data needs of managers, and increasing the value of good forecasts. The costs of forecasting are

[3] The roman numerals refer to quarters of the year.

Table 2
Impact of economic events on forecasting costs.

Economic event	Costs of inaccuracy		
	Effects on accuracy	Effects on information needs	Value of good forecasts
Inflation	Reduces accuracy because of historical data having fewer inflationary effects. Causes variation in variables measured in $ which were previously absent; reduces accuracy.	Creates a need for separate $ and unit forecasts. Creates patterns that differ among industries, thus creating a need for disaggregated forecasts.	Increases because decisions must be made as a function of inflation in inputs and outputs.
Inventory cycle	Reduces dramatically. Affects accuracy of seasonal and trend measures.	Creates a need to distinguish among orders, production, and sales.	Increased because of need to tighten sales, purchasing, and production decisions.
Business cycle Recession Recovery New steady state	Reduces accuracy if naive or time-series methods are employed. Reduces accuracy somewhat if causal methods are employed. Turning points are difficult to measure. Trend estimates for new steady state could be underestimated because of recession experience.	Timing of turning points becomes a major objective. Impact among industries differs, leading to a need for disaggregation.	Increases because of stop and go decision needs.

affected through changes in the desired frequency of model reestimation, the level of detail required, the costs of model specification – including identification of appropriate variables – and the choice of technique.

The conclusions drawn in table 2 are, of course, simplified. Often, the true impact depends upon more complicated factors. The analysis of the table serves as an integrating device for the remainder of the issues raised in the paper. The conclusions drawn will, one hopes, have specific as well as general value to forecasters.

A simple example serves to illustrate clearly some of these issues. Table 3 presents data for 16 time periods for the Hypothetical Company. The customers of

Costs of forecasting			
Frequency of reestimation	Level of detail	Model specification cost	Technique choice
Increases when changes in inflation rate occur often.	Increases because of need for more disaggregation.	Increases because of need to define variables and behavioral relationships more cautiously.	May cause a change to causal models, which are more expensive.
Increases as different phases of cycle occur.	Turning points become more important. Greater disaggregation needs.	Increases because of need to define variables and behavioral relationships more cautiously.	May cause a change to stock adjustment methods, which are more expensive.
Increases as different phases of cycle occur.	Turning points are more important. Increases because of need for more disaggregation.	Increases because of need to define variables and behavioral relationships more cautiously.	Appropriate technique choice becomes more important because the correct time horizon becomes more significant during a cycle.

Hypothetical require its product, a raw material, in strict proportion to their production, which in turn depends upon customer sales. Sales are precisely 10 percent of real *GNP* given in billion of dollars.

The demand for Hypothetical's output comes partly from the customers' raw material demands. We call this demand customer consumption (*CONS*) and it is determined perfectly by *GNP*. Because of steady growth in *GNP* for the first 13 time periods, this portion of demand demonstrates a steady upward trend. Stagnation occurs during period 14, after which a recession and a recovery occur.

A second source of demand comes from adjustments to the raw material inven-

Table 3
Data for the hypothetical company.

Time period	Dollar sales (DSAL)	Unit sales (USAL)	Customer consumption (CONS)	Customer inventory (INV)	Real gross national product- in billions of dollars (GNP)
1	11.00	11.0	10	1	100
2	21.00	21.0	20	2	200
3	31.00	31.0	30	3	300
4	41.00	41.0	40	4	400
5	51.00	51.0	50	5	500
6	61.00	61.0	60	6	600
7	71.00	71.0	70	7	700
8	81.00	81.0	80	8	800
9	91.00	91.0	90	9	900
10	101.00	101.0	100	10	1000
11	111.00	111.0	110	11	1100
12	128.10	122.0	121	12	1210
13	170.20	148.0	133	27	1330
14	136.85	119.0	133	13	1330
15	113.00	113.0	120	6	1200
16	154.00	140.0	133	13	1330

tory (INV) held by Hypothetical's customers. For the first 12 periods, desired inventory levels are simply 10 percent of CONS. Such a policy leads to an increase in inventory demand of one unit per period. [4] Because of the onset of rapid inflation in the raw material's price, customers hoard inventory in period 13. They return to the 10 percent rule in period 14, drop to a 5 percent level because of deflation in period 15, and return to the 10 percent rule in period 16.

By definition, unit sales (USAL) are determined by the following equation:

$$USAL = CONS + \Delta INV \tag{1}$$

Also, customer consumption is related to real GNP as follows:

$$CONS = 0.1 GNP \tag{2}$$

Inflation does not occur in Hypothetical's average selling price until period 12. It

---

[4] This increase in demand occurs because it is the change in inventory stocks (ΔINV) that generates sales by Hypothetical.

becomes dramatic (10%) in period 13, disappears in period 14, turns negative in period 15, and disappears in period 16.

Consider now two regression-based forecasting models for Hypothetical. Model One relates dollar sales to real *GNP* and is given in the following equation:

$$DSAL = a + b(GNP) \tag{3}$$

Alternatively, Model Two relates unit sales to real *GNP* and is given below:

$$USAL = a + b(GNP) \tag{4}$$

Both models are found frequently in practice. Since the behavior in the economy described in the example is fairly typical, if overstated in terms of the magnitude of changes, this example demonstrates the impact of economic change on traditional regression models.

3.1. Model performance during stable economic conditions

The first 12 periods represent the time of stable growth and low inflation rate. Estimation of equations (3) and (4) for this stable period leads to the following results, presented as equations (5) and (6), respectively:

$$
\begin{aligned}
DSAL &= -0.0321 + 0.10237 \,(GNP) & \bar{R}^2 &= 0.9981 \\
(t\text{-values}) \quad &(-0.032) \quad (76.053) & SEE &= 1.615 \\
& & D{-}W &= 1.331
\end{aligned}
\tag{5}
$$

$$
\begin{aligned}
USAL &= 1.0001 + 0.1000(GNP) & \bar{R}^2 &= 1.000 \\
(t\text{-values}) \quad &(22.681)\ (1672.18) & SEE &= 0.0718 \\
& & D{-}W &= 0.065
\end{aligned}
\tag{6}
$$

The entire difference in the two models arises from inflation in period 12, which causes *DSAL* and *USAL* to differ in that period.

Obviously both models are good. They fit past data quite well as the high coefficients of determination and low standard errors show. If one had been forecasting *DSAL* during that period, there would have been no great incentive to switch to a forecast of *USAL* instead. Also, there would have been no incentive to switch to a forecast of *CONS*, although equation (2) above would be the estimated equation and it would have an R^2 equal to one.

3.2. Model performance during changing economic conditions

Two issues arise in evaluating the regression models during periods 13 through 16, the period of cyclical economy-inflation-inventory swings. One occurs in com-

Table 4

Time period	Forecasted DSAL	Actual DSAL	Percentage Error	Forecasted USAL	Actual USAL	Percentage Error
13	136.16	170.20	20.0	134	148.0	9.5
14	136.16	136.85	5	134	119.0	−12.6
15	122.85	113.00	−8.7	121	113.0	−7.1
16	136.16	154.00	11.6	134	140.0	4.3

paring equations (5) and (6) as predictors of *DSAL* and *USAL,* even given perfect foresight of what would happen to *GNP.* [5] The results are given in table 4.

The errors in 3 of the 4 periods are smaller in absolute value when the *USAL* model is used rather than the *DSAL* model. Only in period 14, when no inflation occurred, [6] was the *DSAL* model accidentally a better performer.

Clearly, *USAL* is the better dependent variable. Inflation causes the *DSAL-GNP* relationship to depart from historical patterns. The only reason this relationship held up in the stable period was the constancy of average selling price.

The second issue arises from adjustments in the estimated form of equations (3) and (4) when they are reestimated over the entire 16 periods. These results are:

$$DSAL = -4.393 + 0.111 GNP \qquad \bar{R}^2 = 0.9603$$
$$(t\text{-values}) \quad (-0.828) \quad (19.066) \qquad SEE = 9.584 \qquad (7)$$
$$D-W = 2.155$$

$$USAL = 0.966 + 0.0998 GNP \qquad \bar{R}^2 = 0.9797$$
$$(t\text{-values}) \quad (0.286) \quad (26.943) \qquad SEE = 6.097 \qquad (8)$$
$$D-W = 2.466$$

The differences in adaptation of the *DSAL* and *USAL* models are instructive. The *GNP* coefficient rises in the *DSAL* model, comparing equations (7) and (5). In contrast, the *USAL* models show negligible differences. What little change that does occur in the *GNP* coefficient is negative. If stable growth and lower inflation were to resume, the *DSAL* model would be led astray by the unstable periods and would predict less effectively than would the *USAL* model.

Having established the comparative superiority of the *USAL* model, one can examine the model for other attributes. Clearly, the inventory adaptations were the sole source of errors, since equation (2) is still a perfect model for the customer

---

[5] Clearly, forecasts of *GNP* would be required.
[6] Also the inventory reductions caused the lowered unit sales to be offset by the impact (higher) of previous inflation.

consumption component of demand. Unfortunately, the typical company does not have information on the amount of its product being held as raw material inventory by customers. One prospect would be to employ measures of inventory levels in the economy as a whole or in relevant component industries. These variables could be used as independent variables in a regression model. Another practical approach, if no satisfactory results obtain from using proxy inventory variables, would be to assume that all residuals (or all large ones) in the original *USAL* model are the result of inventory adjustments. By employing lagged residuals,[7] either as independent variables or as adjustments to the predictions of the model, appropriate corrections might be made. In the case of Hypothetical, the residual pattern of +14.0, −15.0, −8.0, +6.0 in the last 4 periods is suggestive. The peak sales in time period 13 caused by inventory buildup meant that the impact of the recession would be more pronounced on *USAL*, owing to inventory disinvestment. Hence the large downswing in *USAL*, more than the drop in real *GNP*, was predictable.

Our hypothetical (but realistic) example demonstrates several points made in table 2. Inflation had several effects: 1) it reduced the accuracy of existing forecasting methods, 2) it created a need for separate dollar and unit sales forecasts, and 3) it caused the estimated form of models to be outdated more quickly. The inventory cycle and recession had similar effects. Since the management value of good forecasts was probably increased by the sequence of economic events and the need to make well-timed management responses, the forecasting cost trade-off is probably tilted toward the employment of more detailed models. More disaggregated, detailed information becomes desirable. Also, fewer influences on real events can be ignored in the model-building process, a conclusion that implies a turn towards causal models and more carefully specified behavioral relationships.

The hypothetical example obviously is rigged for illustrative purposes. However, the economic statistics presented in table 1 and the analysis presented below validate the realistic nature of the example. Majani and Makridakis [8] document events in the French newsprint and printing and writing paper industry and steel industry during the 1970's that are very comparable to the Hypothetical Company example. The report on the U.S. paper industry by the Council on Wage and Price Stability (1976) offers similar evidence [3].

The length of the time period in the example is not specified for purposes of generality. It should be noted that the conclusion will differ significantly, depending upon whether the time period is annual, quarterly, or monthly. For example, if the data are monthly or quarterly, the inventory cycle could cause a classical time-series decomposition model to encounter problems with seasonal index calculations. Unusually large swings in time series could affect the seasonal index of that month or quarter unless care was taken to prevent such an influence. On the other

---

[7] Weighted combinations of residuals of varying lag could also be used. Distributed lag regression techniques might well prove useful.

hand, in an annual or quarterly forecast, the trend calculations in a time-series
model and the slope coefficients in a regression model could be adjusted erroneously because of economic events, as was illustrated above in equations (7) and (8).

3.3. Analyzing the recovery back to historical patterns

During the era of unstable economic conditions from 1974 to 1976, various
industries and companies experienced atypical performance vis-à-vis the economy.
That was partially due to inventory behavior and inflation. An examination of
economic statistics reveals that the Hypothetical example used above was, in fact,
the pattern of events that affected large segments of the U.S. economy. To understand better the behavior of the industry-economy relationship over the unstable
period, let us analyze some generally available statistics.

Consider the typical industrial producer during the unstable period. Table 5 displays, for the period mid-1973 through 1975, the index of industrial production
and the real gross national product. In order to obtain a rough measure of the
behavior of the industrial production—real *GNP* relationship (similar to the *USAL-
GNP* relationship examined above), the ratio of the two variables was calculated.

Table 5
Relationship of industrial production and real *GNP*.

Year and quarter	(1) Index of total industrial production [a]	(2) Real *GNP* [b]	(3) Ratio (col. 1 ÷ col. 2)	(4) Ratio index [c]
1973 III	126.67	1236.3	0.1024	102.81
IV	127.00	1242.6	0.1022	102.61
1974 I	124.90	1230.4	0.1015	101.90
II	125.67	1220.8	0.1029	103.31
III	125.43	1212.9	0.1034	103.81
IV	121.30	1191.7	0.1017	102.10
1975 I	111.67	1161.1	0.0961	96.48
II	110.37	1177.1	0.0937	94.07
III	114.20	1209.3	0.0944	94.77
IV [d]	117.50	1219.2	0.0963	96.68
	Average ratio, 1969–1973 = 0.0996			100.0
	Average ratio, 1976I–1976III = 0.1005			100.90

[a] Averages of three monthly figures (1967 = 100); figures seasonally adjusted.
[b] 1972 dollars.
[c] Ratio average, 1969–1973 = 100.00.
[d] Preliminary data as of January 1976. The series was revised subsequently making comparisons
with previous periods unacceptable, given the data available to the author.
Source: Economic report of the president, 1975 and 1976, various tables.

This ratio was converted to an index by dividing it by the average ratio over the 1969 through 1973 period.

An examination of the ratio index reveals above average figures for the last two quarters of 1973 and for all four quarters of 1974. Despite the fact that real *GNP* turned down after 1973-IV, the index of industrial production did not make a sustained turndown until the middle of 1974. Even then, industrial production declined less than did real *GNP* until 1975-I. Inventory accumulations, caused by inflation, were the obvious cause. The inevitable outcome was a lagged turndown in industrial production that was more pronounced than the recession of real *GNP*. The ratio index values below 100.00 for all of 1975 demonstrate this phenomenon. The average for the 10 periods displayed is 99.85 — evidence of a complete adjustment back to historical levels. The first three quarters of 1976 were back on track, averaging 100.90.

Various industries behaved differently during the unstable period. Table 6 displays ratio indexes for three contrasting market groups: final products, intermediate products, and durable materials. As would be expected, the final products ratio index is relatively stable. [8] Intermediate products seemed to be produced for inventory purposes less than either of the other two categories. [9] But in 1975 that category felt a much stronger recession than did real *GNP*. Durable materials, which experienced very strong inflation from 1973 through 1974, responded quite unstably, as was expected. After inventory adjustments took place, producing hard times in such industries in 1975, recovery back to historical levels seems to have occurred.

The obvious implication of these analyses is that traditional regression models relating industrial sales or production to real *GNP* would have generated large errors during the period studied. However, historical relationships have been accurate recently. The pattern that evolved during the unstable period should be studied for future usefulness. The shortness of the period precludes successful estimation of more careful and intricate econometric relationships, such as inventory models. In most cases, eliminating the data for the unstable period or replacing it with adjusted figures [10] would enhance future forecasting performance.

A similar type of analysis could be made for various classifications of product. For example, the behavior of consumer products and the important distinctions between durables and nondurables, should be compared to other categories. The data for any industry or even every product in a firm can be studied in a similar manner. Table 6 demonstrates that sales to various customer industries for any supplier firm or industry took on different patterns during the 1973–1976 period.

---

[8] Obviously, this index has grown faster than real *GNP* since the early 1970s.

[9] The possible reason that the figures did not go higher — on this series and on all others — is that capacity constraints may have been binding.

[10] These would be figures that are adjusted for inventory anomalies. In the absence of such information, moving averages might suffice.

Table 6
Indexes of ratio of industrial production to real *GNP* by market group.

Year and quarter	Final products	Intermediate products	Durable materials
1973 III	100.53	102.75	107.91
IV	101.66	101.02	108.01
1974 I	101.04	100.82	105.38
II	102.59.	101.98	105.89
III	103.72	101.69	106.49
IV	103.82	99.38	103.86
1975 I	100.43	95.52	93.54
II	99.19	92.34	86.45
III	98.68	91.96	87.87
IV	99.19	93.69	92.52
Average, 1976 I–III	103.34	104.01	104.37 [a]

Note: The economic data for this table are calculated on the same bases as those for Table 5.
[a] This figure was for all materials and is not totally comparable to the other data in the column.

This fact suggests that disaggregation of forecast items could prove useful in improving forecast accuracy. Equally important, management decisions regarding disaggregated variables must be made during periods of rapid economic change.

3.4. Impact on other forecasting methods

Regression methods are not restricted to the employment of economic measures as independent variables. Even when noneconomic variables are used, the effects of inflation, inventory adjustments, and recession might be equally dramatic. A prescription for such situations would be to add appropriate economic variables and then to perform an analysis similar to that described above.

If classical time series decomposition methods were being employed, several issues would arise. First, the units versus dollars problem during inflationary periods would be the same as in the regression situation. Second, the pattern of inventory behavior might cause erroneous adjustments to be made to seasonal and cyclical indexes. Third, the recession would cause adjustments to be made to trend forecasts. Possibly, the trend would be readjusted downward. Other analysts might introduce polynomial trend relationships. That would be an erroneous strategy in most cases, unless some unlikely magic intuition about the regularity of business cycles were obtained.

Time-series decomposition methods usually become less desirable during either a recession or an inventory cycle. Their primary drawback is an inability to predict turning points. On the other hand, the simplicity of the time-series decomposition model allows easy adjustment of forecasts based upon information not embodied in the formal model. A variety of sources of intelligence data about the future can be included in the time-series forecast through the prediction of trend-cycle values. Majani and Makridakis [8] suggest the use of leading indicators to influence trend-cycle forecasts.

The ability to incorporate qualitative, and nonformal, quantitative factors into a forecast is by no means restricted to time-series methods. It is for this reason that causal methods become relatively more attractive during rapid economic change, despite the conceptual simplicity of the time-series decomposition model.

Exponential smoothing and other moving average methods such as *ARMA*, might have had surprisingly respectable performance during the unstable period. Such methods would have, with a lag, adapted to inflationary effects, inventory fluctuations, and recession. Unfortunately, since these events occurred irregularly, these techniques would probably be foretelling upward movements at exactly the time when downward movements were taking place or vice versa. If forecasts of turning points are important, these methods would be unattractive, other factors [11] aside. The more sophisticated software packages employing the advanced versions of these techniques would probably fare no better, since they would attempt to extrapolate the aberrations in the future without regard to the real causes and their likelihood of recurrence. Although a better fit of the past would result, forecasting ability would not be improved.

Some encouraging advances have been made in recent years in combining forecasting techniques so as to allow the best features of various methods to complement one another. The most notable success has been in combining causal methods, such as regression analysis, with time-series methods, such as *ARIMA*.

Pindyck and Rubinfeld [9, pp. 540–544] present a good example of combined forecasts of interest rates on three-month treasury bills. Using a linear regression model to explain variations in monthly rates over the period from January 1958 to January 1970, they generated simulated values over the period from January 1968 to January 1970. These simulations, a forecast of sorts, had a root-mean-square error (*RMS*) of 0.542. Ex-post forecasts of the interest rate over the period from January 1970 to June 1970 also were produced, resulting in an *RMS* error of 0.750. The residuals of the regression were then analyzed by using a time-series model. An *ARIMA* (4, 0, 0) model was employed. By combining regression model forecasts of the interest rate with *ARIMA* model forecasts of the error term, simulated values over the period from January 1968 to January 1970 had an *RMS* error of 0.269. Ex-post forecasts of the period from January 1970 to June 1970 had an *RMS* error of 0.340. Thus the combined forecast reduced the *RMS* error by a large factor in both tests of accuracy.

As described above, a period of rapid economic change causes reductions in forecast accuracy and increases the value of turning point forecasts and of accuracy in general. These circumstances argue persuasively for a combined forecast approach. If time-series or naive methods were previously employed alone, the case

---

[11] Cost would be one such factor.

for causal models that include carefully specified behavioral relationships has been established above. If causal models were previously the sole basis for forecasts, the value of reducing the increased inaccuracy during the unstable period argues in favor of applying time-series methods to the residuals of the regression.

Another forecasting method employed by many analysts is the leading indicators approach. Two comments can be made about the impact of recent experience on this method. First, some traditional lead-lag relationships were altered during the recent past because of new forces at work. As was the case for regression analysis, carefully considered lead-lag relationships were either not affected or changed predictably. Second, the need to foresee turning points made leading indicators very attractive during an active business cycle. Either as independent variables in a regression or as independent checks of forecasts, leading indicators have gained in attractiveness.

4. Prescriptions for improved forecasting

The overwhelmingly obvious result of this analysis thus far has been to demonstrate why sloppy forecasting practices were tolerable during stable economic periods and inadequate during the recent past. This analysis leads to prescription 1 and a corollary:

Prescription 1: Statistical fit and demonstrated forecasting accuracy are necessary, but not sufficient, attributes of a good forecasting system.

Corollary: Logical choice of variables and their functional form is another necessary attribute. When combined with fit and accuracy, it implies a successful forecasting experience.

The ability to have seen, for example, that unit sales relationships were superior to dollar sales relationships in a large number of situations would have paid off in neither a significantly higher fit nor a significantly better forecasting track record during stable economic conditions. Yet we demonstrated the value of the units approach during inflationary periods. There may be trade-offs associated with using logical relationships instead of measures that maximize fit or forecasting accuracy. The accuracy — model-building cost trade-off during rapid economic change periods is tilted toward more effort in model specification and toward experimentation with techniques that might overcome the problem of reduced accuracy.

Having demonstrated that the impact of the 1973–1975 period differed among industries, one is led to an important suggestion:

Prescription 2: For durable products, stock adjustment or other adaptive expectations models might prove to be valuable in specifying inventory adjustments or other [12] adaptive behavior.

---

[12] Gauging the impact of recycled scrap or substitution towards used products instead of new ones are examples of such behavior.

Stock adjustment models are based upon the supposition that, for certain durable products, the desired stock of the product held by consumers is behaviorally related to other measures such as *GNP* and wealth. Demand for the product which is a flow derives from adjustments of the actual stock to a desired level which, in turn, adjusts to external changes. This approach has proven useful for forecasting such durables as automobiles and for understanding inventory demand. The econometric problems generated by stock adjustment approaches are somewhat complicated, but have been solved quite satisfactorily (see Harberger [5], and Houthakker and Taylor [6] for good treatments of this topic).

Hymans [7] found stock adjustment models superior in predicting consumer durable spending. He predicted consumer expenditures on autos and parts as a function of lagged disposable personal income, the lagged index of consumer sentiment and a dummy variable that corrected for the influence of strikes. That and other single-equation regression models were compared to various stock adjustment models, which included also income, consumer sentiment, unemployment, relative price, and strike variables. Over the period from 1954 to 1968, using quarterly data, the stock adjustment model generates a better fit, $\overline{R}^2$ being 0.963 as compared to 0.950 in the conventional model. In forecasting the period from 1969-I through 1970-II, the stock adjustment model achieves better accuracy, the *RMS* error being 1.71 as compared to 2.54 for the conventional model.

Feldstein and Auerbach [4] studied the behavior of inventories in durable manufacturing industries over the period from 1959 to 1976. Their results are of general interest to forecasters for several reasons: 1) they employ a target-adjustment model that outperforms stock adjustment models; 2) they obtain good forecasting performance, even during the period from 1974-I to 1976-I, and they predict turning points; 3) their dependent variable, inventory levels, is the most troublesome component of sales forecasts during rapid change periods, as discussed in detail above; and 4) they employ disaggregated data to improve their forecasting accuracy. This last point will be discussed further below.

The success of Feldstein and Auerbach in forecasting a volatile time series during the unstable economic period with a carefully specified causal model lends strength to the conclusions drawn in table 2. Their ability to outperform the stock adjustment model offers hope for improving forecasting performance in the future. Their forecasts of durable manufacturing inventories can, in fact, be employed as a predictor of major deviations from historical production and sales relationships.

The author took the changes in predicted durables-manufacturing inventory levels ($\Delta \hat{I}$), as forecast by Feldstein and Auerbach for 1974-I through 1975-IV, and compared them to a variable representing net inventory production (*NIP*) in durable materials, that is the difference between the durable materials ratio index in table 6 and 100.0. Despite the fact that only eight data points were analyzed and this period was extremely turbulent in durable materials industries, the results were very strong. The variables $\Delta \hat{I}$ and *NIP* had a correlation of 0.9913, and the turning point of *NIP* in 1975-I was correctly predicted by a turning point in $\Delta \hat{I}$. A regression analysis yields:

$$NIP = -2.098 + 6.748\Delta\hat{I} \tag{9}$$

(*t*-statistics)   (−4.90) (18.48)

$$\bar{R}^2 = 0.9799 \quad \overline{SEE} = 1.21 \quad D{-}W = 1.90$$

Similar results could perhaps be obtained from employing predicted inventory changes in the appropriate industry in an augmentation or adjustment of models that predict unit sales of a firm or industry. [13]

As another example of the attractiveness of adaptive behavior models, consider the behavior of the U.S. Paper and Paperboard industry during the period from 1955 to 1975. Census data on apparent consumption of all grades of paper and paperboard per billion dollars of real *GNP* was converted to index number form, making it similar in concept to the ratio index employed above. During the period, the variable was quite well behaved, with the exception of 1975. By subtracting 100.0, the base, from the ratio index, a variable similar to *NIP* was obtained. The *NIP* variable runs in cycles of small magnitudes. In only four years was it significantly negative: 1957, 1958, 1967, and 1975, all recession years. In the first three years this number was between −2.1 and −2.8. In 1975 it was −12.16. However, the 1969–1974 period showed a large inventory buildup. The sum of those six values of *NIP* was 12.60, a number remarkably close in magnitude to the negative value for 1975. Furthermore, the annual values of changes in predicted inventory levels, $\Delta\hat{I}$, of Feldstein and Auerbach is accurate in predicting the turning point in *NIP*.

The differential impact of the unstable period among industries, demonstrated in table 6, suggests another promising avenue of analysis:

Prescription 3: The level of aggregation in forecasting ought to be examined carefully. Data could be disaggregated by: 1) product, 2) customer industry, 3) region or nation of customers, and/or other attributes which might logically lead to better explanatory power.

Forecasting sales of producers goods offers an example of the potential benefit from disaggregation. The demand for a product generated by sales to final-product customers would differ dramatically from the demand generated by sales to durable raw material producers, for example. The ability to predict the disaggregated components might not prove to be of incremental usefulness under stable economic conditions, but could be especially useful when there is a different pattern of insta-' bility among customer industries.

---

[13] As of August 1977, Feldstein and Auerbach are engaged in a study of inventory investment for two-digit *SIC* industries, with disaggregation into three stages of fabrication. Their results could aid the process of industry and firm sales forecasting.

There is very little evidence on the general value of disaggregation strategies in forecasting. It has been suggested that disaggregation is a two-edged sword, depening upon how the forecast is used. [14] Disaggregation may lead to better insights into the behavior of particular markets. In table 2 we have emphasized the increased value of such insights for management making decisions under conditions of rapid economic change. Feldstein and Auerbach [4] achieved improved understanding of inventory investment by disaggregating into two subcomponents: 1) inventories of materials and goods in process, and 2) finished-goods inventories. On the other hand, disaggregation may lead to increased error in all of the forecasts owing to the law of large numbers.

Under unstable economic conditions — when the impact of economic events differs among products, regions, customer industries, or other attributes — the likelihood of reducing error by disaggregated analysis improves. When combined with the increased management value of disaggregated forecasts, there is a strong case for disaggregation in forecasting. Given the dearth of empirical evidence on the topic, it appears to be a promising avenue for future research. Until such time as more evidence is collected, prescription 3 will remain an intuitively sound, but unproven, suggestion.

The discussion has not yet treated the time horizon of the forecast as a consideration. Normally, short-term forecasting methods, such as smoothing and time series, are inadequate for longer horizon forecasts. But such methods usually fare well, relative to their cost, for shorter horizon forecasts. Regression models are usually better suited for forecasts of one quarter to two years. This comparative statement was shown to be accurate during the recent period of rapid change. The correctly chosen regression model was shown in our hypothetical example to be relatively accurate in making forecasts of a year or more into the future. More importantly, the reestimated model was not thrown off by the inventory cycle. Short-term methods might have been more responsive to short-term fluctuations, but such response would have made the models inaccurate for periods further into the future.

During stable economic periods, the choice of optimal technique is not as important as it is during unstable periods. In unstable conditions the forecaster must be more careful. As indicated in table 2 and demonstrated above, the use of causal models, or at least noncausal models supported by a causal adjustment analysis, is strongly advised under conditions of inflation, inventory cycle or business cycle. Perhaps an even better strategy is to combine causal and time-series methods.

Recent forecasting experience probably has been poor for most corporations. One extreme response to these inadequacies would be to drop formal, forecasting efforts. Such a response would assume either that no managerial responses to changing conditions can be planned or that judgmental forecasts are adequate. Since both

---

[14] This suggestion was made by an anonymous referee of this paper to whom the author is grateful.

of these circumstances are less true under rapidly changing conditions, the decision to drop formal forecasting efforts would be erroneous and costly.

The other extreme would be to overreact by implementing more sophisticated but less understood forecasting methodology. The greater the sophistication, the more likely that forecasting activity will be removed farther from management control and understanding. When change is rampant, the ability of management to understand and respond to deviant performance is crucial. One strength of causal models is the logical nature of relationships employed. Recent experience makes causal models even more attractive, given a need to understand the forecasting system better.

It may seem somewhat paradoxical, however true, that a period in which traditional economic relationships underwent dramatic shocks has led to prescriptions to pay more attention to received theory and a priori common sense. If the experience reinforces careful methodology, the state of forecasting practice will benefit immeasurably. At the very least, we will learn from our mistakes.

References

[1] G.E.P. Box and G.M. Jenkins, Time series analysis: forecasting and control (Holden-Day, San Francisco, 1976).

[2] J.C. Chambers, S.K. Mullick and D.D. Smith, How to choose the right forecasting technique, Harvard Business Review (1971) 45–74.

[3] Council on Wage and Price Stability, Price increases and capacity expansion in the paper industry (Council on Wage and Price Stability, 1976).

[4] M. Feldstein and A. Auerbach, Inventory behavior in durable-goods manufacturing: The target-adjustment model, Brookings Papers on Economic Activity (1976) 351–408.

[5] A.C. Harberger (ed.) (1976) The demand for durable goods (University of Chicago Press, Chicago, 1960).

[6] H.S. Houthakker and L.D. Taylor, Consumer Demand in the United States, 1929–1970: Analyses and Projections (Harvard University Press, Cambridge, 1966).

[7] S. Hymans, Consumer durable spending: Explanation and prediction, Brookings Papers on Economic Activity 2 (1970) 173–199.

[8] B. Majani and S. Makridakis, Can recessions be predicted? Long Range Planning 10 (1977) 31–40.

[9] R.S. Pindyck and D.L. Rubinfeld, Econometric Models and Economic Forecasts (McGraw-Hill, New York, 1976).

TIMS Studies in the Management Sciences 12 (1979) 265–278
© North-Holland Publishing Company

AUTOMATIC FORECASTING USING THE FLEXICAST SYSTEM

Lewis W. COOPERSMITH

Health Products Research, Inc. and Rider College

Industrial forecasters must regularly make short- to medium-term forecasts to support operational planning. Many have neither the time, the training, nor the experience for proper selection of the appropriate forecasting technique. These limitations suggest the need for an automatic method, or black box, that selects models and gives meaningful and accurate forecasts without human intervention. Criteria for the design of better black boxes are set forth in this paper and a specific implementation, the FLEXICAST system, is described. The paper also discusses the techniques and statistical decision rules used in automatic model selection including details of a unique method of piecewise linear regression used to model trend after the removal of extreme points and adjustment for autocorrelated residuals. A description of experience with the FLEXICAST System is also presented along with suggestions for further research.

1. Short- to medium-term forecasting in industry

Forecasts three months to two years ahead are needed regularly to support operational planning for numerous business activities. Accurate forecasts of historical data, such as product demand and manpower requirements, make more efficient production and inventory control and more effective cash flow management possible. The volume of these forecasts can be large; many business and government organizations forecast more than several hundred items monthly or quarterly (see Lawrence [11] p. 58). The total cost of generating a forecast, which includes analyst's time and computation, must therefore be kept low if there is to be any overall benefit from the greater accuracy of sophisticated computer-based models.

High speed computers, especially interactive time-sharing, have played a significant role in the development of techniques that require little analyst's time while increasing forecast accuracy. Many models and techniques have been developed for computer systems. Most are univariate time-series techniques that model only past observations of the series to be forecasted. Many early computer forecasting systems included exponential smoothing (see Brown [3]). This technique emphasizes computational efficiency rather than accurate behavioral modeling. Currently, behaviorally based time-series models have gained popularity as a result of the availability of computer programs for the analytical methods of Box and Jenkins [2]. To further facilitate the use and understanding of various computer techniques, many time-sharing firms offer systems that have their own simple conversational languages so that users can perform different analyses, try different techniques and compare results (see Makridakis, Wheelwright and Hodgsdon [14]).

Even with the advances in modeling methods and computer applications, recent surveys show that managers still rely heavily on nonautomated methods (see Naylor and Schauland [15]; Bernard and Scheuing [2]). Wheelwright and Clarke [19] found that most companies with under 500 million in sales devote less than five staff members and under $ 50,000 per year to short- to medium-term forecasting efforts.

As these surveys point out, there are many obstacles to widespread acceptance of computer techniques. First, although interactive computer programs have made sophisticated methods more convenient, some time for model evaluation, model selection, and parameter estimation is still required to obtain the most effective results. When many forecasts are needed, this time requirement can be significant and the costs for analysts' time and computation become prohibitive. Second, the more sophisticated methods, such as Box and Jenkins' techniques, require extensive training and experience to be properly applied. Forecast analysts who do not have this background can easily misuse these techniques. Finally, businessmen have more confidence in using forecasts based on assumptions they understand, even if these assumptions are oversimplified. Recently developed sophisticated techniques go far beyond the use of popular straight-line or percentage growth models. This complexity makes simple business explanations of how models work impossible and prevents managers from determining causes for inaccuracies and making proper revisions.

The objective of the research discussed in this paper is to satisfy the need for more widely acceptable forecasting techniques. This objective can be achieved by developing better black boxes — completely automatic forecasting techniques. Many current forecasting systems are black boxes that contain one or two simple models. Better black boxes can completely automate the technically sophisticated process of model selection to produce forecasting models and forecasts that are meaningful to modern businessmen. Such a tool allows a nontechnical manager to easily obtain forecasts in which he has confidence. It also guides the technical analyst to more advanced methods when the need is warranted. To gain a proper perspective of the use of better black boxes, the various approaches to short-term forecasting are first classified and described. Next the general requirements for better black box design and implementation are discussed. The final sections describe the development of the FLEXICAST system — a black box technique that is currently operational — and discuss experience in its use.

2. Alternative philosophies on computer-based short-term forecasting

2.1. Single model systems

Brown [3], in his pioneering work on forecasting, proposes three criteria for design of forecasting techniques — accuracy, simplicity of computation, and flexibility to adjust to changes in directional movement. Following Brown's recommendation, early systems included one or two methods, such as simple or double exponential smoothing, to model trend. Later, McLaughlin and Boyle [13] developed a system that uses Bureau of Census methods to account for seasonal effects. These systems satisfied the criterion of computational efficiency and are acceptably accurate for short-term forecasting. Some judgment and preparation time is still required to select from two or more trend models or to specify the values of smoothing parameters, but the major disadvantage of systems based on one or two models is that they are optimal for narrow classes of underlying behavior (see Cogger [6]). As a result, misspecification leads to highly inaccurate forecasts as the forecasting horizon increases beyond three time periods.

2.2. System of models

Advances in computer technology significantly lowered the time and cost of computation, thus reducing the importance of computational efficiency. This development led to forecasting systems that included a greater variety of models to represent underlying behavior. Some systems of models use regression to fit several time functions to history and require the user to select the best model based on goodness-of-fit statistics. Box and Jenkins [2] structure the methodology of designing and estimating autoregressive integrated moving average, ARIMA, models that can represent a rich variety of behavior. Unfortunately, the features of model selection and model sophistication that have made these methods attractive to technical specialists have limited their use in business. Managers, and even skilled technical experts, are not necessarily capable of interpreting the behavioral meaning of many models that fit the data well (see Chatfield and Prothero [5]). Meaningless and sometimes explosive forecasts resulting from misuse of these techniques have led to their abandonment before realization of their full potential. When many forecasts are needed regularly the significant expense of an analyst's time for model design is a further drawback.

2.3. System of techniques

Most recently, system design has centered on the philosophy that one technique or model cannot provide satisfactory results under all combinations of desired accuracy and costs of preparation. These systems of techniques such as SIBYL-RUNNER developed by Makridakis, Wheelwright and Hodgsdon [14], are available through a number of time-sharing companies and feature simple self-contained conversational languages to aid in analysis. The user is offered a wide selection of techniques and analytical tools, such as autocorrelations and graphical displays, that aid in the choice of meaningful and reliable models. In addition to appealing to the user's artistic sense, these systems serve an educational function; the users can start with simple techniques and experiment with more sophisticated ones until the technical skills and experience are gained to use them effectively.

Although the system of techniques approach reduces the need for technical skills and makes computer-assisted forecasting more attractive to management, significant time is still required for analysis and model selection. For large volumes of short- to medium-term forecasts, preparation time makes the system of techniques approach expensive and possibly infeasible for use in every case. Development of better black boxes would significantly reduce the need for costly analytical time while satisfying the requirement of proper technique selection. The structure of better black boxes and criteria for their design are discussed in the next section.

3. The black box approach to automatic forecasting

The black box approach is similar to the system of techniques approach in that different models are used to represent a wide range of patterns of historical variation. However, interactive data analysis and model selection are replaced by an automated logic of model selection based on statistical criteria. The ideal black box would produce acceptably accurate forecasts for any given series of historical data. There would be no need for model selection or parameter estimation. Safeguards would be built in so that selected models and estimated parameters would make sense to all those using forecasts in making decisions.

Historically, the need for accurate and easy to use forecasting systems has motivated the development of black boxes. The development of exponential smoothing was based on the philosophy of automation, which demands that information should be untouched by human hands from the original input to final output. Black boxes have been built that include exponential smoothing models and more recently, ARIMA time-series models. These latter models require regular model review and updating because of the lack of stationarity in the order of differencing, the AR order, or the MA order.

Chatfield and Prothero [5] have examined the practical use of the modeling techniques of Box and Jenkins. They conclude that the technical skills and time required for proper analysis in choice of model prohibit the use of these techniques in large scale application. They make the following recommendation:

If a large number of items are involved, say several hundred, then for production planning and stock control purposes it may be useful to set up a computer forecasting system to allow routine forecasts to be made without human intervention. The high initial cost of Box and Jenkins procedure will probably make it unsuitable in this sort of situation (Chatfield and Prothero [5, p. 312]).

Articles on the use of forecasting technqiues in business suggest that better black boxes would fill an unmet need. A survey conducted by Wheelwright and Clarke [19] indicates that sophisticated methods could be used more effectively if management were less dependent on management scientists or statisticians. They conclude that forecasting computer programs and forecasting methods should be made easier for managers to use. Informal discussions with management confirm these survey results. Chambers, Mullick and Smith [4] predict the development of total forecasting systems in which several techniques are tied together and, as confidence is gained in their use, human intervention is continuously reduced.

The popularity of automatic forecasting using exponential smoothing is evidence of the importance of eliminating the time needed for data analysis and model selection. But dissatisfaction with the accuracy and interpretation of results of these techniques shows that black box methods are only as good as the models and techniques they contain. Thus, good design of black boxes is critical to their acceptance and the scope of their applicability. However, since no one technique or model is universally optimal, a black box must also provide analytical statistics for evaluating the results of model selection. These can also be used to measure the degree of improvement that might be obtained by further analysis through the system of techniques approach.

The challenge, therefore, is to design black boxes that can forecast effectively with little need for the use of other techniques. The following criteria should be useful in designing black boxes with both a broad scope of application and acceptability to management.

3.1. Robust model selection

The automatic modeling technique should guarantee acceptable forecasting accuracy for many types of time series that differ according to characteristic patterns of trend, seasonality, and autocorrelation. The technique should be sensitive to recent changes in these patterns, and data of questionable projectability should be modified or eliminated. Thus, extreme one-time events such as strikes and promotions would have little effect, if any, on model selection or parameter estimation.

3.2. Meaningfulness of selected models

Decision makers should be able to assign meaning to model parameters. This criterion is particularly important in evaluating the way forecasts might change because of recent changes in the business environment.

3.3. Computational efficiency

Efficient computation is important because in many industries where thousands of forecasts are needed regularly, inefficient computational procedures could increase costs significantly and discourage usage.

4. Black box implementation – the FLEXICAST system

4.1. Technique selection

The FLEXICAST system was designed as a black box that would satisfy the criteria outlined above. It has been implemented and is currently operational. Individual techniques were evaluated based on their ability to accurately represent one or more components of time-series behavior. The meaningfulness of model parameters and computational efficiency were also considered. The techniques included were chosen because they could be tied together to provide the most satisfactory results for a wide variety of time series. The process of selection is described below.

4.1.1. Trend/cycle modeling

Long-term directional movement results from trends or long term cycles – those with periods greater than one year. As Granger [7] and Jenkins and Watts [10] indicate, identification of long-term cycles requires many years of historical data and extensive analysis. Judgment is also needed to identify and select long-term cycles, which prohibits the use of automatic modeling methods. However, the possibility of their existence should not be ignored. Thus, a technique of trend estimation was sought that would given information on possible cyclical movement. The user could then either make proper manual adjustment of projected trends or use more sophisticated cyclical modeling.

Straight-line trend projection is cited by Naylor and Schauland [15] as a widely accepted and meaningful practical technique. Projections of short-term trends with the straight-line model limit the chance of specification error inherent in curvilinear models. Theoretically, curve fitting by piecewise linear sections is appropriate for smooth secular trends. By fitting pieces of linear sections, changes in growth rate, or slope, that might result from long-term cyclical movement or product life cycles can be identified. Thus, a computationally efficient piecewise linear regression, PLR, procedure was developed, which is described below.

Double exponential smoothing and second order differencing were also considered for inclusion, since these techniques are sensitive to changes in slope. However, PLR was selected because of the following combination of advantages:

1. *Meaningfulness*. Changes in trends are often associated with dramatic changes in policy or the environment. Unlike other techniques that were considered, PLR identifies the origin of the current trend and its rate of change. See Guthery [8], McGee and Carleton [12] and Quandt [16] for a discussion of PLR and the economic justification of its use in forecasting.

2. *Reliability*. PLR gives measures of residual variance that can be used to automatically identify and exclude extreme points, which results in more robust estimation of trend parameters. Occasionally, information on residual variance is lost by extreme point removal, but extreme points should be removed when they represent

events of a nonstatistical nature, such as sales promotions or strikes.

3. *Interface with residual modeling.* PLR assures a mean zero residual process. The correlogram of this process can be easily determined and a stationary time-series model can be identified as described below.

4.1.2. Seasonality

Three seasonal modeling techniques were considered: multiplicative and additive seasonal adjustment and twelfth order differencing. The Bureau of Census X-11 variant of the census method II seasonal adjustment for 1967 [18] was selected mainly because it produces meaningful multiplicative seasonal indices with which most businessmen are familiar. This technique has been used effectively by McLaughlin and Boyle [13] in the development of the FORAN sales forecasting system. This method provides good insight into the seasonal nature of economic data such as sales or manpower ability. Other reasons for selection of this technique include:

1. *Built in tests for seasonality.* An *F*-test measuring the significance of the seasonal index is computed and can be used with criteria for rejection of the use of seasonality.

2. *Extreme point adjustment.* The seasonal nature is not significantly affected by extreme one-time variation from the trend/cycle because these points are automatically adjusted to within levels of normal variation.

3. *Allowance for changing seasonality.* Smooth seasonal indices are used in seasonal adjustment and projected seasonal indices are computed for forecasting. These moving seasonal indices allow for the possibility that the seasonal component may not be stationary.

4.1.3. Irregular

After adjustment for seasonality and trend removal, autocorrelation of the residual or irregular component could result from natural adaptation or reaction to movement away from the trend. In addition, the use of automatic trend modeling procedures, such as PLR, could occasionally produce a lack of fit resulting in short-term positive autocorrelation. The general class of ARMA models were considered as possible models for the irregular component. Autoregressive, AR, models, as opposed to the more parsimonious ARMA models, were selected because they are more meaningful and parameter estimation is more computationally efficient.

The use of stationary time-series models is, in itself, difficult for most businessmen to understand. Moving average, MA, models that use unobservable random shocks, are difficult to interpret, even by well-qualified experts (see Chatfield and Prothero [5, p. 310]). The restriction of using only AR models is theoretically acceptable, because of the property of invertibility, which assures that any stationary process can be closely approximated by a sufficiently high order AR model. In practice it is important that efficient and reliable procedures exist for the automatic identification and estimation of AR models of any order.

4.2. Decision rules and system implementation

The methods selected for use in the FLEXICAST system produce estimates of the forecasting model:

$$\hat{Y}_T(t) = [\hat{a}_c + \hat{b}_c(T + t - t_c) + \hat{R}_T(t)]SF(T + t), \tag{1}$$

where t is the forecast horizon from the final observation, $Y(T)$,
a_c, b_c, t_c are the intercept, slope, and origin of the most current trend, and
$SF(T + t)$ is the seasonal factor for the month at $T + t$.
$\hat{R}_T(t)$ is the forecasted residual, given by

$$\hat{R}_T(t) = \sum_{i=1}^{p} \hat{\phi}_i \hat{R}_T(t - i) \tag{2}$$

where p is the AR order,
$\hat{\phi}_i$ are the AR coefficients,
$\hat{R}_T(t - i)$ is the forecast at $T + t - i$ if $t > i$, and is the observed residual at $T + t - i$ if $t \leqslant i$.

Decision rules and model selection involve criteria and testing procedures for automatic identification of:
1. significant seasonality
2. the location of changes in trend direction, $t_0, t_1, ..., t_c$
3. the order, p, of the AR model of the residuals

A flowchart of the steps followed in automatic model selection and parameter estimation for the FLEXICAST system is depicted in fig. 1. This section gives details of the logic followed in this flowchart and describes computational methods.

4.2.1. Seasonality

For monthly data, the X-11 method is used first to estimate seasonal indices and to provide a seasonally adjusted series for use in trend and residual model selection. Seasonality is rejected if the F-statistic is not significant at the 5% level; seasonal indices are then set at 1.0. The projected seasonal indices are retained for the forecasting model.

4.2.2. PLR technique

The seasonally adjusted data is then fit by a unique PLR procedure that sequentially identifies and estimates linear pieces. A set of control parameters, *MNINV*, *MNBBK*, *MNPSB*, and *MNEND* are used to assure meaningful and reliable trend fitting. The identification of changes in trend — breakpoints — involves evaluation of a historical interval (τ_0, τ_1) initially set at $(1, MNINV)$. The control parameter *MNINV* should be small enough so that it is unlikely that more than one change in trend would occur in the interval. Thus, one can test for a breakpoint at points

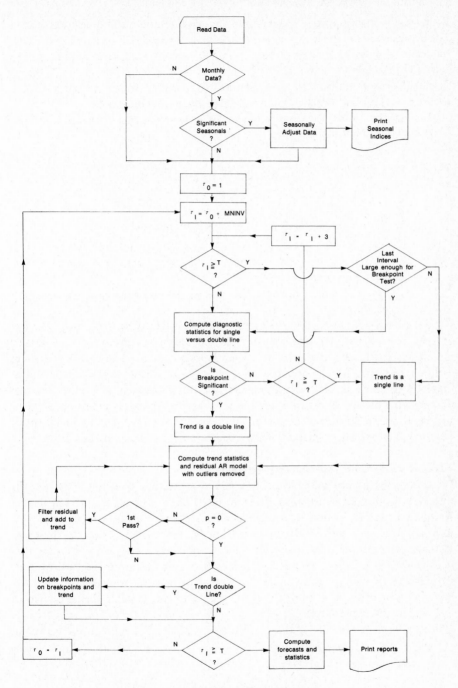

Figure 1. FLEXICAST system flowchart.

within the interval provided they are not too close to either end. Breakpoints may not be separated by an interval of length less than *MNBBK*. This rule prevents trend modeling of behavior that may be best represented by short-term residual movement. To the right of potential breakpoints a sufficient length of data, *MNPSB*, is required to assure reliable trend estimation. Thus, each point in the interval $(\tau_0 + MNBBK - 1, \tau_I - MNPSB + 1)$ is evaluated as a potential breakpoint.

The statistic to test for the significance of a change in trend is given in McGee and Carleton [12] as the *F*-statistic

$$
F_{(2,m+n-4)} = \frac{\left[\sum_{t=1}^{m+n} \hat{R}_C^2(t) - \sum_{j=1}^{m} \hat{R}_L^2(j) - \sum_{k=1}^{n} \hat{R}_R^2(k)\right]\Big/2}{\left[\sum_{j=1}^{m} \hat{R}_L^2(j) + \sum_{k=1}^{n} \hat{R}_R^2(k)\right]\Big/(m+n-4)}
\tag{3}
$$

where $\hat{R}_L, \hat{R}_R, \hat{R}_C$ are the residuals of the left, right, and combined linear fit, respectively, and

m and n are the number of points in the left and right line segment, respectively.

If the breakpoint with the maximum *F*-statistic is not significant, the evaluation interval is extended by three time periods and testing is repeated. Once a breakpoint is selected, the parameters of the left line segment are estimated as described below, and testing for the next breakpoint is repeated starting with the new breakpoint. When the last observation is included in the evaluation interval, a straight line is automatically fit by using data from the last breakpoint if no new one is identified. *At least MNEND observations* before the last one are used to provide sufficient data for reliable estimation of the slope, b_c, of the trend used in forecasting.

4.2.3. Robust features of parameter estimates

As straight-line segments are defined, either up to a breakpoint or up to the last observation, the parameters a_i and b_i are estimated after removal of extreme points, and after adjusting for residual autocorrelation. A double-pass estimation procedure is used. The first pass identifies up to 10% of the data as extreme points; these are defined as observations lying outside a 99% confidence range computed from the estimated variance about the least squares line. A correlogram of the least squares residuals (excluding extreme points) of all observations up to the most recently selected breakpoint is then used to identify and estimate an AR model as described below. The filtered residuals

$$
\hat{R}_F(t) = \hat{R}(t) - \sum_{i=1}^{p} \hat{\phi}_i \hat{R}(t-i)
\tag{4}
$$

are added back to the first pass fitted line. A second pass least squares fit to these

Table 1
Upper bounds on the maximum AR order.

Observations used in correlogram estimation	p_{max}
Less than 24	4
25–35	6
36–47	9
48–59	12
>60	14

adjusted data is then estimated by the same steps used in the first pass. This double-pass procedure is suggested by Hannan [9, p. 110] to obtain more efficient parameter estimates.

4.2.4. AR model identification and parameter estimation

AR models are determined in two steps: first, the order, p, is identified and, second, the AR coefficients are estimated. Several controls must be exercised in selecting the AR order to assure that a reliable portion of the correlogram is used and that the model is unlikely to be explosive. One control is to set a maximum allowable order, p_{max} and test it for significance. An upper bound for p_{max} is set based on the amount of observations used in estimating the correlogram. Table 1 lists these limits.

As a second control, the partial autocorrelation coefficient – the pth coefficient of an estimated AR (p) model, $\hat{\phi}_{pp}$ – is examined to determine an appropriate order. Stationarity demands that $\hat{\phi}_{pp}$ be equal to the product of p numbers each with absolute value less than 1. Thus, $\hat{\phi}_{pp}$ is restricted from becoming too high by automatic reduction of p_{max} if $\hat{\phi}_{pp}$ is greater than $(\alpha_u)^{p-1}$ where α_u is selected near but below 1.0. Then $\hat{\phi}_{pp}$ is tested as being significantly greater than zero. The test statistic, α_L, for the null hypothesis that $\hat{\phi}_{jj} = 0$ for $j \geqslant p$ is based on the assumption that $\hat{\phi}_{ii}$ is approximately normally distributed, $N(0, 1/\sqrt{T_i})$, where T_i is the number of included observations. Thus, if $\hat{\phi}_{pp} > \alpha_L$ (95%), p is fixed as the order, otherwise an order $\hat{\phi}_{p-1, p-1}$ is tested and the procedure repeated until an order is set or independence is indicated – that is, $p = 0$. Computational efficiency of this procedure is guaranteed through iterative estimation of AR coefficients for models of any order, as described by Whittle [20, p. 37].

4.3. Setting of control parameters

The control parameters of the FLEXICAST system were determined by testing thirty series of historical data. Nine series from the Survey of Current Business fifteen company sales histories, and series from several other sources were used.

Series were selected by reviewing their graphs and classifying them according to visual differences in trend and seasonality. For example, some series were selected with no changes in trend, while others had one or more.

The selected series were then divided into three sets of ten series, with three years, five years, and seven years of monthly data respectively. Forecasts for a horizon of twelve months were compared to actuals by using the mean absolute percentage error, $MAPE$,

$$\frac{(100)}{12} \sum_{i=1}^{12} |(f_i - a_i)|/a_i, \tag{5}$$

where i is the forecast horizon,
         a_i is the actual observation, and
         f_i is the forecast.

The lowest $MAPE$ for most series was obtained for control parameters settings of $MNINV = 25$, $MNBBK = 12$, $MNPSB = 5$, $MNEND = 10$ and $\alpha_u = 0.93$. Table 2 displays details of the results of the test. These show that the black box mechanism of the FLEXICAST system is accurate to within 15% of actual values for over three-quarters of the series for horizons up to six months ahead. As would be expected, the median absolute percentage error shifts upward from 6.3 to 18.8% as the forecast horizon increases from one to twelve periods ahead.

Data on international airline passengers modeled by Box and Jenkins [2, pp. 531, 300–322] were forecasted 12 periods ahead and compared to similar results for the Box-Jenkins seasonal ARIMA model. The FLEXICAST forecasts were significantly closer to actuals for ten of the twelve forecasts. The mean squared errors for the twelve forecasts were 86.92 for the Box-Jenkins model and 16.35 for the automatically selected FLEXICAST model.

Table 2
Results of the test of FLEXICAST.

Absolute percentage error range	Forecast horizon (periods ahead)			Annual total
	1 period ($t = 1$)	6 periods ($t = 6$)	12 periods ($t = 12$)	
0–5.00	37	23	17	23
5.01–10.00	27	20	17	23
10.01–15.00	13	30	10	30
15.01–25.00	7	17	30	13
More than 25.00	16	10	27	10
Median % error	6.3%	12.6%	18.8%	10.2%

Note: Table entries show the percentage of forecasts for the various time horizons that fall within the error range labeled for each row. For example, 30 percent (9 series) of the forecasts for 6 periods ahead had absolute percentage error between 10.01 and 15 percent.

5. Experience with FLEXICAST

The FLEXICAST system has been used by many companies in the past year for a variety of forecasting needs. Feedback from users indicates that the system has succeeded in reducing time and costs for obtaining meaningful forecasts. Test results suggest that acceptable accuracy has been achieved in many practical applications.

The current system also contains override options that allow users to obtain more stable patterns of historical data to be modeled and projected by the black box technique. For example, those extreme deviations from the trend that are not caused by seasonal influences can be adjusted to evaluate the effects of one-time events, such as strikes and sales promotions. The overrides do not, however, allow the user to change models selected by the black box technique. That would be inconsistent with the black box philosophy. Technical users of FLEXICAST have mentioned that it has occasionally been a helpful guide to proper selection of more sophisticated models when improved accuracy was desired.

Experience with FLEXICAST identified a number of situations in which poor forecasting occurred. As with other time-series modeling methods, the FLEXICAST system cannot forecast noncyclical turning points. An override option is available to evaluate alternative hypotheses on turning points in trend. Discrete jumps in trend can also cause forecasting inaccuracy. These jumps can sometimes be large enough to cause an oscillatory piecewise trend fit, since the current FLEXICAST system assumes continuous underlying trends. An alternate version was developed that modeled noncontinuous trend pieces, which provided more accurate forecasts for these situations. Inaccurate forecasts also result from recurring, but infrequent, residual patterns caused by influences such as promotions for sales histories and speculative behavior for security and commodity prices. Use of the extreme point adjustment override has helped to improve forecasting accuracy for these situations.

The FLEXICAST system is one implementation of a better black box. It is hoped that further research will broaden the scope of application to a greater variety of time series – perhaps automatic modeling of long-term cycles or nonlinear trends. For example, quadratic or exponential models might improve the degree of fit. However, results would have to be expressed in a meaningful manner, and controls would be needed to prevent explosive or other meaningless trend projections.

References

[1] R.M. Bernard and E. Eberhard, Scheuing, Improving forecast accuracy, Medical Marketing and Media 11 (1976) 9, 15–25.
[2] G.E.P. Box and G.M. Jenkins, Time Series Analysis, Forecasting and Control, revised edition (Holden-Day, San Francisco, 1976).
[3] R.G. Brown, Smoothing, Forecasting and Prediction of Discrete Time Series (Prentice-Hall, Englewood Cliffs, N.J., 1963).

[4] J.C. Chambers, S.K. Mullick and D.D. Smith, How to choose the right forecasting technique, Harvard Business Review (July-August 1971) 45–74.

[5] C. Chatfield and D.L. Prothero, Box-Jenkins seasonal forecasting: Problems in a case study, Journal of the Royal Statistical Society 136 (1973) 295–336.

[6] K.O. Cogger, The optimality of general-order exponential smoothing, Operations Research 22 (1974) 858–867.

[7] C.W.J. Granger, Spectral Analysis of Economic Time Series (Princeton University Press, Princeton, N.J., 1964).

[8] S.B. Guthery, Partition regression, Journal of the American Statistical Association 348 (1974) 945–947.

[9] E.J. Hannan, Time Series Analysis (Wiley, New York, 1960).

[10] G.M. Jenkins and D.G. Watts, Spectral Analysis and Its Applications (Holden-Day, San Francisco, 1968).

[11] M.J. Lawrence, An integrated inventory control system, Interfaces 7 (1977) 55.

[12] V.E. McGee and W.T. Carleton, Piecewise regression, Journal of the American Statistical Association 331 (1970) 1109–1124.

[13] R.L. McLaughlin and J.J. Boyle, Short Term Forecasting (American Marketing Association, New York, 1968).

[14] S. Makridakis, S.C. Wheelwright and A. Hodgsdon, An Interactive Forecasting System, The American Statistician 28 (1974) 4.

[15] T.H. Naylor and H. Schauland, A survey of users of corporate planning models, Management Science 22 (1976) 927–937.

[16] R.E. Quandt, New approach to estimating switching regressions, Journal of the American Statistical Association 338 (1972) 306–310.

[17] Survey of Current Business, Office of Business Economics, U.S. Department of Commerce, vols. 43–49, 1963–1969.

[18] U.S. Bureau of the Census, The X-11 Variant of the Census Method II Seasonal Adjustment Program, Technical Paper No. 15 (U.S. Government Printing Office, Washington, D.C., 1967).

[19] S.C. Wheelwright and D.G. Clarke, Corporate Forecasting: promise and reality, Harvard Business Review (November–December 1976) 40.

[20] P. Whittle, Prediction and Regulation (D. Van Nostrand, Princeton, N.J., 1963).

TIMS Studies in the Management Sciences 12 (1979) 279–296
© North-Holland Publishing Company

FORECASTING BY SMOOTHED REGRESSION: DEVELOPMENT AND AN APPLICATION TO PREDICTING CUSTOMER UTILITY BILLS

Charles P. BONINI and James R. FREELAND

Graduate School of Business, Stanford University

This paper develops the methodology of regression smoothing models, then applies it to the problem of forecasting usage rates for individual utility customers. Regression models are useful for making forecasts when observable independent variables are correlated with the variable to be predicted. Smoothing models are useful in forecasting time series when a large number of individual forecasts are required. The methodology developed here combines the two ideas. The approach is applicable when many forecasts must be made each time period and when independent variables are available. The regression smoothing models allow for modifying the forecasting model over time in response to forecasting errors. They have the advantage of producing relatively accurate forecasts, but are still computationally simple, require little data storage, and are adaptive to changes.

Regression smoothing models are applied to forecasting monthly usage of water, gas, and electricity for individual customers of a city-owned utility. The models are found to significantly outperform other simple forecasting methods in this application.

1. Introduction

In certain time-series forecasting situations, the variable to be predicted may be influenced by a set of observable independent variables. A traditional forecasting procedure to use is a regression model. However, if the forecasting process is to be repeated over time, the basic underlying relationship between the dependent variable and the independent variables, and hence the regression coefficients, may change. In such cases a methodology should be used that recognizes and incorporates these changes into the model.

This paper develops a methodology for time-series forecasting by using a single or multiple regression framework in conjunction with an adaptive procedure for updating the regression coefficients in a computationally simple way. The methodology merges exponentially weighted smoothing models, which have found wide usage in situations such as inventory control systems where a large number of items must be forecast [3], and multiple regression procedures.

This regression smoothing idea is then used for a specific application: the forecasting of individual customers' utility bills. It was found that for most customers, utility usage was closely correlated with weather, although the specific relationship varies across individual customers. Hence a series of simple regression models relating usage of each commodity — gas, water and electricity — to temperature for each customer is a reasonable forecasting scheme. However, these regressions do not remain stable over time. Customers get new appliances and change their usage patterns because of energy conservation awareness or changes in family size. In addition, houses are sold and new owners often have different usage patterns from those of previous occupants. Hence it is necessary to use simple methods to identify when usage patterns change and to modify the parameters of the forecasting model when necessary. Since this must be done for thousands of customers and for each commodity, the procedures must be systematic, simple, and computationally efficient. These requirements led the authors to an examination of the class of models called regression smoothing models.

2. Smoothed regression model

The smoothed regression model developed by the authors operates by making a forecast for some time-series variable, based upon the correlation with a set of independent variables. The actual result is observed. The model is then reestimated and a new forecast made for the next period, and so on.

The parameters of an ordinary regression model are estimated by minimizing the sum of squared error terms, each term receiving the same weight. For the smoothed regression model, the parameters are estimated by minimizing the sum of weighted squared error terms, with the most recent observation receiving the most weight and the weights declining exponentially with time. In addition, the parameters for the smoothed regression can be estimated in recursive fashion, so that only the previous parameters, the basic correlation matrix, and the most recent observation are required to revise or update the regression estimates. See [1] and [7] for related recursive estimation formulations.

The basic model is:

$$y_t = b'_t x_t + e_t,$$

where y_t is the actual value of the dependent variable in period t,

         e_t is the residual (or error) term for period t,

         x_t is an n-dimensional column vector representing the n independent variables at time t, and

         b_t is an n-dimensional column vector of regression coefficients estimated at time period t.

If a constant term is to be included in the model, the first independent variable, x_1, is always 1, and the first regression coefficient, b_1, is the constant term.

If one makes the usual assumptions that the e_t terms have expectation zero, common variance o^2, and are uncorrelated, the normal equations arrived at by minimizing the weighted errors squared are

$$X'_t W_t X_t b_t = X'_t W_t y_t,$$

where $X_t = \begin{bmatrix} x_{11} & x_{12} & \cdots & x_{1n} \\ x_{21} & x_{22} & \cdots & x_{2n} \\ \vdots & & & \\ x_{t1} & x_{t2} & \cdots & x_{tn} \end{bmatrix} = \begin{bmatrix} x'_1 \\ x'_2 \\ \vdots \\ x'_t \end{bmatrix}$

in which x_{ij} refers to the value of the jth independent variable in period i.

$$W_t = \begin{bmatrix} \alpha(1-\alpha)^{t-1} & 0 & \cdots & 0 \\ 0 & \alpha(1-\alpha)^{t-2} & \cdots & 0 \\ \vdots & & & \\ 0 & 0 & \cdots & \alpha \end{bmatrix},$$

$$b_t = \begin{bmatrix} b_{t1} \\ b_{t2} \\ \vdots \\ b_{tn} \end{bmatrix}, \qquad y_t = \begin{bmatrix} y_1 \\ y_2 \\ \vdots \\ y_t \end{bmatrix}$$

in which b_{ti} refers to the coefficient for variable i estimated in period t, and y_i is the value of the dependent variable in period i. Assuming that the matrix $X'_t W_t X_t$ is nonsingular, then

$$b_t = (X'_t W_t X_t)^{-1} X'_t W_t y_t. \tag{1}$$

The matrix $(X'_t W_t y_t)$ for period t can be written in recursive form by using the matrix of the previous period and the recent values of the independent variables:

$$X'_t W_t y_t = (1-\alpha)(X'_{t-1} W_{t-1} y_{t-1}) + \alpha x_t y_t, \tag{2}$$

where

$$X_{t-1} = \begin{bmatrix} x_{11} & x_{12} & \cdots & x_{1n} \\ x_{21} & x_{22} & \cdots & x_{2n} \\ \vdots & & & \\ x_{t-1,1} & x_{t-1,2} & \cdots & x_{t-1n} \end{bmatrix}$$

and

$$
W_{t-1} = \begin{bmatrix} \alpha(1-\alpha)^{t-2} & 0 & \cdots & 0 \\ 0 & \alpha(1-\alpha)^{t-3} & \cdots & 0 \\ \vdots & & & \\ 0 & 0 & \cdots & \alpha \end{bmatrix}
$$

In a similar fashion, the estimated coefficients for period t can be expressed as a recursive function of the previous values for $t-1$:

$$
b_t = b_{t-1} - \alpha[(X_t'W_tX_t)^{-1}x_t']\,e_t. \tag{3}
$$

This result is developed in the appendix. Note that, when the above formula is used, the regression coefficients are estimated by correcting the previous values as a function of the smoothing constant α and the error in the current period e_t.

The special case of simple regression is of particular interest because of its wide applicability and because the application to be discussed in this paper is of this type. Hence the formulas for this case are developed in more detail. Here $n = 2$, and

$$
X_t = \begin{bmatrix} 1 & x_1 \\ 1 & x_2 \\ \vdots & \\ 1 & x_t \end{bmatrix}
$$

where the subscript on the x variable now refers only to the time period.

The recursive estimation formula now becomes

$$
b_t = b_{t-1} - \alpha \begin{bmatrix} \alpha\sum_{i=1}^{t}(1-\alpha)^i & M_t \\ M_t & S_t \end{bmatrix} x_t'\,e_t,
$$

where

$$
\left.\begin{array}{l} M_t = \alpha x_t + (1-\alpha)M_{t-1} \\ S_t = \alpha(x_t^2) + (1-\alpha)S_{t-1} \end{array}\right\} \tag{4}
$$

That is, M_t is an exponentially weighted average of the independent variable x values, and S_t is an exponentially weighted average of the x^2 values.

For larger values of t, the term $\alpha \Sigma_{i=1}^{t}(1 - \alpha)^i$ is approximately 1. Using common notation for simple regression gives

$$b_t = \begin{bmatrix} a_t \\ b_t \end{bmatrix},$$

then

$$a_t = a_{t-1} + \alpha \left[1 - M_t \left(\frac{x_t - M_t}{S_t - M_t^2} \right) \right] e_t, \tag{5}$$

and

$$b_t = b_{t-1} + \alpha \left[\frac{x_t - M_t}{S_t - M_t^2} \right] e_t. \tag{6}$$

Note that this methodology requires storing only the values for M_t, S_t, and the coefficients a_t and b_t. These values are updated each period based upon the current error term e_t and the current value for the independent variable x_t. The forecast for period $t + 1$ is given as

$$\text{forecast } y_{t+1}^* = a_t + b_t x_{t+1} \tag{7}$$

2.1. Projection smoothing method for simple regression

Projection smoothing — the meaning of the name will become apparent shortly — was developed to further simplify the computations and storage requirements for the simple regression case. This procedure is heuristic in nature and designed specifically for the utility forecasting situation.

Suppose at the end of period t the regression line is as shown in fig. 1, with values of b_{t-1} for slope and a_{t-1} for intercept. The initial line may be estimated by least squares to get the system started. Suppose that the mean μ and range of the independent variable x are reasonably well known. Two perpendicular lines are drawn at an equal distance on either side of the mean of x. These lines should be close to the lower and upper ranges of the x values. In fig. 1, the lines are shown as $x = \mu - k$ and $x = \mu + k$. A forecast is made for period t by using equation (7), and after the value of y_t is known, the forecast error e_t is computed as:

$$e_t = y_t - y_t^* = y_t - a_{t-1} - b_{t-1} x_t.$$

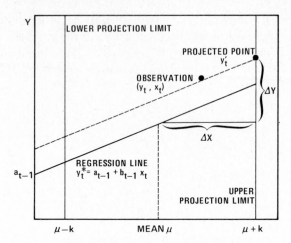

Fig. 1. Projection smoothed method.

The values of a and b are to be revised taking into account the size and direction of the forecast error. The value a is a measure of the height of the regression line. Hence if the observed value is above the line, meaning a positive forecast error, the line should move up somewhat. Similarly, if the actual is below the line, meaning a negative forecast error, the line should move down. In short, the height or value of the line should be expected to move in the same direction as the error, and the distance should be proportionate to the size of the error. That provides the rational for the updating formula for the intercept a:

$$a_t = a_{t-1} + \alpha e_t, \qquad 0 < \alpha < 1, \tag{8}$$

where α is the weighting factor.

The calculation of the new slope b_t is more complicated. As a first step, the new observation is projected onto the nearest limit (either $x = \mu - k$ or $\mu + k$). This projection gives the name to the method. That is, the projected point $y'_t = a_{t-1} + b_{t-1}(\mu \pm k) + e_t$ is determined (see fig. 1). Thus the projected point is the same distance above or below the regression line but is out on the nearest limit line. The new estimate of the slope will be determined from the values of Δx and Δy as shown in fig. 1. The value Δy is the incremental amount the projected point is above or below the mean:

$$\Delta y = y'_t - \mu_y$$

$$= [a_{t-1} + b_{t-1}(\mu \pm k) + e_t] - (a_{t-1} + b_{t-1}\mu)$$

$$= \pm b_{t-1}k + e_t,$$

where the + sign is used if the projection point is on the line $x = \mu + k$ and the minus sign if the projected point is on $x = \mu - k$. The value Δx represents the distance between the mean and the limit line, and hence:

$$\Delta x = k \quad \text{if } x \geqslant \mu, \qquad \Delta x = -k \quad \text{if } x < \mu.$$

A new estimate of the slope $b(\text{est})$ can be obtained from $\Delta y / \Delta x$:

$$b(\text{est}) = \Delta y / \Delta x = (\pm b_{t-1} k + e_t)/(\pm k) = b_{t-1} \pm e_t/k).$$

The new value for b_t can then be obtained by weighting $b(\text{est})$ and the old value b_{t-1}. The same weighting value α as above may be used, but there is no reason why it must be the same. In this paper another weight, β, will be used. Then

$$b_t = \beta b(\text{est}) + (1 - \beta)b_{t-1}$$

$$= \beta[b_{t-1} \pm (e_t/k)] + (1 - \beta)b_{t-1}$$

$$= b_{t-1} \pm \beta(e_t/k),$$

where the $\pm$ sign depends on whether x_t is above or below the mean

$$b_t = b_{t-1} + \beta(e_t/k) \quad \text{if} \quad x_t \geqslant \mu, \tag{9}$$

$$b_t = b_{t-1} - \beta(e_t/k) \quad \text{if} \quad x_t < \mu.$$

The simplicity of these formulas is appealing. The slope and intercept are updated by very simply weighting in the error of the last observation. Only the slope and intercept of the previous period need to be saved from period to period. Since the formulas are heuristic, their value depends on how well they work, which will be discussed in a later section.

3. Application of regression smoothing to forecasting utility usage rates

The regression smoothing models were developed for a specific application: the forecasting of utility (water, gas, and electricity) usage rates for both residential and small commercial establishments of a city in northern California. Currently the city reads the utility meters every 30 days or so. If reasonable forecasts could be made, the city would like to bill customers on alternate months on the basis of the forecast, thus substantially reducing the cost of reading meters. Of course, any forecast errors are automatically corrected when the meter is read in the subsequent month. There are approximately 50,000 different meters and a 30% turnover in customers per year.

There are a large number of time-series models for handling seasonality that are computationally simple and can adjust to changes in parameter values (see [2,3,6, 10,11]). However, in the application here, utility usage is much less related to the time of year than it is to the weather. In addition, the length of a period may differ depending on the scheduling of meters, for example, one time a forecast may be desired over 25 days, while another time a forecast for 35 days may be needed. For these reasons only regression models in which the independent variables depend on observable variables, which may depend on time, were considered. Furthermore, since there were 50,000 different meters to individually forecast and since custom- ers' usage patterns change, the class of regression smoothing models was considered the most appropriate.

3.1. Data analysis

A random sample of utility usage for 53 customers — 43 residential and 10 com- mercial establishments — was collected. The data were in the form of meter read- ings for gas, water, and electricity for 39 months covering the period from January 1973 to April 1976. During this period the utility meters had been read approxi- mately every 30 days. It was tentatively proposed that utility usage was correlated with the temperature. Information was available about the maximum and minimum temperature for each day in the sample period. The variable degree days was calcu- lated by finding the difference between the average of max and min temperatures and $65°F$. Two other variables were also calculated: cold degree days — considering only days with average temperature below $65°F$ — and hot degree days — days with the average above $65°F$. Table 1 illustrates these calculations. The sample data showed the cold degree days variable, to be more strongly correlated to utility usage than the other variables shown in table 1. Fig. 2 shows graphs of the average daily usage of each utility versus the average number of cold degree days per day for one customer. As one can see, gas usage is strongly correlated with temperature $(r = 0.99)$, while water and electricity are somewhat related to temperature $(r =$

Table 1
Sample calculations for degree days.

Day	Maximum temperature	Minimum temperature	Average temperature	Degree days	Cold degree days	Hot degree days
1	73	63	68	3	0	3
2	72	46	59	−6	6	0
3	75	55	65	0	0	0

Average degree days   = −1.0
Average cold degree days = 2
Average hot degree days = 1

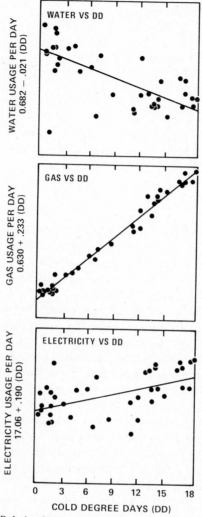

Fig. 2. Relationships between utility usage and degree days.

0.66 and 0.55 respectively). In this area, water is used extensively during warmer months for lawn watering, and air conditioning does not seem to be a major factor. It probably would be possible to improve the accuracy of prediction by adding other variables such as the amount of rainfall or hours of sunlight, but then the amount of storage and computation effort increase. The model would also be more difficult to implement and more difficult to explain.

The model proposed was

$$\begin{bmatrix} \text{estimated utility usage} \\ \text{per day for customer } i \\ \text{during period } t \end{bmatrix} = a_i + b_i \begin{bmatrix} \text{average cold degree days per} \\ \text{day during period } t \end{bmatrix}$$

and

$$\begin{bmatrix} \text{forecast usage for} \\ \text{period } t \text{ for customer } i \end{bmatrix} = \begin{bmatrix} \text{estimated utility usage} \\ \text{per day for customer } i \\ \text{during period } t \end{bmatrix} \begin{bmatrix} \text{number of days} \\ \text{during period } t \end{bmatrix}.$$

3.2. Procedure for testing the models

Several different procedures were used to estimate and update the parameters of the model. For each procedure the first twelve readings (approximately twelve months) were used to initially estimate the parameters for each customer in the sample. Two different runs were then made for each procedure. In the first run a forecast was computed for periods 13, 15, ..., 39. To begin, a forecast was made for period 13 for each utility and customer. The forecast was compared to the actual usage in period 13 and the error tabulated for each utility (in terms of units per day) and for the dollar error for the entire bill of the customer. A forecast was next computed for periods 13 and 14 together. Information about the forecast error for periods 13 and 14 together was used to update the estimates of *a* and *b* for each customer and utility. Next a forecast was prepared for period 15 and the errors tabulated. Thus, in the first run the forecast was compared to the actual for the odd numbered periods. The reason the error for periods 13 and 14 together was used to update the parameters is that when the system is implemented, actual readings will be made only every two periods so that updating will be based on the two-period error. In the second run a forecast was made for the even numbered months — 14, 16, and so on. In this manner errors can be tabulated for $39 - 12 = 27$ months.

For each customer, tabulations were made for the average error, average absolute error, average absolute percentage error, and the average absolute error as a percentage of the mean usage for water, gas, electricity, and the dollar value of the entire bill. Frequency distributions were also prepared for the percentage errors on the bill in dollars. For this particular application the best single summary measure of performance — the one most visible to the customer — probably relates to the errors in the total utility bill. The city administration has expressed a strong preference for an unbiased procedure with the average dollar error equal to zero. Overbilling creates complaints for obvious reasons and underbilling creates complaints because the next time an actual reading is made the charge will be for more than was actually used in the previous month. Although the average absolute error is a measure of the variance in the errors (see Brown [3], pp. 282–287), customers with large utility bills tend to have larger dollar value errors than customers with smaller bills. Thus for purposes of choosing between models, the criterion of average absolute percentage error was used.

3.3. Models tested

Several different procedures were used to estimate the usage equations.

3.3.1. Three-month average of past usage
The somewhat naive method of averaging periods of past usage was used to get a basis for comparison with other procedures. Usage per day in period t was computed as the average daily usage over certain previous periods. In particular, the previous periods used included the most recent actual daily usage and the actual daily usage for the two-month period, 12 periods ago. For example, the forecast for average daily usage in January 1975 would be computed as the average of the daily usages for December 1974, January 1974, and February 1974.

3.3.2. Moving regression model
The moving regression idea is similar to that of ordinary moving averages [1]. For example, estimates of a_{12} and b_{12} were computed at the end of period 12 by using information about the actual average usage per day and the average number of degree days per day for each of the previous 6 two-month periods. Then a forecast was prepared by using

$$y^*_{12+1} = a_{12} + b_{12}x_{12+1}.$$

At the end of period 14 the parameters a and b (that is, a_{14}, b_{14}) are recomputed based on the most recent 6 two-month periods.

3.3.3. Smoothed regression
For the smoothed regression model, discussed earlier, estimates of a and b are computed at the end of period t by using equations (5) and (6). Equation (7) is used to forecast for period $t + 1$. The best value for the smoothing constant α was chosen by trying different values in the range 0.1 to 0.5. Higher values were not tested because it was felt too much weight might be put on the most recent observation (see Brown [3] pp. 106–108). A value of $\alpha = 0.4$ was chosen because it produced the lowest average absolute percentage error for the dollar amount of the bill.

3.3.4. Projection regression smoothing
For the projection smoothing model, estimates of a and b are computed at the end of period t using equations (8) and (9). Equation (7) is used to forecast for period $t + 1$. As with the smoothed regression model, the best values for the

smoothing constants, α and β, were chosen by a search over several different values. Values of 0.5 for α and 0.1 for β were chosen.

3.3.5. Adaptive methods.

Some situations may require further adaptation. When there is turnover by the customer there may be changes in the usage patterns. For example, fig. 3 displays the average daily electricity usage for each month as a function of the month's average cold degree days. For the first 18 months the customer's usage decreased as the average degree days increased. In month 19 a turnover of ownership occurred. As one can see, the usage pattern changed dramatically. In addition, during the last 8 months the pattern again changed dramatically. The last change was not caused by a change in the customer but probably by the acquisition of a new appliance. The city utility company knows when there is a customer turnover, and it would seem advisable to use this information when updating a and b. The natural procedure would be to increase the weight of the most recent observations in determining a and b. With a smoothing procedure, the smoothing constant could be increased temporarily. When demand patterns change for reasons unknown to the utility company, it might be advisable to have control procedure for detecting

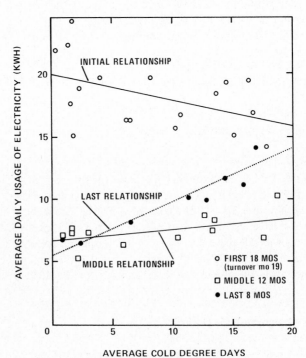

Fig. 3. Electricity usage for customer 2050.

these changes and automatically giving more weight to the recent observations. In the context of smoothing models several adaptive type models have been proposed [6,8].

Two different adaptive approaches, the Trigg–Leach procedure [9] and a procedure suggested by Whybark [12], were tested in conjunction with both the smoothed regression model and the projection smoothed model. With the Trigg–Leach procedure a tracking signal, Q_t, is computed each period by using the formula:

$$Q_t = d_t/\Delta_t$$

where

$$d_t = \text{smoothed average error} \tag{10}$$

$$= \delta e_t + (1 - \delta)d_{t-1},$$

and

$$\Delta_t = \text{smoothed absolute average error} \tag{11}$$

$$= \delta |e_t| + (1 - \delta)\Delta_{t-1} \qquad 0 < \delta < 1.$$

Then the smoothing paramter α is set equal to $|Q_t|$. The Whybark procedure involves increasing the smoothing parameter if the error in any period is large relative to the smoothed absolute average error (Δ_t).

3.4. Implementation of the adaptive procedures

The use of the adaptive procedures for regression smoothing models and for this particular data required some minor modifications to the Trigg–Leach and Whybark procedures. First, upper and lower bounds were established on the smoothing constant α in the Trigg–Leach procedure; if the tracking signal was outside the limits, α was set at the bound. An upper bound $\alpha = 0.7$ was used in all cases. Based on experiments with the lower bound for the smoothed regression model, a lower bound of $\alpha = 0.3$ seemed appropriate and was used for subsequent analysis.

For the Whybark procedure, if an out of control observation was obtained the value of the smoothing constant was set equal to 0.7, the smoothing constant was then reduced to 0.5 in the subsequent period, then returned to normal. Several different normal values for the smoothing constant were tested. Values of $\alpha = 0.2$ and 0.3 were about the same, and a normal value of 0.3 was chosen for subsequent work.

Another modification of the Whybark procedure was raising the smoothing constant to a maximum value of 0.7 if there was a turnover in a customer. Turnover information is available to the utility and allows faster adaption to changes in usage patterns.

The adaptive models require a smoothing parameter for the error. A value of δ = 0.1 was used for this purpose in equations (10) and (11).

In the smoothed regression model there is only one parameter. However, in the projection smoothing model, the parameter α is used to smooth the intercept a, and the parameter β is used to smooth the slope. Experiments indicated that a low value of β = 0.1 was better, indicating relative stability in the slope.

The Trigg—Leach procedure outperformed the Whybark procedure for the smoothed regression model, but the opposite was true for the projection smoothing model. The difference in results may be caused by having only one smoothing constant in the smooth regression model, while there are two smoothing constant for the projection method, with only α being changed in the adaptive procedure.

3.5. Evaluation

Table 2 shows the summary results over the 53 sample customers for six different models. In each case, the model used the optimum — as far as was searched — set of smoothing parameters and adaptive parameters, the latter were appropriate. That is, the best challenger of each type is shown.

No model is the best across all utilities. The last column in Table 2 , which shows the average absolute error as a % of mean usage, is probably the best measure for each utility separately. That is because for a given commodity the forecast error might be very large relative to a small actual usage, thus causing a very large percentage error. This phenomena was much less true in the total utility bill. The naive model three-month past average, performs quite well on water predictions but is poor on the other utilities. Gas is the most important to predict, since it accounts for a large part of the dollar amount for most customer bills.

Using these measures, the smoothing models clearly outperform the naive average past usage model and the moving regression model. Most of the difference can be attributed to their doing a better job in forecasting gas consumption.

The adaptive procedure models make additional marginal improvements. The fact that the adaptive methods do not make a more dramatic impact is probably due to the very high values for the smoothing parameters used throughout. The addition of the adaptive feature did not help much.

The high values for the smoothing constants result from several factors. One is the high turnover in homes and apartments in the area, a turnover rate of 30% per year. Secondly, the energy crisis of 1974 occurred right in the middle of the data collection period and affected the usage patterns for gas and electricity. Also increasing utility costs have led people to reduce usage. High values for the smooth-

Table 2
Summary of results for different models–average across all 53 customers.

Utility	Average error	Average absolute error	Average absolute percentage error	Average absolute error as a percentage of mean usage
Three-month average of past usage				
Water	0.033	0.193	34.74	27.37
Gas	−0.057	1.082	39.28	20.52
Electricity	−0.232	.2.873	18.85	16.95
Bill	−0.039	5.354	15.28	−
Moving regression model				
Water	0.027	0.197	37.55	28.77
Gas	−0.042	0.917	24.45	18.15
Electricity	−0.317	2.813	20.42	17.38
Bill	−0.118	4.969	14.73	−
Smoothed regression model (nonadaptive), $\alpha = 0.4$				
Water	0.015	0.189	37.24	28.43
Gas	−0.032	0.848	23.62	17.56
Electricity	−0.244	2.633	19.07	16.04
Bill	−0.125	4.695	14.13	−
Projection smoothing (nonadaptive), $\alpha = 0.5, \beta = 0.1$				
Water	0.008	0.182	36.37	27.52
Gas	−0.011	0.832	24.44	17.58
Electricity	−0.117	2.645	19.05	16.22
Bill	0.016	4.68	14.40	−
Adaptive smoothed regression, Trigg-Leach Version (limits on α are 0.6 and 0.3)				
Water	0.021	0.185	36.74	27.80
Gas	−0.30	0.830	23.51	17.33
Electricity	−0.357	2.632	19.45	16.16
Bill	−0.136	4.632	14.03	−
Adaptive projection smoothing, Whybark Version ($\beta = 0.1$; $\alpha = 0.3, 0.5, 0.7$)				
Water	0.016	0.188	35.43	26.98
Gas	−0.039	0.837	24.39	17.42
Electricity	−0.304	2.647	19.08	16.15
Bill	−0.131	4.628	14.20	−

Note: Water is measured in 100 cu ft, gas in therms, electricity in kilowatt hours, and the bill in dollars.

ing parameters allow the models to adapt quickly to changes in individual consumer usage patterns.

The authors actually recommended to the city that either the projection smoothing method or the regression smoothing technique be adopted with an adaptive feature. The adaptive feature was recommended because it did improve the errors slightly in the test and it is intuitively appealing in an environment where usage patterns change frequently.

4. Summary

This paper developed a new class of forecasting models: regression smoothing models. Unlike previous attempts to merge exponential smoothing models and multiple regression [5], this development results in simple formulas that allow the user to update the regression coefficients in an adaptive fashion. The models presented are computationally simple and require little data storage. They are most useful in a situation where many variables must be forecast, but each variable can be related to the same set of observable independent variables. Further, the relationships may change through time.

A special case of the smoothed regression model, a simple regression, was illustrated by an application to forecasting customer utility bills. Although this application would seem to be of some interest in itself, it does not address many of the larger issues in using forecasting in the utility industry (see [4]). It does illustrate, however, a viable procedure for forecasting customer's utility bills that might offer considerable savings in meter reading costs.

Appendix

The notation presented in the section on smoothed regression model is used here to develop the recursive formula for b_t, which is given by equation (3). Using equations (1) and (2) yields

$$b_t = (X_t' W_t X_t)^{-1} [(1 - \alpha) X_{t-1}' W_{t-1} y_{t-1} + \alpha x_t y_t]$$

$$= (X_t' W_t X_t)^{-1} [(1 - \alpha)(X_{t-1}' W_{t-1} X_{t-1})$$

$$\times (X_{t-1} W_{t-1} X_{t-1})^{-1} X_{t-1}' W_{t-1} y_{t-1} + \alpha x_t y_t].$$

But, since

$$b_{t-1} = (X_{t-1}' W_{t-1} X_{t-1})^{-1} X_{t-1}' W_{t-1} y_{t-1}, \tag{A1}$$

then

$$b_t = (X_t'W_tX_t)^{-1}[(1 - \alpha)(X_{t-1}'W_{t-1}X_{t-1})\,b_{t-1} + \alpha x_t y_t]$$

$$+ b_{t-1} - b_{t-1}. \tag{A2}$$

Substituting for the last term in (A2) by using (A1) and rewriting yields

$$b_t = b_{t-1} + \alpha(X_t'W_tX_t)^{-1}x_t y_t + (X_t'W_tX_t)^{-1}$$

$$\times [(X_{t-1}'W_{t-1}X_{t-1})(1 - \alpha) - (X_t'W_tX_t)]\,b_{t-1}. \tag{A3}$$

Note that

$$X_t'W_tX_t = (1 - \alpha)(X_{t-1}'W_{t-1}X_{t-1}) + \alpha x_t x_t'.$$

Hence equation (A3) becomes

$$b_t = b_{t-1} + \alpha(X_t'W_tX_t)^{-1}x_t y_t - (X_t'W_tX_t)$$

$$\times [(X_t'W_tX_t) - \alpha x_t x_t' - X_t'W_tX_t]$$

$$= b_{t-1} + \alpha(X_t'W_tX_t)^{-1}x_t y_t - \alpha(X_t'W_tX_t)^{-1}x_t x_t' b_{t-1}$$

$$= b_{t-1} + \alpha(X_t'W_tX_t)^{-1}x_t(y_t - x_t'b_{t-1})$$

$$= b_{t-1} - \alpha(X_t'W_tX_t)^{-1}x_t\, e_t.$$

References

[1] D.A. Belsley, On the determination of systematic parameter variation in the linear regression models, Annals of Economic and Social Measurement 2 (1973) 487–494.
[2] G.E.P. Box and G.M. Jenkins, Time Series Analysis, Forecasting and Control (Holden-Day, San Francisco, 1970).
[3] R.G. Brown, Smoothing, Forecasting and Prediction (Prentice-Hall, Englewood Cliffs, N.J., 1963).
[4] G.K.C. Chen and P.R. Winters, Forecasting peak demand in an electric utility with a hybrid exponential model, Management Science, 12 (1966) 531–537.
[5] D.B. Crane and J.R. Crotty, A two-stage forecasting model: Exponential smoothing and multiple regression, Management Science 13 (1967) 501–507.
[6] D.C. Montgomery and L.A. Johnson, Forecasting and Time Series Analysis (McGraw-Hill, N.Y., 1976).
[7] J.E. Reinmuth and D.R. Wittink, Recursive models for forecasting seasonal processes, Journal of Financial and Quantitative Analysis 9 (1974) 659–684.

[8] S.D. Roberts and D.C. Whybark, Adaptive forecasting techniques, International Journal of Production Research 12 (1974) 635–645.

[9] D.W. Trigg and A.G. Leach, Exponential smoothing with an adaptive response rate, Operational Research Quarterly 18 (1967) 53–59.

[10] S.C. Wheelwright and S. Makridakis, An examination of the use of adaptive filtering in forecasting, Operational Research Quarterly (Winter, 1973).

[11] S.C. Wheelwright and S. Makridakis, Forecasting methods for management (Wiley, New York, 1977).

[12] D.C. Whybark, A comparison of adaptive forecasting techniques, Logistis Transportation Review 8 (1970).

TIMS Studies in the Management Sciences 12 (1979) 297–312
© North-Holland Publishing Company

ON SELECTING A FORECASTING MODEL

Robert FILDES and Syd HOWELL
Manchester Business School

This paper discusses how to select a quantitative forecasting model. It is argued that even when the forecaster has a strictly specified problem to solve, no "best" method exists. Instead the forecaster must consider the cost effectiveness of the various alternatives. The various classes of model available to help the forecaster face this dilemma are examined. Since no one class is better than any other, general principles need to be developed. It is argued that model sensitivity to data errors and misspecification are important; similarly important is the ability to recognize specification error in the chosen model. The evidence on comparative accuracy is then analyzed, and, together with the theoretical analysis on specification, it is used to support a number of recommendations on the appropriate criteria for selecting a forecasting model.

1. The forecaster's problem

This paper is intended for the practicing forecaster in an organization. It assumes that he wishes to construct a replicable quantitative model to produce forecasts of some important variables. His objective is to improve the economic payoff to a specified set of decisions.

This problem generally involves some model of the decisions to be taken, some model of the data-generating process, and some, probably largely informal, model of the decision maker and his relationship to the forecasting model.

The difficulty that confronts the forecaster is that there is as yet no theoretical basis on which to choose a forecasting model appropriate to his situation. General principles guide him: for example, if the payoff from improved forecasting is slight, he can use an extrapolative model. However, over the past few years even the distinction between extrapolative models, once used particularly for short-term production and inventory decisions, and causal models, used for evaluating policy options, has tended to break down. Thus it was once thought that large-scale econometric models would necessarily be more accurate at forecasting than extrapolative models and that stochastic models of consumer behavior would be more accurate if they were more complex. Such general principles, had they been correct, would have helped in model selection. Unfortunately, now that evidence has accumulated to show that these recommendations are misleading, the forecaster once again finds that any one type of model is comparable with any other. In this paper the broad classes of models available, their accuracy, and their sensitivity to error are examined with a view to developing some general criteria to help the forecaster in model selection.

2. The tools available

Forecasting models come in many shapes, sizes, and disguises. They have often been developed for specific purposes. For example, in macroeconomics one finds separate models developed to analyze short- or medium-term policy options and these models have different desirable characteristics. Despite the fact that models are purpose specific, it remains true that they are all to a large extent competitors to be evaluated in terms of cost effectiveness. Thus, while an extrapolative model may not answer the marketing department's question of how effective a campaign with 2 cents off a pack is likely to be, it can be used to forecast sales, and it may be more accurate at that task than a model that includes a promotions variable. The question a forecaster must answer is which of the two models produces the greater improvement in decision making.

Although such a conclusion is not surprising to an operations researcher, researchers working in their own particular specialties have consistently ignored its implications. Models of consumer behavior have been treated separately from the mathematically similar smoothing models [44], and macroeconomic models have not been compared to their time-series alternatives. Although these distinctions have now broken down, the effect has been that relatively little evidence has accumulated on comparative forecasting performance.

More will be said later about comparative forecast performance. In the next section the various broad classes of forecasting models are described, and the research available on their accuracy, an inevitable substitute measure for cost effectiveness is summarized. The aim is to understand the sensitivity of the various models to likely errors, because the more sensitive they are the more they should be avoided unless there is evidence of their exceptional merit. The classes considered, while not exhaustive, include the major approaches to forecasting.

2.1. Extrapolative models

A number of extrapolative models have been developed for the situation in which only a single series of data is available. These univariate models are discussed first.

2.1.1. Smoothing and ARIMA models

One broad class of univariate forecasting models can best be described by dopting the framework proposed by Box and Jenkins [5]. The autoregressive integrated moving average (ARIMA) models have the mathematical formulation

$$\phi(B)(1 - B)^d Z_t = \delta + \theta(B) e_t,$$

where B is the backshift operator, ϕ and θ are polynomials in B, $\{e_t\}$ is a set of independent identically distributed normal random variables and δ is unknown. Z_t is a transform of the variable we wish to forecast, Y_t, chosen so that $(1 - B)^d Z_t$ is stationary. ARIMA models can include exponential smoothing, moving average decomposition, and trend curve methods as special cases (although approximations are involved) and consequently the remarks made here apply generally to these types of models.

The process of modeling, following Box and Jenkins, stresses the identification of an appropriate model selected from this class. After the chosen model is estimated, diagnostic checking is used to test this preliminary identification. Identification typically requires a sample of at least fifty points to estimate the autocorrelation structure of the series, which is then used in selecting the specific model to be estimated. Usually only two or three parameters are included in the final model, so estimation does not demand as large a sample as identification.

The two basic assumptions made are that 1) the autocorrelation structure of the series is constant and 2) Z_t is stationary. With these assumptions established, Box and Jenkins show that estimation of the selected model is possible using nonlinear least squares, and that assumption 2) can be relaxed somewhat, at least for short lead times.

Exponential smoothing and time-series decomposition models differ from ARIMA models only in that there is little stress on identification. That is so, even though each of the many available variants was developed to meet an earlier model failure. Identification of the appropriate model is typically done subjectively. In the short term, the corresponding loss of accuracy is unimportant. The accuracy of trend curve analysis on the other hand, largely used in medium- and long-term applications, depends quite critically on choice of curve, a choice equivalent to the selection of Z_t in the ARIMA formulation.

The empirical evidence on smoothing models supports Box and Jenkins proposition that identification is a key element in forecast model selection. Thus Groff [31], who took a mechanistic approach to identifying ARIMA models, compares them unfavorably with smoothing variants, while the many studies that favor ARIMA models all took considerable care in model identification. Newbold and Granger [55] have conducted the most extensive tests on 88 series, comparing exponential smoothing models (with trend and seasonal factors) with stepwise autoregression in first differences and with ARIMA models. They found that ARIMA models outperformed the other two some 65% of the time on *ex ante* tests, but that this advantage deteriorated with lead time.

2.1.2. Models with shifting coefficients

The fundamental assumption in ARIMA-type models is a stable autocorrelation structure. However, evidence that this structure does change is fairly widespread, despite the success of fixed parameter models (see [3,36,56]). Harrison and Stevens [32,33] argue in favor of short-term parameter model changes in order to deal with the transients and step changes caused by strikes, holidays, tax changes, product redesign and so forth. They have presented the most extensive approach to shifting coefficient models, which are discussed in greater detail below.

Bayesian forecasting and the Kalman filter. Harrison and Stevens have based their development of Bayesian forecasting on the extremely general dynamic linear model. This model resembles a conventional regression model except that the model parameters are allowed to vary over time. It consists of two equations. The observation equation which relates a vector of dependent variables Y_t to independent variables X_t through using coefficients β_t and added noise v is given as:

$$Y_t = \beta_t X_t + v_t, \quad \text{where} \quad v_t \sim N[0, E(v_t v_t')].$$

It is usual to assume β_t constant over the fitted and forecast periods. Here, however, a second system equation is added that describes random movements of the coefficients β_t by a deterministic component G and a stationary noise component w:

$$\beta_t = G\beta_{t-1} + w_t, \quad \text{where} \quad w_t \sim N[0, E(w_t w_t')].$$

For forecasting Y_t one requires the causal variables X_t and current estimates of the parameters β_t. In univariate applications, X_t is chosen to represent Y_t in terms of a level parameter and a growth parameter.

Kalman [41] showed that if the matrix G is known and X_t and the covariances of v and w are known at time t, an estimate of the current parameters β_t can be calculated recursively from the previous estimates of β and from the most recent observations of Y and X. In practice of course the parameters G, $E(v_t v_t')$ and $E(w_t w_t')$ may not fulfill the above requirement, so standard but difficult methods of estimation have been attempted (Mehra in this publication) while Harrison and Stevens [32] adopt an approximation method of estimation.

Using the Kalman filter as a basis, Harrison and Stevens have constructed multistate models in which alternative process changes are explicitly modeled, for example, step change, large transient value, slope change, and so on. In effect, the overall model includes a number of different submodels any one of which may apply at any one time.

The dynamic linear model is clearly a generalization of autoregressive models, and suggests that an autoregressive model could be made self-tuning and adaptive in the coefficients. Unfortunately, there are no published studies that empirically compare the accuracy of the dynamic linear model with an ARIMA alternative, but Harrison and Stevens [34] and Fildes and Stevens [23] give examples of its use.

Other models with shifting parameters. Several other models with shifting parameters are listed below, but space does not permit a detailed discussion of them here.
1. adaptive exponential smoothing (see Trigg and Leach [68] and Whybark [72])
2. adaptive filtering (see Makridakis and Wheelwright [50])
3. multiple exponential smoothing models (see Brown [7])

There are many variants of adaptive exponential smoothing and users seem to modify the basic techniques substantially to a more fixed form of exponential smoothing. However, the methods are simple and minimize out-of-control interventions by the forecaster. In a large-scale comparative empirical study by Dancer and Gray [17] Whybark's method outperformed that of Trigg and Leach. Adaptive filtering has also encountered theoretical and empirical criticism (see [21,30]).

All of these models lack an underlying statistical model and a sampling theoretical base, and as yet there is little empirical evidence on their performance, so that selecting the appropriate model is a matter of trial and error.

2.2. Multiple time-series models

In addition to the univariate forecasting models, a number of models have been developed for situations in which data are available for multiple time-series.

2.2.1. Single-equation causal models

The single-equation causal method relates a single endogenous variable to a number (often large) of exogenous variables and stresses the inclusion of all relevant variables in the model. Lags in the dependent variables are easily included in the model, as well as autocorrelation in the error term. Estimation is usually by least squares, justified by reference to an assumed normal error distribution. This straightforward approach is defended by Armstrong [2], who has argued that the *ex ante* accuracy of a properly specified single-equation causal model that includes all important influences is not highly sensitive to a range of plausible variations in the estimates of the coefficients.

Two key assumptions in causal models mirror those discussed in the univariate case — stable model parameters and a well-behaved error term. The failure of these assumptions to hold true may undermine forecast accuracy as Newbold and Davies [54] have shown in the case of autocorrelated errors, which can reduce the precision of the parameter estimates. Researchers have examined the effects of relaxing both these assumptions and their work will be discussed next. The aim of these modifications is to find accurate parameter estimates which in turn should produce accurate forecasts.

Shifting coefficients. Harrison and Stevens [32] point out that the Kalman filter technique is valid for single-equation models where parameters change with time. Econometricians have also been working on so-called random coefficient models [39,65]. A special issue of the *Annals of Economic and Social Measurement* (Vol. 2, No. 4, 1973) has been devoted to the problem of shifting coefficients, but as yet there is little evidence that these methods improve the quality of forecasts.

Lag and error structure in the single equation model. The inclusion of lags either in the error term or in the variables causes difficulty because the usual least squares assumptions do not hold in such cases. The basic model is

$$F_0(B) \, Y_t = \sum_i F_i(B) \, X_{it} + e_t,$$

with B the backshift operator. In practice the numbers of coefficients in the polynomials $\{F_i(B)\}$ are too great to estimate, and the profiles must therefore be imitated by a function with fewer parameters. The error structure in a distributed lag model is usually rudimentary, that is, e_t is independent. The problems in identifying the order of the polynomial lag profile are considerable. The penalties of misspecification are also large ([27,29,43,61,63]).

A variant of these lagged models has been developed specifically for forecasting applications by Box and Jenkins – a generalization of their univariate ARIMA approach to indicator models. Simultaneously, the same type of model was developed in the econometrics literature under the name *rational polynomial lag*. In an indicator model, the forecaster adds a small number of causal variables X_i to the basic ARIMA model. Some stationary difference of each independent variable X_i, say R_i, feeds its influence to Z, itself a stationary transform of the dependent variable, through use of a lagged system. The behavior of the lagged system's response to R_i is described by the ratio of two polynomials in the backshift operator, B – ω_i and δ_i. The influence of the causal variables R and of a random noise process are assumed to be additive, as given by

$$Z_t = \delta + \sum_{i=1}^{p} \frac{\omega_i(B)}{\delta_i(B)} R_{i(t-k_i)} + \frac{\theta(B)}{\phi(B)} e_t,$$

where the parameters, k_i describe the pure delay in the effects of each variable.

Box and Jenkins [5] and Newbold [53] discuss the problems of identifying the orders of the various polynominals in B and of estimating the coefficients. The first stage of the identification technique is to construct an ARIMA model of the causal time series X_i. Therefore there is no logical inconsistency or inefficiency in using an extrapolation of the leading indicator itself as part of an *ex ante* model. For remote periods, the combined extrapolation of $\{X_i\}$ and Y will be little better than a (respecified) single-series model of Y alone. It remains to be seen whether the assumptions of this model are as empirically useful as those of the univariate ARIMA models. Box et al. [4], Jenkins [38], Wall et al. [70], Pierce [57]. Box-Jenkins indicator models include the simpler polynomial lag approach [53] and require fewer parameters to be estimated. They are therefore to be preferred on grounds of both simplicity and generality, but applications are few at present.

2.3. Interactive systems models

Econometricians have long considered a natural generalization of the above methods: the case when Y_t and $\{X_{it}\}$ have a mutual influence on each other. Simulation modelers, such as systems dynamicists, start from a different perspective and include feedback between the variables in their models. The increased complexity of this approach stresses the complete economic and behavioral specification of the system rather than its statistical specification. Error structures must necessarily be simple [53] and estimation must be somewhat *ad hoc,* since most systems simulation models are nonlinear.

In a large-scale test of nine macroeconomic systems models one of the simpler models, Fair's, consistently outperforms its competitors on the variables considered by Fromm and Klein, though not sufficiently well as to be decisive. Unfortunately as Christ [12], points out policy effects calculated from the systems coefficents differ so much between models that most models, if not all, must be assumed to be misspecified. As one moves to ever larger nonlinear models, such as the world dynamics modesl of Forrester, the danger of misspecification increases, and as Cole [14] points out, they should no longer be used directly for forecasting because of the very different policy implications of equally plausible models.

3. Common problems in forecasting applications

With so many classes of model available one must search for general principles that help to choose the most cost-effective approach. As will be seen, no "best" approach exists. Consequently, questions of data quality and availability, model complexity, and the possible effect of selecting the wrong model have to be used to limit the search to the more plausible alternatives.

3.1. Data problems

If a forecasting model is unduly sensitive to the data on which it is based, it must be used circumspectly, since the magnitude and consistency of data errors remains unknown. Cole [13] for example, has shown the heavy reliance judgmental macroeconomic forecasters place on provisional government data and their concomitant inaccuracy. Although most economic data includes sampling errors, there is evidence that the accuracy of quantitative forecasting models is not much affected by data errors and data revisions (Denton and Oksanen [19], McDonald [48]). Armstrong [1,66] shows that preliminary data can be combined with a causal model to estimate the likely revision. However, Fildes and Wood [24] point out that often "it is not how you forecast but what you forecast" that is important. Although revisions to a "true" data series are unimportant, the choice of data can be quite critical.

This general problem of data errors affects all models equally, but three further problems in data conditioning should directly influence the choice of model: outlying observations, collinear observations, and the inclusion of noninterval data.

Missing observations and outliers. Model estimation can be seriously impeded by occasional missing or atypical observations. For a discussion of interpolation of missing observations see [10,11,16,20,42]. Robust estimation aims to minimize the effect of outliers. This topic is dealt with by Hinich and Talwar [37] and Wiginton [73]. See also Meyer and Glauber [51] for a forecasting application. Most forecasters remove outliers themselves but not so effectively as the robust methods of estimation [59]. Thus a forecasting method such as the Bayesian approach of Harrison and Stevens, which takes account of outliers, is to be preferred to one that either relies on direct intervention from the modeler, or worse, ignores the problem.

Multicollinearity. Most economic data include substantial collinear trends that distort parameter estimates and consequently forecast performance. Ridge regression is one estimation technique that aims to minimize the effects of multicollinearity. In this technique the fit to the data sets is allowed to deteriorate in return for narrower confidence intervals for the parameters (see McDonald and Galarneau [49] and Vinod [69]). When multicollinearity is intractable and likelihood functions are flat, the use of prior theory may permit the "safe" deletion of variables and can also ensure that the model uses economically neutral null hypotheses about the coefficients, such as that price elasticity is unity, rather than numerically neutral null hypotheses, such as that price elasticity is zero. Dempster et al. [18] present strong support for such a view. Consequently automatic procedures in which theory has played no part and the model coefficients are meaningless should be avoided. Secondly, large systems models are more likely to suffer from effects of multicollinearity than small univariate indicator models.

Scaling properties of the data. Ordinal data can give good regression fits, but in theory the estimated coefficients have no sampling or predictive properties. In effect, however, ordinal variables such as expectations data may often be safely included as their consistent performance in *ex post* and *ex ante* tests can show (Fromm and Klein [26]). For further information see [8,60,64]. Any model that includes noninterval data should however be subject to stringent *ex ante* tests to minimize the possibility of spurious fit.

3.2. Relationship of model fit to forecasting

Ample evidence exists to show that good *ex post* fit does not lead to good (*ex ante*) forecasts, and, more seriously, that *ex ante* forecasting performance does not even correlate closely with *ex post* fit. For example, Armstrong [2] compared two forecasting models — one model chosen by using step-by-step regression and the other on the basis of theory. The stepwise model gave a better fit, but poorer *ex ante* forecasts. Shupack [62] and Ferber [22] offer further evidence on the low correlation between fit and forecasting performance.

In contrast to the often poor performance of fitted models, there is some evidence that models which are well specified, and which include the important characteristics of the system forecast well despite variations in the coefficients. ARIMA models are often insensitive to coefficient changes [74]. Armstrong [1] found that a priori estimates of coefficients were very little inferior to fitted estimates when forecasting *ex ante*. The implication of this evidence is that identification of functional form is more important than estimation, but since the size of samples commonly encountered is small, one is forced to simplify, often using prior theory.

Model identification from small samples. Specification error — that is, the incorrect choice of model form or the omission of a variable or a feedback loop — is a widely recognized problem particularly in econometrics. However, it is possible to "overfit" a model to the available data set, which suppresses the evidence for misspecification as well as improves the fit. For example, ordinary least squares tends to suppress any evidence of autocorrelated errors, owing to downward bias in the estimated autocorrelation coefficients. The standard deviations of the (usually) biased coefficient estimates in the model are likely to be seriously underestimated [40, p. 308]. The indiscriminate addition of variables to this model will spuriously improve the fit, with a secondary adverse effect of concealing those features in the residuals that indicate the original specification error.

If unimportant or spurious variables can appear to improve fit, unfortunately, the reverse holds equally true. Many theoretically important variables are found statistically "insignificant," perhaps because they are observed under the "degenerate" regression conditions of a stable control system (see Pierce [57]).

Thus a purely statistical test of the coefficients is weak in practice, because with misspecification no meaning can be attached to the coefficients' computed standard errors. Overfitting suppresses not only the evidence for misspecification, but along with it, the evidence that the calculated standard errors are invalid. As a consequence the model should include only as many parameters as can be reliably estimated from the available sample. Further degrees of freedom should be reserved for testing the functional specification.

Avoiding overfitting. If the forecaster does not overfit the data, it is at least possible for the evidence of misspecification to appear. If persistent evidence for misspecification does arise, such as autocorrelated error, the forecaster has three main options.
1. He can add variables or parameters; for example, a lag structure in the variables. This approach is likely to improve the forecasts only if it does not use up all the degrees of freedom that are still needed to check for model misspecification. Otherwise, the only improvement may be to the fit in the data set.
2. He can model the autocorrelated error term separately. That is often done in systems modeling, but it poses problems. The original estimates of the parameters may be invalid under the new error specification; for example, it may formally be necessary to perform simultaneous nonlinear estimation of the parameters of the model and of the error structure. More seriously, if the apparent error structure is due to misspecification in the original variables, then any model of the

error term may be overfitting and may impair the forecasts.

3. He can adopt a simpler model with a tractable specification. If all plausible alternatives lead to overfitting, for the purpose of forecasting, as opposed to fitting, it may be better to discard model complexity in the interests of better estimation and a more tractable specification. Evidence in favour of this proposition can be found in the relative success of ARIMA models, discussed earlier and the success of some simpler macroeconomic models (such as the Fair model [12]). A positive correlation (0.41) exists between measures of model size and measures of model error in the study reported on by both Christ [12] and Fromm and Klein [26]. It seems therefore that the improvement in specification and estimation can outweigh the loss of information from the discarded variables.

3.3. Misspecification

It is a truism of forecasting that the model chosen is misspecified. Consequently if several alternative model specifications seem plausible but they produce widely different forecasts, then the model initially chosen is critically undermined.

In extrapolative models the two key assumptions affecting misspecification are stationarity and parameter stability. The first assumption only matters when one is forecasting for periods far ahead of the estimation sample, though Chatfield and Prothero [9] in a situation of almost exponential trend found forecasting accuracy undermined. Box and Jenkins' reply to their findings is not reassuring [6]. With more typical situations later in the product life cycle ARIMA models appear robust. The second assumption of parameter stability can undoubtedly be incorrect and the effects important [24]. Contrary evidence for a large number of similar consumer products is given by Dancer and Gray [17] who found that the gain from using adaptive models was very slight. Winters [74] also supports this conclusion. This conflict can be resolved by reversing the question of sensitivity to ask whether a variable parameter model is substantially less accurate than a correct model with fixed parameters. Dancer and Gray [17] answer this question "no", which resolves the problem. If prior theory attaches some possibility to shifts in the model's parameters, an adaptive extrapolative model such as the univariate Bayesian should be adopted instead.

Misspecification in causal models includes the same problems as the univariate case, stability and choice of functional form. Unfortunately, it offers no guidance on model selection, in the sense that little evidence is available on the robustness of various classes of models to these errors. (See a keyworded bibliography by Fildes et al. [25].) However an additional aspect of causal misspecification is the question of whether the model contains 1) all relevant variables and 2) appropriate feedback loops. Although having all relevant variables is known to be important for precise parameter estimation the likely result is multicollinearity [40]. Its consequences can be avoided by adopting the indicator methods of Box and Jenkins where the omitted variables are approximated by a more complex error and lag structure, a solution which at the same time avoids undesirable autocorrelation. The second misspecification — the omission of feedback — can be quite critical in the long term as has already been noted in the context of world dynamics [14]. However, no general evidence exists on the sensitivity of systems to the omission of feedback, although its unnecessary inclusion is harmless. Unlike the earlier arguments of the section this fact tentatively suggests the acceptance of the increased complexity of a systems model, but the extra costs of that complexity in model estimation are high, and the inclusion of a general lag and error structure is difficult [53].

Questions of misspecification, data errors, and overfitting now constrain the search for the appropriate forecasting model. To progress, one must examine the performance of the different classes of model for further clues, then recommendations on apprpriate criteria for selecting a forecasting model can be proposed.

4. A judicial summing up

4.1. The empirical evidence

Comparative evidence on performance between classes of models is slight. In the section on extrapolative models it was pointed out that the univariate Box-Jenkins model outperformed its competitors, though this advantage diminished with lead time. The inclusion of adaptive models in the comparison does not alter the conclusion, although when shifts in behavior take place an adaptive model is to be preferred [17]. Bayesian models cannot easily be included here because of the limited information on their performance. Unfortunately if one broadens the basis of comparison to include causal and systems models the picture becomes more confusing.

Causal models are now regularly tested against an ARIMA alternative, and this evidence is informative. Where financial variables are concerned the inclusion of causal variables brings about little or no improvement [45,57]. If one examines macroeconomic deflators, again one finds ARIMA models regularly the equal of causal alternatives [15]. If one turns to output variables, the results argue in the opposite direction. Causal models outperform the univariate [12,45,58], although there remains the problem of forecasting the exogenous variables.

Systems models have less forecasting evidence in their favour when compared to simpler alternatives. The success of Fair's small econometric model has already been discussed, and Hendry [35] for example, takes the comparison further to include a single-equation model with a well-specified error structure. He concluded that "'single equation' methods appear to provide value for money." Thus on very limited evidence we can conclude that the principle of parsimony apparently holds: simple, well-specified models outperform their more complex alternatives.

4.2. Recommendations

Because no 'best' model exists, even when one considers the model as being used in a specific context, one is forced to search for general principles. The decision and the value of perfect information limit the models under consideration. The expertise of the forecast user and the likely biases in the forecasting system constrain the analysis further [47]. In many cases the relationship between user and forecaster is so weak that there may be little purpose in expending much effort in seeking the most cost-effective forecast when greater improvements are likely to result for organizational change [71].

With these provisos, certain recommendations follow from the analysis presented here. In general, it has stressed the dangers of using fit as a major criterion of model selection, and the even greater dangers of using *ex post* fit as the prime objective of model building. This conclusion is supported by all the empirical evidence as well as the discussion on data conditioning and model misspecification. On the positive side, the use of prior information, careful *ex ante* testing, robustness, and comprehensibility are recommended as the most appropriate criteria for model selection.

4.2.1. Prior theory

Prior information can be used to discriminate between candidate functional forms and to decide on which variables should be included in the model, both difficult problems with a typically small and collinear data sample. Formal Bayesian methods can be used to combine evidence from the data with the prior likelihoods of the various model forms, the result being the posterior odds in favour of each alternative [28]. The choice can of course be made less formally. Whatever approach is adopted, the automatic selection of the simplest model should be avoided. Similarly, variables are often found to be insignificant when tested against a conventional 'zero effect' null hypothesis. Prior theory can again suggest a more appropriate null hypothesis, and the effect is more accurate forecasting than the use of fit-hunting techniques such as stepwise regression can provide.

This same approach works whenever model coefficients are theoretically important but imprecisely estimated because the prior estimates can then be used in their place. Alternatively prior data can be adjusted to take into account the sample evidence (see [2,66] or standard Bayesian methods).

4.2.2. Ex ante testing

Model performance should be compared by using *ex ante* testing. As has been shown, models that fit the data *ex post* may perform badly in forecasting and vice versa. If insufficient data exist for such testing, a smaller subset of the fitted data should be used to break the unique superiority of the fitted coefficients. Similarly, specification error tests should be used on the unfitted as well as the fitted data (see Muench et al. [52]). Also forecast error distributions for a particular lead time should be derived from *ex ante* forecast errors for that lead time, not from standard deviations computed while fitting.

4.2.3. Robustness

The quality of robustness is important to model performance because whatever the model chosen, specification error is likely to occur during the forecasting period. The discusssion of overfitting showed how tests for misspecification can lose their power. Consequently, it is better to work with a limited model that may well omit relevant variables but includes within its structure the possibility of misspecification; for example, adaptive or indicator models. As noted earlier certain classes of models appear more sensitive to data errors and misspecification. Models should therefore be tested for robustness against the likely range of errors. Robustness can be improved by combining different types of forecasting models [15] since each model may perform well in different circumstances, the respective errors being negatively correlated for example.

4.2.4. Comprehensibility

Because models rely on the forecast user in a number of important ways — for example, his prior estimates of model parameters — the model should be developed to suit user needs and should be easily understandable to the user [71]. The model should also include the possibility of user interventions (see Little [46]), and model parameters should be easily interpreted by the user, for example, price elasticities.

4.2.5. Comparative analysis

These recommendations involve the researcher in a greater responsibility to embed his new ideas in a comparative framework such as that described here. At the present time, only the rare article includes both empirical comparisons with previous research and tests of robustness, minimum prerequisites before a new model can be viewed as desirable. The final recommendation is therefore one for researchers. To help forecasters select the most cost-effective forecasting model, empirical articles on forecasting should discuss *ex ante* testing, a benchmark comparison against a 'best' ARIMA alternative, and robustness of the models under consideration.

References

[1] J.S. Armstrong, An application of econometric models to International Marketing, Journal of Marketing Research 7 (1970) 190–198.
[2] J.S. Armstrong, Longe Range Forecasting: From Crystal Ball to Computer (Wiley, New York, 1978).
[3] R.G. Bodkin and K.S. Murphy, The orders shipment mechanism in Canadian producer goods industries, Journal of the American Statistical Association 68 (1973) 297–305.
[4] G.E.P. Box, S.C. Hilmer and C.G. Tiao, Analysis and modelling of seasonal time series, NBER-CENSUS, Conference on Seasonal Time Series, (NBER, Washington, D.C., 1976).
[5] G.E.P. Box and G.M. Jenkins, Time Series Analysis, Forecasting and Control (Holden-Day, San Francisco, 1970).
[6] G.E.P. Box and G.M. Jenkins, Some comments on a paper by Chatfield and Prothero and on a review by Kendall, Journal of the Royal Statistical Society, Series A, 35 (1973) 337–352.

[7] R.G. Brown, Statistical forecasting for inventory control, (McGraw-Hill, New York, 1959).

[8] S.W. Burch and H.O. Stekler, The forecasting accuracy of consumer attitude data, Journal of American Statistical Association (1968) 1225–1232.

[9] C. Chatfield and D.L. Prothero, Box-Jenkins, seasonal forecasting problems in a case study (with discussion), Journal of the Royal Statistical Society, Series A, 136 (1973) 295–336.

[10] G.C. Chow and A. Lin, Best linear unbiased interpolation, distribution and extrapolation of time series by related series, Review of Economics and Statistics 53 (1971) 372–375.

[11] G.C. Chow and A. Lin, Best linear unbiased estimation of missing observations in an economic time series, Journal of American Statistical Association 71 (1976) 719–721.

[12] C.F. Christ, Judging the performance of econometric models of the U.S. economy, International Economic Review 16 (1975) 54–76.

[13] R. Cole, Data errors and forecasting accuracy, in: J. Mincer, ed., Economic forecasting and expectations (National Bureau of Economic Research, Columbia University Press), 1969.

[14] S. Cole, Accuracy in the long run – where are we now? in: R. Fildes and D. Wood, eds., Forecasting and Planning (Teakfield, Farnborough, 1978).

[15] J.P. Cooper and C.R. Nelson, The ex ante prediction performance of the St. Louis and FRB–MIT–PENN econometric models, and some results on composite predictions, Journal of Money, Credit and Banking 7 (1975) 1–31.

[16] M.G. Dagenais, Further suggestions concerning the utilization of incomplete observations in regression analysis, Journal of the American Statistical Association 66 (1971) 93–98.

[17] R. Dancer and C. Gray, An empirical evaluation of constant and adaptive computer forecasting models for inventory control, Decision Sciences 8 (1977) 228–239.

[18] A.P. Dempster, M. Schatzoff and N. Wermuth, A simulation study of alternatives to ordinary least squares, Journal of the American Statistical Association 72 (1977) 77–90.

[19] F.T. Denton and E.H. Oksanen, A multi-country analysis of the effect of data revision on an econometric model, Journal of the American Statistical Association 67 (1972) 281–291.

[20] H.E. Doran, Prediction of missing observations in the time series of an economic variable, Journal of the American Statistical Association 69 (1974) 546–554.

[21] S. Ekern, Forecasting with adaptive filtering, Operational Research Quarterly 27 (1976) 705–716.

[22] R. Ferber, Are correlations any guide to predictive value, Applied Statistics 5 (1956) 113–122.

[23] R. Fildes and C. Stevens, The role of prior information – an example in Bayesian forecasting, in: R. Fildes and D. Wood, eds., Forecasting and planning (Teakfield, Farnborough, 1978).

[24] R. Fildes and D. Wood, Data and the validity of forecasting models, Journal of Enterprise Management 1 (1978) 97–106.

[25] R. Fildes et al., Forecasting – A Key Worded Bibliography (Teakfield, Farnborough, 1979).

[26] G. Fromm and L.R. Klein, The NBER/NSF model comparison seminar: An analysis of results, Annals of Economic and Social Measurement 5 (1976) 1–28.

[27] P.A. Frost, Some properties of the Almon Lag technique when one searches for degree of polynomial and lag, Journal of the American Statistical Association 70 (1975) 606–612.

[28] K.M. Gaver and M.S. Geisel, Discriminating among alternative models: Bayesian and non-Bayesian methods, in: P. Zarembka, ed., Frontiers in econometrics (Academic Press, New York, 1973).

[29] L.G. Godfrey and D.S. Poskitt, Testing the restrictions of the Almon Lag technique, Journal of the American Statistical Association 70 (1975) 105–108.

[30] E.R. Golder and J.G. Settle, On adaptive filtering, Operational Research Quarterly 27 (1976) 857–868.

[31] G.K. Groff, Empirical comparison of models for short range forecasting, Management Science 20 (1973) 22–31.

[32] P.J. Harrison and C.F. Stevens, A Bayesian approach to short term forecasting, Operational Research Quarterly 22 (1971) 341–362.

[33] P.J. Harrison and C.F. Stevens, Bayesian forecasting, Journal of the Royal Statistical Society, Series B 38 (1976) 205–247.

[34] P.J. Harrison and C.F. Stevens, Bayes forecasting in action: Case studies (mimeographed, University of Warwick, 1976).

[35] D.F. Hendry, Stochastic specification of aggregate demand model of the United Kingdom, Econometrica 42 (1974) 559–578.

[36] M.J. Hinich and R.W. Roll, Measuring non-stationarity in the stochastic process of asset returns, European Institute for Advanced Studies in Management, Working Paper, 74–53 (Brussels, 1975).

[37] M.J. Hinich and P.P. Talwar, A simple method for robust regression, Journal of the American Statistical Association 70 (1975).

[38] G.M. Jenkins, Practical experiences in forecasting, in: Proceedings of the Institute of Statisticians Conference on Forecasting, 1976.

[39] K.H. Johnson and H.L. Lyon, Experimental evidence on combining cross-section and time series information, The Review of Economics and Statistics 55 (1973) 465–474.

[40] J. Johnston, Econometric Methods (McGraw-Hill, New York, 1972).

[41] R.E. Kalman, New methods in Wiener filtering theory, in: J.L. Bogdanoff and F. Kozlin, eds., Proceedings of the First Symposium on Engineering Application of Random Function Theory and Probability (Wiley, New York, 1963).

[42] H.H. Kelejian, Missing observations in multivariate regression: Efficiency of a first order method, Journal of the American Statistical Association 46 (1969) 1609–1616.

[43] B.K. Kimelfeld, Estimating the lags of lag processes, Journal of the American Statistical Association 70 (1975) 603–605.

[44] R. Lawrence, Consumer brand choice – a random walk, Journal of Marketing Research 12 (1975) 314–324.

[45] R.M. Leuthold et al., Forecasting daily hog prices and quantities: A study of alternative forecasting techniques, Journal of the American Statistical Association 65 (1970) 90–107.

[46] J.D.C. Little, Models and managers: The concept of a decision calculus, Management Science 16 (1970) 446–485.

[47] E.A. Lowe and R.W. Shaw, An analysis of managerial biasing: Evidence from a company's budgeting process, Journal of Management Studies 5 (1968) 304–315.

[48] J. McDonald, An analysis of the significance of revisions to some quarterly U.K. national income time series, Journal of the Royal Statistical Society, Series A, 138 (1975) 242–256.

[49] G.C. MacDonald and D. Galarneau, A Monte Carlo evaluation of some ridge type estimators, Journal of the American Statistical Association 79 (1975) 407–416.

[50] S. Makridakis and S.C. Wheelwright, Adaptive filtering: An integrated autoregressive/moving average filter for time series forecasting, Operational Research Quarterly 28 (1977) 425–437.

[51] J.R. Meyer and R.R, Glauber, Investment decisions economic forecasting and public policy (Harvard Business School, Boston, 1964).

[52] T. Muench et al., Tests for structural changes and prediction intervals for the reduced forms of two structural models of the U.S.: The FRB–MIT and Michigan quarterly model, Annals of Economic and Social Measurement 3 (1974) 491–519.

[53] P. Newbold, Bivariate time series model building methods, in: R. Fildes and D. Wood, eds., Forecasting and planning (Teakfield, Farnborough, 1978).

[54] P. Newbold and N. Davies, Error mis-specification and spurious regressions, Department of Mathematics, University of Nottingham, 1976.

[55] P. Newbold and C.W.J. Granger, Experience with forecasting univariate time series and the combination of forecasts (with discussion), Royal Statistical Society, Series A, 137 (1974) 131–165.

[56] L.J. Parsons, The product life cycle and time varying advertising elasticities, Journal of Marketing Research 12 (1975) 476–480.

[57] D.A. Pierce, Relationships – and the lack thereof – between economic time series with special reference to money and interest rates (with discussion), Journal of the American Statistical Association 72 (1977) 11–26.

[58] G. Rausser and A. Oliveiriá, An econometric analysis of wilderness area use, Journal of the American Statistical Association 71 (1976) 276–285.

[59] D.A. Relles and W.H. Rogers, Statisticians are fairly robust estimators of location, Journal of the American Statistical Association 72 (1977) 107–111.

[60] R.D. Rippe and M. Wilkinson, Forecasting accuracy of the McGraw-Hill anticipatory data, Journal of the American Statistical Association 69 (1974) 849–858.

[61] P. Schmidt and R.N. Waud, The Almon lag technique and the monetary versus fiscal debate, Journal of the American Statistical Association 68 (1973) 11–19.

[62] M.P. Schupack, The predictive accuracy of empirical demand analysis, Economic Journal 72 (1962) 550–575.

[63] C.A. Sims, The role of approximate prior restrictions in distributed lag estimation, Journal of the American Statistical Association 67 (1972) 169–175.

[64] B. Strumpel, J.N. Morgan and E. Zahn, eds., Human behaviour in economic affairs: essays in honour of George Katona (Elsevier, Amsterdam, 1972).

[65] P.A.V.B. Swamy, Linear models with random coefficients, in: P. Zarembka ed., Frontiers in econometrics (Academic Press, New York, 1973).

[66] T.H. Tessier and J.S. Armstrong, Improving current sales estimates via econometric methods (mimeographed, 1976).

[67] H. Theil and A.S. Goldberger, On pure and mixed statistical estimation in economics, International Economic Review 2 (1961) 65–78.

[68] D.W. Trigg and A.G. Leach, Exponential smoothing with adaptive response rate, Operational Research Quarterly 18 (1967) 53–59.

[69] H.D. Vinod, Application of new ridge regression methods to a study of Bell System scale economies, Journal of the American Statistical Association 71 (1976) 835–841.

[70] K.D. Wall et al., Estimates of a simple control model of the U.K. economy, in: G.A. Renton, Modelling the economy (Heinemann, London, 1975).

[71] S.C. Wheelwright and D.G. Clarke, Corporate forecasting: Promise and reality, Harvard Business Review 54 (1976).

[72] D.C. Whybark, A comparison of adaptive forecasting techniques, The Logistics Transportation Review 9 (1973) 13–26.

[73] J.C. Wiginton, MSAE estimation, an alternative approach to regression analysis for economic forecasting applications, Applied Economics 4 (1972) 11–21.

[74] P.R. Winters, Forecasting sales by exponentially weighted moving averages, Management Science 6 (1960) 324–342.

TIMS Studies in the Management Sciences 12 (1979) 313–327
© North-Holland Publishing Company

INTUITIVE PREDICTION: BIASES AND CORRECTIVE PROCEDURES

Daniel KAHNEMAN and Amos TVERSKY *

The University of British Columbia and Stanford University

This paper presents an approach to elicitation and correction of intuitive forecasts that attempts to retain the valid component of intuitive judgments while correcting some biases to which they are prone. This approach is applied to two tasks that experts are often required to perform in the context of forecasting and in the service of decision making: the prediction of values and the assessment of credible intervals. The analysis of these judgements reveals two major biases: nonregressiveness of predictions and overconfidence. Both biases are traced to people's tendency to give insufficient weight to certain types of information, for example, the base-rate frequency of outcomes and their predictability. The corrective procedures described in this paper are designed to elicit from the expert relevant information that he would normally neglect and to help him integrate this information with his intuitive impressions in a manner that respects basic principles of statistical prediction.

1. Introduction

Any significant activity of forecasting involves a large component of judgment, intuition, and educated guesswork. Indeed, the opinions of experts are the source of many technological, political, and social forecasts. Opinions and intuitions play an important part even where the forecasts are obtained by a mathematical model or a simulation. Intuitive judgments enter in the choice of the variables that are considered in such models, the impact factors that are assigned to them, and the initial values that are assumed to hold. The critical role of intuition in all varieties of forecasting calls for an analysis of the factors that limit the accuracy of expert judgments, and for the development of procedures designed to improve the quality of these judgments.

* The authors' interest in the debiasing of judgments under uncertainty developed through their contact with the Decision Analysis Group at Stanford Research Institute. They wish to thank J. Matheson, C. Spetzler, and C.A. Staël von Holstein of S.R.I. for many valuable discussions. The authors also thank B. Fischhoff and P. Slovic of Decision Research for their helpful comments on an earlier version of this article. The work was supported in part by grants from the Harry F. Guggenheim Foundation and from the Advanced Research Projects Agency of the Department of Defense, monitored by the Office of Naval Research under Contract N00014/76/0074 (ARPA Order No. 3052).

The question of how people think under conditions of uncertainty has attracted increasing research interest in recent years. A comprehensive review of the findings and their implications has been assembled by Slovic, Fischhoff and Lichtenstein [12], and some common biases have been described and analyzed by Tversky and Kahneman [17]. Several conclusions that emerge from this body of research are especially relevant to our present concern. First, errors of judgment are often systematic rather than random, manifesting bias rather than confusion. Thus, man suffers from mental astigmatism as well as from myopia, and any corrective prescription should fit this diagnosis. Second, many errors of judgment are shared by experts and laymen alike. Studies of stockbrokers [14], electrical engineers [7], intelligence analysts [3] and physicians [20], to cite but a few, confirm the presence of common biases in the professional judgments of experts. Third, erroneous intuitions resemble visual illusions in an important respect: the error remains compelling even when one is fully aware of its nature. Awareness of a perceptual or cognitive illusion does not by itself produce a more accurate perception of reality. It may, however, enable one to identify situations in which the normal faith in one's impressions must be suspended and in which judgement should be controlled by a more critical evaluation of the evidence.

This paper presents an approach to elicitation and correction of intuitive forecasts that attempts to retain what is most valid in the intuitive process while correcting some errors to which it is prone. This approach is applied to two tasks that experts are often required to perform in the context of forecasting or in the service of decision making: the prediction of uncertain quantities and the assessment of probability distributions. The analysis of these tasks reveals two common biases: nonregressiveness of predictions and overconfidence in the precision of estimates. In order to eliminate or reduce these biases, specific procedures are proposed for the elicitation of expert judgments and for the assessment of corrected values. These recommendations assume a dialogue between an expert and an analyst, whose role is to help the expert make most efficient use of his knowledge and avoid some of the common pitfalls of intuition. The expert may, of course, act as his own analyst.

The rationale for these recommendations derives from a psychological analysis of judgmental biases. The authors' limited experience with the implementation of the proposed methods indicates that they are feasible. It should be emphasized, however, that the recommended procedures have not been subjected to systematic evaluation. They should be regarded as suggestions for improved practice and as an illustration of a general approach to debiasing rather than as a well-established methodology of elicitation.

2. Singular and distributional data

Experts are often required to provide a best guess, estimate, or prediction concerning an uncertain quantity such as the value of the Dow-Jones index on a particular day, the future sales of a product, or the outcome of an election. A distinction should be made between two types of information that are available to the forecaster: singular and distributional. Singular information, or case data, consists of evidence about the particular case under consideration. Distributional information, or base-rate data, consists of knowledge about the distribution of outcomes in similar situations. In predicting the sales of a new novel, for example, what one knows about the author, the style, and the plot is singular information, whereas what one knows about the sales of novels is distributional information. Similarly, in predicting the longevity of a patient, the singular information includes his age, state of health, and past medical history, whereas the distributional information consists of the relevant population statistics. The singular information describes the specific features of the problem that distinguish it from others, while the distributional information characterizes the outcomes that have been observed in cases of the same general class. The present concept of distributional data does not coincide with the Bayesian concept of a prior probability distribution. The former is defined by the nature of the data, whereas the latter is defined in terms of the sequence of information acquisition.

Many prediction problems are essentially unique in the sense that little, if any, relevant distributional information is available. Examples are the forecast of demand for nuclear energy in the year 2000, or of the date by which an effective cure for leukemia will be found. In such problems, the expert must rely exclusively on singular information. However, the evidence suggests that people are insufficiently sensitive to distributional data even when such data are available. Indeed, recent research suggests that people rely primarily on singular information, even when it is scanty and unreliable, and give insufficient weight to distributional information [5,18].

The context of planning provides many examples in which the distribution of outcomes in past experience is ignored. Scientists and writers, for example, are notoriously prone to underestimate the time required to complete a project, even when they have considerable experience of past failures to live up to planned schedules. A similar bias has been documented in engineer's estimates of the completion time for repairs of power situations [7]. Although this planning fallacy is sometimes attributable to motivational factors such as wishful thinking, it frequently occurs even when underestimation of duration or cost is actually penalized.

The planning fallacy is a consequence of the tendency to neglect distributional data and to adopt what may be termed an internal approach to prediction in which one focuses on the constituents of the specific problem rather than on the distribution of outcomes in similar cases. The internal approach to the evaluation of plans is likely to produce underestimation. A building can only be completed on time, for example, if there are no delays in the delivery of materials, no strikes, no unusual weather conditions, and so on. Although each of these disturbances is unlikely, the probability that at least one of them will occur may be substantial.

This combinatorial consideration, however, is not adequately represented in people's intuitions [2]. Attempts to combat this error by adding a slippage factor are rarely adequate, since the adjusted value tends to remain too close to the initial value that acts as an anchor [17]. The adoption of an external approach that treats the specific problem as one of many could help overcome this bias. In this approach, one does not attempt to divine the specific manner in which a plan might fail. Rather, one relates the problem at hand to the distribution of completion time for similar projects. It is suggested that more reasonable estimates are likely to be obtained by asking the external question: how long do such projects usually last? and not merely the internal question: what are the specific factors and difficulties that operate in the particular problem?

The tendency to neglect distributional information and to rely mainly on singular information is enhanced by any factor that increases the perceived uniqueness of the problem. The relevance of distributional data can be masked by detailed acquaintance with the specific case or by intense involvement in it. The perceived uniqueness of a problem is also influenced by the formulation of the question that the expert is required to answer. For example, the question of how much the development of a new product will cost may induce an internal approach in which total costs are broken down into components. The equivalent question of the percentage by which costs will exceed the current budget is likely to call to mind the distribution of cost overruns for developments of the same general kind. Thus, a change of units – for example, from costs to overruns – could alter the manner in which the problem is viewed.

The prevalent tendency to underweigh or ignore distributional information is perhaps the major error of intuitive prediction. The consideration of distributional information, of course, does not guarantee the accuracy of forecasts. It does, however, provide some protection against completely unrealistic predictions. The analysts should therefore make every effort to frame the forecasting problem so as to facilitate utilizing all the distributional information that is available to the expert.

3. Regression and intuitive prediction

In most problems of prediction, the expert has both singular information about the specific case and distributional information about the outcomes in similar cases. Examples are the counselor who predicts the likely achievements of a student, the banker who assesses the earning potential of a small business, the publisher who estimates the sales of a textbook, or the economist who forecasts some index of economic growth.

How do people predict in such situations? Psychological research [6,11] suggests that intuitive predictions are generated according to a simple matching rule: the predicted value is selected so that the standing of the case in the distribution of outcomes matches its standing in the distribution of impressions. The following example illustrates this rule. An editor reviewed the manuscript of a novel and was favorably impressed. He said: "This book reads like a best-seller. Among the books of this type that were published in recent years, I would say that only one in twenty impressed me more." If the editor were now asked to estimate the sales of this novel, he would probably predict that it will be in the top 5 percent of the distribution of sales.

There is considerable evidence that people often predict by matching prediction to impression. However, this rule of prediction is unsound because it fails to take uncertainty into account. The editor of our example would surely admit that sales of books are highly unpredictable. In such a situation of high uncertainty, the best prediction of the sales of a book should fall somewhere between the value that matches one's impression and the average sales for books of its type.

One of the basic principles of statistical prediction, which is also one of the least intuitive, is that the extremeness of predictions must be moderated by considerations of predictability. Imagine, for example, that the publisher knows from past experience that the sales of books are quite unrelated to his initial impressions. Manuscripts that impressed him favorably and manuscripts that he disliked were equally likely to sell well or poorly. In such a case of zero predictability, the publisher's best guess about sales should be the same for all books – for example, the average of the relevant category – regardless of his personal impression of the individual book. Predictions are allowed to match impressions only in the case of perfect predictability. In intermediate situations, which are of course the most common, the prediction should be regressive; that is, it should fall between the class average and the value that best represents one's impression of the case at hand. The lower the predictability, the closer the prediction should be to the class average. Intuitive predictions are typically nonregressive: people often make extreme predictions on the basis of information whose reliability and predictive validity are known to be low.

The rationale for regressive prediction is most clearly seen in the prediction of the result of a repeated performance or a replication. The laws of chance entail that a very high score on the first observation is likely to be followed by a somewhat lower score on the second, while a poor score on the first observation is likely to be followed by a higher score on the second. Thus, if one examines a group of firms that did exceptionally well last year one will probably find that, on average, their current performance is somewhat disappointing. Conversely, if one selects firms that did poorly last year one will find that, on average, they are doing relatively better this year. This phenomenon, known as regression towards the mean, is a mathematical consequence of the presence of uncertainty. The best prediction for a repeated performance of an individual, a product, or a company is therefore less extreme – that is, closer to the average – than the initial score. As was pointed out earlier, intuitive predictions violate this principle. People often make predictions as if measures of performance were equally likely to change toward the average and away from it.

The error of nonregressive prediction is common among experts as well as among laymen. Furthermore, familiarity with the statistics of prediction does not eliminate the erroneous strategy of matching predictions to impressions [6]. Thus, when an expert makes an intuitive prediction that is based on impression matching, the analyst has grounds to suspect that the estimate is nonregressive, and therefore nonoptimal.

3.1. A corrective procedure for prediction

How can the expert be guided to produce properly regressive predictions? How can he be led to use the singular and distributional information that is available to him, in accordance with the principles of statistical prediction? In this section a five-step procedure that is designed to achieve these objectives is proposed.

3.1.1. Step 1: selection of a reference class. The goal of this stage is to identify a class to which the case at hand can be referred meaningfully and for which the distribution of outcomes is known or can be assessed with reasonable confidence.

In the predictions of the sales of a book or of the gross earnings of a film, for example, the selection of a reference class is straightforward. It is relatively easy, in these cases, to define an appropriate class of books or films for which the distribution of sales or revenue is known.

There are prediction problems – for example, forecasting the cost of developing a novel product, or the time by which it will reach the market – for which a reference class is difficult to identify because the various instances appear to be so different from each other that they cannot be compared meaningfully. As was noted earlier, however, this problem can sometimes be overcome by redefining the quantity that is to be predicted. Development projects in different technologies, for example, may be easier to compare in terms of percentage of cost overruns than in terms of absolute costs. The prediction of costs calls the expert's attention to the unique characteristics of each project. The prediction of cost overruns, in contrast, highlights the determinants of realism in planning which are common to many different projects. Consequently, it may be easier to define a reference class in the latter formulation than in the former.

More often than not the expert will think of several classes to which the problem could be referred, and a choice among these alternatives will be necessary. For example, the reference class for the prediction of the sales of a book could consist of other books by the same author, of books on the same topic, or of books of the same general type, such as hardcover novels. The choice of a reference class often involves a trade-off between conflicting criteria. Thus, the most inclusive class may allow for the best estimate of the distribution of outcomes, but it may be too heterogeneous to permit a meaningful comparison to the book at hand. The class of books by the same author, on the other hand, may provide the most natural basis for comparison, but the book in question could well fall outside the range of previously observed outcomes. In this example, the class of books on the same topic could be the most appropriate.

3.1.2. Step 2: assessment of the distribution for the reference class. For some problems – for example, sales of books – statistics regarding the distribution of outcomes are available. In other problems, the relevant distribution must be estimated on the basis of various sources of information. In particular, the expert should provide an estimate of the class average and some additional estimates that reflect the range of variability of outcomes. Sample questions are: how many copies are sold, on the average, for books in this category? What proportion of the books in that class sell more than 15,000 copies?

Many forecasting problems are characterized by the absence of directly relevant distributional data. That is always the case in long-term forecasting, where the relevant distribution pertains to outcomes in the distant future. Consider, for example, an attempt to predict England's share of the world market in personalized urban transportation systems in the year 2000. It may be useful to recast this problem as follows: "What is the likely distribution, over various domains of advanced technology, of England's share of the world market in the year 2000? How do you expect the particular case of transportation systems to compare to other technologies?" Note that the distribution of outcomes is not known in this problem. However, the required distribution could probably be estimated on the basis of the distribution of values for England's present share of the world market in different technologies, adjusted by an assessment of the long-term trend of England's changing position in world trade.

3.1.3. Step 3: intuitive estimation. One part of the information the expert has about a problem is summarized by the distribution of outcomes in the reference class. In addition, the expert usually has a considerable amount of singular information about the particular case, which distinguishes it from other members of the class. The expert should now be asked to make an intuitive estimate on the basis of this singular information. As was noted above, this intuitive estimate is likely to be nonregressive. The objective of the next two steps of the procedure is to correct this bias and obtain a more adequate estimate.

3.1.4. Step 4: assessment of predictability. The expert should now assess the degree to which the type of information that is available in this case permits accurate prediction of outcomes. In the context of linear prediction, the appropriate measure of predictability is ρ, the product-moment correlation between predictions and outcomes. Where records of past predictions and outcomes exist, the required value could be estimated from these records. In the absence of such data, one must rely on subjective assessments of predictability. A statistically sophisticated expert may be able to provide a direct estimate of ρ on the basis of his experience. When statistical sophistication is lacking, the analyst should resort to less direct procedures.

One such procedure requires the expert to compare the predictability of the variable with which he is concerned to the predictability of other variables. For example, the expert could be fairly confident that his ability to predict the sales of books exceeds the ability of sportscasters to predict point spread in football games, but is not as good as the ability of weather forecasters to predict temperature two days ahead of time. A skillful and diligent analyst could construct a rough scale of predictability based on computed correlations between predictions and outcomes for a set of phenomena that range from highly predictable — for example, temperature — to highly unpredictable — for example, stock prices. The analyst would then be in a position to ask the expert to locate the predictability of the target quantity on this scale, thereby providing a numerical estimate of ρ.

An alternative method for assessing predictability involves questions such as: If you were to consider two novels that you are about to publish, how often would you be right in predicting which of the two will sell more copies? An estimate of the ordinal correlation between predictions and outcomes can now be obtained as follows: If p is the estimated proportion of pairs in which the order of outcomes was correctly predicted, then $\tau = 2p - 1$ provides an index of predictive accuracy, which ranges from zero when predictions are at chance level to unity when predictions are perfectly accurate. In many situations τ can be used as a crude approximation for ρ.

Estimates of predictability are not easy to make, and they should be examined carefully. The expert could be subject to the hindsight fallacy [4], which leads to an overestimate of the predictability of outcomes. The expert could also be subject to an availability bias [16] and might recall for the most part surprises, or memorable cases in which strong initial impressions were later confirmed.

3.1.5. Step 5: correction of the intuitive estimate. To correct for nonregressiveness, the intuitive estimate should be adjusted toward the average of the reference class. If the intuitive estimate was nonregressive, then under fairly general conditions the distance between the intuitive estimate and the average of the class should be reduced by a factor of ρ, where ρ is the correlation coefficient. This procedure provides an estimate of the quantity, which, one hopes, reduces the nonregressive error.

For example, suppose that the expert's intuitive prediction of the sales of a given book is 12,000 and that, on average, books in that category sell 4,000 copies. Suppose further that the expert believes that he would correctly order pairs of manuscripts by their future sales on 80 percent of comparisons. In this case, $\tau = 1.6 - 1 = 0.6$, and the regressed estimate of sales would be $4000 + 0.6(12,000 - 4000) = 8800$.

The effect of this correction will be substantial when the intuitive estimate is relatively extreme and predictability is moderate or low. The rationale for the computation should be carefully explained to the expert, who will then decide whether to stand by his original prediction, adopt the computed estimate, or correct his assessment to some intermediate value.

The procedure that we have outlined is open to several objections that are likely to arise in the interaction between analyst and expert. First, the expert could question the assumption that his initial intuitive estimate was nonregressive. Fortunately, this assumption can be verified by asking the expert to estimate 1) the proportion of cases in the reference class — for example, manuscripts — that would have made a stronger impression on him and 2) the proportion of cases in reference class for which the outcome exceeds his intuitive prediction — for example, the proportion of books that sold more than 12,000 copies. If the two proportions are approximately the same, the prediction was surely nonregressive.

A more general objection may question the basic idea that predictions should be regressive. The expert could point out, correctly, that the present procedure will usually yield conservative predictions that are not far from the average of the class and is very unlikely to predict an exceptional outcome that lies beyond all previously observed values. The answer to this objection is that a fallible predictor can retain a chance to correctly predict a few exceptional outcomes only at the cost of erroneously identifying many other cases as exceptional. Nonregressive predictions over-predict: they are associated with a substantial probability that any high prediction is an overestimate and any low prediction is an underestimate. In most situations, this bias is costly, and should be eliminated.

4. The overconfidence effect

A forecaster is often required to provide, in addition to his best estimate of a quantity, some indication of confidence in his estimate or, equivalently, some expression of his uncertainty about the value of the quantity (for example see Spetzler [13] and Staël von Holstein [14]). These judgments can take the form of credible intervals or probability distributions. To construct credible intervals, the expert selects a value X_π of the uncertain quantity X, such that he has a probability π that the outcome will fall below X_π, that is, $P(X < X_\pi) = \pi$. Values obtained in this manner are called fractiles. A probability distribution can be constructed by assessing fractiles — for example, $X_{01}, X_{25}, X_{50}, X_{99}$. The range between symmetric fractiles is called a (symmetric) credible interval. For example, the interval between X_{01} and X_{99} is the 98 percent credible interval: the expert's probability is 0.98 that the true value will be contained within the interval and only 0.02 that it will be below X_{01} or above X_{99}.

Consider, for example, a publisher who attempts to forecast the sales of a new textbook. Suppose he thinks that there is only one chance in 100 that the book will sell less than 3000 copies, that is, $X_{01} = 3000$, and that there is a probability of 0.99 that the book will sell less than 25000 copies, that is, $X_{99} = 25000$. The range between 3000 and 25,000 is the 98 percent credible interval for the number of copies that will be sold. Another expert may select $X_{01} = 5000$ and $X_{99} = 15,000$

for the sales of the same textbook. The narrower credible interval of the second expert expresses greater confidence in his ability to predict the sales of the book in question.

Stimulated by the widely cited unpublished work of Alpert and Raiffa [1], a considerable amount of research has established the existence of a highly consistent bias in the setting of credible intervals and probability distributions. The bias can be demonstrated by noting in a large number of problems the proportion of cases in which the actual value of the uncertain quantity falls outside the credible interval. These cases are called *surprises*. If the expert's confidence adequately reflects his knowledge, the true value should fall outside the 98 percent credible interval – that is, below X_{01} or above X_{99} – on approximately 2 percent of problems. If the percentage of surprises is much higher, the judge is said to be *overconfident:* his credible intervals are narrower than his knowledge justifies. Conversely, a proportion of surprises that is much lower than the designated value exhibits *underconfidence.*

A number of studies recently reviewed by Lichtenstein, Fischhoff, and Phillips [8] have reported considerable overconfidence in the estimation of uncertain quantities. For 98 percent credible intervals, where the rate of surprises should be 2 percent, the actual proportion of surprises is typically above 25 percent! All one need do to verify this effect is to select a few quantities from a standard almanac (for example, population of countries, air distance between cities, yearly consumption of various foods), ask a few friends to assess X_{01} and X_{99} for each of these quantities, and record the percentage of surprises.

There is some evidence that the degree of overconfidence increases with ignorance. For example, we found 28 percent of surprises in assessments of the air distance between New Delhi and Peking, which compares to 15 percent for assessments of the air distance between London and Tel Aviv. The two distances, in fact, are approximately equal. Naturally, the credible intervals were considerably wider in the former problem, about which our respondents knew little than in the latter problem, about which they know more. Credible intervals were too narrow in both problems, as indicated by the high rate of surprises, but overconfidence was much more pronounced in the more difficult question.

It seems that overconfidence does not occur when the expert has considerable information about the conditional distribution of the outcomes. In extensive studies of credible intervals given by weather forecasters for the temperature on the next day, Murphy and Winkler [9,10] found that the proportion of surprises corresponded quite precisely to the designated probabilities. This exception to the overconfidence effect appears to be due to the repetitive nature of the situation with which these experts are concerned and to the availability of feedback about the outcome following each forecast. The recurrence of an identifiable pattern of indicators, which is followed by different outcomes on different occasions, allows the expert to learn the distribution of outcomes which is associated with that pattern. In this case, the forecaster could judge the probability of different outcomes in terms of their relative frequency. Since people are fairly accurate in their perception of relative frequency (for example see Vlek [19]), the overconfidence effect is not expected to occur in essentially repetitive situations.

Few forecasting tasks are likely to offer the scope for frequency learning that is available to the meteorologist. In the absence of such distributional data, credible intervals can only be assessed on the basis of singular information, and overconfidence prevails.

Psychological studies of judgment under uncertainty implicate several factors that contribute to the overconfidence effect. First, people are not sufficiently sensitive to some factors that determine the quality of evidence – for example, the amount and the reliability of the available information – and often express high confidence in predictions that are based on small samples of unreliable data. Studies of naive and sophisticated respondents [15,5] showed that the confidence in conclusions based on sample data did not vary sufficiently with the size of the sample. Similarly, it has been shown that people predict a person's occupation with unwarranted confidence from a brief and unreliable description of his personality [6]. Apparently, sample size and reliability have little impact on judgments of confidence, contrary to the normative principles of statistics.

Insensitivity to the quality of evidence could help explain the overconfidence effect. In many problems of prediction and estimation, available information is limited, incomplete, and unreliable. If people derive almost as much confidence from poor data as from good data, they are likely to produce overly narrow credible intervals when their information is of inferior quality. That is, they will have too much confidence in the statement that the actual value of the uncertain quantity is included in a narrow range around the best estimate. This account is supported by the observation that overconfidence is reduced when one has more information about a particular problem, that is when the quality of the evidence is high. In fact, overconfidence could disappear in the presence of a large quantity of reliable data.

Oversensitivity to the consistency of available data is a second cause of overconfidence. People tend to draw more confidence from a small body of consistent data than from a much larger body of less consistent data. For example, when subjects were instructed to predict students' class standing on the basis of grades obtained in the freshman year, they made essentially the same prediction on the basis of a single B in one course and on the basis of A in one course and C in another. However, they expressed much more confidence in predicting from a single grade than from an inconsistent pair of grades, a pattern which is not readily justified on statistical grounds. Similarly, it is likely that the public will have more confidence in a conclusion that was unanimously supported by a panel of three experts than in a conclusion that was supported by ten experts in a panel of twelve. This pattern is also difficult to justify.

The effect of consistency indirectly contributes to overconfidence. In their search for coherence, people often see patterns where none exist, reinterpret data so as to increase their apparent consistency, and ignore evidence that does not fit their views. In this manner, people are likely to overestimate the consistency of data and to derive too much confidence from them.

Two additional factors that contribute to overconfidence in the assessment of uncertain quantities are conditionality and anchoring. Conditionality refers to the adoption of unstated assumptions regarding the assessed quantity. An expert who attempts to estimate the future revenue of a firm, for example, typically assumes normal operating conditions and may not take into account the possibility that these conditions could change because of war, depression, or sabotage. Indeed, experts often claim that their expertise is limited to normal conditions, and that if these conditions are drastically altered all bets are off. A probability distribution that is conditioned on restrictive assumptions reflects only part of the existing uncertainty regarding the quantity and is therefore likely to yield too many surprises.

Anchoring refers to the biasing effect of an initial value on subsequent judgments. When constructing a probability distribution over a quantity, one normally considers a best guess before assessing extreme fractiles. The best guess therefore acts as an anchor, and the extreme fractiles — for example, X_{01} and X_{99} — are pulled toward it. This common bias further contributes to the setting of credible intervals that are overly narrow.

4.1. Debiasing credible intervals

Because the choice of action is often sensitive to the possibility of extreme outcomes, the best estimate of an uncertain quantity may be less relevant to decision making than the 98 percent credible interval. The presence of a large overconfidence bias in the setting of such intervals implies that the element of uncertainty is typically underestimated in risky decisions. The elimination of overconfidence is therefore an important objective in an attempt to improve the quality of the intuitive judgments that serve decision making.

The preceding analysis of overconfidence suggests that this effect may be quite difficult to overcome. Merely acquainting people with the phenomenon and exhorting them to "spread those extreme fractiles!" does little to reduce the bias [1]. The attempt to do so may destroy the intuitive basis for the initial judgment without substituting an alternative for it. How is one to know how far the extreme fractiles should be spread? Indeed, the overconfidence effect may be too large to yield to such blandishments. For most people, a change in the probability of an event from 0.02 to 0.30 is a qualitative shift that alters the character of the events from very unlikely to fairly probable. Since this is the magnitude of the shift that is required to abolish overconfidence, the basic view of the problem must be modified for the corrected fractiles to be intuitively acceptable. That becomes vividly evident when one first constructs a probability distribution, then attempts to reallocate 30 percent of the total area of the distribution outside the original 98 percent credible interval. The attempt could induce a sense of confusion, a loss of any confident intuition about the problem, and a tendency to wild guessing.

What can be done, then, to eliminate the overconfidence bias in intuitive assessments of credible intervals and probability distributions? The most radical suggestion is to replace such assessments by computations. That is sometimes possible when appropriate information is available.

consider, for example, a publisher who wishes to estimate the 90 percent credible interval for the sales of a new textbook. Instead of making an intuitive estimate of the interval, which is likely to be too narrow, the publisher could proceed as follows. First, he should assess X_{05} and X_{95} for the distribution of sales of textbooks in the appropriate reference class. These assessments provide a 90 percent credible interval for the class. The width of the 90 percent credible interval for the particular book can now be estimated from the width of the corresponding interval for the class.

The statistical theory of prediction entails a simple relation between a credible interval for an individual case and the corresponding credible interval for the reference class. This relation is mediated by predictability, that is, by the correlation between predictions and outcomes — for example, between predicted and actual sales. Under standard assumptions of linear regression and normal distributions, the width of the credible interval for an individual case is $c\sqrt{(1 - \rho^2)}$ where c is the width of the interval for the class and ρ is the correlation between predicted and actual values. Thus, if one has assessed ρ to be 0.40, the interval between X_{05} and X_{95} for the particular book should be 92 percent of the interval between the corresponding fractiles in its class $[0.92 = \sqrt{(1-0.40^2)}]$. Many of our students find this statistical relation counterintuitive: a gain of 8 percent in precision is smaller than would be expected on the basis of a correlation of 0.40.

The computational procedure that was illustrated for the prediction of the sales of a book is applicable, in principle, whenever the statistical assumptions are met at least approximately, and when there are sufficient distributional data. If the relevant data are sparse, the assessment of extreme fractiles cannot be reliable. The main advantage of this procedure is that it relies on an assessment of the distribution in the reference class, which is likely to be more precise and less biased than intuitions about a particular case.

In a less radical vein, the computational approach can provide a check on subjective probability distributions obtained in the standard manner. When an expert who admits that predictability is low sets credible intervals for a particular case that are much narrower than corresponding intervals for the reference class, there are strong grounds to suspect that he is overconfident. In such cases, the analyst would do well to suggest to the expert that his credible interval should be bracketed between his initial assessment for the case and his estimate for the class.

The procedures for the debiasing of credible intervals and for the correction of nonregressive predictions share the same rationale. The need for correction arises in both cases because of the inadequate sensitivity of intuition to considerations of predictability. The suggested procedures involve an assessment of predictability and the explicit use of distributional data. The corrections consist of regressing the expert's intuitive best guess toward the average of the reference class and expanding his intuitive credible interval toward the corresponding interval for the class.

5. Concluding remarks

The approach presented here is based on the following general notions about forecasting. First, that most predictions and forecasts contain an irreducible intuitive component. Second, that the intuitive predictions of knowledgeable individuals contain much useful information. Third, that these intuitive judgments are often biased in a predictable manner. Hence, the problem is not whether to accept intuitive predictions at face value or to reject them, but rather how they can be debiased and improved.

The analysis of human judgment shows that many biases of intuition stem from the tendency to give little weight to certain types of information, for example, the base-rate frequency of outcomes and their predictability. The strategy of debiasing presented in this paper attempts to elicit from the expert relevant information that he would normally neglect, and to help him integrate this information with his intuitive impressions in a manner that respects basic principles of statistical prediction. This approach has been illustrated in an analysis of two tasks, the prediction of uncertain values and the assessment of credible intervals. The basic approach of adapting procedures of forecasting and decision making to the recognized limitations of human judgment could be extended to many other activities, such as the evaluation of evidence from multiple sources, the design of effective communication between expert and decision maker, and the weighting of advantages and disadvantages of alternative policies.

References

[1] W. Alpert and H. Raiffa, A progress report on the training of probability assessors, (unpublished manuscript, 1969).
[2] M. Bar-Hillel, On the subjective probability of compound events, Organizational Behavior and Human Performance 9 (1973) 396–406.
[3] R.V. Brown, A.S. Kahr, and C. Peterson, Decision Analysis for the Manager, (Holt, Rinehart and Winston, New York, 1974).
[4] B. Fischhoff, Hindsight ≠ foresight: The effect of outcome knowledge on judgment under uncertainty, Journal of Experimental Psychology: Human Perception and Performance 1 (1975) 288–299.
[5] D. Kahneman and A. Tversky, Subjective probability: A judgment of representativeness, Cognitive Psychology 3 (1972) 430–454.
[6] D. Kahneman and A. Tversky, On the psychology of prediction, Psychological Review 80 (1973) 237–251.

[7] J.B. Kidd, The utilization of subjective probabilities in production planning, Acta Psychologica 34 (1970) 338–347.

[8] S. Lichtenstein, B. Fischhoff and L.D. Phillips, Calibration of probabilities: The state of the art, in: H. Jungermann and G. de Zeeuw (eds.) Decision Making and Change in Human Affairs (Reidel, Amsterdam, 1977).

[9] A.H. Murphy and R.L. Winkler, Subjective probability forecasting experiments in meteorology: Some preliminary results, Bulletin of the American Meteorological Society 55 (1974) 1206–1216.

[10] A.H. Murphy and R.L. Winkler, The use of credible intervals in temperature forecasting: Some experimental results, in: H. Jungermann and G. de Zeeuw (eds.) Decision Making and Change in Human Affairs (Reidel, Amsterdam, 1977).

[11] L. Ross, The intuitive psychologist and his shortcomings: Distortions in the attribution process, in: L. Berkowitz (ed.) Advances in Experimental Social Psychology (Academic Press, New York, 1977) 173–220.

[12] P. Slovic, B. Fischhoff and S. Lichtenstein, Behavioral decision theory, Annual Review of Psychology 28 (1977) 1–39.

[13] C.S. Spetzler and C.A.S. Staël von Holstein, Probability encoding in decision analysis, Management Science 22 (1975) 340–358.

[14] C.A.S. Staël von Holstein, Probabilistic forecasting: An experiment related to the stock-market, Organizational Behavior and Human Performance 8 (1972) 139–158.

[15] A. Tversky and D. Kahneman, The belief in the "law of small numbers", Psychological Bulletin 76 (1971) 105–110.

[16] A. Tversky and D. Kahneman, Availability: A heuristic for judging frequency and pro-bability, Cognitive Psychology 5 (1973) 207–232.

[17] A. Tversky and D. Kahneman, Judgment under uncertainty: Heuristics and biases, Science 185 (1974) 1124–1131.

[18] A. Tversky and D. Kahneman, Causal schemas in judgements under uncertainty, in: M. Fishbein (ed.) Progress in Social Psychology (Laurence Erlbaum Associates, Hillsdale, 1979, in press).

[19] C.A.J. Vlek, Multiple probability learning: Associating events with their probabilities of occurrence, Acta Psychologica 33 (1970) 207–232.

[20] L. Zieve, Misinterpretation and abuse of laboratory tests by clinicians, Annals of the New York Academy of Science 134 (1966) 563–572.

TIMS Studies in the Management Sciences 12 (1979) 329–352
© North-Holland Publishing Company

FORECASTING THE FUTURE AND THE FUTURE OF FORECASTING

Spyros MAKRIDAKIS

INSEAD, Fontainebleau, France

and

Steven C. WHEELWRIGHT

Graduate School of Business Administration, Harvard University

1. Introduction

It should be clear from the papers included in this publication and the diverse backgrounds of their authors that forecasting is becoming a truly interdisciplinary field. The breadth and depth of the field can be measured by the spectrum of methodologies available and the range of situations to which they have been applied. Even though forecasting is still a young field, the diversity of both methods and applications is impressive. Furthermore, the provinces of the majority of existing forecasting methodologies are complementary, rather than mutually exclusive. Consequently, one of the most difficult tasks in forecasting applications is knowing *which* technique to use for a particular forecasting task.

The introduction to this publication sought to address the question of *which* method to use by describing various frameworks for classifying forecasting methodologies and matching them to application requirements. The papers in the second section of the book then dealt with the question of *how* the different methodologies could be applied and *what* those methodologies entailed. Most of those papers also discussed recent developments and examined the theoretical foundations of the major categories of methodologies.

From the range of methodologies covered, it should not be surprising that an appropriate methodology can be matched with a variety of practical forecasting situations. However, because there are so many variables in each new forecasting situation, no single method can deal effectively with all applications. Thus the critical question is not which methodology is better than all the rest, but rather under what conditions should each methodology be selected for different types of applications. Relatively little empirical work addresses this latter question, which is of major interest to practitioners.

For many centuries successful forecasters were those who possessed the qualities of good judgment, intuition, foresight, and knowledge of the environment and were able to use those qualities in forecasting the future. Today forecasting the future is based on much more technical foundations. It is no longer possible for one individual even to be an expert in all of the methodologies currently available. The field is now subdivided into specialized segments, each with its own expertise and advantages and disadvantages for a range of applications. Thus the complaint is not that there are not enough methods, but that there are too many; not that there are not sufficient sophisticated techniques, but that they are too complex for many of the applications for which a forecast is required. Basically the problem is one of too many choices, rather than too few.

The authors believe that there is an urgent need to develop a comprehensive framework, based on empirical research, that can relate these different methodologies and better match them to practitioner requirements. Much of the emphasis to date in the forecasting literature has been on theoretical developments. This emphasis is understandable, because 30 or 40 years ago little knowledge was available. Theory and methodologies were needed so that the field could develop to its present level. However, as with many other fields of management science, forecasting research now needs to shift from the development of theory to the investigation of applications – a shift to studying what the methods ought to do, what they can do, and when or under what circumstances they should be utilized. In the opinion of the authors, this shift is the number one priority for the field.

The tone of the great majority of papers included in this issue is optimistic. Forecasting is viewed as a new, rapidly growing field that has already achieved considerable success and will continue to expand in the future. However, this success does not mean there are no problems or major difficulties; there are many and they cannot be ignored if the field is to reach its full potential.

The remainder of this paper will focus on those problems and difficulties the authors believe to be most important. The future of forecasting will depend in part on how well these difficulties are addressed, which, in turn, will determine how successful forecasting will be and the direction in which it will evolve. Several key problem areas will be discussed first, then some of the major weaknesses in existing forecasting methodologies will be explored. Finally, the authors will present a brief statement of their prediction for the future of forecasting.

2. General problems in forecasting

2.1. Forecasting when patterns change

Few forecasters possess a crystal ball for looking at the future. They must base their predictions on historical evidence, which can vary from quantitative data to subjective experience or knowledge of past events. Table 1 classifies a range of forecasting situations in terms of two dimensions: the availability of data and the type of forecasting required. It is this latter aspect that will be examined here;

Table 1

Information availability, type of forecasting, and appropriate forecasting methods for various situations.

Type of forecasting	Availability and quality of data and information				
	Sufficient quantitative information (data) available		Little or no quantitative information available, but sufficient qualitative knowledge exists		Little or no information available
	Time-series methods	Explanatory or causal methods	Exploratory methods	Normative methods	
Forecasting a continuation of patterns	Predicting the continuation of growth in in sales or GNP	Understanding the effect of prices and advertising on sales	Predicting the speed of transportation around the year 2000	Predicting the design of automobiles in the year 1990	Predicting the effects of interplanetary travel; colonization of the earth by extraterrestial beings; the discovery of a new, very cheap form of energy that produces no pollution.
Forecasting changes in existing patterns or time when changes will occur	Predicting the next recession and its severity	Understanding the effect of price controls or a ban on TV advertising on sales	Forecasting the effect of a large increase in oil prices on the consumption of oil	Having predicted the last oil embargo, which followed the Arab-Israeli war.	

data and information will be discussed in the next section.

If series such as GNP, inflation, the sales of company XYZ, population, oil consumption, and usage of electricity — just to mention a few — are examined, it is not difficult to distinguish two types of activity for each. The first can be labeled *normal* activity, which implies the continuation of a past pattern with no major changes. In the second type of activity, significant deviations from the normal occur. These can take the form of major accelerations or decelerations in the growth rate, or what are frequently called turning points. The authors believe that existing forecasting methodologies deal well only with continuations of existing patterns or relationships and have very serious difficulties forecasting when changes in the patterns or relationships occur. This crucial point is often not well understood by practitioners or academicians and deserves further discussion.

In a comprehensive study of short-term economic forecasts from 1953 to 1963, Zarnowitz [61, p. 7] concludes in appraising errors in turning points

The results here are, on the whole, negative: the record of the numerical forecasts of GNP (like that of qualitative turning-point forecasts) does not indicate an ability to forecast the turn several months ahead. Not only were actual turns missed but also turns were predicted that did not occur.

A similar conclusion is reached by McNees in the article included in this colletion, "Lessons from the track record of macroeconomic forecasts in the 1970s." In that paper the major econometric models of the U.S. economy and their performance during the 1970–1975 period are evaluated. The author found that apart from the 1974–1975 recession, the forecasts of the major econometric models were quite accurate. However, during the major recession of 1974–75, McNees reports:

> The forecasts made in early 1974 produced by far the largest errors in the period for GNP, real GNP, and the unemployed rate – errors 3.75, 4.0, and 6.0 times larger respectively than the normal errors for the early 1970s. These forecasts failed miserably in warning of the severity of the impending recession.

In examining the changes in pattern that occurred in company sales data during the 1974–75 period, the authors have found results similar to those reported by McNees. In one situation, for example, the accuracy of forecasting went from an average of 5 1/2 percent (mean absolute percentage error) in a period of steady growth to over 35 percent within a period of 12 months during the 1974–75 recession [36, pp. 297–299].

The extent of the difficulty incurred when patterns change and the need to understand the magnitude of those changes are illustrated by the data in table 2, which summarizes the U.S. business cycles from 1850 through 1976. These data indicate that even during the relatively short period since World War II the United States has gone through six economic cycles whose duration has varied from 34 to 117 months. The substantial variation in the length of such cycles makes their prediction several periods ahead impossible by time-series methods, which forecast by mechanically extrapolating past patterns. Unfortunately, econometric models and judgmental forecasts do no better, as illustrated by the studies of Zarnowitz and McNees. It seems that the relationships among various economic factors hold only during periods of normal conditions. Either there are not enough recessions or booms to provide data for the model to fit or the conditions that give rise to turning points are not constant from one recession or boom, to the next.

Although the above illustrations are for quantitative methods of forecasting, similar difficulties have been experienced with qualitative or technological methods of forecasting. For example, forecasting when the growth of a new technology will slow as the market becomes saturated is much more difficult than estimating its annual growth rate during the rapid growth phase. Similarly, it is easy to discuss such topics as population growth, food consumption, or raw material utilization, based on extrapolations of historical patterns [38], but these forecasts become meaningless, once basic changes occur that modify the relationship among the

Table 2
U.S. business cycles 1850 through 1976.

Business cycle:			Duration (in months):		
Trough	Peak	Trough	Expansion	Contraction	Full cycle
Dec. 1854	June 1857	Dec. 1858	30	18	48
Dec. 1858	Oct. 1860	June 1861	22	8	30
June 1861	Apr. 1865	Dec. 1867	46	32	78
Dec. 1867	June 1869	Dec. 1870	18	18	36
Dec. 1870	Oct. 1873	Mar. 1879	34	65	99
Mar. 1879	Mar. 1882	May 1885	36	38	74
May 1885	Mar. 1887	Apr. 1888	22	13	35
Apr. 1888	July 1890	May 1891	27	10	37
May 1891	Jan. 1893	June 1894	20	17	37
June 1894	Dec. 1895	June 1897	18	18	36
June 1897	June 1899	Dec. 1900	24	18	42
Dec. 1900	Sept. 1902	Aug. 1904	21	23	44
Aug. 1904	May 1907	June 1908	33	13	46
June 1908	Jan. 1910	Jan. 1912	19	24	43
Jan. 1912	Jan. 1913	Dec. 1914	12	23	35
Dec. 1914	Aug. 1918	Mar. 1919	44	7	51
Mar. 1919	Jan. 1920	July 1921	10	18	28
July 1921	May 1923	July 1924	22	14	36
July 1924	Oct. 1926	Nov. 1927	27	13	40
Nov. 1927	Aug. 1929	Mar. 1933	21	43	64
Mar. 1933	May 1937	June 1938	50	13	63
June 1938	Feb. 1945	Oct. 1945	80	8	88
Oct. 1945	Nov. 1948	Oct. 1949	37	11	48 Postwar
Oct. 1949	July 1953	Aug. 1954	45	13	58 cycles
Aug. 1954	July 1957	Apr. 1958	35	9	44
Apr. 1958	May 1960	Feb. 1961	25	9	34
Feb. 1961	Nov. 1969	Nov. 1970	105	12	117
Nov. 1970	Aug. 1974 [a]	Apr. 1975	43	8	51

[a] There is some disagreement as to whether the start of the recession was November 1973 or August 1974. The latter has been assumed here.

various factors involved. The impact of recent oil price increases on the consumption of oil illustrates this point all too clearly. The growth of oil consumption since 1974 has reversed a pattern of more than 50 years, thus extrapolations of pre-1974 data and post-1974 data, differ by many billions of barrels of oil a year.

The same is true with population series whose rate of growth was constantly increasing until about 1970 when it reached a peak of 1.9 percent for the average of the world. Since then it has declined, reaching 1.7 percent in 1977. This change means that the world population will be 5.5 billion (assuming 1.7 growth rate) by the end of the century instead of 6.7 billion as predicted by United Nations statisticians in 1968. The difference is huge. However, even that gives little information as to what will happen if the 1.7 percent growth rate declines further. Fig. 1 illustrates a set of population forecasts for Great Britain, indicating how misleading predictions can be when serious changes in past patterns do occur.

It is perhaps the case that during the stable economic environment of the sixties, forecasters became complacent, feeling that they could adequately capture the pattern in a range of situations and use that as a basis for forecasting. With the shifting patterns of the seventies likely to continue, methodologies that deal with such changes in pattern need to be developed and extended. It is the authors' expectation that the forecasting field will respond to this need by researching approaches that can handle changes in pattern and/or be used to identify turning

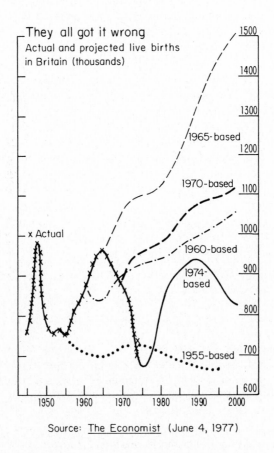

Source: The Economist (June 4, 1977)

Fig. 1. Various population forecasts for Great Britain.

points, thus complementing existing methodologies that mainly identify and predict ongoing patterns.

2.2. Availability and quality of data

Closely related to the type of forecasting situation and the characteristics of the patterns for each situation is the availability of data. There are major problems with the amount of data available and its quality, whether one is dealing with internal factors – those within the organization preparing the forecast – or with external factors, such as general economic data. The accuracy of forecasts and the appropriateness of applying individual methodologies depends on the quantity and quality of available data.

2.2.1. Difficulties with quantitative data. The data most often used in forecasting comes from sampling procedures and thus involves sampling errors. The magnitude of those errors is often greater than practitioners imagine. In a classic study examining the accuracy of macroeconomic data, Morgenstern [41] found that even in such aggregated figures as GNP, which tend to be collected very carefully, the sampling and nonsampling errors were 10 to 15 percent in magnitude. For less aggregated data and for series that receive less attention than GNP, the magnitude of errors was found to be even larger. [1]

A second factor that causes difficulties with some data series is that the most important sources of data can frequently be some of the least accurate. For example, in formulating short-term economic forecasts to be used as a basis for policy formulation, two of the most important series are changes in inventory levels and capacity utilization levels. Data for both of these series are based on sample surveys that are often unreliable because those who respond have no objective way of measuring the item in question. Better approaches for collecting data on these series need to be found. One approach that the authors see as being promising is to develop specialized organizational units with precise tools and procedures, much like those used in the Nielson approach to TV ratings. However, such an approach is costly.

A third difficulty is that for many macroseries, the raw figures are published initially, then subsequently revised. Often the difference between the raw data and the revised data is small, but on some occasions this difference is substantial. This difference creates additional problems for the forecaster, since the raw data, because of its timeliness, often is the basis for individual forecasting applications.

A fourth concern is that data from external macro sources are often reported only in a seasonally adjusted form. As described in the Burman article in this

---

[1] In this collection, Fildes and Howell's article, "On specifying a quantitative forecasting model," identifies some of the problems and difficulties associated with errors in data used as a basis for forecasting.

collection, "Seasonal adjustment – a survey," the methods used to make seasonal adjustment are not without their own problems. Thus seasonally adjusted data may in fact incorporate errors as a result of the adjustment process. These difficulties may be further compounded by the fact that the most recent data available for a series may be the least reliable. Since seasonal adjustment methods involve moving average computations, accurate values for the last few periods are unavailable because of the technique itself.

A fifth problem, and perhaps one of the most important for external data sources, is the timing with which such data become available. It often takes several months or longer to obtain these data in final form so that they can be used in forecasting. Even figures for leading indicators come out one month after the close of the period for which they are collected. New methods for gathering data, and perhaps using weekly rather than monthly or quarterly observations, will need to be developed to overcome this problem.

In addition to these problems with external data sources, there are also problems with data generated inside the organization. For example, one of the most frequent applications of forecasting is in predicting sales demand for a company. The available historical data may be labeled *sales data* but in fact it frequently does not reflect actual demand. Such factors as stockouts, order lead times, and backlogs make sales data an accounting definition of activity in a given period, rather than a demand-based description of that activity. Such problems can be largely overcome through keeping better records within the company and by making specific adjustments to recorded sales data. Other difficulties with internal data are that shipments of a single order may be spread out over several time periods, orders may increase just before an expected or announced price increase, and order patterns may change in anticipation of a strike or other interruptions of normal delivery. Again special adjustments may be necessary to correct for such factors.

Finally, a major problem with internal data is that time periods vary and are usually defined by accountants and not forecasters. Thus, monthly periods may vary in the number of business days, or even the number of weeks. Unusual events may affect the number of production days in a given period, and changes in accounting procedures may make historical data for different periods incomparable. All of these problems require adjustments and modification of procedures so that problems with the data will not detract from the performance of the forecasting approach.

2.2.2. Difficulties with qualitative data. The same problems that affect quantitative data hold in spades for qualitative data. In addition, the information needed to utilize qualitative methods of forecasting is usually derived from nonstandard and subjective sources. Variations in the level of detail available and the completeness of that data make evaluation of specific applications of qualitative forecasting methods almost impossible.

Qualitative methodologies are frequently applied in situations where few historical quantitative data are available, and persons needing the forecast are unwilling to wait until such data can be gathered. This lack of data compounds the problem for the qualitative methodology, since no standard is available as a basis for evaluating forecasting performance. However, the opportunity for improving management decision making, even based on the meager data available, can be very significant.

2.3. Generality of forecasting methodologies

Quantitative forecasting methods are usually mathematical models for which assumptions must be made to apply them in a given situation. Frequently these assumptions are restraining. For example, exponential smoothing models are restrictive in terms of the types of patterns with which they can deal. Simple exponential smoothing cannot deal with seasonal data and does not do well when a linear trend is present. Similarly, decomposition methods are of little value with nonseasonal data, and the Box-Jenkins methodology may not perform well when the generating process is not constant over time. While Kalman filters may be appropriate in this latter case, the information required for their application is usually difficult to obtain.

Generally, the more sophisticated methods require more knowledge and additional information about the situation than do the simpler methods such as exponential smoothing or single equation econometric models. Thus although the more sophisticated methods can deal with a wider range of situations, the forecasting practitioner must make a trade-off between the greater fixed costs of understanding and getting the data necessary to apply such methods, and the time-cost advantage of selecting from several simpler methods one that may not fit the situation quite as well.

This trade-off between generality and simplicity is complicated by the fact that sophisticated methods are not always more accurate than simpler ones. Certainly in many situations adopting a more sophisticated method can improve forecasting performance. However, there are studies that indicate just the opposite. In several studies [4,13,18,23,31,33,35,45] the conclusion was that simpler methods, like exponential smoothing or naive forecasting, did better than more sophisticated methodologies. Haitovsky et al. [24, p. 343] for instance, report: "The most striking finding is that the St. Louis equation (one equation econometric model) outperforms both OBE (Office of Business Economics) and Wharton (both large econometric models) ex-post forecasts for nominal GNP." For many forecasters and experts in the field these results might seem counterintuitive, but that is the experience of several researchers and practitioners.

What is most important is not deciding whether one method is always better than another, which seems to be indeterminable at present, but rather discovering when simpler methods outperform more sophisticated methods and when the reverse is true. It may well be that during periods of cyclical change, the more sophisticated methods do not do as well. That may also be the case when the degree of randomness in a series is large. Unfortunately, the reasons as to why some methods sometimes outperform others are not well understood. As a result, more sophisticated methods are sometimes used when simpler ones would suffice or would do even better.

In the field of qualitative forecasting methodologies, there is also a wide range of methods available that vary in complexity, sophistication, and performance. In this field it is even more difficult to make comparisons based on empirical results. However, extrapolating the results of the research cited above, it might well be that more sophisticated qualitative methods will not necessarily produce better results than simpler ones. Again, the question is when a given method will perform better than the alternatives for a particular situation.

2.4. Organizational blocks to improved forecasting

In addition to these technical problems, organizational and behavioral problems can also be major hindrances to successful forecasting. Unfortunately, the typical forecasting problem is usually classified as *insufficient accuracy*. Classifying the forecasting problem as inaccuracy usually gives a fairly narrow view of the available solutions. Fig. 2 suggests two common approaches to solving a forecasting problem that has been defined as a lack of accuracy. A major shortcoming of this simple diagnosis is that the solution is viewed strictly from a technical perspective and fails to resolve other underlying difficulties.

Through studies of a number of applications the authors have identified six categories of organizational or behavioral problems that impede forecasting [60]. As additional research is performed on each of these areas and as results from other disciplines are brought to bear, substantial improvement should be made in the successful application of forecasting in today's organizations.

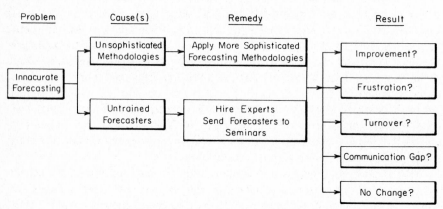

Fig. 2. Common view of forecasting problems.

2.4.1. Bias. In many organizations there is an incentive for the forecast to represent not the most likely future outcome, but rather a self-serving goal. This incentive may be systematic, such as might be caused by a management reward system or some overt manipulation by those who control forecasting. It may also be benign, such as simple sales force optimism or a narrow view of the goals of the business on the part of production management. Whatever the cause, forecasting is often caught in the middle and emerges biased in its representation of the most likely future outcomes.

2.4.2. Credibility and impact. Forecasting often has little impact on decision making. There are several causes for this ineffectiveness. The forecasts may lack relevance in terms of what, when, how, and in what form they are provided. Alternatively, the problem may be interpersonal, as when those who prepare the forecasts and those who use them fail to communicate effectively. Again, the problem may be one of organizational structure; the forecasting may be performed at such a level in the organization that it is highly unlikely to have much impact on decision makers. It is also true that forecasters tend to concentrate on well-behaved situations that can be forecast with standard methodologies and to ignore the rapidly changing situation for which management may most want forecasts.

2.4.3. Lack of recent improvement in forecasting. Problems may arise when forecasting is no longer improving in a company. Sometimes the resources committed to forecasting have become so stretched by maintaining ongoing forecasting procedures that no new developments are possible. At other times the management or staff may not have made sufficient commitment to attain the next level of substantial progress. That often occurs as organizations grow and managerial problems are not recognized.

2.4.4. Lack of a firm base on which to build. A number of problems arise when a firm is just beginning to use forecasting. Resources committed to forecasting may be insufficient for substantial impact. Even when the resources have been committed, knowledge of good forecasting practice and available methodologies may be inadequate. The lack of a systematic plan for improving forecasting may cause this problem even after forecasting is well underway.

2.4.5. Recognition of major flaws in the present approach. Companies frequently describe their forecasting problems in terms of opportunities for improvement. They may be quite happy with what is being done, but feel that substantially more could be done. Certain areas may not yet be handled systematically as part of the forecasting system, or performance may not yet have achieved the expected level. Organizations may also think their forecasting approach is especially vulnerable to changes in the environment, or may recognize that changes in their strategy may require changes in forecasting performance.

2.4.6. Poor communication between forecast preparers and forecast users. As with many technical fields forecasting often involves extensive interaction between a professional applying sophisticated methodologies and a manager seeking to interpret and use the results. If the communication between these two groups is poor, efforts may be focused on inappropriate problems, forecast preparers may not tell users the limitations of forecasting results, and managers may simply ignore forecasts generated by methods they do not understand. Under these conditions, even the best forecaster is likely to have little impact on the decisions being made.

With the increased interest in improving the utilization of existing forecasting methods throughout business and government, substantial future research will probably focus on these six problem areas. This research should be aided by work done in other fields, particularly in the implementation of management science. Certainly the problems that forecasting experiences with organizational and human difficulties will also be encountered by other management science techniques. Thus, the authors expect considerable development in the organizational and applicability aspects of forecasting.

3. Problems and shortcomings in existing methodologies

Since many methods overlap in their ability to meet the requirements of various situations, the basis for making decisions as to which method is most appropriate should be studied. Often the selection of a method is based on emotional rather than objective criteria. For example, academicians tend to prefer the Box-Jenkins methodology over other time-series approaches because of its completeness and statistical features. Other factors, however, such as accuracy, cost, complexity, and data requirements may frequently lead practitioners to select exponential smoothing or other simpler approaches to forecasting.

In order to improve method selection decisions, the characteristics most important to practitioners and the ability of various methods to perform along those dimensions should be studied. Unfortunately, much of the description of individual methodologies deals with their advantages, often under-reporting their disadvantages. The purpose of this section is to examine some of those shortcomings, not to be critical of individual methods, but rather to highlight some of the problems so as to facilitate their recognition and solution.

3.1. Exponential smoothing methods

The major advantages of exponential smoothing methods are their simplicity of application and minimum requirements for data and computations. As indicated earlier, it has not been proven that they are systematically less accurate than more sophisticated methods. Nor has it been shown that they are highly inaccurate in general. However, it must be remembered that there is not a single exponential smoothing method, but rather a class of methods. Thus even when a decision has been made to use exponential smoothing, the exact model and the approach for determining its parameters must still be specified.

With the exception of generalized exponential smoothing, which does not seem to be widely used in practice, other exponential smoothing techniques can deal only with very specific data patterns. Thus the difficulty in their use lies in selecting the appropriate exponential smoothing approach that fits the pattern of the given situation. Unfortunately, the criteria for making this selection decision have not been examined rigorously, and the decision requires judgment, since there is no automated procedure for this task. Furthermore, one would often like to switch from one exponential smoothing method to another when a change in pattern occurs. Again, little research has been reported as to guidelines for when such a switch should be made.

Another difficulty in applying exponential smoothing methods is the need to know whether forecasting errors are random. This need complicates the development of confidence intervals for forecasts and the evaluation of the methods' fit to historical data. Furthermore, procedures for correcting bias so that residuals will be random have not been developed.

3.2. Decomposition methods

The major advantages of decomposition methods are that they are intuitive, easy to use, and easy to interpret. Their ability to provide seasonal indexes for adjusting raw data also makes them especially useful in practice. A substantial number of government-based forecasts, particularly those that are deseasonalized, are based on these methods, and their use in business is expanding. Because they have been in use for several decades, the problems associated with them are perhaps better understood than for many of the more recently developed time-series approaches.

One of the problems is that, like exponential smoothing, there is no guarantee that the residuals will be random. In fact, it has been shown that they usually are not random. Furthermore, if the residuals are not random, there are no systematic procedures available for correcting that condition or modifying the decomposition method to fit the actual pattern better. The user has little choice of models and parameters, once decomposition has been selected as the approach.

Some research is being done on the possibility of modifying decomposition methods — mainly Census II — to make them more flexible so that the user can adapt them to a given situation. However, this increased flexibility might simply mean increased complexity, making it more difficult to select the appropriate form of decomposition.

Decomposition methods have been criticized because of their inability to react to changes in the basic pattern of data. A recent *Business Week* article, "Seasonal maladjustment", reported: "Some charge that in these unsettled times, just when it seems most important to have reliable data, seasonal adjustment has become downright treacherous for many key figures, including the money supply and the unemployment problem" [59].

3.3. Box-Jenkins method

Probably the most talked about advantage of the autoregressive/moving average models, usually called the Box-Jenkins methodology, is their generality. A single methodology can deal effectively with a large class of data patterns. According to some claims [46 and 52], the Box-Jenkins approach performs better than exponential smoothing methods. Furthermore, several studies [6,8,10,33,42,44,56] have concluded that it does as well or better than econometric approaches. Finally, the methodology is statistically complete and built on a sound theoretical base.

Offsetting some of these advantages is the fact that it is frequently too complex for the practitioner to understand and apply intelligently. Its advantages have led to its extensive use in the academic world, but its complexity has limited its use among businesses and government agencies. Perhaps the biggest problem with this approach is identifying the appropriate ARMA model from the class of models available. Unfortunately, no automated selection procedure is currently available. Rather judgment must be used in this step of the process. Parzen's article in this collection suggests an approach that moves toward automation.

Some of the difficulties of both exponential smoothing and the Box-Jenkins method can be better understood by contrasting the two approaches. In the case of exponential smoothing there are many independent models, and the practitioner must select the right one for the given situation. In the case of ARMA models, there is one general class of models, from which the practitioner must choose a specific one. The advantage of the Box-Jenkins method is that if selection is done incorrectly, tests are available to detect it, and another model can be chosen. No such tests exist for exponential smoothing models.

A final problem, although one not frequently discussed in regard to ARMA models, occurs in the optimization procedure used in estimating the parameters. This is the most mechanical part of applying the methodology and ordinarily would be of no concern. However, there are indications that Marquardt's algorithm [37], which is the most commonly applied procedure for this estimation, may result in serious problems [45,49,51]. An alternative explanation of the optimization problem is that the computer programs used to implement nonlinear optimization do so in a nonstandardized fashion. In one survey of such computer programs [34], it was found that different computer programs gave parameter values that differed considerably from one another, even for the same ARMA model. Table 3 illustrates the range of parameter values estimated by different computer codes. Clearly, some standardized computational procedures must be found if the Box-Jenkins methodology is to provide consistent results.

Table 3
Parameter values estimated by different computer programs for ARMA model: $(1 - B)$
$(1 - B^{12})(1 - \phi_1 B)Z_t = (1 - \theta_1 B)(1 - \Theta_{12}B^{12})e_t$
(using 124 data points).

Computer program	Program characteristics:				Parameter values:		
	Mean	Backfore-casting	Nonlinear optimization algorithm	Maximum likelihood	ϕ_1	θ_1	Θ_{12}
1	Constant	No	Marquardts' unconstrained	No	0.051	0.60	0.707
2	Constant	No	Marquardts' unconstrained	No	0.064	0.600	0.824
3	Constant	No	Marquardts' unconstrained	No	0.075	0.610	0.712
4	Constant	No	Marquardts' unconstrained	No	−0.211	0.353	0.775
5	Constant	No	Marquardts' unconstrained	No	−0.198	0.353	0.792
6	Constant	No	Marquardts' unconstrained	No	0.093	0.367	0.782
7	Constant	No	Spiral constraint	No	−0.009	0.541	0.704
8	Constant	No	Spiral constraint	Yes	−0.19	0.344	0.761
9	Constant	No	Simplex constraint	No	−0.069	0.502	0.809
10	Constant	Yes	Marquardts' unconstrained	No	−0.175	0.387	0.817
11	Constant	Yes	Marquardts' unconstrained	No	0.82	0.635	0.82
12	Parameter	Yes	Marquardts' unconstrained	No	−0.274	0.224	0.766
13	Parameter	Yes	Modified simplex constraint	No	−0.31	0.19	0.88
14	Parameter	Yes	Full maximum likelihood	Yes	0.02	0.56	0.79

3.4. Kalman filtering method

According to the supporters of the Kalman filtering forecasting method the Box-Jenkins approach is merely a special case of a Kalman filter [25]. In addition to generality, Kalman filters are extremely flexible and can deal with all types of data patterns and changes in those patterns. Kalman filters need not assume fixed parameters or fixed values of variances or covariances. Thus this approach seems to offer everything that theoreticians might desire.

The problem with Kalman filters is the basic trade-off mentioned earlier: generality and flexibility mean that more parameters must be specified and the practitioner must have increased knowledge of the approach and its application. The difficulties highlighted above for the Box-Jenkins methodology are magnified in the Kalman filtering approach. Finally, the fact that there is very little experience in the application of this approach and no empirical studies comparing it with alternative approaches, limits its applicability.

3.5. Econometric models

Time-series approaches are frequently referred to as *black boxes* because much of what goes on remains unexplained to the user. That is not the case with econometric methods. A major advantage of these latter approaches is that they can be used to improve understanding of the relationship between various factors in a situation. As such, they can be used to perform simulation or sensitivity analysis and to evaluate alternative policy decisions and their impact, as well as to forecast.

The major problem with econometric methods is one of accuracy in relation to cost. Since econometric models are expensive to develop and test, many practitioners would prefer to use them only if their results are substantially more accurate than less costly time-series approaches. Several studies [6,8,10,33,42,43, 44,56] have concluded that univariate ARMA models provide results that are comparable to, if not better than, econometric models in terms of accuracy. However, other studies conclude just the opposite [7].

A potential critical problem with the methodology of these models has recently come to light [21,50]. The essence of the problem is that the R^2 measure of goodness of fit may be artificially large because of a common underlying trend and not because the model has in fact captured the important causal relationships between the independent and dependent variables. One approach that has been suggested for overcoming this problem [50] is to remove at least the trend and possibly other patterns before estimating such econometric relationships [21].

Another difficulty with the use of econometric models in forecasting is that the role and importance of the quantitative model is often overestimated. Apart from the Fair model, most econometric forecasts incorporate a substantial subjective element, reflecting the developer's own personal opinion about the future [16]. Thus there is some question as to how much the quantitative model contributes to better forecasting and how much the judgmental input of the developer affects the, results.

The final difficulty with this methodology is the lack of experience in applying it to areas other than the total economy. Questions related to the accuracy of such models when applied to regions, industries, or a single firm, and questions relating to their costs and benefits cannot be readily assessed until such experience is gained.

3.6. Leading indicators

The leading indicator methodology is perhaps the best developed of those approaches aimed at identifying changes in pattern. The major shortcoming of such an approach is obtaining timely and accurate data on the required indicators.

In a recent article, the business publication *Fortune* [58] took a critical look at the performance of leading indicators. Two of the problems highlighted were that the initial values are at least a month old when published and that there is a substantial difference between those initial values and the final revised figures. As table 4 shows, the leading indicator initially showed a decline in the U.S. economy in the spring of 1975. However, when revised, the figures predicted an upturn, rather than a downturn. Unfortunately, these revised figures were not available until November of 1975, several months after the original series had been published. The Fortune article concludes: "A great deal of high-powered research and analysis goes into constructing the index of leading economic indicators and it would be nice to find some use for it. Unhappily, we can't think of any."

It is the authors' belief that there are many uses for leading indicators. The paired indices approach and the pyramid of leading indicators method [30] provide extremely useful information for the practitioner. Other writers such as Evans [15] have concluded: "[Such] series serve as a valuable historical record and shed light on the causes of the past depression. But as a practical method of forecasting, the leading indicators cannot be used very effectively or accurately."

3.7. Input-output tables

Input-output forecasting is unique in the type of inter-sector information it can provide and the forecasting possibilities it offers. It suffers, however, from some serious deficiencies. First, input-output tables (at least for the United States) are infrequently prepared. Secondly, the published data come with several years of delay (often as many as ten). Finally, the technological coefficients describing

Table 4
Original and revised leading indicator values.

1975	Original Series	Final Revised Series [a]
January	157.4	106.5
February	156.6	106.2
March	154.5	107.1
April	157.8	109.4
May	157.8	111.7
June	155.1	115.2

[a] Published in November 1975.

inter-sector interactions are assumed to be constant, which is usually an unrealistic assumption, given today's rapidly changing environment.

3.8. Qualitative or technological forecasting methods

The major problem with qualitative forecasting methods is the difficulty of estimating the accuracy of the forecasts they provide. As an illustration of the difficulty of using such methods accurately, figs. 1 and 3 report the results of two applications that were studied over an extended period of time. As shown, the forecasts not only changed drastically each time they were revised, but in the end were very inaccurate.

One must question the value of applications that perform as inaccurately as those of fig. 3. More research is required before their value can be adequately deter-

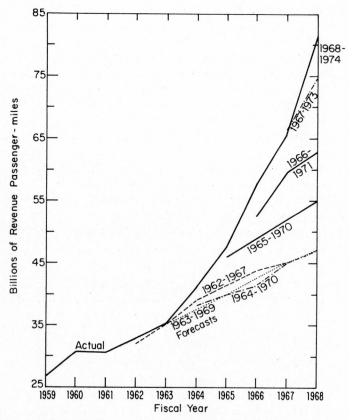

Fig. 3. Inaccuracies in qualitative forecasting methodologies. FAA six-year forecasts and actual, since 1961 – billions of domestic revenue passenger/miles.

mined. Only when the reliability of such approaches can be effectively measured can they gain full credibility for use among practitioners. In a report on the results of a conference of some 1500 key decision makers in the private and public sectors, the following statement was made: "We have witnessed major emergencies, such as the petroleum crisis, the international monetary crisis, the ecological crisis, two-digit inflation, and deep recession... [When the original conference was held in 1972] none of these developments was forecast during the conference" [57].

Another difficulty with qualitative or technological methods is the assumptions that are made to arrive at future forecasts. Ascher [3] in a comprehensive study undertaken to evaluate long-term forecasts, concluded: "In some respects the appraisal of forecasts puts a greater burden on the policy maker than the original task of forecasting itself."

4. The future of forecasting

Based on the number of issues and concerns raised in the two previous sections, one might well consider whether it is appropriate to be optimistic about the future of forecasting. In spite of the problems, the authors would assert that it is. Almost all types of decision making involve the future, and thus require some form of prediction. The basic alternatives are to rely purely on judgmental and informal predictions or to obtain predictions based on systematic and more quantitative forecasting methodologies.

Although most of the concerns raised in previous sections relate to the systematic or more quantitative approaches to forecasting, there would seem to be even more difficulties in using only judgmental approaches. As Kahneman and Tversky point out in their excellent paper, "Intuitive predictions: biases and corrective procedures," ample evidence indicates that in repetitive type situations, quantitative methods outperform clinical judgement [19,26,53,54,55]. In Meehl's review of the literature [39,40] he identified only one case where clinical judgement was superior to a statistical model. This conclusion and a subsequent piece of research [29] have been disputed by Goldberg [20] who reversed the exceptional finding simply by transforming the data. In a recent article Dawes [15] stated that he knew of no other finding that had been reported showing the superiority of clinical judgment.

Outside of the psychological literature, judgmental forecasts have been analyzed in some detail in the area of predicting earnings per share for major companies. A number of researchers have compiled histories of the forecasts of earnings per share made by analysts and based on judgmental approaches. These have then been compared with results obtained from quantitative methods [11,14,22,47]. In all of these studies the researchers concluded that the analysts did not perform as well in forecasting earnings per share as did the quantitative techniques. An exception to this conclusion has been reported by Johnson and Smidt [28] who claim that analysts can do better than more systematic quantitative methods, provided that those analysts have accurate economic and industry information. Unfortunately, these authors make no attempt to identify the existence of a model that can be used if the additional information is available. Thus, their results must be somewhat suspect. In addition, several studies of professionally managed funds whose managers base most of their decisions on judgmental forecasts indicate that those funds do no better than the market as a whole [2,17,27,48,55].

A recent study by Mabert directly compared judgmental forecasts and quantitative forecasts [30]. The study found that forecasts based on opinions of the sales force and corporate executives gave less accurate results over a five-year period than did quantitative forecasts, based on either exponential smoothing, harmonic smoothing, or Box-Jenkins approaches. The study also found that in terms of timeliness and the cost of preparing forecasts, quantitative techniques were more attractive than subjective approaches. In a more complete study involving many subjects in a controlled setting, Adam and Ebert [1] found that Winters' method produced forecasts that were statistically more accurate than those produced by judgmental methods. Finally, Armstrong and Grohman [2] analyzed the accuracy of different models in forecasting the U.S. air travel market during the 1963–1968 period and concluded that judgmental approaches were less accurate than quantitative approaches.

Based on this evidence, it seems reasonable to conclude that managers and experts show systematic bias in forecasting when using only judgmental methods. Thus it is likely that the application of quantitative approaches will continue to increase and supplement or replace many of the applications now handled through purely judgmental approaches.

Of course it must be remembered that just as it is impossible to say which methodology is always best, it is impossible to conclude that quantitative methods are always better than subjective or judgmentally based methods. Human forecasters can process much more information than most of the formalized quantitative methods, and such forecasters are more likely to have knowledge of specific near-term events that need to be reflected in current forecasts. These facts suggest that what might be most useful would be effective ways to combine predictions based on quantitative models with the forecasts prepared by managers and experts. In the initial article of this publication, McLaughlin talked about such an integrated approach and its importance in day-to-day forecasting application. As approaches for formalizing that interaction become defined and tested, substantial improvement should result.

A number of factors external to the forecasting field will also have an impact on future developments in forecasting. One of the most important of these is the computer. With the continuing decline in computing costs and the increase in computational power available to most managers, there will be greater access to existing forecasting methodologies and the data, both internal and external, required for their use.

The future of forecasting can be viewed from two contrasting perspectives. In the first scenario, forecasting methodologies will be improved, the difficulties associated with their usage reduced, and methodologies for integrating judgmentally based forecasts and quantitative forecasts developed. As a result, forecasting accuracy will increase, which will lead to additional commitment from organizations and further improvements in the field. This scenario is a realization of the predictions made by several experts in the field of forecasting.

An alternative scenario presents a pessimistic view: accurate forecasting will become more difficult as relationships and patterns change more rapidly and the rate of change in both social patterns and the economy increases. The result will be increased difficulty in predicting events in the future, and quantitative methods will become less applicable. Firms will reduce their commitment to such approaches and concentrate on training their managers to survey the environment more effectively and subjectively integrate their assessment of likely events into their own decision-making procedures.

It is the authors' view that the optimistic scenario is much more likely to occur than the pessimistic one. Even though some areas may become more difficult to forecast, experience in using existing methodologies and the development of extensions to make them more applicable will increase their use in practice. Based on that experience, further improvements will be made, and the successful integration of judgmental assessments with formal forecasting methodologies will become a reailty.

References

[1] E.E. Adam and R.J. Ebert, A comparison of human and statistical forecasting, AIIE Transaction 8 (1976) 120–127.

[2] J.S. Armstrong and M.C. Grohman, A comparative study for long-range market forecasting, Management Science 19 (1972) 211–227.

[3] W. Ascher, Forecasting: An Appraisal for Policy Makers and Planners (Johns-Hopkins University Press, Baltimore, 1978).

[4] W.S. Bauman, The less popular stocks versus the most popular stocks, Financial Analysts Journal 21 (1965) 61–69.

[5] C. Chatfield and D.L. Prothero, Box-Jenkins seasonal forecasting: Problems in a case study, Journal of the Royal Statistical Association 136 (1973) 295–336.

[6] C.F. Christ, A test of an econometric model of the United States, 1921–1974, Conference on Business Cycles, (National Bureau of Economic Research, New York, 1951).

[7] C.F. Christ, Judging the performance of econometric models of the U.S. economy, International Economic Review 16 (1975) 54–74.

[8] J.P. Clearly and D.A. Fryk, A comparison of ARIMA and econometric models for telephone demand, Proceedings American Statistical Association, Business and Economics Section (1974) 448–450.

[9] W.P. Cleveland and G.C. Tiao, Decomposition of seasonal time series: A model for the Census X-11 Program, Journal of the American Statistical Association, 71 (1976) 581–587.

[10] R.L. Cooper, The predictive performance of quarterly econometric models of the United States, in B.G. Hickman, (ed.), Econometric Models of Cyclical Behavior, (National Bureau of Econometric Research, New York, 1972).

[11] J. Cragg and B. Malkiek, The consensus and accuracy of some predictions of the growth in Corporate Earnings, Journal of Finance (1968) 67–84.

[12] R.M. Dawes, Shallow psychology, in: J.S. Carrall and J.W. Payne (eds.) Cognition and Social Behavior (Laurence Erlbaunn, Hilldale, N.J., 1977).

[13] R.M. Dawes and B. Corrigan, Linear models in decision making, Psychological Bulletin 81 (1974) 95–106.

[14] E.J. Elton and M.J. Gruber, Earnings estimates and the accuracy of expectational data, Management Science, (1972) B409–B424.

[15] M.K. Evans et al., An analysis of the forecasting properties of U.S. econometric models, in: B.G. Hickman, (ed.) Econometric models of cyclical behavior, Vol. 2, (Columbia Press, New York, 1972) 949–1158.

[16] M.K. Evans, Macroeconomic Activity: Theory Forecasting and Control (Harper and Row, New York, 1969).

[17] E.F. Fama, The behavior of the stock market prices, Journal of Business 38 (1965) 34–105.

[18] M.D. Geurts and I.B. Ibrahim, Comparing the Box-Jenkins approach with the exponentially smoothed forecasting model application to Hawaii tourists, Journal of Marketing Research (1975) 182–188.

[19] L.R. Goldberg, Man versus model of man: A rationale, plus some evidence for a method of improving clinical inferences, Psychological Bulletin 73 (1970) 422–432.

[20] L.R. Goldberg, Man versus model of man: Just how conflicting is that evidence? Organizational Behavior and Human Performance 16, (1976) 13–22.

[21] C.W.J. Granger and P.J. Newbold, Spurious regressions in econometrics, Journal of econometrics 2 (1974) 111–120.

[22] D. Green and J. Segall, The predictive power of first-quarter earnings reports, Journal of Business 40 (1967) 44–55.

[23] G.K. Groff, Empirical comparison of models for short-range forecasting, Management Science 20 (1973) 22–31.

[24] Y. Haitovsky, G. Treyz and Y. Su, Forecasts with Quarterly Macroeconometric Models (National Bureau of Econometric Research, New York, 1974).

[25] P.J. Harrison and C.F. Stevens, Bayesian forecasting, Journal of the Royal Statistical Society, Series A, (1976) 206–228.

[26] R.M. Hogarth, Cognitive processes and the assessment of subjective probability distributions, Journal of the American Statistical Association 70 (1975) 271–290.

[27] M.C. Jensen, The performance of mutual funds in the period 1945–1966, Journal of Finance 23 (1968) 389–416.

[28] T.E. Johnson and T.G. Schmitt, Effectiveness of earnings per share forecasts, Financial Management, (1974) 64–72.

[29] R. Libby, Man versus model of man: Some conflicting evidence, Organizational Behavior and Human Performance 16 (1976) 1–12.

[30] V.A. Mabert, Statistical versus sales force – executive opinion short range forecasts: A time series analysis case study, Krannert Graduate School, Purdue University, (Working paper, 1975).

[31] C.A. McCoubrey and W. McKenzie, Jr., Forecasting collections using expert opinions in a deterministic model, ORSA/TIMS Conference, Miami, Fla., November 1976.

[32] R.L. McLaughlin, A new five-phase economic forecasting system, Business Economics, (1975) 49–60.

[33] A. McWhorter, Jr., 1975, Time series forecasting using the Kalman filter: An empirical

study, Proceedings American Statistical Association, Business and Economics Section (1975) 436–446.

[34] S. Makridakis, The applicability of the Box-Jenkins methodology (INSEAD mimeographed paper, 1977).

[35] S. Makridakis and M. Hibon, The accuracy of forecasting: An empirical investigation (with discussion), Journal of the Royal Statistical Society, Series A, no. 142 (1979).

[36] S. Makridakis and S.C. Wheelwright, Interactive forecasting, 2nd ed. (Holden-Day, San Francisco, 1976).

[37] D.W. Marquardt, An Algorithm for least squares estimation of non-linear parameters, Society of Industrial and Applied Mathematics, 11: (1963) 431.

[38] D.H. Meadows et al., The limits to growth (Universe Books, New York, 1972).

[39] P.E. Meehl, Clinical versus statistical prediction, Journal of Experimental Research in Personality 1 (1965) 27–32.

[40] P.E. Meehl, Clinical versus statistical prediction: A theoretical analysis and review of the literature (University of Minnesota Press, Minneapolis, 1974).

[41] O. Morgenstern, On the accuracy of economic observations (Princeton University Press, Princeton, 1963).

[42] G.V.L. Narasimham, On the predictive performance of the BEA Quarterly Econometric Model and a Box-Jenkins type of ARIMA model, Proceedings American Statistical Association, Business and Economics Section (1974) 448–450.

[43] G.V.L. Narasimham et al., A comparison of predictive performance of alternative forecasting techniques: Time series vs. an econometric model, Proceedings American Statistical Association, Business and Economics Section (1975) 459–464.

[44] T.H. Naylor et al., Box-Jenkins methods: An alternative to econometric forecasting, International Statistical Review 40: (1972) 123–137.

[45] P. Newbold, The exact likelihood function for a mixed autoregressive-moving average process, Biometrika 61 (1974) 423–426.

[46] P. Newbold and C.W.J. Granger, Experience with forecasting univariate time series and the combination of forecasts, Journal of the Royal Statistical Society, Series A, Vol. 137, (1974) 131–165.

[47] V. Niederhoffer and D. Regan, 1972, Summarized in Barron's magazine, December 18.

[48] J.W. O'Brien, How market theory can help investors set goals, select investment managers and appraise investment performance, Financial Analysts Journal 26 (1970) 91–103.

[49] D.R. Osborn, Maximum likelihood estimation of moving average processes, Ann. Econ. Soc. Meas., 5 (1976) 75–87.

[50] D.A. Pierce, Relationships – and the lack thereof – between economic time series with special reference to money, reserves and interest rates, Journal of the American Statistical Association 72 (1977) 11–27.

[51] D.L. Prothero and K.F. Wallis, Modelling Macroeconomic time series, Journal of the Royal Statistical Society, Series A, No. 139, 4 (1976) 468–486.

[52] D.J. Reid, A comparative study of time series prediction techniques on economic data, doctoral dissertation, University of Nottingham, England, 1969.

[53] T.R. Sarbin, Contribution to the study of actuarial and individual methods of prediction, American Journal of Sociology 48 (1943) 593–602.

[54] J. Sawyer, Measurement and prediction, clinical and statistical, Psychological Bulletin 66 (1966) 178–200.

[55] P. Slovic, Psychological study of human judgment: Implications for investment decision making, Journal of Finance 27 (1972) 779–799.

[56] H.O. Steckler, Forecasting with econometric models: An evaluation, Econometrica, 36 (1968) 437–463.

[57] A. Van Dam, The future of global business forecasting, Business Horizons (1977) 46–50.

[58] Fortune, Keeping up, Fortune (October, 1977).

[59] Business Week, Seasonal maladjustment, Business Week, (24 October 1977).

[60] S.C. Wheelwright, Improving the marketing organization's forecasts, in: J. LaPlaca, ed., The New Role of the Marketing Professional (American Marketing Assoc., Chicago, 1977).

[61] V. Zarnowitz, An appraisal of short term economic forecasts (National Bureau of Economic Research, New York, 1967).

TIMS Studies in the Management Sciences 12 (1979) 353–375
© North-Holland Publishing Company

APPENDIX I
REVIEWS OF RECENT FORECASTING PUBLICATIONS

O.D. Anderson, **Time Series Analysis and Forecasting** (Butterworths, London, 1976).

Contents: Introduction, Autocorrelation, Box-Jenkins, Autoregressive Processes, Moving Average Processes, Mixed Processes, Identification, Estimation, Verification, Forecasting, Integrated Processes, Seasonal Models, Forecasting — Further Points, How the Models Arise, Realisability, Autoaggregation, Postscripts, Appendices, References, Index. 182 pages.

This book is based on the author's experience in a senior-level undergraduate course on time-series analysis and forecasting. It describes in detail and through several examples the Box-Jenkins approach to time-series analysis, and provides for the reader who does not want to tackle the major book by Box and Jenkins a short introduction that deals with the time domain and discrete data of a time-series nature. This book would be of most interest to students who have a fairly extensive background in mathematics and are seeking to be brought up to data on the Box-Jenkins approach to ARMA models of time-series forecasting.

The book is divided into roughly three segments. The first addresses the properties of linear statistical models known as autoregressive/moving average approaches. In the second major segment, the Box-Jenkins iterative cycle of identification, estimation, and verification is described and numerous illustrations demonstrate how a satisfactory model can be fitted and used in forecasting. This work is also extended to cover certain types of unstable models, as well as the stable ones. In the third segment, the more recent work done under Professor Granger at Nottingham University is reported. The book includes examples which should be helpful to the reader seeking to better understand the strengths and weaknesses of the approach and its ability to deal with a range of known as well as unknown, processes.

J. Scott Armstrong, **Long-range Forecasting: From Crystal Ball to Computer** (John Wiley and Sons, New York, 1978).

Contents: Introduction, The Systems Approach and Other Good Advice, Implementation, Research Strategies, Classifying the Forecasting Methods, Judgmental Methods: The Crystal Ball, Extrapolation Methods, Econometric Methods, Segmentation Methods, Bootstrapping and Other Combined Methods, A Framework for Evaluation, Testing Inputs, Testing Outputs, Costs and Benefits of a Forecasting Method, An Evaluation of Accuracy, Trends in the Use of Forecasting Methods,

Research on Forecasting Methods, Appendices, References, Index. 585 pages.

This book concentrates on methods for long-range forecasting that are applicable to all areas of social, behavioral, and management sciences. It is very readable and written with considerable humor and personality.

The audience for this book is described by the author as the "doers" – people who have done or are doing long-range forecasting. Thus the book is oriented towards how to structure problems, how to tackle them, how to interpret their results, and how to improve upon those results. In addition, the author has included many of his own views regarding research needs in the forecasting area and relevant research results from related fields. The book should be suitable for self-study, for classroom use, and as a reference for those involved in forecasting.

William Ascher, **Forecasting – An Appraisal for Policy Makers and Planners** (The Johns Hopkins University Press, Baltimore, 1978).

Contents: Introduction, The Impact of Expert Forecasting, Population Forecasting, Economic Forecasting, Energy Forecasting, Transportation Forecasting, Technological Forecasting, Conclusion, Index. 238 pages.

This book, intended for users of forecasting in both the public and private sectors, addresses itself to a basic question facing planners and policy-makers: "How accurate will forecasts be?" To answer this question, the author has collected a number of forecasts that have been made in the past century in the areas of population, economy, energy, transportation, and technology. He then computes a measure of the accuracy of these predictions, using various time intervals (such as 5, 10, and 15 years). In this respect the book is unique and provides a great deal of insight into how well long-term forecasting has performed in the past.

In addition to examining forecasting accuracy, the reasons for success and failure in forecasting are discussed and several hypotheses that might explain variations in forecasting performance are formulated. As the author suggests, "In some respect the appraisal of forecasts puts a greater burden on the policy-maker than the original task of forecasting itself." It is this task of appraisal on which the author concentrates. He provides ample evidence of past performance and a thorough examination of the basic assumptions made in order to predict the future.

Daniel Bell, **The Coming of Post-Industrial Society – A Venture in Social Forecasting** (Basic Books, New York, 1976).

Contents: From Industrial to Post-Industrial Society, From Goods to Services – The Changing Shape of the Economy, The Dimensions of Knowledge and Technology, The Subordination of the Corporation, Social Choice and Social Planning, "Who Will Rule?", Politicians and Technocrats in the Post-Industrial Society, An Agenda for the Future, Index. 507 pages.

The author has provided a book that is balanced in terms of being sufficiently scientific to be taken seriously, but provocative and imaginative enough to encourage speculation about the shape of the future. He identifies several significant changes that are already taking place in the economy, class structure, and political institutions of Western industrialized societies. He then argues that forecasting is indeed possible and necessary when one can assume a high degree of rationality on the part of those who influence future events.

The author's predictions for the future are based on his assumptions regarding a continuation of existing trends. His basic scenario builds on a post-industrial society that is in the process of changing the largely traditional industrial fabric of Western countries.

This book is aimed at students and researchers in sociology, but also has direct relevance for students of long-range forecasting. It should also be of considerable practical value to long-range planners and forecasters.

Peter Bloomfield, **Fourier Analysis of Time Series — An Introduction** (John Wiley and Sons, New York, 1976).

Contents: The Search for Periodicity, Harmonic Analysis, The Fast Fourier Transform, Examples of Harmonic Analysis, Complex Demodulation, The Spectrum, Some Stationary Time Series Theory, Analysis of Multiple Theories, Further Topics. 258 pages.

The following time series forecasting methodologies are discussed: (a) harmonic regression — least squares regression on a sinusoid; (b) harmonic analysis — the discrete Fourier transform, periodograph analysis; (c) complex demodulation; and (d) spectrum analysis. The sequence of these topics is correlated with the increasing complexity of the statistical concepts involved. At all stages of the book the practical aspects of applying a particular method to a set of data are considered. The author believes that a critical step in data analysis is to discover some kind of oscillation, as uniform or as regular as possible, through which the data can be analyzed. Oscillations thus identified can be used for various application purposes as well.

Students who are taking a course on time series analysis, and practitioners involved in analyzing time series data may find this book helpful.

Wayne I. Boucher (ed.), **The Study of the Future: An Agenda for Research** (U.S. Government Printing Office, Washington, D.C., July 1977 (NSF/RA-770036)).

Contents: Introduction, A New Perspective on Forecasting Methodology, Validity of Forecasting Systems, The Nature of Unforeseen Developments, Attitudes Towards Forecasting in Political Science and Sociology, Technological Forecasting, On Normative Forecasting, Forecasting in Economics, A Resource Allocation Tool for Decision Making, Forecasting and its Impact on Policy Making, Problems in Futures Research, Forecasting When the Future is Known — The Case of the Soviet Union, The Futures Field, Communication in Futures Research, Monitoring the

Future, Forecasting and/or Futures Research, An Agenda for Futures Research, A Statement of Research Needs, Results from a Survey of Current Forecasting Efforts, Bibliography. 316 pages.

The various beliefs, methods, and results associated with the type of long-term forecasting known as "futures research" are the bases of the eighteen papers published here, the results of a conference held in 1974. The list of contributors includes some of the world's best-known authorities in the field.

Even though a major part of the book gives state-of-the-art descriptions of various approaches for long-term forecasting, many of the contributors venture beyond that to speculate on what can be done to improve the quality and usefulness of these forecasting approaches. There is little doubt that long-term forecasting is attracting increasing attention, but much still remains to be done before it can be completely effective. This book provides a research agenda of steps that must be taken to advance the field. It organizes and evaluates these steps in such a way as to provide directions for future development in futures research.

George E.P. Box and Gwilym M. Jenkins, **Time Series Analysis: Forecasting and Control**, Revised Edition (Holden-Day, San Francisco, 1976).

Contents: Introduction and Summary, The Autocorrelation Function and Spectrum, Linear Stationary Models, Linear Nonstationary Models, Forecasting, Model Identification, Model Estimation, Model Diagnostic Checking, Seasonal Models, Transfer Function Models, Identification, Fitting, and Checking of Transfer Function Models, Design of Feed-Forward and Feed-Back Control Schemes, Some Future Problems in Control, Technical Appendices, References, Index, Exercises and Problems. 575 pages.

This is the basic source book for those interested in autoregressive/moving average methods of time series analysis and forecasting. It is designed mainly as a reference work for researchers and forecasting specialists, but is also suitable as a textbook for graduate courses in engineering and statistics. The authors have done an excellent job of presenting in a single volume all of the major contributions in the field of univariate and multivariate autoregressive/moving average (ARMA) processes. In addition, they have included their own contribution and provided a methodology for dealing with time series data in general.

There is little doubt that this book has contributed a great deal towards the popularization of time series methods. It has done so by providing both a theoretical foundation to the approach and a practical insight into the application of that theory. A great deal can be gained by a careful reading of this book, in spite of the possible difficulties arising from the compact mathematical presentation of the authors. For the advanced student, the practical usefulness of the book is as important as its undisputable theoretical value.

The revised edition, which appeared in 1976, is very similar to the initial edition published in 1970. The major expansion is the addition of a collection of exercises and problem for the individual chapters.

David R. Brillinger, **Time Series – Data Analysis and Theory** (Holt, Rinehardt and Winston, New York, 1975).

Contents: The Nature of Time Series and Their frequency Analysis, Foundations, Analytic Properties of Fourier Transforms and Complex Matrices, Stochastic Properties of Finite Fourier Transforms, The Estimation of Power Spectra, Analysis of a Linear Time Invariant Relation Between a Stochastic Series and Several Deterministic Series, Estimating the Second Order Spectra of Vector Valued Series, Analysis of a Linear Time Invariant Relation Between Two Vector-Valued Stochastic Series, Principal Components in the Frequency Domain, The Canonical Analysis of Time Series, Proofs of Theorems, References, Index. 500 pages.

Designed to serve mainly as a text for graduate level courses in time-series analysis and as a reference work for researchers working in the field of time series, this book generalizes the field of time series beyond the framework provided by the Box-Jenkins methodology. It would be of special value to anyone interested in the theoretical aspects of time series forecasting. (This book is actually the first of two volumes; the second volume, still in preparation, will deal mainly with nonlinear analysis.)

The major focus of the book is on linear analysis of stationary vector-valued time series. The definitions, procedures, techniques, and statistics discussed, however, are simply extensions of existing multiple regression and multivariate analysis techniques. The basis nature of the statistical tools covered indicates the pervasive nature of the procedures that are discussed. The most important contributions made by this work relate to the direct application of statistical theory to time-series methods. The author makes extensive use of discrete Fourier transformations of observed values of a time-series in performing such analysis because of their important computational and mathematical properties.

William F. Butler, Robert A. Kavesh and Robert D. Platt (eds.), **Methods and Techniques of Business Forecasting** (Prentice-Hall, Englewood Cliffs, N.J., 1974).

Contents: The Forecaster's Kit of Tools, Major Approaches to Business Forecasting, Aggregate Forecasting in Practice, Industry and Sales Forecasting, Financial Forecasting, The Accuracy of Forecasts and their Uses by Business and Government. 635 pages.

More than thirty experts in the forecasting field discuss forecasting, giving particular emphasis to the tasks facing macroeconomic forecasters in industry, government, and academia. A wide range of topics is covered, including tools, techniques, problems, and illustrative applications.

Several audiences may find these essays valuable: (a) business economists who might utilize many of the methods covered in preparing or understanding forecasts of business activity; (b) businessmen seeking to gain insight into the workings of the economy and to better supervise and evaluate forecasts; and (c) students of forecasting seeking to gain broad exposure to many applications and many different methodologies.

This book is an expanded and updated version of a similar book of readings by the same editors which was first published in 1966 under the title, How Business Economists Forecast.

George K. Chacko, **Technological Forecontrol** (North-Holland Publishing Company, Amsterdam, 1975).

Contents: Scientific Code Breaking and Democratic Code Making, Anticipating Technological Potential to Acquire Corporate Profits, Technological Forecasting and Code Breaking — From the Promethean Fire to the Fire of Life, Technological Assessment of Code Breaking Consequences — The Specter of Enveloping Environmental Pollution, Technological Dimensions of Policy Making — Code Making for Code Breaking. 457 pages.

Technological forecontrol is a phrase coined to combine the notion of forecasting future breakthroughs in major areas of science and technology with the control of outcomes associated with the promises of such breakthroughs. Thus this methodology does not deal directly with linear or nonlinear projections of the past into the future.

The four parts of the book deal with (1) the practical realities of corporate decision making; (2) the development of corporate strategy in order to utilize technological potential for increased profit; (3) the technological assessment of the consequences of code breaking through technoligical forecasting; and (4) the consequences and portent of the expanding universe of technological reality and the ecological consequences that it introduces. The policy implications, both at the national and international level, are then discussed.

The book is intended mainly for students of long-range forecasting and goes a step beyond much technolgical forecasting by introducing many normative ideas on controls that can be applied in order to guide future technological developments.

John C. Chambers, Satinder K. Mullick and Donald D. Smith, **An Executive's Guide to Forecasting** (John Wiley, New York, 1974).

Contents: Strategic Importance of Forecasting in Decision-Making, Manager-Analyst Roles in Forecasting, Forecasting Techniques, Decision-Making During the Product Life Cycle, The Pre-Product and Technology Development Stage, The Product Development Stage: An Existing Market, The Product Development Stage: A New Market, The Testing and Introduction Stage, The Rapid Growth Stage, The Steady State Stage: Time Series Analysis and Projection, The Steady State Stage: Causal Model, The Phasing Out Stage, Tracking and Warning, Inventions, Innovations, and Forecasting, Forecast Management, Forecasting Techniques of the Future, Bibliography, Index. 308 pages.

These authors have sought to present a nontechnical description of forecasting aimed mainly at decision makers who desire an awareness of available techniques — their accuracy, strengths, and limitations — and of their own role in the forecasting process. The book does not contain detailed mathematical descriptions, but is mainly concerned with how different techniques can be used. Included are numerous examples of industrial and business applications of forecasting.

This book represents an extension of a widely read article published by the authors in the Harvard Business Review, July-August 1971, entitled "How to Choose the Right Forecasting Technique". This was one of the early articles that pointed out the availability of a wide range of forecasting methods and summarized their actual and potential usefulness to business organizations. Factors such as accuracy, cost, complexity, and appropriateness for stages in the product life cycle were discussed in that article and followed up in detail in this book. The influence of each of these factors on the choice of a specific forecasting method and the problems associated with these various methods of forecasting are also described by the authors.

C. Chatfield, **The Analysis of Time Series: Theory and Practice** (John Wiley and Sons, New York, 1975).

Contents: Introduction, Simple Descriptive Techniques, Probability Models for Time Series, Estimation and the Time Domain, Forecasting, Stationary Processes and the Frequency Domain, Spectral Analysis, Bivariate Processes, Linear Systems, Some Other Topics, Technical Appendices, References, Answers to Exercises, Index. 263 pages.

The intent of this book is to provide an introduction to the topic of time series and to bridge the gap between theory and practice in that field. A difficulty with the book, however, is that its length is insufficient to cover enough examples or to provide enough detail on the theory to accomplish completely its stated objectives. The original work by Box and Jenkins, although published several years prior to this book, seems to provide more detail and a clearer discussion, along with many more examples of the same set of topics covered here.

The book is intended for students and forecasting specialists with some previous background in probability and statistical inference, and a major interest in time series analysis.

Samprit Chatterjee and Bertram Price, **Regression Analysis by Example** (John Wiley and Sons, New York, 1977).

Contents: Simple Linear Regression, Detection and Correction of Model Violations — Simple Linear Regression, Multiple Regression Models, Qualitative Variables as Regressors, Weighted Least Squares, The Problem of Correlated Errors, Analysis of Colinear Data, Biased Estimation of Regression Coefficients, Selection of Variables and a Regression Equation. 228 pages.

In an approach broader than the usual one taken by statisticians, regression analysis is viewed as a set of data analysis techniques that is useful in understanding the interrelationships among a given set of variables. The emphasis of the book is not on formal statistical tests and probability computations, but rather argues for an informal analysis which is directed towards uncovering patterns from the data that can be used subsequently to develop regression equations.

The book relies heavily on graphical presentation of the data, particularly on plots of the residuals. The authors feel that more information is obtained from an informal examination of various plots of the residuals than from the formal tests of statistical significance of limited null-hypotheses. In short, their presentation is guided by the principles and concept of exploratory data analysis, rather than the traditional approaches of formal regression analysis.

The book is intended for anyone involved in analyzing data. Specifically, it could be used as a textbook for courses on regression analysis designed for students who are not specialists in statistics. It could be used by practitioners whose present approach to analyzing multifactor data consists of looking at standard computer outputs – tests, F-tests, R-squared, standard errors, etc. – but who want to go beyond these summaries for a more thorough analysis.

Fred Emery, **Futures We Are In** (H.E. Stenfert Kroese b.v. Leiden, 1977).

Contents: Intoduction, From Evolving Systems to Evolving Environments, Three Patterns of Maladaptive Response to Turbulence – Three Possible Scenarios, The Doomsday Scenarios, Active Adaptation – The Energency of Ideal Seeking Systems, The Most Probable Future for Western Society, A Scenario for Asia and the West, Notes for a World Schenario, Epilogue – Social Sciences and Social Futures, Appendix – Social Forecasting. 230 pages.

This book attempts to further study the kinds of social environments that man creates and the ways in which these evolve or regress. The author employs a wide variety of source materials and uses scenarios in a wide range of situations. The scenarios developed include the following:

(1) General scenarios – maladaptive and adaptive; (2) the future for Western societies, including identifying the main changes in the nature of work, leisure, family organization, education, and lifestyle; (3) the future for major Asian powers – China, Japan, and India; (4) a world scenario built around the first two scenarios, but also aimed at locating within this pattern the most probable future for smaller societies and underdeveloped countries.

This book was originally written in 1973 and revised in 1976. The revised edition includes a more optimistic outlook on some of the scenarios discussed and includes several additional chapters. Emery's pioneering work has been characterized by a high degree of intellectual stimulation, and this standard has been maintained. The book is intended mainly for those who would like to gain insight regarding the future environment and for policy makers and planners who must act now to avoid or alter future unwanted outcomes.

Robert Fildes and Douglas Wood (eds.), **Forecasting and Planning** (Saxon House, in Association with Gower Press, Farnbourough, England, 1978).

Contents: Introduction, Macroeconmic Forecasting and Planning, Long-Range Planning, Quantitative Forecasting Models, Company Planning and Decision Models, Planning and Forecasting. 190 pages.

This collection of readings attempts to deal with the application of advanced forecasting techniques in practice. Thirteen papers are included, plus an introduction by the editors. The introduction was presented at a conference held in May, 1976. The stated objective of these papers is to explore different aspects of the link between forecasting, planning, and decision making in an attempt to identify areas in which improvements in forecasting effectiveness can best be made.

The main audience of the book is business practitioners, even though academicians may find many useful insights from a review of the book.

Michael Firth, **Forecasting Methods in Business and Management** (Edward Arnold Limited, London, 1977).

Contents: The Role of Forecasting in Management, Forecasting Situations and the Characteristics of Forecasting Techniques, Time-Series Forecasting — Smoothing Techniques, Time-Series Forecasting — Classical Decomposition Analysis, Adaptive Methods of Time-Series Forecasting, The Monitoring of Time-Series Forecasting Methods, An Introduction to Simple Regression and Correlation, Forecasting by Multiple Regression/Causal Models, The Building of Causal Models, Other Techniques — Input/Output Analysis, Leading Indicators, Subjective Probabilistic Forecasting and Decision Analysis Techniques, Qualitative Methods of Forecasting, Data Sources for Forecasting, The Selection and Implementation of Forecasting Techniques. 300 pages.

Directed at general managers, this book describes the applicability, usefulness, and limitations of a range of formal forecasting techniques, but does not seek to give a detailed description of the mathematics required for each of those. A comprehensive reference section at the end of each chapter enables the interested reader to pursue various topics in greater detail.

The book begins with two introductory chapters describing the role of forecasting in management and the broad characteristics of forecasting techniques. It then describes a wide range of forecasting methodologies and concludes with chapters related to data requirements for forecasting and the application of specific methodologies in a given situation.

The stated purpose of the book is to introduce students seeking a career in middle- and senior-management to the area of forecasting. It is not intended for the operational researcher or the statistian who would require a more detailed introduction to the subjects covered. It is also aimed at practicing managers seeking to bring themselves up to date on recent developments in forecasting.

Warren Gilchrist, **Statistical Forecasting** (John Wiley, New York, 1976).

Contents: An Introduction to Forecasting Models, Forecasting Criteria, The Constant Mean Model, Linear Trend Models, Regression Models, Stochastic Models, Seasonal Models, Growth Curves, Probabilistic Models, Multivariate Models, Forecasting Methods and Models, Data, Adaptive Methods and Other Extensions. The Analysis and Comparison of Methods, Forecast Control, Two-Stage Forecasting, Problems and Practice, Appendices, Index. 308 pages.

The aim of this book is to provide the reader with an understanding of a broad range of statistical forecasting methods and their use in practice. The main audience for the book is students who have a basic background in mathematics. The author not only describes the fundamentals of each of the methods covered, but provides numerous examples of their application and discusses the criteria to be considered in selecting a method for specific situations. One difficulty of the book is that it is too short to provide complete coverage of each topic that it considers.

The book is divided into three main parts. Part I provides a general introduction to some of the basic concepts and terms used in statistical forecasting. Part II deals with the development of statistical forecasting methods that are applicable to a variety of situations. Part III looks at several topics related to the application of forecasting in practice. Those methods developed in Part II are described in Part III in terms of the processes used in managing their application. In addition the author explores alternative ways of improving forecasting accuracy. The appendices cover statistical concepts that are useful in the development of the methods discussed in Part II, but which some readers may not have been exposed to previously.

Peter Graff, **Die Wirtschaftsprognose** (J.C.B. Mohr, Tubingen, 1977).

Contents: Introduction, Historical Developments of Trend Functions, Mathematical Trend Functions, Empirical Section, Theoretical Section, General Review, Appendices. 447 pages.

This book describes the analysis and utilization of long-term trends for forecasting. It traces the development of ideas related to trend functions from an early historical perspective to their present day mathematical representation. To support his findings the author has analyzed several time series representing a wide range of products and subjects (economics, biology, population, etc.). A major conclusion of this exhaustive and comprehensive survey is that a great majority of time series can be best approximated by the probability density function of a normal distribution. The author has accordingly devised special graph paper to analyze time series in such a way that an estimate can be made of the saturation point for any specific data pattern.

The author warns statisticians and those working the field of forecasting that trend extrapolation can give results that are far from accurate. To avoid such difficulties an appropriate method of decomposing and analyzing trends and time series is suggested. This method enables the user to avoid the usual pitfalls. It is suggested that a trend can be separated into primary, secondary, and cursory trends, each of which can be analyzed and predicted individually.

The book provides a student of forecasting with a wide variety of data and forecasts for a range of situations. In addition, a thorough bibliography is included. The text is presently in German, but an English translation will probably be forthcoming, since the book has much to offer both practitioners and academicians.

C.W.J. Granger and Paul Newbold, **Forecasting Economic Time Series** (Harcourt Brace Jovanovich, New York, 1977).

Contents: Introduction to the Theory of Time Series, Spectral Analysis, Building Linear Time Series Models, The Theory of Forecasting, Practical Methods for Univariate Time Series Forecasting, Forecasting from Regression Models, Multiple Series Modeling and Forecasting, The Combination and Evaluation of Forecasts, Nonlinearity, Nonstationarity, and Other Topics, References, Index. 333 pages.

The main audiences for this book are graduate students and researchers working in the field of forecasting. This book presents a good blend of the theoretical aspects of time series forecasting and its applied aspects. In addition to providing basic coverage of univariate time series methods, the authors discuss multivariate methods and consider the question of forecast evaluation. Numerous examples are included, based mainly on economic situations.

This book approaches the analysis of economic data along the lines of two different philosophies. These are the newer time series approaches (ARMA methods) and the more classical econometric approach. Although the authors favor the former, they treat both as having a great deal to contribute to better forecasting.

In addition to combining time series and econometric forecasts, the authors generalize by describing how other forecasting methodologies might be combined so as to minimize their weighted mean squared error. The authors include numerous examples in which overall forecasting accuracy is improved by developing such a combination of forecast results.

Charles W. Gross and Robin T. Peterson, **Business Forecasting** (Houghton Mifflin Company, Boston, 1976).

Contents: Introduction to Forecasting, Judgmental Methods, Trend Analysis, Regression and Correlation, Time-Series Analysis, Forecasting by Surveys and Test Markets, Models Based on Learned Behavior, Model Building and Simulation, Indirect Methods, Assessment and Implementation, Summary and Conclusions, Index. 314 pages.

After first presenting a basic framework — a model of the forecasting process — the authors then relate various methodologies and management issues to that framework as an over-all structure for the book. Written primarily as a text but also suitable for practitioners, it is designed as an introduction to business forecasting, with emphasis on forecasting at the firm and industry level, as opposed to aggregate economic forecasting.

The authors have covered a range of forecasting methodologies, including both subjective and judgmental methods, as well as quantitative methods such as time-series analysis and regression. In addition, they have sought to address some of the organizational and behavioral aspects of applying forecasting in practice. Questions for further study are provided at the end of each chapter, as well as suggested further reading, but no teacher's manual is available.

Yoel Haitovsky, George Treyz and Vincent Su, **Forecasts with Quarterly Macro-econometric Models** (National Bureau of Economic Research, New York, 1974).

Contents: Introduction and Summary, Description of the Model, Sample Period Simulations and Mechanical Ex-Post Forecasts, The Decomposition of Forecasting Error – Methodology, The Decomposition of Forecasting Error – The Wharton Model, The Decomposition of Forecasting Error – The OBE Model, Comparisons of Macroeconomic Forecasts, and Appendix (Microfiche). 353 pages.

The main objective of this book is an examination of macroeconomic forecasting models in order to analyze the magnitude and source of errors in the resulting forecast. Other purposes include improving evaluation techniques for such situations and identifying the need for further research in this area. This book is intended for researchers in the field of econometrics.

It consists of two main parts. In Part I, the authors study several econometric model forecasts, based on observed rather than projected values for the exogenous variable, when no subjective judgment is used to adjust the equations in the model. The authors next look at the changes in forecasting error that result either from adding anticipation variables to the specification, or from altering the statistical method used to determine coefficients for various subsets of equations. Part II examines several econometric models and their application in forecasting. Various adjustments to each of these models are analyzed and human judgment as a factor affecting forecasting accuracy is examined. Based on this analysis, the resulting forecasting errors are studied and decomposed into several components. Finally, the authors contrast forecasts derived from econometric models with those derived by other means, such as mechanical forecasts using univariate time-series methods and the relatively simple forecasting model used by the Federal Reserve Bank of St. Louis.

Maurice Kendall, **Multivariate Analysis** (Charles Griffin and Company, Ltd., London, 1975).

Contents: Introduction, Principal Components, Classification and Clustering, Factor Analysis, Canonical Correlations, Some Distributiom Theory, Problems in

Regression Analysis, Functional Relationships, Tests of Hypotheses, Discrimination, Categorized Multivariate Data. 210 pages.

This book describes in fairly detailed terms the full range of multivariate statistical techniques presently available. Its outlook is practical and avoids overrefinement of the mathematics involved. Equal attention is devoted to topics which are specific to multivariate analysis — such as discrimination component analysis and functional relationships — and to topics that are extensions of basic concepts — such as multiple regression. The treatment throughout is applications-oriented, and the most effective methods for dealing with different data are outlined for a wide range of problems.

The book is intended for students of statistics at all levels and for researchers addressing the topic of multivariate forecasting techniques. In addition, it can serve as a reference for statisticians working in the industrial and public sectors.

Marice Kendall, **Time Series** Second Edition (Charles Griffin and Company, Ltd., London, 1976).

Contents: General Ideas, Tests of Randomness, Trend, The Choice of a Moving Average, Seasonality, Stationary Time Series, Problems in Sampling, Serial Correlation and Correlogram, Spectrum Analysis, Forecasting by Auto-Projective Methods, Multivariate Series, Forecasting from Lag Relationships, Notes on Some Problems of Estimation and Significance, Appendices. 197 pages.

Most of the univariate time series methods are given precise and well-written treatment, describing the basic ideas and techniques of time-series analysis and forecasting, and including many examples that require a minimum of mathematical sophistication for understanding. The stated purpose of the book is to close the gap between statistical theory and practical application. Thus it attempts to bring together the extensive literature that exists in scientific and professional journals into a single book that deals comprehensively with the subject of time series.

It is an appropriate text for a basic course on time-series analysis (at the graduate level). It would also be useful to statisticians, economists, and engineers seeking additional references on the subject of time-series forecasting. The second edition does not differ significantly from the first, except that several mistakes have been corrected and additional references have been added.

Colin E. Lewis, **Demand Analysis and Inventory Control** (Saxon House/Lexington Books, Lexington, Mass., 1975).

Contents: Introduction to Demand Analysis Short-Term Forecasting, Short-Term Forecasting Techniques Used in Stationary Demand Situations, Short-Term Forecasting Techniques Used in Nonstationary Demand Situations, Monitoring Forecasting Systems and Adaptive Forecasting, Advanced Forecasting Methods — Adaptive Filtering, Practical Problems of Implementing Forecasting Techniques — Man-

agement by Exception, Introduction to Inventory Control – The Link with
Demand Analysis and Short-Term Forecasting, Stochastic Reorder Level Inventory
Model – The Traditional Approach, Stochastic Cyclical Inventory Models – The
Traditional Approach, Stochastic Inventory Model – Recent Developments, Inventory Policies of Situations Where Demand is Known (or Partially Known) in Advance, Simulation of Inventory Problems, Practical Problems of Implementing
Inventory Control Techniques – Grouping Methods and Restrictive Capital, Statistical Tables, Reference, Index. 234 pages.

The focus of this book is to bring together elements of those mathematical theories developed for demand analysis and inventory control, and to deal with their
application in the day-to-day tasks of analyzing demand and controlling inventories.
Approximately half of the book deals with short-term forecasting methodolgies
that are particularly suitable for production planning and control systems. The second half deals with inventory models and the interface between the forecasting system and the production planning and inventory control system.

While this book is somewhat narrower in its focus than the other books on forecasting currently available, it does an excellent job of integrating forecasting into a
specific field of application, that of production planning and control. This book has
been used as a text for an elective course on Production Planning and Inventory
Management. It is also suitable as a reference for practitioners working in the materials management area and concerned with the interface between forecasting and
production and inventory control.

Harold A. Linstone and Devendra Sahal (eds.), **Technological Substitution – Forecasting Techniques and Applications** (Elsevier, New York, 1976).

Contents: Introduction, Basic Models, Determinants of Substitution Rate, Economic Analysis, Application to Energy Production, Diffusion Processes, The Future, Selected Bibliography, Index. 280 pages.

Technological substitution can be used as a long-term forecasting procedure. The
technique is based on an idea originally developed by Ralph Lenz, who identified
an analogy between functional technology and biological growth patterns. The
essence of this analogy is that technological advancements follows the same basic
S-curve pattern that is widespread in biological activities. Applying this technique
requires predicting the saturation point of existing technologies, which will inevitably signal the coming of new technological capabilities. In the final analysis it will
be these new technologies, the market place, and constraints on resources that will
determine the rate of technological substitution and provide the basis for the technological forecasts.

This book of readings contains sixteen articles taken largely from the Journal of
Technological Forecasting and Social Change and it is aimed at the researcher working on long-term technological forecasting and practitioners involved in long-range
planning.

Harold A. Linstone and Murray Turoff, (eds.), **The Delphi Method – Techniques and Applications** (Addison-Wesley, Reading, Mass., 1975).

Contents: Introduction, Philosophy, General Application, Evaluation, Special Cross Impact Analysis, Specialized Techniques, Computers and the Future of Delphi, Eight Basic Pitfalls – A Checklist, Delphi Bibliography, and Index. 620 pages.

The richness of the Delphi Method is illustrated by exposing the reader to a diverse set of applications and a number of different perspectives on the method. The authors provide an excellent framework on the underlying philosophy of the Delphi approach and give illustrations of numerous variations and applications.

At the outset the authors admit that "if anything is true about Delphi today, it is that in its design and use Delphi is more of an art than of a science." Based on this point of view, the authors' emphasis is not on the results of a particular application, but rather on a discussion of why Delphi was used and how it was implemented. From such illustrations the reader can determine the usefulness and applicability of Delphi.

This is a collection of twenty six papers gathered into a framework covering eight basic areas. Each of these areas is introduced with a short piece by the editors. At the conclusion of the book, a comprehensive bibliography on the Delphi Method is provided.

The book is likely to have three main audiences: researchers, practitioners who would like to use Delphi as a forecasting methodology, and students of technological forecasting. All three groups should find the book interesting and good in its coverage of the latest developments in the field.

G.S. Maddala, **Econometrics** (McGraw-Hill Book Company, New York, 1977).

Contents: Preface, Data/Variables/Models, Probability, Random Variables and Probability Distributions, Classical Statistical Inference, Bayesian Inference and Decision Theory, Descriptive Measures, Simple Linear Regression, Multiple Regression, Demivariables/Lag Variables/Nonlinearities in Multiple Regression, Some Further Topics on Multiple Regression, Introduction to Simultaneous-Equation Models, Heteroscedasticity and Autocorrelation, Errors in Variables and Non-normal Errors, Covariance Analysis and Cooling Cross-Section in Time-Series Analysis, Trend/Seasonal Variation/Forecasting, Distributed-Lag Models, Varying Parameter Models, Bayesian Methods in Econometrics, Appendices, Index. 516 pages.

While the author indicates that the book was originally intended for undergraduates, it has in fact ended up being most suitable for the graduate level. In addition, the author feels that the book as a whole can be used by applied econometricians and in government and industry.

The major purpose of the book is to bring together significant concepts and issues that relate to econometrics and to present the essential aspects of their theory, as well as the empirical results of their application. The author has intentionally minimized the amount of algebra appearing in the basic text of each chapter and has put what was still felt to be essential in the Appendices.

Spyros Makridakis and Steven C. Wheelwright, **Forecasting – Methods and Applications** (Wiley-Hamilton, Santa Barbara, California, 1978).

Contents: Introduction, Fundamentals of Quantitative Forecasting, Smoothing Methods, Decomposition Methods, Simple Regression, Multiple Regression, Econometric Models and Forecating, Time/Series Analysis, Generalized Adaptive Filtering, The Box-Jenkins Method, Multivariate Time-Series Analysis (Transfer Functions), Predicting the Cycle, Subjective Assessment Methods, Qualitative and Technological Methods, Forecasting and Planning, Comparison and Selection of Forecasting Methods, Data Procurement/Preparation and Handling, Organizational and Behavioral Aspects of Forecasting, Statistical Tables, Glossary of Forecasting Terms, Index. 740 pages.

This comprehensive text describes the fundamentals of a wide range of forecasting methodologies. Guidelines are provided that summarize the strengths and weaknesses of the various methods. These guidelines can be used by practitioners in a variety of application situations.

A number of examples and sample problems are included in the text, and several have solutions included to aid the learning process. The authors have sought to be complete and comprehensive in their coverage of both quantitative and qualitative forecasting methods and also in their coverage of organizational and behavioral aspects of applying forecasting in practice. The chapters are structured so that the practitioner desiring mainly an understanding of those aspects of the methods necessary for their application can obtain that from early sections of each chapter. The latter sections in each chapter provide the statistician and professional foreccater additional background information on the fundamentals of various forecasting approaches. This book also includes a glossary of forecasting terms and a comprehensive list of references of the forecasting literature. It should be suitable as a text for comprehensive courses in forecasting and as a reference publication for forecasters and managers.

Spyros Makridakis and Steven C. Wheelwright, **Interactive Forecating – Univariate and Multivariate Methods** Second Edition (Holden-Day Inc., San Francisco, 1978).

Contents: Cases for Interactive Forecasting, Introduction to the Interactive Forecasting System, Introduction to Time-Series Analysis and Forecasting, Autocorrelation Analysis, Moving Averages, Single Exponential Smoothing, Brown's One Parameter Linear Exponential Smoothing, Holt's Two Parameter Linear Exponential Smoothing, Brown's One Parameter Quadratic Exponential Smoothing, Winters' Three Parameter Linear and Seasonal Exponential Smoothing, Single and Linear Moving Averages, Trend Analysis, S-Curve and Exponential Growth Models, Harrison's Smoothing, The Classical Decomposition Method, Census II Decomposition Method, Generalized Adaptive Filtering, The Box-Jenkins Methodology, Choosing a Forecasting Method (SIBYL), Predicting the Cycle, Predicting the Longer Term Trend – Cycle Growth, Tracking Trend-Cycle and Budget Movement, Multiple Regression, Introduction to Multivariate Time-Series Analysis and Forecasting, Cross Autocorrelation Analysis, Multivariate Box-Jenkins Methodology (Transfer Functions), Multivariate Generalized Adaptive Filtering, Preparing the Executive Forecast, Data Management, Glossary of Forecasting Terms, Index. 650 pages.

This book provides a basic description of a wide range of both univariate and multivariate time-series and regression forecasting methodologies. The authors have also prepared a set of interactive forecasting programs available on a number of time-sharing service bureaus and available to individual corporations for in-house use. Numerous examples are included in each chapter illustrating how each method develops forecasts. The strengths and weaknesses of each of the quantitative approaches are also covered in the text. Furthermore, a complete numerical solution illustrating how computations are carried out is provided for each method.

This book is suitable both as a user's manual to those having access to SIBYL/ RUNNER interactive forecasting programs and also as a reference work on the basic mathematics and application of most of the major quantitative forecasting approaches. The book includes a number of practical case examples of forecasting and a detailed, comprehensive glossary of forecasting terms that can be used as a quick reference for the student or practitioner who may not be familiar with forecasting terminology. An extensive teacher's manual is also available for this book and provides teaching notes and application results for each of the exercises and case studies included in the book.

Nathaniel J. Mass, **Economic Cycles: An Analysis of Underlying Causes** (Write-Allen Press, Cambridge, Mass., 1975.

Contents: Introduction, Classification of Business-Cycle Theories, Inventory-Work Force Interactions, Inventory-Capital Interactions, A Production Sector, Including Labor and Capital as Factors of Production, Summary and Suggestions for Further Work, Appendices, Bibliography, Index. 185 pages.

A series of system dynamics models are developed in order to explore the basic factors underlying short-term and long-term cyclical movements in the economy. These system dynamics models are the type first proposed by Jay Forrester and widely used in his work on industrial, urban, and world dynamics. The book provides an overview of existing theories of economic cycles and develops a general framework for evaluating the impact of social and economic factors on economic cycles of various periodicities. The main contribution of this work is its attempt to analyze the causes of economic cycles and to develop hypotheses about their possible control. Specifically, the author relates employment and inventory policies, short-term cyclical movements, and capital outlays for fixed investment as the primary factors in generating longer-term cycles.

This book is useful for the student of business cycles and for practitioners seeking to obtain additional ideas on approaches to simulate the effects of business cycles for their organization. Though originally written as a doctoral thesis, in its present form the book is well-organized and does a good job of presenting some mathematical models and simple but provocative reasoning as to how and why cycles occur.

Thomas E. Milne, **Business Forecasting – A Managerial Approach** (Longman Group Limited, London, 1975).

Contents: Forecasting and Managerial Action, The Firm in the Economy, Forecasts Based on Mathematical Trends, Further Analysis of Time Series, Automatic Forecasting Systems, Relationships Among Economic Variables, Economic Forecasts, Surveys as a Basis for Forecasting, Using Forecasts for Decision Making, Managing Forecasting, References, Index. 204 pages.

This book is aimed at the nontechnical or managerial reader interested in forecasting and seeking to gain a basic appreciation for the methodologies available and their application in practice. The author has covered a wide range of approaches, including subjective methods such as survey techniques, as well as time series, decomposition, and regression approaches. In addition, the author has sought to illustrate each of these methods and the problems and opportunities associated with their application by describing several managerial problems for which they might be used.

This book has been used as an introductory text for students of management seeking to learn about forecasting. It is pragmatic in its approach and seeks to minimize the amount of mathematics required for understanding the methods that it covers. While it does not present an overall framework for relating the various methodologies and the issues that are raised, it is easy to read and discusses a number of ideas that must be addressed by the manager before he can make effective use of forecasting.

Douglas C. Montgomery and Lynwood A. Johnson, **Forecasting and Time Series Analysis** (McGraw-Hill, New York, 1976).

Contents: Introduction to Forecasting Systems, Regression Methods and Moving Averages, Exponential Smoothing Methods, Discounted Least Squares and Direct Smoothing, Smoothing Models for Seasonal Data, Forecasting, Analysis of Forecast Errors, Adaptive Control Forecasting Methods, The Box-Jenkins Model, Bayesian Methods in Forecasting, Statistical Tables, Time Series Data for Exercises, Computer Programs (Multiple Exponential Smoothing and Winters' Method), References, Index. 304 pages.

This book covers the full range of short-term forecasting methods in an introductory manner. It provides an excellent description of almost all exponential smoothing methods, the Box-Jenkins approach, and Bayesian forecasting. Furthermore, it provides a bridge between exponential smoothing models and ARMA methods by showing that the former are special cases of the latter. The authors give numerous examples using actual time series data in order to illustrate the application of the methods described. Computer programs for several exponential smoothing methods are included and important aspects relating to their application in forecasting are discussed.

The book is intended primarily for undergraduate and graduate students with some mathematical background. A secondary audience would be professional practitioners involved in the development and maintenance of forecasting systems.

James O'Toole and The University of Southern California, **Energy and Social Change** (Center for Futures Research, MIT Press, Cambridge, MA, 1976).

Contents: The Past-Historical Perspective, The Present-Data Base for the Future, The Near-Future, Mitigated Pessimism, The Long-Term Future-Realizing the Opportunity of Energy Options, Results of the Delphi Study. 185 pages.

This book is concerned with an experiment designed to explore the potential of futures research and related methodology to contribute useful and imaginative data for long-range planning by top management in the public and private sectors. The study focuses on investigations undertaken by three task forces at the University of California. It is based on papers written on this study, on a Delphi inquiry undertaken by Helmer, and an analysis based on traditional, historical, economic, and systems methods. This report is the synthesis of the findings after inconsistencies and disagreements have been smoothed and/or eliminated. It provides some insightful conclusions about the importance of energy in the future and the types of technological and social environments that may be associated with it.

This book is intended for students of long range forecasting and those who are interested in energy and its implications for society.

Robert S. Pindyck and Daniel L. Rubinfeld, **Econometric Models and Economic Forecasts** (McGraw-Hill, New York, 1976).

Contents: Introduction to the Regression Model, The Two Variable Regression Model, The Multiple Regression Model, Serial Correlation and Heteroscedasticity, Instrumental Variables in Two-Stage Least Squares, Forecasting with a Single Equation Regression Model, Single-Equation Information — Advanced Topics, Models of Qualitative Choice, Simultaneous Equation Estimation, Introduction to Simulation Models, Dynamic Behavior of Simulation Models, Examples of Simulation Models, Properties of Stochastic Time Series, Linear Time Series Models, Estimation of Time Series Models, Forecasting with Time Series Models, Examples of Time Series Applications, Statistical Tables, Solutions to Selective Problems, Index. 576 pages.

The authors describe their book as "an introduction to the science and art of building and using models". What the authors describe broadly as econometrics (including time series methods) becomes a vehicle through which the science and art of model building can be illustrated. Although mainly a book on econometrics, the authors do a fairly complete job of enlarging the topic and relating it to model building in general.

Three aspects of model building are explored — single equation models, multiple equation models, and time-series models. The authors categorize all three groups under econometrics by arguing that time-series methods are actually single equation regression models. This allows the authors to apply directly the tools developed in Part I of the book, which deals with single equation regression methods. While not everyone would agree with such a classification scheme, since there is a basic difference between econometric models — which are explanatory or causal in nature — and time series models — which are mechanistic or black box in nature — the book is well structured and gives good coverage of both econometric and time series techniques.

Joel Popkin (ed.), **Analysis of Inflation: 1965—1974** (Ballinger Publishing Company for the National Bureau of Economic Research, Cambridge, MA, 1977).

Contents: Introduction, A Monetary Interpretation of Inflation, Econometrics of Inflation 1965—1974, An Appraisal of the Wage-Price Control Program, Controls and Inflation — An Overview, Price and Wage Behavior in the U.S. Aggregate Economy and in Manufacturing Industries, The Effects of Phases I, II and III on Wages, Prices and Profit Margins in the Manufacturing Sector of the United States, Measurement and Price Effects of Aggregate Supply Constraints, A Technique for Analyzing and Decomposing Inflation, Survey Measures of Expected Inflation and and Their Potential Usefulness, The Impact of Econometric Models of the Present Treatment of Smog and Safety Devices in Economics Statistics: A Comment, Canadian Experience with Recent Inflation as Viewed Through CANDIDE, Price Linkage in an Interdependent World Economy, Index. 487 pages.

Twelve papers, each followed by a summary and comments, discuss US inflation in the decade ending in 1974. These papers were presented at the Conference on Price Behavior, held November 21—23, 1974 in Bethesda, Maryland.

Inflation has recently become a major point of concern for both government policy makers and managers. This timely book looks at the variety of inflationary forces and the policies designed to combat them. The impact of price and wage controls, the increases in oil prices, the shift to floating exchange rates, and the increased interdependence of national economies are some of the factors analyzed for their impact on inflation. In addition, the type of policies needed to minimize the influence such factors have on other price rises are considered.

This book looks at inflation from different points of view and provides a chronology of the events affecting inflation during the 1965—1974 period. It should be of interest to those concerned with predicting inflation, as well as those seeking to understand government policies aimed at limiting its impact.

William G. Sullivan and W. Wayne Claycombe, **Fundamentals of Forecasting** (Reston Publishing Company, Reston, Virginia, 1977).

Contents: An Introduction to Forecasting, The Essential Materials of Forecasting, The Choice of Appropriate Techniques for Implementing a Forecasting Strategy, Forecasting Based on Regression Techniques, Moving Averages and Exponential Smoothing, The Use of Subjective Information in Forecasting, Technological Forecasting, Advanced Forecasting Techniques, A Manager's Primer on Forecasting, Tests for Serial Correlation in Regression Analysis, Statistical Tests for Regression Methods, Forecasting High Consequence-Low Probability Events, Index. 292 pages.

The stated objective of this book is to enable the nonstatistical reader to apply popular forecasting techniques and be aware of their strengths and limitations. A range of forecasting methodologies is covered with the basic mathematics commonly taught at the graduate level included in the Appendices in the book. The authors have drawn on a number of practical writings related to production and inventory control and sales management in order to supplement their own experience in the forecasting field.

This book includes listings of computer programs that implement some of the simpler methodologies covered in the text. The authors also have used illustrations and included questions at the end of each chapter to provide focus for additional thought and discussion. However, these are not exercises and no teacher's manual is available for the book.

Steven C. Wheelwright and Spyros Makridakis, **Forecasting Methods for Management** Second Edition (John Wiley and Sons, New York, 1977).

Contents: Forecasting and Management — An Introduction, The Evaluation of Forecasting Techniques, Forecasting with Smoothing Techniques, Forecasting with Adaptive Filtering, Simple Regression and Correlation, The Classical Decomposition Method of Time-Series Forecasting, Multiple Regression and Correlation, Other Quantitative Methods of Forecasting, Data Acquisition and Handling in Forecasting, Forecasts Based on Subjective Estimates, Qualitative Approaches to Forecasting, Matching the Forecasting Method with the Situation, Organizing and Implementing a Corporate Forecasting Function, Corporate Forecasting Report — Promise and Reality, Index. 266 pages.

The practitioner who seeks to better understand the wide range of forecasting methods and their major advantages and disadvantages may find this book helpful. The mathematics of the methodologies described have been kept at a minimum, and the emphasis has been placed on describing what the practicing forecaster and management user need to know about forecasts prepared with each method in order to use those forecasts appropriately.

In its first edition (1973), this book was the first available that sought to cover a a broad range of methods — time-series, regression, econometrics and qualitative approaches — as well as to address organizational, behavioral and application aspects of forecasting. The second edition has added material related to the states of forecasting in major US companies and the phases that companies tend to go through in adopting more sophisticated forecasting methodologies. This book is suitable for the practitioner and manager, and also for introductory courses on forecasting.

Douglas Woods and Robert Fildes, **Forecasting for Business** (Longman, New York, 1976).

Contents: Forecasting and Managerial Decisions, The Value of Forecasts as Decision Inputs, Forecast Timing and Structure for Management Decisions, Smoothing and Interpreting Information Flows, An Introduction to Linear Regression, Multiple Regression, Benchmark Forecasting, Causal Models of Cost and Demand, Forecasting the Business Environment (The National Economy), Long-Range Forecasting and Technological Change, Appendices, Index. 280 pages.

The authors stress the concept that forecasting is a managerial activity and as such must be measured against the needs of management that it meets, rather than against some absolute or narrow technical standard. The authors also see a need for explicit forecasting systems and structures in order for management to improve effectively its own forecasting activity. Based on these premises, the book aims at stating in managerial terms many of the technical aspects of forecasting and the implications that a manager must understand to apply specific methodologies.

The aim of the book is to provide the practicing manager or student of management with the tools and the framework necessary to produce a good forecast without having to become a statistician or econometrician. It is designed so it can be used for independent study or for reference, as well as for classroom use. The book contains numerous examples, and the Appendices include additional references and technical guidelines for handling some of the more sophisticated methodologies.

U.S. Army Engineer Institute for Water Resources, **Handbook of Forecasting Techniques** (Kingman Building, Ft. Belvoir, Virginia 22060 under contract No. EACW 31-75-C-0027, IWR Contract Reports 75-7, December 1975).

Contents: Introduction, Selection and Comparison of Forecasting Techniques, Forecasting Techniques Using Time Series and Projections, Forecasting Techniques Using Models and Simulations, Qualitative and Holistic Forecasting Techniques, References, Forecasting Techniques Examined, Glossary of Terms, Index. 314 pages.

This volume was designed to help planners at the Corps of Engineers Civil Works Program improve their professional expertise in long-range forecasting. The report covers 12 basic techniques that the authors thought would be suitable for a wide range of technological, economic, social, and environmental forecasting. Those techniques are compared on a variety of dimensions, and each of them is described in terms of its use, types of results, time and personnel requirements, costs, and several other characteristics. In addition, instructions are given on procedures for applying each method, along with illustrations, many of which are drawn from the Corps' experience.

This volume is straightforward and easy to read and particularly appropriate as a reference for practitioners faced with problems similar to those faced by planners at the corps of Engineers. References are cited for further study, and the Appendices present supporting information on various techniques and a Glossary of terms for the planner who is new to the forecasting area. This work is particularly good in its coverage of qualitative methods of forecasting and in addressing management science techniques, such as simulation and queueing, that are often overlooked as possible methodologies for handling forecasting problems.

Recent forecasting publications

[1] O.D. Anderson, Time Series Analysis and Forecasting (Butterworths, 1976).
[2] J.S. Armstrong, Long-Range Forecasting: From Crystal Ball to Computer (John Wiley and Sons, New York, 1978).
[3] W. Ascher, Forecasting: An Appraisal for Policy Makers and Planners (The Johns Hopkins University Press, Baltimore, 1978).
[4] D. Bell, The Coming of Post-Industrial Society – A Venture in Social Forecasting (Basic Books, New York, 1976).
[5] P. Bloomfield, Fourier Analysis of Time Series – An Introduction (John Wiley and Sons, New York, 1976).
[6] W.I. Boucher (ed.), The Study of the Future: An Agenda for Research (U.S. Government Printing Office, Washington, D.C., July 1977 (NSF/RA-770036)).
[7] G.E.P. Box and G.M. Jenkins, Time Series Analysis: Forecasting and Control (Holden-Day, San Francisco, 1976).
[8] D.R. Brillinger, Time Series – Data Analysis and Theory (Holt, Rinehardt, and Winston, New York, 1975).
[9] W.F. Butler, R.A. Kavesh and R.D. Platt (eds.) Methods and Techniques of Business Forecasting (Prentice-Hall, Englewood Cliffs, N.J., 1974)).
[10] G.K. Chacko, Technological Forecontrol (North Holland Publishing Company, Amsterdam, 1975).
[11] J.C. Chambers, S.K. Mullick and D.D. Smith, An Executive's Guide to Forecasting (John Wiley and Sons, New York, 1974).
[12] C. Chatfield, The Analysis of Time Series: Theory and Practice (John Wiley and Sons, New York; 1975).
[13] S. Chatterjee and B. Price, Regression Analysis by Example (John Wiley and Sons, New York, 1977).
[14] F. Emery, Futures We Are In. (H.E. Stenfert Kroese b.v., Leiden, 1977).
[15] R. Fildes and D. Wood (eds.), Forecasting and Planning (Saxon House, In Association with Gower Press, Farnborough, England, 1978).
[16] M. Firth, Forecasting Methods in Business and Management (Edward Arnold Limited, London, 1977).
[17] W. Gilchrist, Statistical Forecasting (John Wiley and Sons, New York, 1976).

[18] D. Graff, Die Wirtschaftsprognose (J.C.B. Mohr, Tubingen, 1977).

[19] C.W.J. Granger and P. Newbold, Forecasting Economic Time Series (Harcourt Brace Jovanovich, New York, 1977).

[20] C.W. Gross and R.T. Peterson, Business Forecasting (Houghton Mifflin Company, Boston, 1976).

[21] Y. Haitovsky, G. Treyz and V. Su, Forecasts with Quarterly Macroeconometric Models (National Bureau of Economic Research, New York, 1974).

[22] M. Kendall, Multivariate Analysis (Charles Griffin and Company, Ltd., London, 1975).

[23] M. Kendall, Time Series, Second Edition (Charles Griffin and Company, Ltd., London, 1976).

[24] C.E. Lewis, Demand Analysis and Inventory Control (Saxon House/Lexington Books, Lexington, Mass., 1975).

[25] H.A. Linstone and D. Sahal (eds.), Technological Substitution – Forecasting Techniques and Applications (Elsevier, New York, 1976).

[26] H.A. Linstone and M. Turoff (eds.), The Delphi Method – Techniques and Applications (Addison-Wesley, Reading, Massachusetts, 1975).

[27] G.S. Maddala, Econometrics (McGraw-Hill Book Company, New York, 1977).

[28] S. Makridakis and S.C. Wheelwright, Forecasting – Methods and Applications (Wiley-Hamilton, Santa Barbara, California, 1978).

[29] S. Makridakis and S.C. Wheelwright, Interactive Forecasting – Univariate and Multivariate Methods – Second Edition (Holden-Day, Inc., San Francisco, 1978).

[30] N.J. Mass, Economic Cycles: An Analysis of Underlying Causes (Write-Allen Press, Cambridge, Massachusetts, 1975).

[31] T.E. Milne, Business Forecasting – A Managerial Approach (Longman Group Limited. London, 1975).

[32] D.C. Montgomery and L.A. Johnson, Forecasting and Time Series Analysis (McGraw-Hill, New York, 1976).

[33] J. O'Toole and The University of Southern California Center for Futures Research, Energy and Social Change (The MIT Press, Cambridge, Mass., 1976).

[34] R.S. Pindyck and L. Rubinfield, Econometric Models and Economic Forecasts (McGraw-Hill, New York, 1976).

[35] J. Popkin (ed.), Analysis of Inflation: 1965–1974 (Ballinger Publishing Company for the National Bureau of Economic Research, Cambridge, Mass., 1977)

[36] W.G. Sullivan and W.W. Claycombe, Fundamentals of Forecasting (Reston Publishing Company, Reston, Virginia, 1977).

[37] S.C. Wheelwright and S. Makridakis, Forecasting Methods for Management, Second Edition (John Wiley and Sons, New York, 1977).

[38] D. Woods and R. Fildes, Forecasting for Business (Longman, New York, 1976).

[39] U.S. Army Engineer Institute for Water Resources, Handbook of Forecasting Techniques (Kingman Building, A. Belvoir, Virginia, under contract No. EACW 31-75-C-0027, IWR Contract Reports 75-7, December 1975).

TIMS Studies in the Management Sciences 12 (1979) 377–382
© North-Holland Publishing Company

APPENDIX II: REFEREES

Referee *	Address
David Aaker	School of Business Administration University of California Berkeley, CA 94720
Oliver D. Anderson	Civil Service College 11 Belgrave Road London SW1V 1RB England
Ahmed Aykac	CEDEP/INSEAD 77305 Fontainebleau France
Alan R. Beckenstein	Graduate School of Business Administration University of Virginia Charlottesville, VA 22906
William Berry	Graduate School of Business Indiana University Bloomington, IN 47401
William Berry	Ohio State University Hagerty Hall 1775 College Road Columbus, OH 43210
Steve Beveridge	Faculty of Business Administration University of Alberta Edmonton, Alberta, Canada
John E. Bishop	Graduate School of Business Administration Harvard University Boston, MA 02163
Warren Boe	Department of Business Administration University of Iowa Iowa City, IA 52242
Charles P. Bonini	Graduate School of Business Stanford University Stanford, CA 94305
Stan Buchin	Applied Decision Systems 15 Walnut Street Wellesley Hills, MA 02181

* Several of the referees were kind enough to review more than one manuscript.

Appendix II

Referee	Address
Alan V. Cameron	School of Engineering University of California Irvine, CA 92715
Robert Carbone	College of Administrative Science Ohio State University Columbus, OH 43210
Darral G. Clarke	Department of Business Management 395 JKB Brigham Young University Provo, UT 84602
Kenneth Cogger	School of Business The University of Kansas Lawrence, KS 66045
Lewis Coopersmith	Health Products Research 3520 U.S. Route 22 Somerville, NJ 08876
Tim Davidson	Applied Decision Systems 15 Walnut Street Wellesley Hills, MA 02181
Jose de la Torre	INSEAD 77305 Fontainebleau France
James Dyer	Graduate School of Management University of California Los Angeles, CA 90024
Claude Faucheux	CESA 78305 Jouy-en-Josas France
Robert Fildes	Manchester Business School University of Manchester Booth Street West Manchester M15 6PB England
A. Dale Flowers	Texas Tech University College of Business Administration Box 4320 Lubbock, TX 79409
James R. Freeland	Graduate School of Business Stanford University Stanford, CA 94305
Michael D. Geurts	395 JKB Dept. of Business Management Brigham Young University Provo, UT 84602

Referee	Address
Charles Gross	School of Business Administration Wayne State University Detroit, MI 48202
Arnoldo Hax	Alfred P. Sloan School of Management Massachusetts Institute of Technology Cambridge, MA 02139
Robin Hogarth	INSEAD 77305 Fontainebleau France
Arthur V. Hill	College of Business Administration University of Minnesota Minneapolis, MN 55455
Steven Hillmer	The University of Kansas 1210 W. Dayton Madison, WI 53706
Barbara Jackson	Graduate School of Business Administration Harvard University Boston, MA 02163
Lynwood A. Johnson	School of Industrial and Systems Engineering Georgia Institute of Technology Atlanta, GA 30332
Peter Jones	Graduate School of Business Administration Harvard University Boston, MA 02163
Carl Kallina	Business System Manager Sales and Marketing Consumer Businesses American Can Company American Lane Greenwich, CT 06830
James R. Kearl	Department of Economics Brigham Young University Provo, UT 84602
Jean-Jacque Lambin	Catholique University of Louvain Belgium
Andre Laurent	INSEAD 77305 Fontainebleau France
Robert A. Leone	Graduate School of Business Administration Harvard University Boston, MA 02163
Colin Lewis	University of Aston Management Center 158 Corporation Street Birmingham B46 TE England

Referee	Address
John Lintner	Graduate School of Business Administration Harvard University Boston, MA 02163
Vincent A. Mabert	Department of Management College of Business Administration Bowling Green State University Bowling Green, OH 43402
Bernard Majani	Aussedat Rey 1 rue de Petit Clamart 78140 Velizy Villacoulday France
Spyros Makridakis	INSEAD 77305 Fontainebleau France
George W. McKinney, III	Corning Glass Works Corning NY 14830
Robert L. McLaughlin	Micrometrics, Inc. 99 Mill Street Waterbury, CT 06720
Raman K. Mehra	Scientific Systems, Inc. 186 Alewife Brook Parkway Cambridge, MA 02138
John R. Meyer	Graduate School of Business Administration Harvard University Boston, MA 02163
Claude Michaud	CEDEP 77305 Fontainebleau France
Jeffrey G. Miller	Graduate School of Business Administration Harvard University Boston, MA 02163
Douglas C. Montgomery	School of Industrial and Systems Engineering Georgia Institute of Technology Atlanta, GA 30332
G.W. Morrison	Computing Applications Department Computer Sciences Division Union Carbide Corporation Nuclear Division P.O. Box X Oak Ridge, TN 37830
Satinder K. Mullick	Chief Economist Corporate Finance Division Corning Glass Works Corning, NY 14830

Referee	Address
Paul Newbold	Department of Mathematics University of Nottingham University Park Nottingham NG7 2RD England
Maxwell Noton	Cumulus Systems Russell House 59-61 High Street Rickmansworth, Herts. WD3-IRH, England
David J. Pack	College of Administrative Science Ohio State University Columbus, OH 43210
Emanuel Parzen	Institute of Statistics Texas A and M University College Station, TX 77843
David H. Pike	Computer Sciences Division Oak Ridge National Laboratory P.O. Box X Oak Ridge, TN 37830
Robert S. Pindyck	Alfred P. Sloan School of Management Massachusetts Institute of Technology Cambridge, MA 02139
Charles Plosser	Graduate School of Business Stanford University Stanford, CA 94305
James E. Reinmuth	College of Business Administration Office of the Dean University of Oregon Eugene, OR 97403
Dominique Scaglia	CISI 35 Boulevard Brune 75680 Paris Cedex 14 France
Robert Schlaifer	Graduate School of Business Administration Harvard University Boston, MA 02163
Grahame Settle	Department of Computational and Statistical Science The University of Liverpool P.O. Box 147 Liverpool L69 3BX England
Bert M. Steece	College of Business Administration University of Oregon Eugene, OR 97403

Referee	Address
M. Robert Sultan	CISI 35 Boulevard Brune 75680 Paris Cedex 14 France
Curt Tompkins	Department of Industrial Engineering West Virginia University Morgantown, WV 26506
Walter Vandaele	Graduate School of Business Administration Harvard University Boston, MA 02163
David Weinstein	INSEAD 77305 Fontainebleau France
Steven C. Wheelwright	Graduate School of Business Administration Harvard University Boston, MA 02163
Clay Whybark	Krannert Graduate School Purdue University West Lafayette, IN 47907
Gary Wicklund	College of Business Administration University of Iowa Iowa City, IA 52242
Bernard Widrow	Department of Electrical Engineering Stanford University Stanford, CA 94305
Steven D. Wood	Arizona State University College of Business Administration Tempe, AZ 88281
Douglas Wood	Manchester Business School University of Manchester Manchester, M15 6PB England

TIMS Studies in the Management Sciences 12 (1979) 383-389
© North-Holland Publishing Company

NOTES ABOUT AUTHORS

Bruce Bagamery ("Input-Output Methods in Forecasting") is a Ph.D. candidate in the Department of Finance at Northwestern University's Graduate School of Management, Evanston, Illinois 60201. His research deals with the application of input-output based measures of industry interrelatedness in explaining the variability of firms' returns and its relationship to well-known capital-asset pricing model.

Alan R. Beckenstein ("Forecasting Considerations in a Rapidly Changing Economy") is currently Associate Professor of Business Economics at The Colgate Darden Graduate School of Business, University of Virginia, Charlottesville, Virginia 22906. He received an A.B. (Economics) from Lafayette College and an A.M. and Ph.D. (Economics) from the University of Michigan. His teaching, research, and consulting interests are in the areas of economics, public policy (antitrust), and forecasting. He is the coauthor of *The Economics of Multi-Plant Operation* (Harvard University Press, 1976) and has had a number of articles published in economics and management journals.

Jean-Marie Blin ("Input-Output Methods in Forecasting") is Associate Professor of Managerial Economics and Decision Sciences at Northwestern University's Graduate School of Management, Evanston, Illinois 60201. He holds an M.S. and Ph.D. (Economics) from Purdue University. His research deals with forecasting methodologies applied to corporate planning, input-output analysis, multiple-criteria decision making, and social choice theory. His publications include *Patterns and Configurations in Economic Science* (D. Reidel Publishing Co., 1973), and numerous articles which have appeared in such journals as *Economics of Planning, Econometrica, IEEE Transactions, Management Science, Public Choice,* and *The Review of Economics and Statistics.*

Charles P. Bonini ("An Application of Regression Smoothing for Forecasting Customer Utility Bills") is Associate Professor of Management Science at the Graduate School of Business, Stanford University, Stanford, California, 94305. He received his Ph.D. from Carnegie-Mellon University. He is coauthor of texts in Statistics and Quantitative Methods as well as journal articles. He is a past president of AIDS and a member of TIMS and ASA.

J. Peter Burman ("Seasonal Adjustment − A Survey") is the advisor on statistical techniques at the Bank of England, Threadneedle Street, London EC2R 8AH, England. Apart from three years secondment to the Research Department of the International Monetary Fund, he has been at the Bank since 1946. He has published papers on the design of experiments and sequential sampling, but his current interests are seasonal adjustment and the term structure of interest rates.

Kenneth O. Cogger ("Time Series Analysis in Forecasting with an Absolute Error

Criterion") is Associate Professor of Business and Director of Research, School of Business, University of Kansas, Lawrence, Kansas 66045. He holds a B.S. (Ch.E.), M.B.A., and Ph.D. from the University of Michigan. His primary research and consulting interests involve forecasting and applied statistics. He has published in *Management Science, Operations Research, Journal of the American Statistical Association,* and other professional journals. He is currently a member of TIMS, ORSA, AIDS, and ASA.

Lewis W. Coopersmith ("Automatic Forecasting Using the FLEXICAST System") is an Assistant Professor at Rider College and Vice President of Health Products Research, Somerville, New Jersey 08876. He holds an A.B. from the University of Pennsylvania and an M.S. and Ph.D. from New York University. He has held department management positions with the FDA and Johnson and Johnson. He has published and presented papers on research related to forecasting, design and analysis of sample surveys, and marketing planning. Professional affiliations include TIMS and ASA.

Vittorio Corbo ("An Econometric Approach to Forecasting Demand and Firm Behavior: Canadian Telecommunications") is Associate Professor of Economics and Director at the Institute of Applied Economic Research at Concordia University, Montreal, Quebec, Canada. He is also a Research Associate of the National Bureau of Economic Research. He holds a degree in economics from Universidad de Chile, and a Ph.D. (economics) from MIT. His areas of interest are trade and development, economic development, telecommunications economics, and econometrics. He is author or coauthor of several books, monographs and major reports, and of numerous articles appearing in journals such as *Annals of Economic and Social Measurement, Southern Economic Journal, Economia Internazionale,* and *American Economic Review.*

Robert Fildes ("On Selecting a Forecasting Model") is a lecturer in business forecasting at the Manchester Business School, University of Manchester, Manchester M15 6PB, England. He received a Bachelor's degree (mathematics) from Oxford and a Ph.D. (statistics) from the University of California. He is coauthor of *Forecasting for Business* (Longmans, 1976) and an editor of *Forecasting and Planning* (Teakfield, 1978). He has also authored several articles on forecasting and applied statistics and served as a consultant in these fields. During 1978 he taught at the University of British Columbia and the University of California Berkeley.

James R. Freeland ("An Application of Regression Smoothing for Forecasting Customer Utility Bills") is an Associate Professor of Decision Sciences in the Graduate School of Business, Stanford University, Stanford, California 94305. He received a B.S.I.E. from Bradley University and an M.S.I.E. and Ph.D. (Industrial and Systems Engineering) from Georgia Tech. His recent publications have appeared in *Management Science, Decision Sciences, Omega,* and *Engineering Economist.* He is a member of TIMS, ORSA, AIDS, AIIE and APICS.

Michael D. Geurts ("A Multideterministic Approach to Forecasting") is an

Associate Professor in Business Management at Brigham Young University. He previously has been employed by the University of Hawaii, University of Oregon, Banquet Foods, and IBM, and has consulted with several firms on forecasting and marketing problems. He has published in the *Journal of Marketing, Management Science, Journal of Retailing, Decision Sciences,* and *Systems Management.*

Olaf Helmer ("The Utility of Long-Term Forecasting") has most recently been associated with the International Institute for Applied Systems Analysis, Schloss Laxenburg, Austria. He joined Project Rand in 1946 and was a senior staff member of the Mathematics Department (of the Rand Corporation) until 1968. He was a founder of the Institute for the Future and has served as President and Director of Research. His faculty positions in the field of forecasting have included positions at the University of Chicago, UCLA and USC. His publications include *Social Technology* (Basic Books, 1966) and numerous articles in such journals as *Management Science, Science Journal,* and *Futures.*

Sydney D. Howell ("On Selecting a Forecasting Model") is a Research Fellow in Inflation Accounting at Manchester Business School, University of Manchester, Manchester M15 6PB, England. He received an M.A. in English from Cambridge University and a Ph.D. in Applied Decision Theory and Forecasting Behavior from Manchester Business School. His professional activities include research and consulting in production planning and inventory control, forecasting, and the application of multivariate statistics.

Lynwood A. Johnson ("Forecasting with Exponential Smoothing and Related Methods") is Professor of Industrial and Systems Engineering at the Georgia Institute of Technology, Atlanta, Georgia 30332. He holds a B.I.E., M.S.I.E., and Ph.D. (industrial engineering) from the Georgia Institute of Technology. In addition to being an educator, he has experience as an industrial engineer for E.I. Du Pont, as a management consultant for Kurt Salmon Associates, and as an independent consultant for a number of organizations. He is coauthor of three books: *Operations Research in Production Planning, Scheduling, and Inventory Control; Forecasting and Time Series Analysis;* and *Introduction to Linear Programming with Application.* He is a member of TIMS, ORSA, AIIE, and ASQC.

Daniel Kahneman ("Intuitive Predictions: Biases and Corrective Procedures") is Professor of Psychology at the University of British Columbia, Vancouver, B.C., Canada V6T 1W5. He has a B.A. (Psychology and Mathematics) from Hebrew University and a Ph.D. (Psychology) from the University of California, Berkeley. From 1961 to 1977 he taught at the Hebrew University of Jerusalem, with periods of research at the University of Michigan, Harvard, Oregon Research Institute and the Center for Advanced Studies in the Behavioral Sciences. He divides his research time between the study of attention and perceptual organization, and the study of judgment and decision making under risk, in which he has collaborated with Amos Tversky for a decade.

Spyros Makridakis ("Forecasting: Framework and Overview" and "Forecasting the Future and the Future of Forecasting") is Professor of Management Science at

INSEAD, 77305 Fontainebleau, France. He received his degree from the School of Industrial Studies in Greece and his M.B.A. and Ph.D. from New York University. He has published extensively in the areas of general systems and forecasting and has coauthored *Computer-Aided Modeling for Managers* (Addison-Wesley, 1972), *Forecasting Methods for Management, Second Edition* (Wiley, 1977), *Interactive Forecasting, Second Edition* (Holden-Day, 1978), and *Forecasting: Methods and Applications* (Wiley-Hamilton, 1978). He is the coeditor of this special issue and an associate editor of *Management Science.*

Robert L. McLaughlin ("Organizational Forecasting: Its Achievements and Limitations") is President of Micrometrics, Inc., Waterbury, Connecticut. He is a graduate of Notre Dame and Syracuse University. He has been Marketing Research Manager for General Electric's Electronic Communications Department and Director of Corporate Commercial Research for Scovill Manufacturing Company. He is a member of McGraw-Hill's Economic Panel and recently received the Abrahamson Award of the National Association of Business Economists. In addition to his many publications on forecasting, since 1969 he has been the publisher of *Turning Points,* a monthly forecasting newsletter.

Stephen K. McNees ("Lessons from the Track Record of Macroeconomic Forecasts in the 1970s") is Assistant Vice President and Economist at the Federal Reserve Bank of Boston, Boston, Massachusetts, 02106. He received a B.A. from Swarthmore College and a Ph.D. from the Massachusetts Institute of Technology. As head of the National Business Conditions Section, he advises the Board of Directors and the President of the Bank on the economic outlook and current policy issues. He has published several articles on economic forecasting and econometric models.

Raman K. Mehra ("Kalman Filters and Their Application to Forecasting") is President, Scientific Systems, Cambridge, Massachusetts 02138. He received a B.S. (Electrical Engineering) from Punjab Engineering College (India) and an M.S. and Ph.D. (Control System Theory) from Harvard University. His fields of specialization are optimal control and estimation, numerical solution of optimization problems, system identification, stochastic control and time series analysis. He is the author of numerous papers on topics in these fields and has taught courses on these and related subjects as a past member of the faculty of Harvard University.

Douglas C. Montgomery ("Forecasting with Exponential Smoothing and Related Methods") is Professor of Industrial and Systems Engineering at the Georgia Institute of Technology, Atlanta, Georgia 30332. He received a B.S.I.E., M.S., and Ph.D. from Virginia Polytechnic Institute. His research and teaching interests are in engineering statistics – including forecasting, design of experiments, and statistical model building – and in the use of operations research methodology in the analysis of production and distribution problems. He is the author or coauthor of four books and a number of journal articles and is a member of the editorial board of *AIIE Transactions* and *RAIRO-Operations Research.* He is a member of TIMS, ORSA, AIIE, ASQC, and ASA, and has held several offices in AIIE and ASQC.

Geoffrey H. Moore ("Inflation's Turn") is Director, Business Cycle Research, National Bureau of Economic Research, New York, and Senior Research Fellow, Hoover Institute, Stanford University, Stanford, California 94305. He received a B.S. and M.S. (Agriculture) from Rutgers University and a Ph.D. (Agricultural Economics) from Harvard University. His major interests include analysis and forecasting of business cycles and he has published numerous books, monographs, and articles in that field.

Paul Newbold ("Time Series Model Building and Forecasting: A Survey") is Reader in Econometrics, Department of Mathematics, University of Nottingham, Nottingham NG7 2RD, England. He has held visiting appointments in the Department of Economics, University of California, San Diego; the Graduate School of Business, University of Chicago; and the Mathematics Research Center, University of Wisconsin. He holds a B.Sc. (Econ) from the London School of Economics and a Ph.D. from the University of Wisconsin. He is coauthor with C.W.J. Granger of *Forecasting Economic Time Series* (Academic Press, 1977) and has published articles on time series analysis and forecasting in the *Journal of the Royal Statistical Society, Biometrika, Journal of Econometrics, International Economic Review, Applied Economics,* and *Operational Research Quarterly.* He has also consulted on a range of industrial forecasting problems.

Emanuel Parzen ("Forecasting and Whitening Filter Estimation") is Distinguished Professor of Statistics at Texas A&M University, College Station, Texas 77843. His current research is on general approaches to multiple time series modeling and the density-quantile function approach to statistical inference and data analysis. He is the author of *Modern Probability Theory and its Applications* (Wiley, 1960) and *Stochastic Processes* (Holden-Day, 1962).

Robert S. Pindyck ("An Econometric Approach in Forecasting Demand and Firm Behavior") is Associate Professor in the Sloan School of Management at MIT, Cambridge, Massachusetts 02139. He received a B.S. and M.S. (Electrical Engineering) and a Ph.D. (Economics) from MIT. His research has been in the application of control theory to economic policy, and in the economics of energy and natural resources. He is the author of *Optimal Planning for Economic Stabilization* (North-Holland Publishing Co.), and *The Structure of World Energy Demand* (MIT Press), the coauthor of *The Economics of the Natural Gas Shortage: 1960-1980* (North-Holland), *Price Controls and the Natural Gas Shortage* (American Enterprise Institute), and *Econometric Models and Economic Forecasts* (McGraw-Hill), and the editor of *Advances in the Economics of Energy and Resources* (JAI Press). He has written a number of articles on applied econometrics, economic policy formulation, and the economics of energy and natural resource markets.

James E. Reinmuth ("A Multideterministic Approach to Forecasting") is Professor and Dean, College of Business Administration, University of Oregon, Eugene, Oregon, 97403. He received a B.S. in mathematics from the University of Washington and an M.S. and Ph.D. in statistics from Oregon State University. His research and consulting interests currently involve the application of multivariate and time series methods to problems in marketing and real estate analysis. His publications have appeared in various professional journals directed to business and applied science. He is a member of AIDS, ORSA, TIMS, and the Society of Sigma Xi.

Bert M. Steece ("A Cost Minimization Forecasting Methodology for a Classified Inventory Environment") is on the faculty at the University of Oregon, Eugene, Oregon 97403. Before his appointment at Oregon, he was a member of the Technical Staff (Statistics), Jet Propulsion Laboratory, California Institute of Technology. He received a Ph.D. from the University of Southern California in 1974. His articles have appeared in several journals, including *Management Science, Biometrika,* and *Metron.*

Edward Stohr ("Input-Output Methods in Forecasting") is Associate Professor of Managerial Economics and Decision Sciences at the Graduate School of Management, Northwestern University, Evanston, Illinois, 60201. He has a B.S. (Engineering) from Melbourne University and an M.B.A. and Ph.D. (Business Administration) from the University of California, Berkeley. Currently he is Chairman of the Management Information Systems Curriculum Committee for the Graduate School of Management. His research interests are in the area of Management Information Systems with a special emphasis on computer-aided planning systems. He has published articles in *Management Science, Operations Research, Naval Research Logistics Quarterly, Annals of Economic and Social Measurement,* and *Proceedings of the ACM.*

Amos Tversky ("Intuitive Predictions: Biases and Corrective Procedures") is Professor of Psychology, Stanford University, Stanford, California, 94305. He received a B.A. from the Hebrew University, Jerusalem, and a Ph.D. (Mathematical Psychology) from the University of Michigan. He has taught at the Hebrew University and the University of Michigan as well as at Stanford University. His work deals with intuitive inference, the evaluation of evidence, decision making, and measurement theory. He has a variety of publications on topics in these fields.

Steven C. Wheelwright ("Forecasting: Framework and Overview" and "Forecasting the Future and the Future of Forecasting") is Associate Professor, Graduate School of Business Administration, Harvard University, Boston, Massachusetts 02163. He received his B.S. (mathematics) from the University of Utah and his M.B.A. and Ph.D. from Stanford University. His research and consulting interests concentrate on forecasting, operations planning, and manufacturing strategy, and his publications have appeared in such journals as *Operational Research Quarterly, TIMS/North-Holland Studies in the Management Sciences, The American Statistician,* and *Harvard Business Review.* He is the coauthor of *Computer-Aided Modeling for Managers* (Addison-Wesley, 1972), *Forecasting Methods for Management, Second Edition* (Wiley, 1977), *Interactive Forecasting, Second Edition* (Holden-Day, 1978), and *Forecasting: Methods and Applications* (Wiley-Hamilton, 1978). He is the coeditor of this special issue and an associate editor for *Decision Sciences.*

Steven D. Wood ("A Cost Minimization Forecasting Methodology for a Classified Inventory Environment") is a member of the faculty of the College of Business Administration, Arizona State University, Tempe, Arizona 85281. He received his Ph.D. in Quantitative Business Analysis from the University of Wisconsin, Madison. He is an active consultant and researcher in the areas of health care, property tax assessment, and information systems. He has authored several articles in journals such as *Land Economics, Management Science,* and *Health Services Research.*

TIMS Studies in the Management Sciences 12 (1979) 391–392
© North-Holland Publishing Company

AUTHORS' ADDRESSES

Alan R. Beckenstein
  The Colgate Darden Graduate School of Business Administration, University of Virginia, Box 6550, Charlottesville, VA 22906

Jean Blin
  Nathaniel Leverone Hall, Graduate School of Management, Northwestern University, Evanston, IL 60201

Charles P. Bonini
  Graduate School of Business, Stanford University, Stanford, CA 94305

J. Peter Burman
  Bank of England, Threadneedle Street, London EC2R 8AH, England

Kenneth O. Cogger
  The School of Business, The University of Kansas, Lawrence, KS 66045

Lewis W. Coopersmith
  Health Products Research, Inc., 3520 U.S. Route 22, Somerville, NJ 08876

Vittorio Corbo
  Concordia University, Montreal, Quebec, Canada

Robert Fildes
  Manchester Business School, University of Manchester, Booth Street West, Manchester M15 6PB, England

James R. Freeland
  Graduate School of Business, Stanford University, Stanford, CA 94305

Michael D. Geurts
  College of Business, Brigham Young University, Provo, UT 84601

Olaf Helmer
  International Institute for Applied Systems Analysis, A-2361 Laxenburg, Schloss Laxenburg, Austria

Syd Howell
  Manchester Business School, University of Manchester, Booth Street West, Manchester M15 6PB, England

Lynwood A. Johnson
  Georgia Institute of Technology, School of Industrial and Systems Engineering, Atlanta, GA 30332

Daniel Kahneman
  Center for Advanced Study in the Behavioral Sciences, 202 Junipero Serra Blvd., Stanford, CA 94305

Bernard Majiani
  Audsedot-Rey, 1 Reu de Pettit Claimont, Veligy, France

Spyros Makridakis
  INSEAD, Boulevard de Constance, 77305 Fontainebleau, France

Robert L. McLaughlin
  Micrometrics, 99 Mill Street, Waterbury, CT 06720

Stephen K. McNees
  Federal Reserve Bank of Boston, Boston, MA 02106

Raman K, Mehra
  President, Scientific Systems, Inc., 1640 Massachusetts Avenue, Cambridge, MA 02138

Douglas C. Montgomery
  Georgia Institute of Technology, School of Industrial and Systems Engineering, Atlanta, GA 30332

Geoffrey H. Moore
  National Bureau of Economic Research, Inc., 261 Madison Avenue, New York, NY 10016

Paul Newbold
University of Chicago, Graduate School of Business, 5836 Greenwood Avenue, Chicago, IL 60637

Emanuel Parzen
Institute of Statistics, Texas A&M University, College Station, TX 77843

Robert S. Pindyck
Alfred P. Sloan School of Management, Massachusetts Institute of Technology, Cambridge, MA 02139

James E. Reinmuth
College of Business Administration, Office of the Dean, University of Oregon, Eugene, OR 97403

Bert M. Steece
College of Business Administration, University of Oregon, Eugene, OR 97403

Amos Tversky
Stanford Research Institute, Ravenswood Avenue, Menlo Park, CA

Steven C. Wheelwright
Graduate School of Business Administration, Harvard University, Soldiers Field, Boston, MA 02163

Steven D. Wood
College of Business Administration, Arizona State University, Tempe, AZ 852281

JUE